Larousse

POCKET FACTFINDER

Larousse

POCKET FACTFINDER

Editor
Min Lee

Assistant editor
Nicolas McDowell

LAROUSSE

KINGFISHER
Kingfisher Publications Plc
New Penderel House
283–288 High Holborn
London WC1V 7HZ

First published by Kingfisher Publications Plc 1995
10 9 8 7 6 5 4
4TR / 0399 / WKT / -- / 128KMA
This edition © Kingfisher Publications Plc 1995

A CIP catalogue record for this book is available from the
British Library.

ISBN 0 7523 0029 6

Printed in Hong Kong / China

CONTENTS

THE EARTH

NATURAL HISTORY

SCIENCE AND TECHNOLOGY

COMMUNICATION

THE WORLD

HISTORY

THOUGHT AND BELIEF

ARTS AND CULTURE

SPORT AND GAMES

GENERAL KNOWLEDGE

ALPHABETICAL CONTENTS

PREFACE

The purpose of this book is to give quick and easy access to an enormous number of facts, ranging across areas which include diverse information on geology, astronautics, natural history, astronomy, physics, measurement, language, history, politics, geography, religion, the arts, sport and general knowledge.

The facts are arranged clearly in tables, lists and charts, and include concise biographies of prominent people, with details of their achievements.

There are two tables of contents so that the information can be accessed either by subject area or by specific table.

ABBREVIATIONS USED IN THIS BOOK

AD	Anno Domini	Ital	Italian
admin	administration	Jap	Japanese
BC	Before Christ	kg	kilogram(s)
c	century	km	kilometre(s)
c.	circa	l	litre(s)
C	Celsius (Centigrade)	Lat	Latin
C	central	lb	pounds(s)
Chin	Chinese	m	metre(s)
cm	centimetre(s)	ml	mile(s)
cont.	continued	mm	millimetre(s)
cu	cubic	N	north(ern)
cwt	hundredweight(s)	no.	number
dm	decimetre	oz	ounce(s)
E	east(ern)	p(p)	page(s)
eg	for example	pop	population
est.	estimated	pt	pint(s)
e	estimate	Russ	Russian
F	Fahrenheit	S	south(ern)
fl oz	fluid ounce(s)	sec	second(s)
Fr	French	Span	Spanish
ft	foot (feet)	sq	square
g	gram(s)	St	saint
gall	gallons	Sta	Santa
Ger	German	TV	Television
Gr	Greek	UT	Unified Team
h	hour(s)	W	west(ern)
I(s)	Island(s)	yd	yard(s)
ie	that is (id est)	Z	zodiac
in	inch(es)		

THE EARTH

There are no universally agreed estimates of the natural phenomena given in this section. Surveys make use of different criteria for identifying natural boundaries, and use different techniques of measurement. The sizes of continents, oceans, seas, deserts, and rivers are particularly subject to variation.

VITAL STATISTICS

Earth

Age	4 500 000 000 years (accurate to within a very small percentage of possible error)
Area	509 600 000 sq km/197 000 000 sq ml
Mass	$5\,976 \times 10^{27}$ grams
Land surface	148 000 000 sq km/57 000 000 sq ml (c.29% of total area)
Water surface	361 600 000 sq km/140 000 000 sq ml (c.71% of total area)
Circumference of equator	40 076 km/24 902 ml
Circumference of meridian	40 000 km/24 860 ml

CONTINENTS (in order of size)

	Area	
Name	sq km	sq ml
Asia	44 493 000	17 179 000 (29.6%)
Africa	30 293 000	11 696 000 (20.2%)
North America	24 454 000	9 442 000 (16.3%)
South America	17 838 000	6 887 000 (11.9%)
Antarctica	13 975 000	5 396 000 (9.3%)
Europe[1]	10 245 000	3 956 000 (6.8%)
Oceania	8 945 000	3 454 000 (5.9%)

[1] Including the former western USSR

OCEANS

Name	Area		Greatest depth	m	ft
	sq km	sq ml			
Arctic	13 986 000	5 400 000 (3%)	Eurasia Basin	5 122	16 804
Altantic	82 217 000	31 700 000 (24%)	Puerto Rico Trench	8 648	28 372
Indian	73 426 000	28 350 000 (20%)	Java Trench	7 725	25 344
Pacific	181 300 000	70 000 000 (46%)	Mariana Trench	11 040	36 220

LARGEST SEAS

Name	Area[1] sq km	sq ml
Coral Sea	4 791 000	1 850 200
Arabian Sea	3 863 000	1 492 000
S China (Nan) Sea	3 685 000	1 423 000
Mediterranean Sea	2 516 000	971 000
Bering Sea	2 304 000	890 000
Bay of Bengal	2 172 000	839 000
Sea of Okhotsk	1 590 000	614 000
Gulf of Mexico	1 543 000	596 000
Gulf of Guinea	1 533 000	592 000
Barents Sea	1 405 000	542 000
Norwegian Sea	1 383 000	534 000
Gulf of Alaska	1 327 000	512 000
Hudson Bay	1 232 000	476 000
Greenland Sea	1 205 000	465 000
Arafura Sea	1 037 000	400 000
Philippine Sea	1 036 000	400 000
Sea of Japan	978 000	378 000
E Siberian Sea	901 000	348 000
Kara Sea	883 000	341 000
E China Sea	664 000	256 000
Andaman Sea	565 000	218 000
North Sea	520 000	201 000
Black Sea	508 000	196 000
Red Sea	453 000	175 000
Baltic Sea	414 000	160 000
Arabian Gulf	238 000	92 200
St Lawrence Gulf	238 300	92 000

Oceans are excluded.

[1] Areas are rounded to the nearest 1 000 sq km/sq ml.

LARGEST ISLANDS

Name	Area[1] sq km	sq ml
Greenland	2 131 600	823 800
New Guinea	790 000	305 000
Borneo	737 000	285 000
Madagascar	587 000	227 600
Baffin	507 000	196 000
Sumatra	425 000	164 900
Honshu (Hondo)	228 000	88 000

Name	Area[1]	
	sq km	sq ml
Great Britain	219 000	84 400
Victoria, Canada	217 300	83 900
Ellesmere, Canada	196 000	75 800
Celebes	174 000	67 400
South I, New Zealand	151 000	58 200
Java	129 000	50 000
North I, New Zealand	114 000	44 200
Newfoundland	109 000	42 000
Cuba	105 000	40 500
Luzon	105 000	40 400
Iceland	103 000	39 700
Mindanao	94 600	36 500
Novaya Zemlya (two islands)	90 600	35 000
Ireland	84 100	32 500
Hokkaido	78 500	30 300
Hispaniola	77 200	29 800
Sakhalin	75 100	29 000
Tierra del Fuego	71 200	27 500
Tasmania	67 900	26 200

[1] Areas are rounded to the nearest 100 sq km/sq ml.

LARGEST LAKES

Name/location	Area[1]	
	sq km	sq ml
Caspian Sea, Iran/Russia/ Turkmenistan/Kazakhstan/ Azerbaijan	371 000	143 240[2]
Superior, USA/Canada	82 260	31 760[3]
Aral Sea, Uzbekistan/ Kazakhstan	64 500	24 900[2]
Victoria, E Africa	62 940	24 300
Huron, USA/Canada	59 580	23 000[3]
Michigan, USA	58 020	22 400
Tanganyika, E Africa	32 000	12 350
Baikal, Russia	31 500	12 160
Great Bear, Canada	31 330	12 100
Great Slave, Canada	28 570	11 030
Erie, USA/Canada	25 710	9 920[3]
Winnipeg, Canada	24 390	9 420
Malawi/Nyasa, E Africa	22 490	8 680
Balkhash, Kazakhstan	17 000–22 000	6 500–8 500[2]
Ontario, Canada	19 270	7 440[3]

LARGEST LAKES (cont.)

Name/location	Area[1] sq km	sq ml
Ladoga, Russia	18 130	7 000
Chad, W Africa	10 000–26 000	4 000–10 000
Maracaibo, Venezuela	13 010	5 020[4]
Patos, Brazil	10 140	3 920[4]
Onega, Russia	9 800	3 800
Rudolf, E Africa	9 100	3 500
Eyre, Australia	8 800	3 400[4]
Titicaca, Peru	8 300	3 200

The Caspian and Aral Seas, being entirely surrounded by land, are classified as lakes.

[1] Areas are rounded to the nearest 10 sq km/sq ml.
[2] Salt lakes
[3] Average of areas given by Canada and USA
[4] Salt lagoons

HIGHEST MOUNTAINS

Name/location	Height[1] m	ft
Everest, China-Nepal	8 850	29 030
K2, Kashmir-Jammu	8 610	28 250
Kangchenjunga, India-Nepal	8 590	28 170
Lhotse, China-Nepal	8 500	27 890
Kangchenjunga S Peak, India-Nepal	8 470	27 800
Makalu I, China-Nepal	8 470	27 800
Kangchenjunga W Peak, India-Nepal	8 420	27 620
Llotse E Peak, China-Nepal	8 380	27 500
Dhaulagiri, Nepal	8 170	26 810
Cho Oyu, China-Nepal	8 150	26 750
Manaslu, Nepal	8 130	26 660
Nanga Parbat, Kashmir-Jammu	8 130	26 660
Annapurna I, Nepal	8 080	26 500
Gasherbrum I, Kashmir-Jammu	8 070	26 470
Broad-highest, Kashmir-Jammu	8 050	26 400
Gasherbrum II, Kashmir-Jammu	8 030	26 360
Gosainthan, China	8 010	26 290
Broad-middle, Kashmir-Jammu	8 000	26 250
Gasherbrum III, Kashmir-Jammu	7 950	26 090
Annapurna II, Nepal	7 940	26 040
Nanda Devi, India	7 820	25 660
Rakaposhi, Kashmir	7 790	25 560
Kamet, India	7 760	25 450

Name/location	Height[1]	
	m	ft
Ulugh Muztagh, Tibet	7 720	25 340
Tirich Mir, Pakistan	7 690	25 230
Muz Tag Ata, China	7 550	24 760
Communism Peak, Tajikistan	7 490	24 590
Pobedy Peak, China-Kirghizia	7 440	24 410
Aconcagua, Argentina	6 960	22 830
Ojos del Salado, Argentina-Chile	6 910	22 660

[1] Heights are given to the nearest 10 m/ft.

LARGEST DESERTS

Name/location	Area[1]	
	sq km	sq ml
Sahara, N Africa	8 600 000	3 320 000
Arabian, SW Asia	2 330 000	900 000
Gobi, Mongolia and NE China	1 166 000	450 000
Patagonian, Argentina	673 000	260 000
Great Victoria, SW Australia	647 000	250 000
Great Basin, SW USA	492 000	190 000
Chihuahuan, Mexico	450 000	175 000
Great Sandy, NW Australia	400 000	150 000
Sonoran, SW USA	310 000	120 000
Kyzyl Kum, Kazakhskan	300 000	115 000
Takla Makan, N China	270 000	105 000
Kalahari, SW Africa	260 000	100 000
Kara Kum, Turkmenistan	260 000	100 000
Kavir, Iran	260 000	100 000
Syrian, Saudi Arabia/Jordan/ Syria/Iraq	260 000	100 000
Nubian, Sudan	260 000	100 000
Thar, India/Pakistan	200 000	77 000
Ust'-Urt, Kazakhstan	160 000	62 000
Bet-Pak-Dala, S Kazakhstan	155 000	60 000
Simpson, C Australia	145 000	56 000
Dzungaria, China	142 000	55 000
Atacama, Chile	140 000	54 000
Namib, SE Africa	134 000	52 000
Sturt, SE Australia	130 000	50 000
Bolson de Mapimi, Mexico	130 000	50 000
Ordos, China	130 000	50 000
Alashan, China	116 000	45 000

[1] Desert areas are very approximate, because clear physical boundaries may not occur.

LONGEST RIVERS

Name	Outflow	Length[1] km	ml
Nile-Kagera-Ruvuvu-Ruvusu-Luvironza	Mediterranean Sea (Egypt)	6 690	4 160
Amazon-Ucayali-Tambo-Ene-Apurimac	Atlantic Ocean (Brazil)	6 570	4 080
Mississipi-Missouri-Jefferson-Beaverhead-Red Rock	Gulf of Mexico (USA)	6 020	3 740
Chang Jiang (Yangtze)	E China Sea (China)	5 980	3 720
Yenisey-Angara-Selenga-Ider	Kara Sea (Russia)	5 870	3 650
Amur-Argun-Kerulen	Tartar Strait (Russia)	5 780	3 590
Ob-Irtysh	Gulf of Ob, Kara Sea (Russia)	5 410	3 360
Plata-Parana-Grande	Atlantic Ocean (Argentina/Uruguay)	4 880	3 030
Huang Ho (Yellow)	Yellow Sea (China)	4 840	3 010
Congo (Zaire)-Lualaba	Atlantic Ocean (Angola-Zaire)	4 630	2 880
Lena	Laptev Sea (Russia)	4 400	2 730
Mackenzie-Slave-Peace-Finlay	Beaufort Sea (Canada)	4 240	2 630
Mekong	S China Sea (Vietnam)	4 180	2 600
Niger	Gulf of Guinea (Nigeria)	4 100	2 550

[1] Lengths are given to the nearest 10 km/ml, and include the river plus tributaries comprising the longest watercourse.

HIGHEST WATERFALLS

Name/location	Height[1] m	ft
Angel (upper fall), Venezuela	807	2 648
Itatinga, Brazil	628	2 060
Cuquenan, Guyana-Venezuela	610	2 000
Ormeli, Norway	563	1 847
Tysse, Norway	533	1 749
Pilao, Brazil	524	1 719
Ribbon, USA	491	1 612
Vestre, Mardola, Norway	468	1 535
Kaieteur, Guyana	457?	1 500?
Cleve-Garth, New Zealand	450?	1 476?

[1] Height denotes individual leaps.

DEEPEST CAVES

Name/Location	Depth[1] m	ft
Jean Bernard, France	1 494	4 900
Snezhnaya, Caucasus	1 340	4 397

Name/location	Depth[1] m	ft
Puertas de Illamina, Spain	1 338	4 390
Pierre-Saint-Martin, France	1 321	4 334
Sistema Huautla, Mexico	1 240	4 067
Berger, France	1 198	3 930
Vqerdi, Spain	1 195	3 921
Dachstein-Mammuthhle, Austria	1 174	3 852
Zitu, Spain	1 139	3 737
Badalona, Spain	1 130	3 707
Batmanhöhle, Austria	1 105	3 626
Schneeloch, Austria	1 101	3 612
G E S Malaga, Spain	1 070	3 510
Lamprechstofen, Austria	1 024	3 360

MAJOR VOLCANOES

Name	Height[1] m	ft	Last eruption (year)
Aconcagua (Argentina)	6 960	22 831	extinct
Ararat (Turkey)	5 198	18 350	extinct
Awu (Sangihe Is)	1 327	4 355	1968
Bezymianny (Russia)	2 800	9 186	1984
Coseguina (Nicaragua)	847	1 598	1835
El Chichón (Mexico)	1 349	4 430	1982
Erebus (Antarctica)	4 023	13 200	1986
Etna (Italy)	3 236	10 625	1986
Fuji (Japan)	3 776	12 388	1707
Galunggung (Java)	2 180	7 155	1982
Hekla (Iceland)	1 491	4 920	1981
Helgafell (Iceland)	215	706	1973
Hudson (Chile)	1 740	5 742	1991
Jurullo (Mexico)	1 330	4 255	1774
Katmai (Alaska)	2 298	7 540	1931
Kilauea (Hawaii)	1 247	4 100	1991
Kilimanjaro (Tanzania)	5 930	19 450	extinct
Klyuchevskoy (Russia)	4 850	15 910	1985
Krakatoa (Sumatra)	818	2 685	1980
La Soufrière (St Vincent)	1 232	4 048	1979
Laki (Iceland)	500	1 642	1784
Lamington (Papua New Guinea)	1 780	5 844	1956
Lassen Peak (USA)	3 186	10 453	1921
Mauna Loa (Hawaii)	4 172	13 685	1984
Mayon (Philippines)	2 462	8 084	1993
Nyamuragira (Zaire)	3 056	10 026	1984

MAJOR **VOLCANOES** (cont.)

Name	Height[1] m	ft	Last eruption (year)
Paricutin (Mexico)	3 188	10 460	1952
Pelée, Mont (Martinique)	1 397	4 584	1932
Pinatubo, Mt (Philippines)	1 462	4 795	1991
Popocatepetl (Mexico)	5 483	17 990	1943
Rainier, Mt (USA)	4 392	14 416	1882
Ruapehu (New Zealand)	2 796	9 175	1986
St Helens, Mt (USA)	2 549	8 364	1987
Santorini/Thira (Greece)	1 315?	4 316?	1950
Stromboli (Italy)	931	3 055	1986
Surtsey (Iceland)	174	570	1967
Taal (Philippines)	1 448	4 752	1977
Tambora (Sumbawa)	2 868	9 410	1880
Tarawera (New Zealand)	1 149	3 770	1973
Unzen (Japan)	1 360	4 461	1991
Vesuvius (Italy)	1 289	4 230	1944
Vulcano (Italy)	502	1 650	1890

MAJOR EARTHQUAKES

All magnitudes on the Richter scale.
The energy released by earthquakes is measured on the logarithmic Richter scale. Thus

2 Barely perceptible   5 Rather strong   7+ Very strong

Location	Year	Magnitude	Deaths
Kobe	1995	7.2	4 000+
Los Angeles	1994	6.6	57
Futuna (French Pacific)	1993	6.3	5
Guam	1993	8.1	—
Latur (India)	1993	6.5	9 748
North and East Japan	1993	7.8	2
Papua New Guinea	1993	6.8	60
Cairo	1992	5.9	552
California	1992	7.4	2
Erzinicum (Turkey)	1992	6.7	2 000
Kirgizstan	1992	7.5	50
Nusa Tenggara	1992	6.8	2 500
Uttar Pradesh (India)	1991	6.1	1 000
Costa Rica/Panama	1991	7.5	80
Georgia	1991	7.2	100
Afghanistan	1991	6.8	1 000
Pakistan	1991	6.8	300
Cabanatuan City	1990	7.7	1 653

Location	Year	Magnitude	Deaths
NW Iran	1990	7.5	40 000
N Peru	1990	5.8	200
Romania	1990	6.6	70
Philippines	1990	7.7	1 600
San Francisco	1989	6.9	100
Armenia	1988	7.0	25 000
SW China	1988	7.6	1 000
Nepal/India	1988	6.9	900
Mexico City	1985	8.1	7 200
N Yemen	1982	6.0	2 800
S Italy	1980	7.2	4 500
El Asnam (Algeria)	1980	7.3	5 000
NE Iran	1978	7.7	25 000
Tangshan (China)	1976	8.2	242 000
Guatemala City	1976	7.5	22 778
Kashmir	1974	6.3	5 200
Managua (Nicaragua)	1972	6.2	5 000
S Iran	1972	6.9	5 000
Chimbote (Peru)	1970	7.7	66 000
NE Iran	1968	7.4	11 600
Anchorage (USA)	1964	8.5	131
NW Iran	1962	7.1	12 000
Agadir (Morocco)	1960	5.8	12 000
Erzincan (Turkey)	1939	7.9	23 000
Chillan (Chile)	1939	7.8	30 000
Quetta (India)	1935	7.5	60 000
Gansu (China)	1932	7.6	70 000
Nan-shan (China)	1927	8.3	200 000
Kwanto (Japan)	1923	8.3	143 000
Gansu (China)	1920	8.6	180 000
Avezzano (Italy)	1915	7.5	30 000
Messina (Italy)	1908	7.5	120 000
Valparaiso (Chile)	1906	8.6	20 000
San Francisco (USA)	1906	8.3	500
Ecuador/Colombia	1868	*	70 000
Calabria (Italy)	1783	*	50 000
Lisbon (Portugal)	1755	*	70 000
Calcutta (India)	1737	*	300 000
Hokkaido (Japan)	1730	*	137 000
Catania (Italy)	1693	*	60 000
Caucasia (Caucasus)	1667	*	80 000
Shensi (China)	1556	*	830 000
Chihli (China)	1290	*	100 000
Silicia (Asia Minor)	1268	*	60 000
Corinth (Greece)	856	*	45 000
Antioch (Turkey)	526	*	250 000

* Magnitude not available

EARTHQUAKE SEVERITY MEASUREMENT

Mercalli and Richter Scales

Mercalli		Richter
1	detected only by seismographs	<3
2	**feeble**	3–3.4
	just noticeable by some people	
3	**slight**	3.5–4
	similar to passing of heavy lorries	
4	**moderate**	4–4.4
	rocking of loose objects	
5	**quite strong**	4.5–4.8
	felt by most people even when sleeping	
6	**strong**	4.9–5.4
	trees rock and some structural damage is caused	
7	**very strong**	5.5–6
	walls crack	
8	**destructive**	6.1–6.5
	weak buildings collapse	
9	**ruinous**	6.6–7
	houses collapse and ground pipes crack	
10	**disastrous**	7.1–7.3
	landslides occur, ground cracks and buildings collapse	
11	**very disastrous**	7.4–8.1
	few buildings remain standing	
12	**catastrophic**	>8.1
	ground rises and falls in waves	

GREAT ICE AGES

Precambrian era	Early Proterozoic
Precambrian era	Upper Proterozoic
Palaeozoic era	Upper Carboniferous
Cenozoic era	Pleistocene[1]
	(Last 4 periods of glaciation)
	Gunz (Nebraskan or Jerseyan) 520 000–490 000 years ago
	Mindel (Kansan) 430 000–370 000 years ago
	Riss (Illinoian) 130 000–100 000 years ago
	Wurm (Wisconsan and Lowan) 40 000–18 000 years ago

[1] The Pleistocene epoch is synonymous with 'The Ice Age'.

GEOLOGICAL TIME SCALE

Eon	Era	Period	Epoch	Million years before present
Phanerozoic	Cenozoic	Quaternary	Holocene	0.01–
			Pleistocene	2–0.01
		Tertiary	Pliocene	7–2
			Miocene	25–7
			Oligocene	38–25
			Eocene	54–38
			Palaeocene	65–54
	Mesozoic	Cretaceous		140–65
		Jurassic		210–140
		Triassic	Late	
			Middle	250–210
			Early	
	Palaeozoic	Permian	Late	
			Early	290–250
		Carboniferous	Pennsylvanian	
			Mississippian	360–290
		Devonian		410–360
		Silurian		440–410
		Ordovician		505–440
		Cambrian		580–505
Proterozoic	Precambrian			4 500–580

NATURAL HISTORY

CEREALS

English name	Species	Area of origin
barley	*Hordeum vulgare*	Middle East
maize (or corn, sweet corn, Indian corn)	*Zea mays*	C America
millet, common	*Panicum miliaceum*	tropics, warm temperate regions
millet, foxtail or Italian	*Setaria italica*	as common millet
millet, bulrush	*Pennisetum americanum*	as common millet
oats	*Avena sativa*	Mediterranean basin
rice	*Oryza sativa*	Asia
rye	*Secale cereale*	Mediterranean, SW Asia
sorghum (or Kaffir corn)	*Sorghum bicolor*	Africa, Asia
wheat	Genus *Triticum*, 20 species	Mediterranean, W Asia

VEGETABLES

English Name	Species	Part eaten	Area of origin
artichoke, Chinese	*Stachys affinis*	tuber	China
artichoke, globe	*Cynara scolymus*	buds	Mediterranean
artichoke, Jerusalem	*Helianthus tuberosus*	tuber	N America
asparagus	*Asparagus officinalis*	young shoots	Europe, Asia
aubergine (or eggplant)	*Solanum melongena*	fruit	Asia, Africa
avocado	*Persea americana*	fruit	C America
bean sprouts	*Vigna radiata*	shoots	China
beans, blackeyed	*Vigna unguiculata*	seeds	India, Iran
beans, borlotti (or Boston or pinto)	*Phaseolus vulgaris*	seeds	America
beans, broad	*Vicia faba*	seeds and pods	Africa, Europe
beans, flageolot	*Phaseolus vulgaris*	seeds	America
beans, French	*Phaseolus vulgaris*	pods	America
beans, haricot	*Phaseolus vulgaris*	seeds	America
beans, kidney	*Phaseolus vulgaris*	seeds	America
beans, runner	*Phaseolus coccineus*	pod	America
beans, soya	*Glycine max*	seeds	E Asia
beetroot	*Beta vulgaris*	root	Mediterranean
broccoli	*Brassica oleracea*	buds and leaves	Europe

English Name	Species	Part eaten	Area of origin
Brussels sprout	*Brassica oleracea* (Gemmifera)	buds	N Europe
cabbage	*Brassica oleracea* (capitata)	leaves	Europe, W Asia
cardoon	*Cynara cardunculus*	inner stalks and flower heads	Mediterranean
carrot	*Daucus carota*	root	Asia
cauliflower	*Brassica oleracea* (Botrytis)	flower buds	Middle East
celeriac	*Apium graveolens* var. *rapaceum*	root	Mediterranean
celery	*Apium graveolens* var. *dulce*	stalks	Europe, N Africa, America
chayote (or chocho)	*Sechium edule*	fruit	America
chick-pea	*Cicer arietinum*	seed	W Asia
chicory	*Cichorium intybus*	leaves	Europe, W Asia
chinese leaf	*Brassica pekinensis*	leaf stalks	E Asia, China
chives	*Allium schoenoprasum*	leaves	Europe, N America
courgette (or zucchini)	*Cucurbita pepo*	fruit	S America, Africa
cucumber	*Cucumis satius*	fruit	S Asia
eggplant *see* aubergine			
endive	*Cichorium endivia*	leaves	S Europe, E Indies, Africa
fennel, Florentine	*Foeniculum vulgare* var. *azoricum*	leaf stalks	Europe
kale (or borecole)	*Brassica oleracea* (Acephala)	leaves	Europe
kohlrabi	*Brassica oleracea* (Gongylodes)	stem	Europe
laver	*Porphyra leucosticta*, *P. umbilicalis*	leaves and stems	Europe
leek	*Allium porrum*	stem and leaves	Europe, N Africa
lentil	*Lens culinaris*	seed	S Asia
lettuce	*Lactuca sativa*	leaves	Middle East
marrow	*Cucurbita pepo*	fruit	America
mooli	*Raphanus sativus*	roots	E Africa
mushroom	*Agaricus campestris*	fruiting body	worldwide
okra	*Abelmoschus esculentus*	pods and seeds	Africa
onion	*Allium cepa*	bulb	Central Asia
parsnip	*Pastinaca sativa*	root	Europe

VEGETABLES (cont.)

English Name	Species	Part eaten	Area of origin
pea	*Pisum sativum*	pods and seeds	Asia, Europe
pepper	*Capsicum annuum*	fruit	S America
potato	*Solanum tuberosum*	tuber	S America
pumpkin	*Cucurbita pepo*	fruit	S America
radish	*Raphanus sativus*	root	China, Japan
salsify	*Tragopogon porrifolius*	roots	S Europe
sorrel	*Rumex acetosa*	leaves	Europe
spinach	*Spinacea oleracea*	leaves	Asia
squash, winter	*Cucurbita maxima*	fruit	America
squash, summer	*Cucurbita pepo*	fruit	America
swede	*Brassica napus* Napobrassica	root	Europe
sweet potato	*Ipomoea batatas*	tuber	C America
swiss chard	*Beta vulgaris* subsp. *cicla*	leaves and stems	Europe
tomato	*Lycopersicon esculentum*	fruit	S America
turnip	*Brassica rapa*	root	Middle East
watercress	*Nasturtium officinale*	leaves and stems	Europe, Asia
yam	Genus *Dioscorea* 60 species	tuber	tropics
zucchini *see* courgette			

HERBS

Herbs may be used for medicinal, cosmetic or culinary purposes. Any part of those marked * may be poisonous when ingested.

English name	Species	Origin	Part of plant used
aconite* (or monkshood, winter aconite)	*Aconitum napellus*	Europe, NW Asia	tuber
agrimony	*Agrimonia eupatoria*	Europe	flowers
alecost (or costmary)	*Balsamita major*	E Mediterranean	leaves, flowers
aloe	*Aloe vera*	Africa	leaves
anise	*Pimpinella anisum*	Egypt	fruits (seed heads)
basil	*Ocimum basilicum*	Middle East	leaves, flowering shoots
borage	*Borago officinalis*	Mediterranean	leaves, flowers
celandine	*Chelidonium majus*	Europe	buds
celery	*Apium graveolens*	Europe	roots, stems, leaves
chamomile	*Chamaemelum nobile*	Europe, Asia	flowers
chervil	*Anthriscus cerefolium*	Europe, Asia	leaves

English name	Species	Origin	Part of plant used
chicory	*Cichorium intybus*	Europe	leaves, roots
chives	*Allium schoenoprasum*	Europe, America	leaves
coriander	*Coriandrum sativum*	N Africa, W Asia	leaves, fruits
dandelion	*Taraxacum officinalis*	Europe	leaves, roots
deadly nightshade*	*Atropa bella-donna*	Europe, Asia	root
dill	*Anethum graveolens*	S Europe	leaves, fruits (seeds)
elder	*Sambucus nigra*	Europe	flowers, fruits
epazote	*Chenopodium ambrosioides*	C and S America	leaves
fennel, Florentine	*Foeniculum vulgare* var. *azoricum*	Mediterranean	leaves, stems, fruits (seeds)
feverfew	*Tanacetum parthenium*	SE Europe, W Asia	leaves, flowers
foxglove*	*Digitalis purpurea*	Europe	leaves
garlic	*Allium sativum*	Asia	bulbs
gentian	*Gentiana lutea*	Europe	rhizomes, roots
ginseng	*Panax pseudo-ginseng*	China	roots
guaiacum	*Guaiacum officinale*	Caribbean	leaves
heartsease (or wild pansy)	*Viola tricolor*	Europe	flowers
hemlock*	*Conium maculatum*	Europe	all parts
hemp (ganja, cannabis, or marijuana)	*Cannabis sativa*	Asia	leaves, flowers
henbane	*Hyoscyamus niger*	Europe, W Asia, N Africa	leaves, fruits (seeds)
henna	*Lawsonia inermis*	Asia, Africa	leaves
horseradish	*Armoracia rusticana*	SE Europe, W Asia	roots, flowering shoots, leaves
hyssop	*Hyssopus officinalis*	S Europe	leaves, flowers
juniper	*Juniperus communis*	Mediterranean	fruits (berries), wood
lavender	*Lavandula officinalis*	Mediterranean	flowers, stems
leek	*Allium porrum*	Europe	stem, leaves
lemon	*Citrus limon*	Asia	fruits
lemon balm	*Melissa officinalis*	S Europe	leaves
lily of the valley	*Convallaria majalis*	Europe, N America	leaves, flowers
lime, small-leaved	*Tilia cordata*	Europe	flowers
liquorice	*Glycyrrhiza glabra*	Egypt	roots
lovage	*Levisticum officinale*	W Asia	leaves, shoots, stems, roots
mandrake	*Mandragora officinarum*	Himalayas, SE Europe, W Asia	roots

HERBS (cont.)

English name	Species	Origin	Part of plant used
marjoram	*Origanum majorana*	Africa, Asia, Mediterranean	leaves, shoots, stems
marsh mallow	*Althaea officinalis*	Europe, Asia	leaves, roots
maté	*Ilex paraguariensis*	S America	leaves
monkswood *see* aconite			
mugwort	*Artemisia vulgaris*	Europe, Asia	leaves
myrrh	*Commiphora myrrha*	Arabia, Africa	resin
myrtle	*Myrtus communis*	Asia, Mediterranean	leaves, flower heads, fruits (berries)
nasturtium	*Tropaeolum majus*	Peru	leaves, flowers, fruits
onion	*Allium cepa*	Asia	bulbs
oregano	*Origanum vulgare*	Mediterranean	leaves, shoots, stems
parsley	*Petroselinum crispum*	Mediterranean	leaves, stems
peony	*Paeonia officinalis*	Europe, Asia, N America	roots, seeds
peppermint	*Mentha x piperita*	Europe	leaves
poppy*, opium	*Papaver somniferum*	Asia Minor	fruits, seeds
purslane	*Portulaca oleracea*	Europe	leaves
rosemary	*Rosmarinus officinalis*	Mediterranean	leaves
rue	*Ruta graveolens*	Mediterranean	leaves, stems, flowers
saffron	*Crocus sativus*	Asia Minor	flowers
sage	*Salvia officinalis*	N Mediterranean	leaves
sorrel	*Rumex acetosa*	Europe	leaves
spearmint	*Mentha spicata*	Europe	leaves
tansy	*Tanacetum vulgare*	Asia	leaves, flowers
tarragon, French	*Artemisia dracunculus*	Asia, E Europe	leaves, stems
thyme	*Thymus serpyllum*	Mediterranean	leaves, stems, flowers
valerian	*Valeriana officinalis*	Europe, Asia	rhizomes, roots
vervain	*Verbena officinalis*	Europe, Asia, N Africa	leaves, flowers
watercress	*Nasturtium officinale*	Europe, Asia	leaves, shoots, stems
witch hazel	*Hamamelis virginiana*	N America, E Asia	leaves, shoots, bark
wormwood	*Aretemisia absinthium*	Europe	leaves, flowering shoots
yarrow (or milfoil)	*Achillea millefolium*	Europe, W Asia	flower heads, leaves

SPICES

English name	Species	Origin	Part of plant used
allspice	*Pimenta dioica*	America, W Indies	fruits
annatto	*Bixa orellana*	S America, W Indies	seeds
asafoetida	*Ferula assa-foetida*	W Asia	sap
bay	*Laurus nobilis*	Mediterranean, Asia Minor	leaves
caraway	*Carum carvi*	Europe, Asia	seeds
cardamom	*Elettaria cardamomum*	SE Asia	seeds
cayenne	*Capsicum annuum*	America, Africa	fruit pods
chilli pepper	*Capsicum annuum*	America	fruit pods
cinnamon	*Cinnamomum verum*	Ceylon	bark
cloves	*Syzygium aromaticum*	Moluccas	buds
cocoa	*Theobroma cacoa*	S America	seeds (beans)
coconut	*Cocos nucifera*	Polynesia	fruits
coriander	*Coriandrum sativum*	S Europe	fruits
cumin	*Cuminum cyminum*	Mediterranean	fruits (seed heads)
curry leaf	*Murraya koenigii*	India	leaves
fennel	*Foeniculum vulgare*	S Europe	fruits
fenugreek	*Trigonella foenum-graecum*	India, S Europe	seeds
horseradish	*Armoracia rusticana*	E Europe	roots
ginger	*Zingiber officinale*	SE Asia	rhizomes
mace	*Myristica fragrans*	Moluccas	seeds
mustard, black	*Brassica nigra*	Europe, Africa, Asia, America	seeds
mustard, white	*Sinapis alba*	Europe, Asia	seeds
nutmeg	*Myristica fragrans*	Moluccas	seeds
paprika	*Capiscum annuum*	S America	fruit pods
pepper	*Piper nigrum*	India	seeds
sandalwood	*Santalum album*	India, Indonesia, Australia	heartwood, roots
sassafras	*Sassafras albidum*	N America	root bark
sesame	*Sesamum indicum*	tropics	seeds
soya	*Glycine max*	China	fruit (beans)
tamarind	*Tamarindus indica*	Africa	fruits
turmeric	*Curcuma longa*	SE Asia	rhizomes
vanilla	*Vanilla planifolia*	C America	fruit pods

EDIBLE FRUITS (Temperate and Mediterranean)

English name	Species	Area of origin
apple	*Malus pumila*	temperate regions
apricot	*Prunus armeniaca*	Asia
bilberry	*Vaccinium myrtillus*	Europe, N Asia
blackberry	*Rubus fruticosis*	N hemisphere
blackcurrant	*Ribes nigrum*	Europe, Asia, Africa
blueberry	*Vaccinium corymbosum*	America, Europe
cherry (sour)	*Prunus cerasus*	temperate regions
cherry (sweet)	*Prunus avium*	temperate regions
clementine	*Citrus reticulata* cv. Clementine	W Mediterranean
cranberry	*Vaccinium oxycoccus*	N America
damson	*Prunus institia*	temperate regions
date	*Phoenix dactylifera*	Persian Gulf
fig	*Ficus carica*	W Asia
gooseberry	*Ribes uva-crispa*	Europe
grape	*Vitis vinefera*	Asia
grapefruit	*Citrus x paradisi*	W Indies
greengage	*Prunus domestica*	temperate regions
kiwi fruit	*Actinidia chinensis*	China
kumquat	*Fortunella margarita*	China
lemon	*Citrus limon*	India, S Asia
lime	*Citrus aurantiifolia*	SE Asia
loganberry	*Rubus loganobaccus*	America
loquat	*Eriobotrya japonica*	China, Japan
lychee	*Litchi chinensis*	China
mandarin (or tangerine)	*Citrus reticulata*	China
medlar	*Mespilus germanica*	SE Europe, Asia
melon	*Cucumis melo*	Egypt
minneola *see* tangelo		N America
mulberry	*Morus nigra*	W Asia
nectarine	*Prunus persica*	China
orange	*Citrus sinensis*	China
peach	*Prunus persica* var. *nectarina*	China
pear	*Pyrus communis*	Middle East, E Europe
persimmon (or date-plum)	*Diospyros kaki*	E Asia
physalis (or Cape gooseberry)	*Physalis alkekengi*	S America
plum	*Prunus domestica*	temperate regions
pomegranate	*Punica granatum*	Persia
pomelo	*Citrus maxima*	Malaysia
quince	*Cydonia oblonga*	Iran
raspberry	*Rubus idaeus*	N hemisphere
redcurrant	*Ribes rubrum*	Europe, Asia, Africa
rhubarb	*Rheum rhabarbarum*	Asia
satsuma	*Citrus reticulata*	Japan

English name	Species	Area of origin
strawberry	*Fragaria*	Europe, Asia
tangelo	*Citrus* x *tangelo*	N America
tangerine *see* mandarin		
ugli *see* tangelo		
water melon	*Citrullus lanatus*	Africa
white currant	*Ribes rubrum* cv.	W Europe

EDIBLE FRUITS (Tropical)

English name	Species	Area of origin
acerola	*Malpighia glabra*	America
avocado	*Persea americana*	C America
banana	*Musa acuminata*	India, S Asia
breadfruit	*Artocarpus altilis*	Malaysia
carambola	*Averrhoa carambola*	S China
cherimoya	*Annona cherimola*	Peru
guava	*Psidium guajava*	S America
mango	*Mangifera indica*	S Asia
papaya	*Carica papaya*	tropics
passion fruit	*Passiflora edulis*	S America
pineapple	*Ananas comosus*	S America
sapodillo plum	*Manilkara zapota*	C America
soursop	*Annona muricata*	America
tamarind	*Tamarindus indica*	Africa, S Asia

TREES (Europe and N America)

English name	Species	Continent of origin
alder, common	*Alnus glutinosa*	Europe
almond	*Prunus dulcis*	W Asia, N Africa
apple	*Malus pumila*	Europe, W Africa
apple, crab	*Malus sylvestris*	Europe, Asia
ash, common	*Fraxinus excelsior*	Europe
aspen	*Populus tremula*	Europe
bean tree, Red Indian	*Catalpa bignonioides*	America, E Asia
beech, common	*Fagus sylvatica*	Europe
beech, copper	*Fagus purpurea* 'Atropunicea'	Europe
beech, roble	*Nothofagus obliqua*	S America
birch, silver	*Betula pendula*	Europe, America, Asia
box*	*Buxus sempervirens*	Europe, N Africa
Brazil nut*	*Bertholletia excelsa*	S America
camellia, deciduous	*Stewartia pseudo-camellia*	Asia

TREES (Europe and N America) (cont.)

English name	Species	Continent of origin
castor-oil tree, prickly	*Eleutherococcus pictus*	tropics
cedar of Lebanon	*Cedrus libani*	Asia
cedar, smooth Tasmanian	*Athrotaxis cupressoides*	Australia
cedar, white	*Thuja occidentalis*	America
cherry, morello (or sour)	*Prunus cerasus*	Europe, Asia
cherry, wild (or gean)	*Prunus avium*	Europe
chestnut, horse	*Aesculus hippocastanum*	Asia, SW Europe
chestnut, sweet (or Spanish)	*Castanea sativa*	Europe, Africa, Asia
cypress, Lawson	*Chamaecyparis lawsoniana*	America
deodar	*Cedrus deodara*	Asia
dogwood, common	*Cornus sanguinea*	Europe
elm, Dutch	*Ulmus* x *hollandica*	Europe
elm, English	*Ulmus procera*	Europe
elm, wych	*Ulmus glabra*	Europe
fig	*Ficus carica*	Asia
fir, douglas	*Pseudotsuga menziesii*	America
fir, red	*Abies magnifica*	America
ginkgo	*Ginkgo biloba*	Asia
grapefruit	*Citrus* x *paradisi*	Asia
gum, blue	*Eucalyptus globulus*	Australia
gum, cider	*Eucalyptus gunnii*	Australia
gum, snow	*Eucalyptus panciflora*	Australia
gutta-percha tree	*Eucommia ulmoides*	China
hawthorn	*Crataegus monogyna*	Europe
hazel, common	*Corylus avellana*	Europe, W Asia, N Africa
hemlock, Western	*Tsuga heterophylla*	America
holly	*Ilex aquifolium*	Europe, N Africa, W Asia
hornbeam	*Carpinus betulus*	Europe, Asia
Joshua-tree	*Yucca brevifolia*	America
Judas-tree	*Cercis siliquastrum*	S Europe, Asia
juniper, common	*Juniperus communis*	Europe, Asia
laburnum, common	*Laburnum anagyroides*	Europe
larch, European	*Larix decidua*	Europe
larch, golden	*Pseudolarix kaempferi*	E Asia
leatherwood	*Eucryphia lucida*	Australia
lemon	*Citrus limon*	Asia
lime	*Citrus aurantiifolia*	Asia
lime, small-leafed	*Tilia cordata*	Europe
locust tree	*Robinia pseudoacacia*	America
magnolia (or white laurel)	*Magnolia virginiana*	America
maple, field (or common)	*Acer campestre*	Europe
maple, sugar	*Acer saccharum*	America
medlar	*Mespilus germanica*	Europe
mimosa	*Acacia dealbata*	Australia, Europe
mockernut	*Carya tomentosa*	America

English name	Species	Continent of origin
monkey puzzle*	*Araucaria araucana*	S America
mulberry, common	*Morus nigra*	Asia
mulberry, white	*Morus alba*	Asia
myrtle, orange bark*	*Myrtus apiculata*	S America
nutmeg, California*	*Torreya californica*	America
oak, California live	*Quercus agrifolia*	America
oak, cork*	*Quercus suber*	S Europe, N Africa
oak, English (or common)	*Quercus robur*	Europe, Asia, Africa
oak, red	*Quercus rubra*	America
olive*	*Olea europaea*	S Europe
orange, sweet*	*Citrus sinensis*	Asia
pagoda-tree	*Sophora japonica*	China, Japan
pear	*Pyrus communis*	Europe, W Asia
pine, Austrian*	*Pinus nigra* subsp. *nigra*	Europe, Asia
pine, Corsican*	*Pinus nigra* subsp. *laricio*	Europe
pine, Monterey*	*Pinus radiata*	America
pine, Scots	*Pinus sylvestris*	Europe
plane, London	*Platanus x hispanica*	Europe
plane, Oriental	*Platanus orientalis*	SE Europe, Asia
plum	*Prunus domestica*	Europe, Asia
poplar, balsam	*Populus balsamifera*	America, Asia
poplar, black	*Populus nigra*	Europe, Asia
poplar, Lombardy	*Populus nigra* 'Italica'	Europe
poplar, white	*Populus alba*	Europe
quince	*Cydonia oblonga*	Asia
raoul	*Nothofagus procera*	S America
rowan (or mountain ash)	*Sorbus aucuparia*	Europe
sassafras, American	*Sassafras albidum*	America
service tree, true	*Sorbus domestica*	Europe
silver fir, common*	*Abies alba*	Europe
spruce, Norway*	*Picea abies*	Europe
spruce, sitka*	*Picea sitchensis*	America, Europe
strawberry tree*	*Arbutus unedo*	Europe
sycamore (plane)	*Acer pseudoplatanus*	Europe, W Asia
tamarack	*Larix laricina*	N America
tree of heaven	*Ailanthus altissima*	China
tulip tree	*Liriodendron tulipifera*	America
walnut, black	*Juglans nigra*	America
walnut, common	*Juglans regia*	Europe, Asia
whitebeam	*Sorbus aria*	Europe
willow, pussy, goat or sallow	*Salix caprea*	Europe, Asia
willow, weeping	*Salix babylonica*	Asia
willow, white	*Salix alba*	Europe
yew, common*	*Taxus baccata*	N temperate regions

*Evergreen

TREES (Tropical)

Name	Species	Continent of origin
African tulip tree*	*Spathodea campanulata*	Africa
almond, tropical	*Terminalia catappa*	Asia
angel's trumpet	*Brugmansia* x *candida*	S America
autograph tree*	*Clusia rosea*	Asia
avocado*	*Persea americana*	America
bamboo	*Schizostachyum glauchifolium*	America
banana[1]	*Musa* x *paradisiaca*	Asia
banyan*	*Ficus benghalensis*	Asia
baobob (or dead rat's tree)	*Adansonia digitata*	Africa
beach heliotrope*	*Argusia argentea*	S America
bo-tree	*Ficus religiosa*	Asia
bombax	*Bombax ceiba*	Asia
bottle brush*	*Callistemon citrinus*	Australia
breadfruit*	*Artocarpus altilis*	Asia
brownea*	*Brownea macrophylla*	C America
calabash*	*Crescentia cujete*	America
candlenut*	*Aleurites moluccana*	Asia
cannonball*	*Couroupita guianensis*	S America
chinaberry (or bead tree)	*Melia azedarach*	Asia
Christmas-berry*	*Schinus terebinthifolius*	America
coconut palm*	*Cocos nucifera*	Asia
coffee tree*	*Coffea liberica*	Africa
Cook pine*	*Araucaria columnaris*	Oceania (New Caledonia)
coral tree	*Erythrina coralloides*	C America
coral shower	*Cassia grandis*	Asia
cotton, wild	*Cochlospermum vitifolium*	C and S America
crape myrtle	*Lagerstroemia indica*	Asia
date palm*	*Phoenix dactylifera*	Asia and Africa
dragon tree*	*Dracaena draco*	Africa (Canary Is)
durian*	*Durio zibethinus*	Asia
ebony*	*Diospyros ebenum*	Asia
elephant's ear	*Enderolobium cyclocarpum*	S America
flame tree	*Delonix regia*	Africa (Madagascar)
gold tree	*Cybistax donnell-smithii*	Asia
golden rain	*Koelreuteria paniculata*	Asia
golden shower	*Cassia fistula*	Asia
guava*	*Psidium guajava*	S America
ironwood (or casuarina)	*Casuarina equisetifolia*	Australia and Asia
jacaranda	*Jacaranda mimosifolia*	S America
jackfruit (or jack)*	*Artocarpus heterophyllus*	Asia
kapok tree	*Ceiba pentandra*	Old and New World tropics
koa*	*Acacia koa*	Oceania (Hawaii)
lipstick tree*	*Bixa orellanna*	America

Name	Species	Continent of origin
lychee*	*Litchi chinensis*	China
macadamia nut*	*Macadamia integrifolia*	Australia
mahogany*	*Swietenia mahogoni*	S America
mango*	*Mangifera indica*	Asia
mesquite*	*Prosopis pallida*	America
monkeypod (or rain tree)*	*Albizia saman*	S America
Norfolk island pine*	*Araucaria heterophylla*	Oceania (Norfolk I)
octopus tree*	*Schefflera actinophylla*	Australia
ohi' a lehua*	*Metrosideros collina*	Oceania (Hawaii)
pandanus (or screw pine)*	*Pandanus tectorius*	Oceania
paperbark tree*	*Melaleuca quinquenervia*	Australia
powderpuff*	*Calliandra haematocephala*	S America
royal palm*	*Roystonea regia*	America (Cuba)
sandalwood	*Santalum album*	Asia
sand-box tree	*Hura crepitans*	Americas
sausage tree*	*Kigelia pinnata*	Africa
scrambled egg tree*	*Cassia glauca*	Americas
Surinam cherry*	*Eugenia uniflora*	S America
teak tree*	*Tectona grandis*	Asia
tiger's claw	*Erythrina variegata*	Asia
yellow oleander*	*Thevetia peruviana*	Americas (W Indies)

* Evergreen
[1] Plant dies after fruiting.

FLOWERS (Shrubs)

English name	Genus/family	Country/continent of origin
abelia	*Abelia*	Asia, China, Mexico
abutilon	*Abutilon*	S America
acacia (or mimosa or wattle)	*Acacia*	Australia, tropical Africa, tropical America
almond, dwarf	*Prunus*	Asia, Europe
ampelopsis	*Ampelopsis*	Far East
anthyllis	*Anthyllis*	Europe
azalea	*Rhododendron*	N hemisphere
berberis	*Berberis*	Asia, America, Europe
bottle brush	*Callistemon*	Australia
bougainvillea	*Bougainvillea*	S America
broom	*Cytisus*	Europe
buckthorn	*Rhamnus*	N hemisphere
buddleia	*Buddleja*	China, S America
cactus	Cactaceae	America
calico bush (or mountain laurel)	*Kalmia*	China

FLOWERS (Shrubs) (cont.)

English name	Genus/family	Country/continent of origin
camellia	*Camellia*	Asia
caryopteris	*Caryopteris*	Asia
ceanothus	*Ceanothus*	N America
ceratostigma	*Ceratostigma*	China
Chinese lantern	*Physalis*	Japan
cistus	*Cistus*	Europe
clematis	*Clematis*	N temperate regions
clerodendrum	*Clerodendrum*	China
colquhounia	*Colquhounia*	Himalayas
cornelian cherry	*Cornus*	Europe
coronilla	*Coronilla*	S Europe
corylopsis	*Corylopsis*	China, Japan
cotoneaster	*Cotoneaster*	Asia
currant, flowering	*Ribes*	N America
desfontainia	*Desfontainia*	S America
deutzia	*Deutzia*	Asia
diplera	*Diplera*	China
dogwood	*Cornus*	Europe, SW Asia
embothrium	*Embothrium*	S America
escallonia	*Escallonia*	S America
euchryphia	*Euchryphia*	Chile, Australasia
euryops	*Euryops*	S Africa
fabiana	*Fabiana*	S America
firethorn	*Pyracantha*	China
forsythia	*Forsythia*	China
frangipani	*Plumeria*	tropical America
fuchsia	*Fuchsia*	C and S America, New Zealand
gardenia	*Gardenia*	tropics
garland flower	*Daphne*	Europe, Asia
garrya	*Garrya*	America (California and Oregon)
gorse, furze, whin	*Ulex*	Europe, Britain
hawthorn	*Crataegus*	N America, Europe, N Africa
heath, winter-flowering	*Erica*	Africa, Europe
heather	*Calluna*	Europe, W Asia
hebe	*Hebe*	New Zealand
helichrysum	*Helichrysum*	Australia, S Africa
hibiscus	*Hibiscus*	China, India
honeysuckle	*Lonicera*	temperate regions
hydrangea	*Hydrangea*	Asia, America
hyssop	*Hyssopus*	S Europe, W Asia
indigofera	*Indigofera*	Himalayas
ipomoea (or morning glory)	*Ipomoea*	tropical America
japonica	*Chaenomeles*	N Asia
jasmine	*Jasminum*	Asia
Jerusalem sage	*Phlomis*	Europe

English name	Genus/family	Country/continent of origin
kerria	*Kerria*	China
kolkwitzia	*Kolkwitzia*	China
laburnum	*Laburnum*	Europe, Asia
lavender	*Lavandula*	Europe
leptospermum	*Leptospermum*	Australasia
lespedeza	*Lespedeza*	China, Japan
leycesteria	*Leycesteria*	Himalayan
lilac (or syringa)	*Syringa*	Europe (Balkans)
lion's tail	*Leonotis*	S Africa
magnolia	*Magnolia*	China, Japan
mahonia	*Mahonia*	Japan
malus	*Malus*	N America, Asia
menziesa	*Menziesa*	Japan
mimosa *see* acacia		
mimulus	*Mimulus*	N America
mock orange	*Philadelphus*	Europe, Asia, N America
moltkia	*Moltkia*	Greece
morning glory *see* ipomoea		
mother-of-pearl	*Symphoricarpus*	N America
mountain ash *see* rowan		
myrtle	*Myrtus*	Europe
oleander	*Nerium*	Europe (Mediterranean)
olearia	*Olearia*	New Zealand
oleaster	*Elaeagnus*	Europe, Asia, N America
osmanthus	*Osmanthus*	China
pearl bush	*Exochorda*	China
peony	*Paeonia*	Europe, Asia, N America
pieris	*Pieris*	China
poinsettia	*Euphorbia*	America (Mexico)
potentilla	*Potentilla*	Asia
rhododendron	*Rhododendron*	S Asia
rhus	*Rhus*	Europe, N America
ribbon woods	*Hoheria*	New Zealand
robinia	*Robinia*	N America
rock rose (or sun rose)	*Helianthemum*	Europe
rose	*Rosa*	N temperate regions
rosemary	*Rosmarinus*	Europe, Asia
rowan (or mountain ash)	*Sorbus*	Europe, Asia
sage, common	*Salvia*	S Europe
St John's wort	*Hypericum*	Europe, Asia
sea buckthorn	*Hippophae*	SW Europe
senecio	*Senecio*	New Zealand
skimmia	*Skimmia*	Japan, China
snowberry	*Symphoricarpos*	N America
spiraea	*Spiraea*	China, Japan
stachyurus	*Stachyurus*	China
staphylea	*Staphylea*	Europe, Asia

FLOWERS (Shrubs) (cont.)

English name	Genus/family	Country/continent of origin
sun rose *see* rock rose		
syringa *see* lilac		
tamarisk	*Tamarix*	Europe
thyme	*Thymus*	Europe
veronica	*Veronica*	New Zealand
viburnum	*Viburnum*	Europe, Asia, Africa
Virgina creeper	*Parthenocissus*	N America
wattle *see* acacia		
weigela	*Weigela*	N China
winter sweet	*Chimonanthus*	China
wisteria	*Wisteria*	China, Japan
witch-hazel	*Hamamelis*	China, Japan

FLOWERS (Herbaceous)

English name	Genus/family	Country/continent of origin
acanthus	*Acanthus*	Europe
African violet	*Saintpaulia*	Africa
alum root	*Heuchera*	N America
alyssum	*Alyssum*	S Europe
anchusa	*Anchusa*	Asia, S Europe
anemone	*Hepatica*	Europe, Caucasus
asphodel	*Asphodelus*	S Europe
aster	*Aster*	Europe, Asia, N America
astilbe	*Astilbe*	Asia
aubrietia	*Aubrieta*	SE Europe
begonia	*Begonia*	S America, the Pacific
bellflower	*Campanula*	N temperate regions
bergamot	*Monarda*	N America
bistort	*Polygonum*	Japan, Himalayas
bleeding heart	*Dicentra*	China, Japan, N America
bugbane	*Cimicifuga*	N America, Japan
busy lizzie	*Impatiens*	tropics
buttercup	*Ranunculus*	temperate regions
carnation	*Dianthus*	temperate regions
catmint	*Nepeta*	Europe, Asia
celandine, giant	*Ranunculus*	Europe
Christmas rose	*Helleborus*	Europe
chrysanthemum	*Chrysanthemum*	China
cinquefoil	*Potentilla*	Europe, Asia
columbine (or granny's bonnet)	*Aquilegia*	Europe
Cupid's dart	*Catananche*	Europe

English name	Genus/family	Country/continent of origin
dahlia	*Dahlia*	Mexico
daisy	*Bellis*	Europe
delphinium	*Delphinium*	Europe, N America
echinacea	*Echinacea*	N America
edelweiss	*Leontopodium*	Europe, Asia
evening primrose	*Oenothera*	N America
everlasting flower (or immortelle)	*Helichrysum*	Australia
everlasting flower, pearly	*Anaphalis*	N America, Himalayas
fleabane	*Erigeron*	Australia
forget-me-not	*Myosotis*	Europe
foxglove	*Digitalis*	Europe, Asia
fraxinella	*Dictamnus*	Europe, Asia
gentian	*Gentiana*	temperate regions
geranium	*Pelargonium*	temperate regions, subtropics
geum	*Geum*	S Europe, N America
goat's beard	*Aruncus*	N Europe
golden rod	*Solidago*	Europe
granny's bonnet *see* columbine		
gypsophila	*Gypsophila*	Europe, Asia
Hattie's pincushion (or the melancholy gentleman)	*Astrantia*	Europe
heliopsis	*Heliopsis*	N America
hellebore	*Helleborus*	Asia, Greece
herb Christopher	*Actaea*	N America
hollyhock	*Alcaea*	Europe, China
hosta	*Hosta*	China, Japan
immortelle *see* everlasting flower		
kaffir lily	*Schizostylis*	S Africa
kirengeshoma	*Kirengeshoma*	Japan
liatris	*Liatris*	N America
lobelia	*Lobelia*	Africa, N America, Australia
loosestrife	*Lysimachia*	Europe
lotus	*Lotus*	Asia, America
Lupin	*Lupinus*	N America
marigold, African, French	*Tagetes*	America (Mexico)
marigold, pot	*Calendula*	unknown
meadow rue	*Thalictrum*	Europe, Asia
mullein	*Verbascum*	Europe, Asia
nasturtium	*Tropaeolum*	S America, Mexico
orchid	*Orchidaea*	tropics
ox-eye	*Buphthalmum*	Europe
pansy	*Viola*	temperate regions
peony	*Paeonia*	Asia, Europe

FLOWERS (Herbaceous) (cont.)

English name	Genus/family	Country/continent of origin
Peruvian lily	*Alstroemeria*	S America
petunia	*Petunia*	S America
phlox	*Phlox*	America
poppy	*Papaver*	N temperate regions
primrose	*Primula*	N temperate regions
primula	*Primula*	N temperate regions
red-hot poker	*Kniiphofia*	S Africa
salvia	*Salvia*	S America, Europe, Asia
sea holly	*Eryngium*	Europe, S America
sidalcea	*Sidalcea*	N America
snapdragon	*Antirrhinum*	Europe, Asia, S America
speedwell	*Veronica*	Europe, Asia
spiderwort	*Tradescantia*	N America
stokesia	*Stokesia*	N America
sunflower	*Helianthus*	N America
sweet pea	*Lathyrus*	Mediterranean
sweet william	*Dianthus*	S Europe
thistle, globe	*Echinops*	Europe, Asia
thistle, Scotch (or cotton)	*Onopordum*	Europe
violet	*Viola*	N temperate regions
water chestnut	*Trapa*	Asia
water lily	*Nymphaea*	worldwide
wolfsbane	*Aconitum*	Europe, Asia
yarrow	*Achillea*	Europe, W Asia

FLOWERS (Bulbs, corms, rhizomes and tubers)

English name	Genus/family	Country/continent of origin
African lily (or lily-of-the-Nile)	*Agapanthus*	S Africa
agapanthus	*Agapanthus*	S Africa
allium	*Allium*	Asia, Europe
amaryllis (or belladonna lily)	*Amaryllis*	S Africa, tropical America
anemone	*Anemone*	Mediterranean, Asia, Europe
belladonna lily *see* amaryllis		
bluebell	*Hyacinthoides*	Europe
camassia	*Camassia*	N America
chionodoxa (or glory of the snow)	*Chionodoxa*	Greece, Turkey
crinum	*Crinum*	S Africa
crocosmia	*Crocosmia*	S Africa

English name	Genus/family	Country/continent of origin
crocus	*Crocus*	Mediterranean, Asia, Africa
crown imperial	*Fritillaria*	N India
cyclamen	*Cyclamen*	Asia, Mediterranean
daffodil (or narcissus)	*Narcissus*	Mediterranean, Europe
dog's tooth violet *see* erythronium		
erythronium (or dog's tooth violet)	*Erythronium*	Europe, Asia
fritillaria	*Fritillaria*	Europe, Asia, N America
galtonia	*Galtonia*	S Africa
gladiolus	*Gladiolus*	Europe, Asia, NE Africa
glory of the snow *see* chionodoxa		
harebell	*Campanula*	N temperate regions
hippeastrum	*Hippeastrum*	tropical America
hyacinth	*Hyacinthus*	S Europe, Asia
hyacinth, grape	*Muscari*	Europe, Mediterranean
hyacinth, wild	*Scilla*	Asia, S Europe
iris	*Iris*	N temperate regions
Ithuriel's spear	*Brodiaea*	N America
lapeirousia	*Lapeirousia*	S Africa
lily	*Lilium*	China, Europe, America
lily-of-the-Nile *see* African lily		
lily-of-the-valley	*Convallaria*	Europe, Asia, America
naked ladies	*Colchicum*	Asia, Europe
nerine	*Nerine*	S Africa
ornithogalum	*Ornithogalum*	S Africa
peacock (or tiger flower)	*Tigridia*	Asia
rouge, giant	*Tigridia*	Mexico
snake's head	*Fritillaria*	Europe
snowdrop	*Galanthus*	Europe
snowflake	*Leucojum*	S Europe
solfaterre	*Crocosmia* x *crocosmiflora*	S Africa
Solomon's seal	*Polygonatum*	Europe, Asia
squill	*Scilla*	Europe, Asia, S Africa
sternbergia	*Sternbergia*	Europe
striped squill	*Puschkinia*	Asia
tiger flower *see* peacock		
tiger lily	*Lilium*	Asia
tulip	*Tulipa*	Europe, Asia
wand flower	*Dierama*	S Africa
winter aconite	*Eranthis*	Greece, Turkey

INVERTEBRATES

The invertebrates are animals with no backbone. Some have no skeleton at all, but many have external skeletons or shells that give them a rigid shape and provide anchorage for their muscles. There are about 30 major groups or phyla of invertebrates although the great majority of species belong to just two phyla — the Mollusca and the Arthropoda. The latter includes the insects, spiders, crustaceans and several other groups, all of which have segmented bodies and jointed legs. The majority of invertebrates are quite small, but examples of the largest — the giant squid — have been recorded as much as 15m/49ft long and may weigh well over a tonne.

For molluscs, lengths given are normally maximum shell lengths, but (b) indicates body length; for spiders, lengths are body lengths, although legs may be much longer.

Molluscs: Phylum Mollusca

Name	Size cm[1]	Notable features	Range and habitat
Slugs and snails/Gastropoda	*(c.*50 000 species)		
albalone haliotis (several species)	< 30	collected for food/pearly shells	warm seas worldwide
common limpet	< 5.5	conical shell pulled tightly down on rocks when tide is out	worldwide
common periwinkle	< 2.5	thick, dull brown shell; the fishmonger's winkle	N Atlantic and adjacent seas; rocky shores
conch (several species)	< 33	shells often used as trumpets	tropical seas
cone shell (*c.*600 species	< 23	some species dangerous to man; beautiful shells much sought after	warm seas worldwide
cowrie (*c.*150 species in several genera)	< 10	shiny, china-like shells, were once used as money	warm seas worldwide
giant African snail	< 15	agricultural pest; lays hard-shelled eggs as big as those of a thrush	originally Africa, now tropical Asia and Pacific
great grey slug	< 20 (b)	common in gardens; mates in mid-air, hanging from a rope of slime	Europe
great ramshorn snail	< 3	shell forms a flat spiral; body has bright red blood	Europe; still and slow-moving freshwater
roman snail	< 5	often a pest, but cultivated for food in some areas	C and S Europe; lime soils
sea butterfly (*c.*100 species in several genera)	< 5	swims by flapping wing-like extensions of the foot	oceans worldwide; most common in warm waters
slipper limpet	< 6	a serious pest in oyster and mussel farms	originally N America, now common on coasts of Europe
whelk	< 12	collected for human food	N Atlantic and neighbouring seas

Name	Size cm[1]	Notable features	Range and habitat
Bivalves/Lamellibranchia		**(c.8 000 species)**	
common cockle	< 5	important food for fish and wading birds	European coasts
common mussel	< 11	farmed on a large scale for human food	coasts of Europe and eastern N America
great scallop	< 15	strongly ribbed, eared shells with one valve flatter than other	European coasts; usually below low tide level
oyster	< 15	farmed in huge numbers for human food	coasts of Europe and Africa
piddock	< 12	uses rasp-like shell to bore into soft rocks and wood	coasts of Europe and eastern N America
pod razor-shell	< 20	long, straight shell, with open ends	European coasts

Name	Size cm[1]	Notable features	Range and habitat
Squids and octopuses/Cephalopoda		**(c.750 species)**	
blue-ringed octopus	10 (span)	the only octopus known to have killed people	Australian coasts
common cuttlefish	< 30	flat, oval body can change colour	coastal waters of Atlantic and nighbouring seas
common octopus	< 300 (span)	not dangerous to people	Atlantic and Mediterranean coastal waters
common squid	< 50	deep pink in life, fading to grey after death	Atlantic and Mediterranean coastal waters
giant squid	< 1500	main food of the sperm whale	oceans worldwide

Crustaceans: Phylum Arthropoda

Name	Size cm[1]	Notable features	Range and habitat
Crustacea		**(c.30 000 species)**	
acorn barnacle	< 1.5 (diam.)	cemented to intertidal rocks	worldwide
common prawn	< 10	scavenger; almost transparent in life	European coasts; usually stony or rocky shores

Name	Size cm[1]	Notable features	Range and habitat
common shrimp	< 7	much used for human food	coasts of Europe and eastern N America

[1] To convert cm to in, multiply by 0.3937.

INVERTEBRATES (cont.)

Crustaceans (cont.)

Name	Size cm[1]	Notable features	Range and habitat
edible crab	< 20	widely caught for human food	Eastern N Atlantic and neighbouring seas
fiddler crab (many species)	< 3	male has one big, colourful claw	tropical seashores and mangrove swamps
hermit crab (several species and genera)	< 15	soft-bodied crab that inhabits empty seashells	worldwide; mainly in coastal waters
krill	< 5	main food of the whalebone whales	mainly the southern oceans
common lobster	< 70	overfished; rare in many places	European coasts
noble crayfish	< 15	reared for human food, especially in France	Europe
Norway lobster	< 25	marketed as scampi	European seas
robber crab	< 45	related to hermit crab; often climbs trees	islands and coasts of Indian and Pacific oceans
spiny lobster	< 45	a popular food in S Europe; also known as crawfish	Mediterranean and Atlantic; rocky coasts
water flea (many species)	< 0.5	major food of small fish	worldwide; freshwater
woodlouse (many genera and species)	< 2.5	only major group of terrestrial crustaceans, lives in damp places	worldwide

Spiders: Phylum Arthropoda

Name	Size cm[1]	Notable features	Range and habitat
Arachnida		**(c.40 000 species)**	
bird-eating spider (c.800 species in several genera)	< 10	often found in trees, where they sometimes capture nestling birds; venom not dangerous to people	warmer parts of the Americas and southern Africa
black widow	< 1.6	caused many human deaths, but bites are now cured with antivenin	most warm climates including S Europe
bolas spider (several species and genera)	< 1.5	catches moths by whirling a single thread of silk	N and S America, Africa and Australasia
crab spider (c.3 000 species in numerous genera)	< 2	mostly crab-like spiders that lie in wait for prey — often in flowers	worldwide
funnel-web spider (several species)	< 5	among the deadliest spiders, inhabit tubular webs	Australia
garden spider	< 1.2	black to ginger, with a white cross on the back	N Hemisphere

Name	Size cm[1]	Notable features	Range and habitat
gladiator spider (several species)	< 2.5	makes sticky webs which it throws at passing prey, usually at night	warm regions and some cooler parts of N America and Australia
house spider (c.90 species)	< 2	harmless, long-legged, fast-running spider	mostly N Hemisphere
jumping spider (c.4 000 species in many genera)	< 1.5	large-eyed spider that leaps onto prey; often brilliantly coloured	worldwide
money spider (many species and genera)	< 0.6	believed to bring wealth or good fortune	worldwide, but most common in cooler areas of N Hemisphere
orb-web spider (c.2 500 species in many genera)	< 3	the makers of the familiar wheel-shaped webs, up to a metre or more in diameter	worldwide
raft spider (c.100 species)	< 2.5	hunting spiders that lurk at the edge of pools or on floating objects	worldwide
spitting spider	0.6	catches prey by spitting strands of sticky, venom-coated gum	worldwide; normally only in buildings
tarantula	< 3	a wolf spider whose bite was believed to be curable only by performing a frantic dance — the tarantella	S Europe
trapdoor spider (c.700 species in several genera)	< 3	live in burrows closed by hinged lids of silk and debris	most warm parts of the world, including S Europe
water spider	< 1.5	only truly aquatic spider, lives in air-filled web fixed to water plants	Eurasia; in ponds and slow-moving streams
wolf spider (c. 2 500 species in many genera)	< 3	large-eyed hunting spiders, generally harmless but some of the larger species have dangerous bites	worldwide, but most common in cooler parts of N Hemisphere
zebra spider	< 0.6	black and white jumping spider; commonly hunts on rocks/walls	N Hemisphere; often in and around houses

Insects: Phylum Arthropoda

Name	Size cm[1]	Notable features	Range and habitat
Bristletails/Thysanura		**(c.600 species)**	
silverfish	2	wingless scavenger of starchy food	worldwide

[1] To convert cm to in, multiply by 0.3937.

INVERTEBRATES (cont.)

Insects (cont.)

Name	Size cm[1]	Notable features	Range and habitat
Mayflies/Ephemeroptera		(*c.*2 500 species) flimsy insects with 2 or 3 long 'tails'; adults only live for a few hours	worldwide
Dragonflies/Odonata	< 10	(*c.*5 000 species) long-bodied; gauzy wings; most catch insects in mid-air	
Crickets and grasshoppers/Orthoptera		(*c.*17 000 species)	
bush cricket (thousands of species)	< 15	like grasshoppers but with very long antennae; several N American species are called katydids	worldwide, apart from coldest areas
desert locust	8.5	swarms periodically destroy crops	Africa and Asia
house cricket	2	scavenger in houses/ rubbish dumps	worldwide
migratory locust	< 5	swarm in Africa, but solitary in Europe	Africa and S Europe
Stick insects and leaf insects/Phasmida		(*c.*2 500 species, mostly tropical)	
stick insect (over 2 400 species)	< 3	stick-like green or brown bodies; often kept as a 'pet'	warm areas, including S Europe
leaf insect (*c.*50 species)	< 12	very flat, leaf-like, green or brown bodies	SE Asia
Earwigs/Dermaptera	< 3	(*c.*1 300 species) slender, brownish insects with prominent pincers at rear	originally Africa, now worldwide
Cockroaches and mantids/Dictyoptera		(*c.*5 500 species)	
American cockroach	4	scavenger, living outside (if warm) or in buildings	worldwide
praying mantis (*c.*2 000 species)	< 15	catch other insects with spiky front legs	all warm areas

Name	Size cm[1]	Notable features	Range and habitat
Termites/Isoptera		**(over 2 000 species)** colonies in mounds of earth, in dead wood or underground; many are timber pests	mostly tropical
Bugs/Hemiptera aphid (numerous species)	< 0.5	**(c.70 000 species)** sap-sucking insects; many are serious pests	worldwide
bedbug	0.5	blood-sucking; feeds at night	worldwide
cicada (numerous species)	< 20 (w)[2]	males make loud, shrill sounds; young stages live underground	worldwide, mainly in warm climates
froghopper	0.6	young stages live in froth, often called cuckoo-spit	N Hemisphere
pondskater	1	skims across surface of still water	N Hemisphere
Thrips/Thysanoptera		**(over 3 000 species)** cause much crop damage; fly in huge numbers in thundery weather	worldwide
Lacewings/Neuroptera antlion	9 (w)	**(over 6 000 species)** larvae make pits in sandy soil and feed on insects that fall into them	Eurasia
green lacewing (several genera and many species)	< 5	feed on aphids and other small insects	worldwide
Scorpion flies/Mecoptera		**(c.400 species)** male abdomen is ususally turned up like a scorpion's tail; harmless	worldwide
Butterflies and moths/Lepidoptera *Butterflies (c.18 000 species)*		**(c.150 000 species)**	
birdwing butterfly (several genera and species)	< 30 (w)	include the world's largest butterflies; many becoming rare through collecting/loss of habitat	SE Asia and N Australia
cabbage white butterfly	<: 7 (w)	caterpillar is a serious pest of cabbages and other brassicas	Eurasia and N Africa

[1] To convert cm to in, multiply by 0.3937.

INVERTEBRATES (cont.)

Butterflies and moths/Lepidoptera (cont.)

Name	Size cm[1]	Notable features	Range and habitat
fritillary butterfly (numerous genera and species)	< 8 (w)	mostly orange with black spots above and silvery spots below	mostly N hemisphere
monarch butterfly	< 10 (w)	orange with black markings; hibernates in huge swarms in Mexico and southern USA	mostly N America and Pacific area
skipper butterfly (many genera and species)	< 8 (w)	mostly small brown or orange grassland insects with darting flight	worldwide
swallowtail butterfly (numerous genera and species)	< 12 (w)	prominent 'tails' on hindwings; many becoming rare through collecting and loss of habitat	worldwide, but mostly tropical
Moths (c.132 000 species)			
burnet moth (many species)	4 (w)	protected by poisonous body fluids and gaudy black and red colours	Eurasia and N Africa
clothes moth (several species)	< 1.5 (w)	caterpillars damage woollen fabrics	worldwide
death's head hawkmoth	< 13.5 (w)	skull-like pattern on its thorax	Africa and Eurasia
hummingbird hawkmoth	< 6 (w)	produces a loud hum as it hovers	Eurasia
pine processionary moth	< 4	larvae feed in long processions at night; forest pest	S and C Europe
silk moth	< 6 (w)	cream coloured moth bred for fine silk obtained from cocoon; all cultured moths flightless	native of China; now unknown in the wild
tiger moth (many genera and species)	< 10	mostly brightly coloured and hairy, with poisonous body fluids	worldwide
True flies/Diptera		**(*c.*90 000 species, a few without wings)**	
crane-fly or leather-jacket (many genera and species)	< 6 (w)	slender, long-legged flies; larvae of many are leather-jackets that damage crop roots	worldwide

Name	Size cm[1]	Notable features	Range and habitat
house-fly	0.7	abundant on farms and rubbish dumps; becoming less common in houses; breeds in dung and other decaying matter and carries germs	worldwide
hover-fly (many genera and species)	< 4	many have amazing hovering ability; many are black and yellow mimics of bees and wasps	worldwide
mosquito (many genera and species)	< 1.5	blood-suckers; spread malaria and other diseases	worldwide
tsetse-fly (c.20 species)	1	bood-suckers; spread human sleeping sickness and cattle diseases	tropical Africa
Fleas/Siphonaptera		**(c.1 800 species)** wingless, blood-sucking parasites; long hind legs enable them to jump many times their own length	worldwide
Bees, wasps and ants/ Hymenoptera		**(over 120 000 species)**	
army ant (several genera and species)	< 4	live in mobile colonies, some of over a million ants	tropics
bumble bee (many species)	< 3.5	plump, hairy bees living in annual colonies	worldwide, except Australia
honey bee	< 2	less hairy than bumble bees; live in permanent colonies, mostly in artificial hives; store honey	worldwide (probably native of SE Asia)
honeypot ant (several genera and species)	< 2	some workers gorge themselves with sugar-rich food and become living food for other ants	deserts across the world
ichneumon (thousands of genera and species)	< 5	parasites of other insects	worldwide
leaf-cutter ant (several species)	< 1.8	workers carry leaves to large underground nests; feed on fungi that grow on the chewed leaves	tropical America

[1] To convert cm to in, multiply by 0.3937.
[2]Sizes given are normally body lengths, but (w) indicates wingspan.

INVERTEBRATES (cont.)

Bees, wasps and ants (cont.)

Name	Size cm[1]	Notable features	Range and habitat
sawfly (numerous families)	< 5	saw-like ovipositor in most females, used to cut slits in plants before laying eggs	worldwide
weaver ant (several species)	1	nest made from leaves joined by sticky silk	old world tropics
Beetles/Coleoptera		**(over 350 000 species, front wings usually form casing over body)**	
burying beetle (several species)	< 2.5	bury small dead animals, on which they lay their eggs	worldwide
click beetle or wireworm (many genera and species)	< 4	bullet-shaped; flick into the air to turn over — making a loud click; larvae damage crop roots	worldwide
colorado beetle	1	seriously damage potato crops	N America and now Europe
deathwatch beetle	0.7	tunnelling larvae do immense damage to old building timbers; adults tap wood as mating call	N Hemisphere
devil's coach-horse	2.5	called cocktail for its habit of raising its rear end	Eurasia
glow-worm	1.5	wingless female glows with greenish light to attract males	Europe
furniture beetle or woodworm	0.5	cause much damage to furniture and building timbers	worldwide
goliath beetle (several species)	< 15	world's heaviest beetles	Africa
grain weevil	0.3	destroys all kinds of stored grain	worldwide
ladybird (c.3 500 species in many genera)	1	aphid-eating habits make them friends of gardeners	worldwide
scarab beetle (many species)	< 3	some form dung into balls and roll it round before burying it; introduced into Australia to deal with sheep and cattle dung	most warm parts of the world
stag beetle	5	males wrestle rivals with huge antler-like jaws	Eurasia

[1] To convert cm to in, multiply by 0.3937.

FISH

Name	Size cm[1]	Range and habitat	Notable features
albacore	to 130	tropical, warm temperate	food and sport fish
anchovy	9–12	temperate	important food fish
angler fish	5–8	tropical, temperate	large jaws
barracuda	30–240	tropical, warm temperate	carnivorous; large teeth
blenny	20–49	temperate, tropical	devoid of scales
bonito	to 90	temperate, warm	food fish; sport fish
bream	41–80	temperate (N Europe)	deep-bodied; food fish
brill	to 70	temperate	flat fish; food fish
butterfly fish	to 15	tropical	brightly coloured
carp	51–61	temperate	important food fish
catfish	90–135	temperate (N America)	important food fish
chub	30–60	temperate (Europe)	popular sport fish
cod	to 120	temperate, N hemisphere	common cod important food fish
conger eel	274	temperate	upper jaw longer than lower
dab	20–40	temperate (Europe)	flatfish; food fish
dace	15–30	temperate (Europe, former USSR)	sport fish
damsel fish	5–15	tropical, temperate	brightly coloured
dogfish	60–100	temperate (Europe)	food fish (sold as rock salmon)
dolphin fish (dorado)	to 200	tropical, warm temperate	prized sport fish; food fish
dory	30–60	temperate	deep-bodied; food fish
eagle ray	to 200	tropical, temperate	'wings'; young born live
eel	to 50 (male), to 100 (female)	temperate	elongate cylindrical body form; important food fish
electric eel	to 240	Orinoco, Amazon basins (S America)	produces powerful electric shocks
electric or torpedo ray	to 180	tropical, temperate	produces strong electric shocks
file fish	5–13	tropical, warm temperate	food fish
flounder	to 51	temperate (Europe)	flatfish; locally important food fish
flying fish	25–50	tropical, warm temperate	can jump/glide above water surface
goat fish see red mullet			
goby	1–27	tropical, temperate	pelvic fins form a sucker-like fin
goldfish	to 30	temperate	popular ornamental fish
grenadier see rat-tail			

[1] To convert cm to in, multiply by 0.3937.

FISH (cont.)

Name	Size cm[1]	Range and habitat	Notable features
grey mullet	to 75	tropical, temperate	food fish
grouper	5–370	tropical, warm temperate	prized sport and food fish
gurnard (or sea robin)	to 75	tropical, warm temperate	many produce audible sounds
hake	to 180	temperate	head and jaws large; food fish
halibut	to 250	temperate (Atlantic)	prized food fish
herring	to 40	temperate (N Atlantic, Arctic)	important food fish
lamprey	to 91	temperate (N Atlantic)	primitive jawless fish; food fish
lantern fish	2–15	tropical, temperate	body has numerous light organs
lemon sole	to 66	temperate	feeds on polychaete worms; food fish
loach	to 15	temperate (Europe, Asia)	popular aquarium fish
mackerel	to 66	temperate (N Atlantic)	important food fish
manta ray	120–900 (width)	tropical	fleshy 'horns' at side of head
minnow	to 12	temperate (N Europe, Asia)	locally abundant
monkfish	to 180	temperate (N Atlantic, Mediterranean)	cross between shark and ray in shape
moorish idol	to 22	tropical (Indo-Pacific)	bold black/white stripes with yellow
moray eel	to 130	temperate, tropical	pointed snout; long, sharp teeth
parrot fish	25–190	tropical	teeth fused to form parrot-like beak
perch	30–50	temperate	food fish; sport fish
pike	to 130	temperate	prized by anglers
pilchard (or sardine)	to 25	temperate (N Atlantic, Mediterranean)	important food fish, often canned
pipefish	15–160	tropical, warm temperate	males of some species carry eggs in brood pouch
plaice	50–90	temperate (Europe)	flatfish; eyes on right side
puffer	3–25	tropical, warm temperate	often spiny; Japanese food delicacy
rat-tail (or grenadier)	40–110	temperate, tropical	large head, tapering body
ray	39–113	temperate	front flattened with pectoral fins
red mullet (or goat fish)	to 40	tropical, temperate	food fish
remora	12–46	tropical, warm temperate	large sucking disc on head
roach	35–53	temperate (Europe, former USSR)	popular sport fish

Name	Size cm[1]	Range and habitat	Notable features
sailfish	to 360	tropical, warm temperate	long tall dorsal fin; prized sport fish
salmon	to 150	temperate	prized sport and food fish
sandeel	to 20	temperate (N hemisphere)	very important food for seabirds
sardine *see* pilchard			
scorpion-fish	to 50	tropical, temperate	distinctive fin and body spines
sea bass	60–100	tropical, temperate	food fish; popular sport fish
sea robin *see* gurnard			
sea-bream	35-51	tropical, temperate	food fish; sport fish
seahorse	to 15	tropical, warm temperate	horse-like head; swims upright
shark, basking	870–1 350	tropical, temperate	second largest living fish
shark, great white	to 630	tropical	fierce; young born, not hatched
shark, hammerhead	360–600	tropical, warm temperate	head flattened into hammer shape
shark, tiger	360–600	tropical, warm temperate	vertical stripes on body; fierce
shark, whale	1 020–1 800	tropical	largest living fish; feeds on plankton
skate	200–285	temperate	food fish
smelt	20–30	temperate	related to salmon and trout
sole	30–60	tropical, temperate	flat fish; food fish
sprat	13–16	temperate	food fish (white bait when small)
squirrel fish	12–30	tropical	brightly coloured; nocturnal
stickleback	5–10	temperate (N hemisphere)	male builds nest, guards eggs
stingray	106–140	tropical, temperate	tail whip-like, with poison spine(s)
sturgeon	100–500	temperate (N hemisphere)	eggs prized as caviar
sunfish	to 400	tropical, warm temperate	tail fin absent; body almost circular
surgeon fish (or tang)	20–45	tropical, subtropical	spine on tail erected for defence
swordfish	200–500	tropical, temperate	upper jaw forms flathead 'sword'
tang *see* surgeon fish			
trigger fish	10–60	tropical	dorsal spine erected for defence

[1] To convert cm to in, multiply by 0.3937.

FISH (cont.)

Name	Size cm[1]	Range and habitat	Notable features
trout	23–140	temperate	prized food fish
tuna, skipjack	to 100	tropical, temperate	important food fish
tuna, yellow fin	to 200	tropical, warm temperate	elongated body; important food fish
turbot	50–100	temperate (N Atlantic)	flat fish; prized food fish
wrasse	7–210	tropical, warm temperate	brightly coloured

AMPHIBIANS AND REPTILES

The Amphibians are a class of cold blooded vertebrates including frogs, toads, newts and salamanders. There are approximately 4 000 species. They have a moist, thin skin without scales, and the adults live partly or entirely on land, but can usually only survive in damp habitats. They return to water to lay their eggs, which hatch to form fish-like larvae or tadpoles that breathe by means of gills, but gradually develop lungs as they approach adulthood.

Reptiles are egg-laying vertebrates of the class Reptilia, having evolved from primitive amphibians; 6 547 species divided into Squamata (lizards and snakes), Chelonia (tortoises and turtles), Crocodylia (crocodiles and alligators) and Rhynococephalia (the tuatara).

Most reptiles live on the land, breathe with lungs, and have horny or plated skins. Reptiles require the rays of the sun to maintain their body temperature, ie they are cold-blooded or ectothermic. This confines them to warm, tropical and sub-tropical regions, but does allow some species to exist in particularly hot desert environments in which mammals and birds would find it impossible to sustain life.

Extinct species of reptile include the dinosaur and pterodactyl.

Amphibians

Name	Size cm[1]	Distribution	Special features
common spadefoot	to 8	C Europe	a toad with a pale-coloured tubercle (the spade) on its hind foot
frog, arrow poison	0.85–1.24	C and S America	smallest known amphibian; skin highly poisonous
frog, common	to 10	Europe except Mediterranean region and most of Iberia	most widespread European frog
frog, edible	to 12	S and C Europe	often heavily spotted; whitish vocal sacs
frog, goliath	to 81.5	Africa	world's largest frog
frog, leopard	5–13	N America	usually has light-edged dark spots on body
frog, marsh	to 15	SW and E Europe and SE England	extremely aquatic
frog, painted	to 7	Iberia and SW France	usually smooth and yellow-brown, grey or reddish with dark spots

Name	Size cm[1]	Distribution	Special features
frog, parsley	to 5	W Europe	slender bodied, with a whitish underside
hellbender	to 63	USA	a salamander with wrinkled folds of flesh on body
mudpuppy	18–43	N America	a salamander with bright red external gills
natterjack	to 10	SW and C Europe	a toad with a bright yellow stripe along its back
newt, alpine	to 12	C Europe	dark, mottled back and a uniformly orange belly and bluish spotted sides
newt, Bosca's	7–10	Iberian Peninsula	similar to smooth newt without a dorsal crest
newt, marbled	to 15	Iberia and W France	bright red, yellow or orange stripe on velvety green and black mottled back
newt, palmate	to 9	W Europe	palmate (webbed) feet; short filament at the end of breeding male's tail
newt, smooth	to 11	Europe	breeding male develops a wavy crest
newt, warty (great crested newt)	to 17	Europe except Iberia and Ireland	bright orange or yellow spotted belly and warty skin
salamander, alpine	to 15	C Europe	large glands on back of head
salamander, fire	to 25	C and S Europe	large glands on sides of head contain venomous secretion
salamander, giant chinese	114 (average)	China	world's largest amphibian
salamander, gold-striped	15–16	Iberian Peninsula	thin with shiny skin
salamander, spectacled	to 11	W Italy	only European salamander with four toes on hind feet
toad, common	to 15	Europe except N Scandinavia, Ireland and some Mediterranean islands	largest European toad; usually brownish or greyish with warty skin
toad, green	to 10	E Europe	distinctive colouring—grey or greenish with darker marbled markings
toad, marine	to 23.8	S America	world's largest toad
toad, midwife	to 5	W Europe	male carries strings of eggs wrapped around hind legs

[1] To convert cm to in, multiply by 0.3937.

AMPHIBIANS AND REPTILES (cont.)

Amphibians (cont.)

Name	Size cm[1]	Distribution	Special features
toad, surinam	to 20	S America	female incubates eggs on her back
toad, yellow-bellied	to 5	C and S Europe	bright yellow or orange, black-blotched belly
treefrog, common	to 5	S and C Europe	usually bright green; often found in trees high above ground

Reptiles

Name	Size cm[1]	Distribution	Special features
alligator	200–550	S USA, C and S America and E China	although rare, attacks can cause human fatalities; endangered species apart from American alligator
anguid	6–30	N and S America, Europe, Asia and NW Africa	bony-plated scales which reach round its underside give a rigid appearance
boa	200–400	West N America, S America, Africa, Madagascar, Asia, Fiji, Solomons and New Guinea	famous constricting snake, includes species of anaconda
chameleon	2–28	Africa outwith the Sahara, Madagascar, Middle East, S Spain, S Arabian peninsula, Sri Lanka, Crete, India and Pakistan	noted for its ability to change colour to blend with its environment
crocodile	150–750	pantropical and some temperate regions of Africa	distinguished from the alligator by the visible fourth tooth in the lower jaw; several species endangered
gecko	1.5–24	N and S America, Africa, S Europe, Asia and Australia	noted for its vocalization and ability to climb; able to shed its tail for defence
iguana	to 200	C and S America, Madagascar, Fiji and Tonga	terrestrial and tree-dwelling lizard; able to survive in exceptionally high temperatures
lizard, beaded	33–45	SW United States, W Mexico to Guatemala	possesses mildy venomous bite
lizard, blind	12–16.5	SE Asia	eyes concealed within the skin

Name	Size cm[1]	Distribution	Special features
lizard, Bornean earless	to 20	Borneo	no external ear opening; partly accuatic
lizard, chisel-tooth	4–35	Africa, Asia and Australia	distinctive teeth; family includes the flying dragon
lizard, girdle-tailed	5-27.5	Africa south of the Sahara, Madagascar	terrestrial; active by day; adapted to arid environments
lizard, monitor	12–150	Africa, S Asia, Indo-Australian archipelago, Philippines, New Guinea and Australia	includes the Komodo dragon, the largest living lizard which can kill pigs and small deer
lizard, night	3.5–12	C America	most species active by night
lizard, snake	6.5–31	New Guinea and Australia	snake-like appearance; broad but highly extensible tongue
lizard, wall and sand	4–22	Europe, Africa, Asia and Indo-Australian archipelago	open and sandy environments; terrestrial, active by day
lizard, worm	15–35	subtropical regions of N and S America, Africa, Middle East, Asia and Europe	worm-like, burrowing reptile; some species have rare ability to move backwards and forwards
pipesnake	less than 100	S America, SE Asia	tail has brilliantly coloured red underside; eats other snakes
python	100–1 000	tropical and subtropical Africa, SE Asia, Australia, Mexico and C America	capable of killing humans, especially children, by constriction
skink	2.8–35	tropical and temperate regions	terrestrial, tree-dwelling or burrowing species, including highly adept swimmers
snake, dawn blind	11–30	C and S America	short tail, indistinct head, one or two teeth in the lower jaw
snake, front fanged	38–560	worldwide in warm regions	highly venomous family with short fangs
snake, harmless	13–350	worldwide	most species cannot produce venomous saliva
snake, shieldtail	20–50	S India and Sri Lanka	tail forms a cylindrical shield
snake, thread	15–90	C and S America, Africa, Asia	small and exceptionally slender burrowing snake

[1] To convert cm to in, multiply by 0.3937.

AMPHIBIANS AND REPTILES (cont.)

Reptiles (cont.)

Name	Size cm[1]	Distribution	Special features
snake, typical blind	15–90	C and S America, Africa south of the Sahara, SE Europe, S Asia, Taiwan and Australia	burrowing snake with tiny, concealed eyes and no teeth on lower jaw
tortoise	10–140	S Europe, Africa, Asia, C and S America	includes smallest species of turtle, the Speckled Cape tortoise and one of the longest lived turtles, the spur-thighed tortoise
tuatara	45–61	islands off New Zealand	third eye in the top of its head
turtle, Afro-American side-necked	12–90	S America, Africa, Madagascar, Seychelles and Mauritius	bottom-dweller that rarely requires to come to the surface
turtle, American mud and musk	11–27	N and S America	lives mostly in freshwater, produces evil smelling secretion
turtle, Austro-American side-necked	14–48	S America, Australia and New Guinea	includes the matamata, the most adept of the ambush-feeders at the gape and suck technique of capturing prey
turtle, big-headed	20	SE Asia	large head cannot be retracted
turtle, C American river	to 65	Vera Cruz, Mexico, Honduras	freshwater creature with well-developed shell
turtle, Mexican musk	to 38	Mexico to Honduras	freshwater creature dwelling in marshes and swamps
turtle, pig-nosed softshell	55 or over	New Guinea and N Australia	specialized swimmer; plateless skin and fleshy, pig-like snout
turtle, pond and river	11.4–80	N and C America, S Europe, N Africa, Asia and Argentina	family ranges from tiny bog turtle to the largest of the river turtles, the Malaysian giant turtle
turtle, sea	75–213	pantropical, and some subtropical and temperate regions	rapid movement through water contrasts with slow movements of turtles on land
turtle, snapping	47–66	N and C America	large-headed, aggressive bottom dweller

Name	Size cm[1]	Distribution	Special features
turtle, softshell	30–115	N America, Africa, Asia and Indo-Australian archipelago	leathered, plateless skin; noted for its prominent, pointed snout
viper	25–365	N and S America, Africa, Europe and Asia	venomous; includes rattlesnake and sidewinder
whiptail and racerunner	37–45	N and S Asia	eaten by S American Indians, used in traditional medicines
xenosaur	10–15	Mexico, Guatemala and S China	terrestrial, sedentary and secretive

BIRDS

Birds are warm-blooded, egg-laying, and, in the case of adults, feathered vertebrates of the class Aves; there are approximately 8 600 species classified into 29 Orders and 181 Families. Birds are constructed for flight. The body is streamlined to reduce air resistance, the fore-limbs are modified as feathered wings, and the skeletal structure, heart and wing muscles, centre of gravity, and lung capacity are all designed for the act of flying.

Two exceptions to this are the ratites or flightless birds which have become too large to be capable of sustained flight, eg the ostrich, kiwi and emu, and the penguin which has evolved into a highly aquatic creature.

Birds have evolved from reptiles, their closest living relative being the crocodile.

Flightless Birds

Name	Size cm[1]	Distribution	Special features
cassowary	150	Australia and New Guinea	claws can be lethal
emu	160–190	Australia	highly mobile
kiwi	35–55	New Zealand	smallest of Ratitae order
ostrich	275	dry areas of Africa	fastest animal on two legs
rhea	100–150	grasslands of S America	live in flocks
tinamou	15–49	C and S America	able to sustain short flights

Birds of prey

Name	Size cm[1]	Distribution	Special features
barn owl	30–45	worldwide	feathered legs
falcon	15–60	worldwide	excellent flying skills/vision
buzzard	80	worldwide except Australasia and Malaysia	perches often, kills prey on ground
condor	60–100	the Americas	Andean condor has largest wingspan of any living bird

[1] To convert cm to in, multiply by 0.3937.

BIRDS (cont.)

Birds of prey (cont.)

Name	Size cm[1]	Distribution	Special features
eagle, bald	80–100	N America	white plumage on head/neck
eagle, golden	80–100	N hemisphere	kills with talons
eagle, harpy	90	C America to Argentina	world's largest eagle
eagle, sea	70–120	coastline worldwide	breeds on sea cliffs
harrier	50	worldwide	hunts using search pattern
kite	52–58	worldwide	most varied group of hawks
sparrowhawk	to 27 (male), to 38 (female)	Eurasia, NW Africa, C and S America	long tail, small round wings
osprey	55–58	worldwide	feet adapted to catch fish
owl	12–73	worldwide	acute sight and hearing
secretary bird	100	Africa	walks up to 30km/20ml daily
vulture (New World)	60–100	the Americas	lives in colonies
vulture (Old World)	150–270 (wingspan)	worldwide except the Americas	no sense of smell

Songbirds

Name	Size cm[1]	Distribution	Special features
accentor	14–18	Palaearctic	complex social organization
American warbler	10–16	N and S America	well developed songs
Australian tree-creeper	15	Australia and New Guinea	forages for food on trunks
bird of paradise	12.5–100	New Guinea, Moluccas and Eastern Australia	brilliantly ornate plumage
bowerbird	25–37	Australia and New Guinea	male builds bowers to attract female
bulbul	13–23	Africa, Madagascar, S Asia and the Philippines	beautiful singing voice
bunting	15–20	worldwide	large family
butcherbird	26–58	Australia, New Guinea and New Zealand	highly aggressive, known as 'bushman's clock'
chaffinch	11–19	Europe, N and S America, Africa and Asia	strong bill, melodious
cowbird	17–54	N and S America	gaping movements of bill
crow	20–66	worldwide, except New Zealand	complex social systems
cuckoo-shrike	14–40	Africa, S Asia	peculiar courtship display
dipper	17–20	Europe, S Asia and W regions of N and S America	strong legs and toes allow mobility to walk underwater

Name	Size cm[1]	Distribution	Special features
drongo	18–38	S Asia and Africa	pugnacious
flowerpecker	8–20	SE Asia and Australasia	tongue adapted for feeding
flycatcher (Old World)	9–27	worldwide except N and S America	tropical species brightly coloured
flycatcher, silky	to 14	N and S America	feeds on the wing
Hawaiian honeycreeper	10–20	Hawaiian Islands	varying bills between species
honeyeater	10–32	Australasia, Pacific Islands, Hawaii and S Africa	brush tongue adapted for nectar feeding
lark	11–19	worldwide	ground-dwelling
leafbird	12–24	S Asia	forest dwellers
magpie-lark	19–50	Australasia and New Guinea	adapted to urban environment
mockingbird	20–33	N and S America	ability to mimic
nuthatch	14–20	worldwide except S America and New Zealand	European species can break open nuts
oriole	18–30	Europe, Asia, Philippines, Malaysia, New Guinea, and Australia	melodious singing voice
palmchat	18	Hispaniola and W Indies	integrated nesting
robin	13	worldwide except New Zealand	territorial singing
shrike	15–35	Africa, N America, Asia and New Guinea	sharply hooked bill
sparrow	10–20	African tropics in origin, now worldwide	some species noted for urban adaptability
starling	16–45	Europe, Asia and Africa	nests in colonies
sunbird	8–16	Africa, SE Asia and Australasia	bright plumage
swallow	12–23	worldwide	strong and agile flight
thrush	12–26	worldwide, except New Zealand	loud and varied song
tit	11–14	N America, Europe, Asia and Africa	nests in holes
tree-creeper	12–15	N hemisphere and S Africa	forages on trees for food
vanga shrike	12–30	Madagascar	some endangered species
vireo	10–17	N and S America	thick/slightly hooked bill
wagtail	14–17	worldwide, although rare in Australia	spectacular song in flight
wattle-bird	25–53	New Zealand	fleshy fold at base of bill
waxbill	9–13.5	Africa, SE Asia and Australasia	several species drink by sucking
waxwing	18	W hemisphere	waxlike, red tips on secondary flight feathers
white-eye	12	Africa, SE Asia and Australasia	ring of tiny white feathers around eye

[1] To convert cm to in, multiply by 0.3937.

BIRDS (cont.)

Songbirds (cont.)

Name	Size cm[1]	Distribution	Special features
wood-swallow	15–20	tropical Asia and Australasia	tends to huddle together in small groups in trees
wren	8–15	N and S America, Europe and Asia	nests play ceremonial role in courtship

Waterfowl

Name	Size cm[1]	Distribution	Special features
duck	wide range	worldwide	gregarious, migratory
flamingo	90–180	tropics, N America, S Europe	red/pink colour of plumage
goose	wide range	N hemisphere	migratory
grebe	22–60	worldwide	highly aquatic
hammerhead	56	Africa S of the Sahara, Madagascar, and S Arabia	remarkably elaborate nest
heron	30–140	worldwide	mainly a wading bird
ibis	50–100	warmer regions of all continents	includes spoonbill named for shape of bill
loon	66–95	High latitudes of the N hemisphere, migrating to temperate zones	highly territorial/aggressive
screamer	69–90	warmer parts of S America	trumpet-like alarm call
shoebill	120	E Africa	large head on a short neck
stork	60–120	S America, Asia, Africa and Australia	long bill and long neck
swan	100–160	worldwide, freshwater, sheltered shores and estuaries	very long neck

Shorebirds

Name	Size cm[1]	Distribution	Special features
auk	16–76	cold waters of the N hemisphere	include varieties of puffin and guillemot
avocet	29–48	worldwide, except high latitudes	particularly graceful walk
courser	15–25	Africa, S Europe, Asia and Australia	inhabits dry, flat savanna, grassland, river shores
crab plover	38	coasts of E Africa, India, Persian Gulf, Ceylon and Madagascar	single species with mainly white and black plumage gull
gull	31–76	worldwide, scarce in the tropics	elaborate communication system

Name	Size cm[1]	Distribution	Special features
jacana	17–53	tropics	known as lily trotters
oystercatcher	40–45	tropical and temperate coastlines, except tropical Africa and S Asia	powerful bill for breaking shells; do not eat oysters
painted snipe	19–24	S America, Africa, S Asia and Australia	spectacular female plumage
phalarope	19–25	high latitudes of N hemisphere	wading bird; often swims
plover	15–40	worldwide	swift runner; strong flyer
sandpiper	12–60	worldwide	spectacular flight patterns
seedsnipe	17–28	W coast of S America	named after its diet
sheathbill	35–43	sub-Antarctic and E coast of S America	commmunal and quarrelsome scavenger
skimmer	37–51	tropics and subtropics of N and S America, Africa and S Asia	uniquely shaped bill aids capture of prey in shallow waters
skua	43–61	mainly high latitudes of the N hemisphere	chases other seabirds until they disgorge their food
stone-curlew	36–52	Africa, Europe, Asia, Australia and parts of S America	leg joints give alternative name thickknee

Seabirds

Name	Size cm[1]	Distribution	Special features
albatross	70–140	S Hemisphere	noted for powerful flight
cormorant (or shag)	50–100	worldwide	marine equivalent of falcons
darter	80–100	tropical, sub-tropical, temperate regions	distinctive swimming action
diving-petrel	16–25	S Hemisphere	greatly resembles the auk
frigatebird	70–110	tropical oceans	enormous wings; good flier
fulmar	to 60	N and S oceans	comes to land only to breed
gannet	up to 90	worldwide	complex mating behaviour
guillemot	38–42	N Hemisphere	egg shape adapted for cliffside dwelling
pelican	140–180	tropics and subtropics	known for its long bill
penguin	40–115	S Hemisphere	wings modified as flippers
puffin	28–32	N Hemisphere	nests in burrows
shag *see* cormorant			
shearwater	28–91	subantarctic and subtropical zones	many species known for long migrations
storm-petrel	12–25	high latitudes of N and S Hemispheres	considerable powers of migration
tropicbird	25–45	tropical seas	long central tail feathers

[1] To convert cm to in, multiply by 0.3937.

BIRDS (cont.)

Arboreal birds

Name	Size cm¹	Distribution	Special features
barbet	9–32	tropics, except Australasia	nests in rotten timber holes
bee-eater	15–38	Africa, Asia and Australia	colourful plumage
cuckoo	15–90	worldwide	some species lay their eggs in other birds' nests
cuckoo-roller	38–43	Madagascar and Comoros Islands	diminishing population
honeyguide	10–20	Africa and S Asia	eats wax from honeycombs
hoopoe	31	Africa, SE Asia and S Europe	distinctive 'hoo hoo' call
hornbill	38–126	tropics of Africa and Australasia	long, heavy bill
jacamar	13–30	tropical America	long, slender bill
kingfisher	10–46	worldwide	colourful plumage
motmot	20–50	tropical America	distinctive long tail feathers
mousebird	30–35	Africa, S of the Sahara	crest and long tail
parrot	10–100	mainly tropics of S Hemisphere	mainly sedentary; unmelodic voice
pigeon	17–90	worldwide, except high latitudes	distinctive cooing sound
puffbird	14–32	tropical America	stout, puffy appearance
roller	27–38	Africa, Europe, Asia, Australia	distinctive courtship display
sandgrouse	25–48	Africa, S Europe and S Asia	mainly terrestrial birds
tody	10–12	Greater Antilles	captures insects from underside of leaves/twigs
toucan	34–66	S America	bright plummage; huge bill
trogon	25–35	tropics, except Australasia	colourful plummage
turaco	35–76	Africa S of the Sahara	loud and resounding call
woodhoopoe	21–43	Africa S of the Sahara	graduated tail; hooked bill
woodpecker	10–58	worldwide, except Australasia and Antarctica	excavates wood and tree bark for food

Aerial feeders

Name	Size cm¹	Distribution	Special features
crested swift	17–33	SE Asia and New Guinea	prominent crest on head
frogmouth	23–53	SE Asia and Australasia	distinctively shaped bill
hummingbird	6–22	N and S America	wings hum when hovering
nightjar	19–29	worldwide	nocturnal
oilbird	53	tropical S America	only nocturnal fruit-eater
potoo	23–51	tropical C and S America	nocturnal; 'tree-nighthawk'
owlet-nightjar	23–44	Australasia	upright owl-like perch
swift	10–25	worldwide	most of life spent flying

Passerines[2]

Name	Size cm[1]	Distribution	Special features
antbird	8–36	parts of S America and W Indies	some species follow army of ants to prey
bellbird	9–45	C and S America	long metallic sounding call
broadbill	13–28	tropical Africa and Asia, and the Philippines	colourful broad bill
false sunbird	15	Madagascar	blue and emerald wattle develops around male's eye during breeding season
flycatcher (New World)	9–27	N and S America	feeds on the wing
gnateater	14	parts of S America	long thin legs; short tail
lyrebird	80–90	SE Australia	tail resembles Greek lyre
manakin	9–15	C and S America	elaborate courtship display
New Zealand wren	8–10	New Zealand	thought to have colonized islands in Tertiary Period[3]
ovenbird	to 25	S America	one species builds nests like mud-ovens
pitta	15–28	Africa, SE Asia and Australasia	long legs; short tail; colourful plumage
plantcutter	18–19	western S America	bill adapted for fruit-feeding
scrub-bird	16–21	E and SW Australia	small terrestrial bird
tapaculo	8–25	S and C America	movable nostril flap covers
tyrant flycatcher	5–14	N and S America, W Indies and Galapagos	spectacular aerial courtship display
woodcreeper	20–37	S America and W Indies	stiff tail feathers used as climbing support

Game-birds and cranes

Name	Size cm[1]	Distribution	Special features
bustard	37–132	Africa, S Europe, Asia and Australia	frequent pauses for observation whilst walking
button quail	11–19	Africa, S Asia and Australia	secretive; terrestrial
coot	14–51	worldwide	loud nocturnal vocal strains
crane	80–150	worldwide, except S America and Antarctica	long legs
currasow	75–112	Southern N America and S America	noted for running along branches before taking off

[1] To convert cm to in, multiply by 0.3937.
[2] Any bird of the worldwide order *Passeriformes* ('perching birds'), which comprises more than half the living species of birds; landbirds
[3] *see* GEOLOGICAL TIMESCALE p 11

BIRDS (cont.)

Game-birds and cranes (cont.)

Name	Size cm[1]	Distribution	Special features
finfoot	30–62	tropics of America, Africa and SE Asia	long, slender neck
grouse	30–90	N Hemisphere	threatened by hunting
guinea fowl	45–60	Africa	virtually unfeathered head
hoatzin	60	tropical S America	musky odour; top heavy
kagu	56	New Caledonia	sole species
limpkin	60–70	C and S America	sole species; wailing voice
mesite	25–27	Madagascar	terrestrial; sedentary
pheasant	40–235	worldwide	elaborate courtship display
plains wanderer	16	SE Australia	male incubates eggs and raises young
seriema	75–90	S America	heavily feathered head
sunbittern	46	forest swamps of C and S America	complex markings
trumpeter	43–53	tropical S America	trumpeting call of alarm
turkey	90–110	N America	male strutting display

MAMMALS

Mammals are the group of animals to which humans belong. They are characterized by the presence of mammary glands in the female which produce milk on which the young can be nourished. They are divided into monotremes or egg-laying mammals; marsupials in which the young are born at an early stage of development and then grow outside the mother's womb, often in a pouch; placental mammals in which the young are nourished in the womb by the mother's blood and are born at a late stage of development. A crucial aspect of mammals is the fact that their hair and skin glands allow them to regulate their temperatures from within, ie they are endothermic (warm-blooded). This confers on them the ability to adapt to more varied environments than the reptiles from which they are descended.

There are over 4 000 species of mammals, most of which are terrestrial, the exceptions being species of bat which have developed the ability to fly and the whale which leads an aquatic existence.

Generally, size denotes length from head to tip of tail.

Monotremes

Name	Size cm[1]	Distribution	Special features
echidna, long-beaked	45–90	New Guinea	prominent beak
echidna, short-beaked	30–45	Australia, Tasmania and New Guinea	fur covered in protective spines
platypus	45–60	E Australia and Tasmania	duck-like snout

Marsupials

Name	Size cm[1]	Distribution	Special features
bandicoot	15–56	Australia and New Guinea	highest reproductive rate of all marsupials
brushtail possum	34–70	Australia, New Guinea, Solomon Is and New Zealand	the most commonly encountered of all Australian mammals
kangaroo	to 165	Australia and New Guinea	bounding motion and prominent female pouch
koala	78	E Australia	revived population
marsupial mole	13–15	Australia	specialized in burrowing
oppossum	7–55	C and S America	known for its smell
rat kangaroo	28.4–30	Australia and New Guinea	rabbit-sized version of its larger namesake
wombat	870–115	SE Australia and Tasmania	poor eyesight; keen senses of smell and hearing

Placental Mammals

Name	Size cm[1]	Distribution	Special features
aardvark	105–130	Africa S of the Sahara	tubular snout; nocturnal
anteater	16–22	C and S America	elongated snout
antelope, dwarf	45–55	Africa	female larger than male
armadillo	12.5–100	southern N America, C and S America	protective suit of armour
ass	200–210	Africa and Asia	renowned as man's reluctant beast of burden
baboon and mandrill	56–80	Africa	can walk long distances
badger	50–100	Africa, Europe, Asia and N America	black and white markings on European species
bat	15–200 (wingspan)	worldwide except for the Arctic and Antarctic	only vertebrate, apart from birds, capable of flight
bear, black	130–180	N America	more adaptable than brown or grizzly bears
beaver	80–120	N America, Asia and Europe	constructs dams and lodges in water
bison, American	to 380	N America	exists in parks and refuges
bison, European	to 290	former USSR	extinct in wild in 1919, but now re-established in parts of the former USSR
boar	58–210	Europe, Africa and Asia	intelligent and adaptable
buffalo, wild water	240–280	SE Asia	adept at moving through its muddy habitat
bush baby	12–32	Africa and S Asia	highly agile; arboreal
bushbuck	110–145	Africa S of the Sahara	dark brown or chestnut coat with white markings

[1] To convert cm to in, multiply by 0.3937.

MAMMALS (cont.)

Placental Mammals (cont.)

Name	Size cm[1]	Distribution	Special features
camel	190–230 (height of hump)	Mongolia	two humps
capybara	106–134	S America	largest living rodent
capuchin monkey	25–63	S America	lives in social groupings
cat	20–400	worldwide	acute sense of vision and smell
cattle	180–200	worldwide	long-horned and polled or hornless breeds
chamois	125–135	Europe and Asia	adapted to alpine and subalpine conditions
cheetah	112–135	Africa	fastest of all land animals
chimpanzee	70–85	W and C Africa	most intelligent of the great apes
chinchilla	25	S America	hunted for food and fur
civet	33–84	Africa and Asia	cat-like carnivore
colugo	33–42	SE Asia	stretched membrane allows it to glide from tree to tree
coyote	70–97	N America	unique howling sound
coypu	50	S America	highly aquatic rodent
deer	41–152	N and S America, Europe, and Asia	male uses antlers to attack other males during the rutting period
dingo	150	Australasia	descendant of the wolf
dog	20–75	worldwide	first domesticated animal
dolphin	120–400	worldwide	highly developed social/communication systems
dolphin, river	210–260	SE Asia and S America	highly sensitive system of echo location
dormouse	6–19	Europe, Africa, Turkey, Asia and Japan	nocturnal rodent; hibernates during winter
dromedary	190–230 (height of hump)	SW Asia, N Africa and Australia	camel with one hump; source of wool and milk
duiker	55–72	Africa S of the Sahara	dives into cover when disturbed
eland	250–350	Africa	spiral horned antelope
elephant, African	600–750	Africa S of the Sahara	largest living mammal
elephant-shrew	10.4–29.4	Africa	long, pointed snout
fox	24–100	N and S America, Europe, Asia and Africa	noted for its cunning intelligence
gazelle	122–166	Africa	birth peaks coincide with abundance of feeding vegetation during spring

Name	Size cm[1]	Distribution	Special features
gerbil	6–7.5	Africa and Asia	wide field of vision; low frequency hearing
gerenuk	140–160	Africa	graceful and delicate
gibbon	45–65	SE Asia	swings among trees using arms
giraffe	380–470	Africa S of the Sahara	mottled coat and long neck
gnu	194–209	Africa	massive head and mane
goat, mountain	to 175	N America	ponderous rock climber
goat, wild	130–140	S Europe, Middle East and Asia	subspecies includes domestic goat
gopher	12–22.5	N America	highly adapted burrower
gorilla	150–170	C Africa	largest living primate
grizzly or brown bear	200–280	NW America and former USSR	large size (up to half a ton)
guinea pig	28	S America	tailless rodent
hamster	5.3–10.2	Europe, Middle East, former USSR and China	aggressive towards own species in the wild
hare	40–76	N and S America, Africa, Europe, Asia and Arctic	well-developed ability to run from predators
hare, Patagonian	45	S America	strictly monogamous
hartebeest	195–200	Africa	long face, sloping back
hedgehog	10–15	Europe, Asia and Africa	protective spined back
hippopotamus	150–345	Africa	barrel-shaped; stumpy legs
horse	200–210	worldwide in domesticated form; Asia, N and S America and Australia in the wild	historically useful to man as a beast of burden, means of transport, in agriculture, the military, and recreation
hyena	85–140	Africa and Asia	scavenger and hunter
ibex	85–143	C Europe, Asia and Africa	large horns; saved from extinction in C Europe
impala	128–142	Africa	fawn and mahogany coat
jackal	65–106	Africa, SE Europe and Asia	unfair reputation as cowardly scavenger
jaguar	112–185	C and S America	only cat in the Americas
jerboa	4–26	N Africa, Turkey, Middle East and C Asia	moves by hopping and jumping with long hind legs
lemming	10–11	N America and Eurasia	Norway lemming is noted for its mass migration
lemur	12–70	Madagascar	mainly nocturnal/arboreal
leopard	100–190	Africa and Asia	nocturnal hunters
lion	260–330	Africa	the most socially organized of the cat family
llama	230–400	S America	S American beast of burden
lynx	67–110	Europe and N America	well-adapted to snow
macaque	38–70	Asia and N Africa	big built; partly terrestrial

[1] To convert cm to in, multiply by 0.3937.

MAMMALS (cont.)

Placental Mammals (cont.)

Name	Size cm[1]	Distribution	Special features
marmoset	17.5–40	S America	squirrel-like monkey
marten	30–75	N America, Europe and Asia	one species, the fisher, unique for its ability to penetrate the quilled defences of the porcupine
mole	2.4–7.5	Europe, Asia and N America	almost exclusively subterranean existence
mongoose	24–58	Africa, S Asia and SW Europe	stands up on hind legs/tail, known as tripod position
mountain beaver	30–41	Pacific Coast of Canada and USA	land-dwelling and burrowing animal
mouse *see* rat			
narwhal	400–500	former USSR, N America and Greenland	distinctive tusk in the male can measure up to 300 cm
okapi	190–200	Zaire	mixture of giraffe and zebra
orang-utan	150	forests of N Samutra and Borneo	sparse covering of red-brown hair
otter	40–123	N and S America, Europe, Asia and Africa	only truly amphibious member of weasel family
panda, giant	70–80	China	rare; poor breeder
polar bear	250–300	N polar regions	large size; white coat
porcupine (New World)	30–86	N and S America	arboreal; excellent climber
porcupine (Old World)	37–47	Africa and Asia	heavily quilled/spiny body
porpoise	120–150	N temperate zone, W Indo-Pacific, temperate and sub-antarctic waters of S America and Auckland Islands	large range of sounds for the purpose of echo location
puma	105–196	N and S America	wide-ranging hunter
rabbit, European	38–58	Europe, Africa, Australia, New Zealand and S America	burrowing creature; opportunistic animal in widespread environment
racoon	55	N, S and C America	black masked face
rat (New World)	5–8	N and S America	highly adaptable
rat (Old World)	4.5–8.2	Europe, Asia, Africa and Australia	one of the most adaptable mammals
reedbuck	110–176	Africa	whistling sounds; leaping
rhinoceros	250–400	Africa and tropical Asia	horn grows from snout
seal	117–490	mainly polar, subpolar and temperate seas	graceful swimmer and diver
sheep, American bighorn	168–186	N America	large horns and body similar to an ibex

Name	Size cm[1]	Distribution	Special features
sheep, barbary	155–165	N Africa	horns up to 84 cm in length
sheep, blue	91 (shoulder height)	Asia	blue coat; curved horns
shrew	3.5–4.8	Europe, Asia, Africa, N America and northern S America	generally poor eyesight compensated for by acute sense of smell and hearing
skunk	40–68	N and S America	evil-smelling defence
sloth, three-toed	56–60	S America	smaller version of the two-toed sloth
sloth, two-toed	58–70	S America	arboreal; nocturnal; slow
springbuck	96–115	S Africa	herds migrate together
springhare	36–43	S Africa	burrowing creature; like a miniature kangaroo
squirrel	6.6–10	N and S America, Europe, Africa and Asia	include arboreal, burrowing and flying species
tapir	180–250	C and S America and SE Asia	nocturnal mammal with distinctive snout
tarsier	11–14	islands of SE Asia	ability to rotate neck
tiger	220–310	India, Manchuria, China and Indonesia	solitary hunters, stalk for prey
vole	10–11	N America, Europe, Asia and the Arctic	population fluctuates in regular patterns or cycles
walrus	250–320	Arctic seas	thick folds of skin, twin tusks
waterbuck	177–235	Africa	shaggy coat and heavy gait
weasel	15–55	Arctic, N and S America, Europe, Asia and Africa	certain species have been exploited for their fur, eg mink, ermine
whale, beaked	400–1 280	worldwide	dolphin-like beak
whale, blue	to 3 000	Arctic and subtropics	largest animal that has lived
whale, grey	1 190–1 520	N Pacific	long migration to breed, from Arctic to subtropics
whale, humpback	1 600	worldwide	highly acrobatic; wide range of sounds
whale, killer	900–1 000	worldwide in cool coastal waters	toothed; dorsal fin narrow and vertical
whale, long-finned pilot	600	temperate waters of the N Atlantic	best known for mysterious mass strandings on beaches
whale, sperm	to 2 070	widespread in temperate and tropical waters	largest of the toothed whales; deep sea diver
whale, white	300–500	N Russia, N America and Greenland	white skin; range of bodily, facial and vocal expressions

[1] To convert cm to in, multiply by 0.3937.

MAMMALS (cont.)

Placental Mammals (cont.)

Name	Size cm[1]	Distribution	Special features
wild cat	50–80	Europe, India and Africa	domestic cat may descend from the African wild cat
wolf, grey	100–150	N America, Europe, Asia and Middle East	noted for hunting in packs
wolverine	to 83	Arctic and subarctic regions	heavily built; long, dark coat of fur
zebra	215–230	Africa	black and white stripes

ENDANGERED ANIMALS

Name	Where last seen	Est. no.
Asiatic buffalo	India, Nepal	2 200
Blue whale	World oceans	7 500
Bontebok (antelope)	South Africa	800
Crested ibis (wading bird)	Japan	<12
European bison	Poland	>1 000[2]
Everglades kite	Florida	100
Florida panther	Florida	<300
Giant panda	China	200
Imperial eagle	Spain	100
Indian rhinoceros	India, Nepal	<600
Java rhinoceros	Indonesia	<100
Kakapo (parrot)	New Zealand	<100
Key deer	N America	600
Mediterranean monk seal	Mediterranean Sea	500
Orang-utan	Borneo, Sumatra	5 000
Père David's deer	China	600[2]
Polar bear	Arctic	8 000
Przewalski's horse	Central Asia	40–60[2]
Siberian tiger	Russia, China, Korea	<200
Southern bald eagle	N America	600
Whooping cranes	N America	About 50

[1] To convert cm to in, multiply by 0.3937.
[2] Saved from extinction by zoos

SCIENCE AND TECHNOLOGY

THE UNIVERSE

PLANETARY DATA

Planet	Distance from sun (million km) Maximum	Minimum	Planet year	Planet day (equatorial)	Diameter (equatorial) km
Mercury	69.4	46.8	88 d	59 d	4 878
Venus	109.0	107.6	224.7 d	243 d	12 104
Earth	152.6	147.4	365.26[1]	23h 56 m	12 756
Mars	249.2	207.3	687 d	24 h 37 m	6 794
Jupiter	817.4	741.6	11.9 y	9 h 50 m	142 800
Saturn	1 512	1 346	29.5 y	10 h 14 m	120 000
Uranus	3 011	2 740	84 y	16–28 h[2]	52 000
Neptune	4 543	4 466	164.8 y	18–20 h[2]	48 600
Pluto	7 364	4 461	248.5 y	6 d 9 h	1 145

[1]365 d 5 h 48 m 46 s
[2]Different latitudes rotate at different speeds.
y: earth years d: earth days h: hours m: minutes

ANNUAL METEOR SHOWERS

Meteors appear to radiate from named star region.

Name	Dates	Star region
Quadrantids	1–6 January	Beta Boötis
Lyrids	19–22 April	Nu Herculis
Eta Aquarids	1–8 May	Eta Aquarii
Delta Aquarids	15 July–10 August	Delta Aquarii
Perseids	27 July–17 August	Eta Persei
Orionids	15–25 October	Nu Orionis
Leonids	14–20 November	Zeta Leonis
Andromedids	26 November–4 December	Gamma Andromedae
Geminids	9–13 December	Castor
Ursids	20–22 December	Kocab

TOTAL & ANNULAR SOLAR ECLIPSES 1995–2006

In an annular eclipse a ring-shaped part of the sun remains visible.

Date	Extent of eclipse	Visible from parts of[1]
29 April 1995	Annular	S Pacific, S America
24 October 1995	Total	Middle East, S Asia, S Pacific
9 March 1997	Total	C & N Asia, Arctic
26 February 1998	Total	Mid-Pacific, C America, N Atlantic
22 August 1998	Annular	Indonesia, S Pacific, Indian Ocean
16 February 1999	Annular	Indian Ocean, Australia
11 August 1999	Total	N Atlantic, N Europe, Middle East, N India
21 June 2001	Total	S Atlantic, S Africa, Madagascar
14 December 2001	Annular	Pacific, C America
10 June 2002	Annular	Indonesia, Pacific, Mexico
4 December 2002	Total	S Africa, Indian Ocean, Australia
31 May 2003	Annular	Iceland, Greenland
23 November 2003	Total	Antarctic
8 April 2005	Annular/Total	Pacific, Panama, Venzuela
3 October 2005	Annular	Atlantic, Spain, Libya, Indian Ocean
29 March 2006	Total	Atlantic, Libya, Turkey, Russia
22 September 2006	Annular	Guyana, Atlantic, Indian Ocean

[1] The eclipse begins in the first country named.

LUNAR ECLIPSES 1995–2006

Date	Percentage eclipsed	Time of mid-eclipse	Where visible
15 April 1995	Partial	12.19	Pacific, Australia, SE Asia
4 April 1996	Total	00.11	Africa, SE Europe, S America
27 September 1996	Total	02.55	C and S America, part of N America, W Africa
24 March 1997	Partial	04.41	C and S America, part of N America, W Africa
16 September 1997	Total	18.47	S Africa, E Africa, Australia
28 July 1999	Partial	11.34	Pacific, Australia, SE Asia
21 January 2000	Total	04.45	N America, part of S America, SW Europe, W Africa
16 July 2000	Total	13.57	Pacific, Australia, SE Asia
9 January 2001	Total	20.22	Europe, Asia, Africa
5 July 2001	Partial	14.57	Asia, Australia, Pacific
16 May 2003	Total	03.41	Americas, Europe, Africa
9 November 2003	Total	01.20	Americas, Europe, Africa, W Asia
4 May 2004	Total	20.32	Europe, Africa, Asia
28 October 2004	Total	03.05	Americas, Europe, Africa
17 October 2005	Partial	12.05	E Asia, Pacific, N America
7 September 2006	Partial	18.53	Australia, Asia, E Africa

THE LUNAR 'SEAS'

Latin name	English name	Latin name	English name
Lacus Somniorum	Lake of Dreams	Mare Serenitatis	Sea of Serenity
Mare Australe	Southern Sea	Mare Smythii	Smyth's Sea
Mare Crisium	Sea of Crises	Mare Spumans	Foaming Sea
Mare Fecunditatis	Sea of Fertility	Mare Tranquillitatis	Sea of Tranquillity
Mare Frigoris	Sea of Cold	Mare Undarum	Sea of Waves
Mare Humboldtianum	Humboldt's Sea	Mare Vaporum	Sea of Vapours
Mare Humorum	Sea of Humours	Oceanus Procellarum	Ocean of Storms
Mare Imbrium	Sea of Showers	Palus Epidemiarum	Marsh of Epidemics
Mare Ingenii	Sea of Geniuses	Palus Putredinis	Marsh of Decay
Mare Marginis	Marginal Sea	Palus Somnii	Marsh of Sleep
Mare Moscoviense	Moscow Sea	Sinus Aestuum	Bay of Heats
Mare Nectaris	Sea of Nectar	Sinus Iridum	Bay of Rainbows
Mare Nubium	Sea of Clouds	Sinus Medii	Central Bay
Mare Orientale	Eastern Sea	Sinus Roris	Bay of Dew

THE CONSTELLATIONS

Latin name	English name	Latin name	English name
Andromeda	Andromeda	Coma Berenices	Berenice's Hair
Antlia	Air Pump	Corona Australis	Southern Crown
Apus	Bird of Paradise	Corona Borealis	Northern Crown
Aquarius (Z)	Water Bearer	Corvus	Crow
Aquila	Eagle	Crater	Cup
Ara	Altar	Crux	Southern Cross
Aries (Z)	Ram	Cygnus	Swan
Auriga	Charioteer	Delphinus	Dolphin
Boötes	Herdsman	Dorado	Swordfish
Caelum	Chisel	Draco	Dragon
Camelopardalis	Giraffe	Equuleus	Little Horse
Cancer (Z)	Crab	Eridanus	River Eridanus
Canes Venatici	Hunting Dogs	Fornax	Furnace
Canis Major	Great Dog	Gemini (Z)	Twins
Canis Minor	Little Dog	Grus	Crane
Capricornus (Z)	Sea Goat	Hercules	Hercules
Carina	Keel	Horologium	Clock
Cassiopeia	Cassiopeia	Hydra	Sea Serpent
Centaurus	Centaur	Hydrus	Water Snake
Cepheus	Cepheus	Indus	Indian
Cetus	Whale	Lacerta	Lizard
Chamaeleon	Chameleon	Leo (Z)	Lion
Circinus	Compasses	Leo Minor	Little Lion
Columba	Dove	Lepus	Hare

THE CONSTELLATIONS (cont.)

Latin name	English name	Latin name	English name
Libra (Z)	Scales	Pyxis	Mariner's Compass
Lupus	Wolf	Reticulum	Net
Lynx	Lynx	Sagitta	Arrow
Lyra	Harp	Sagittarius (Z)	Archer
Mensa	Table	Scorpius (Z)	Scorpion
Microscopium	Microscope	Sculptor	Sculptor
Monoceros	Unicorn	Scutum	Shield
Musca	Fly	Serpens	Serpent
Norma	Level	Sextans	Sextant
Octans	Octant	Taurus (Z)	Bull
Ophiuchus	Serpent Bearer	Telescopium	Telescope
Orion	Orion	Triangulum	Triangle
Pavo	Peacock	Triangulum Australe	Southern Triangle
Pegasus	Winged Horse	Tucana	Toucan
Perseus	Perseus	Ursa Major	Great Bear
Phoenix	Phoenix	Ursa Minor	Little Bear
Pictor	Easel	Vela	Sails
Pisces (Z)	Fishes	Virgo (Z)	Virgin
Piscis Austrinus	Southern Fish	Volans	Flying Fish
Puppis	Ship's Stern	Vulpecula	Fox

Z: Found on the Zodiac

MAJOR SPACE 'FIRSTS'

Date	Mission	Nation/Agency	Event description
1957	Sputnik 1	USSR	Earth satellite
1957	Sputnik 2	USSR	Dog Laika
1958	Explorer 1	USA	Discovered radiation belt (Van Allen)
1959	Luna 1	USSR	Escaped earth gravity
1959	Vanguard 2	USA	Earth photo
1959	Luna 2	USSR	Lunar impact
1959	Luna 3	USSR	Lunar photo (far side)
1960	TIROS 1	USA	Weather satellite
1960	Transit 1B	USA	Navigation satellite
1960	ECHO 1	USA	Communications satellite
1960	Sputnik 5	USSR	Two dogs recovered alive
1961	Vostok 1	USSR	Manned orbital flight
1962	Mariner 2	USA	Venus flyby
1963	Vostok 6	USSR	Woman in orbit
1964	Ranger VII	USA	Close-up television pictures of the moon
1964	Mariner 4	USA	Mars flyby pictures
1965	Early Bird	USA	Commercial geostationary communications satellite
1966	Venera 3	USSR	Venus impact

Date	Mission	Nation/Agency	Event description
1965	A-1 Asterix	France	French launched satellite
1965	Gemini 7	USA	Manned rendezvous
1965	Gemini 6	USA	Manned rendezvous
1966	Luna 9	USSR	Lunar soft landing
1966	Gemini 8	USA	Manned docking
1966	Luna 10	USSR	Lunar orbiter
1966	Surveyor 1	USA	US soft landing on moon
1966	Lunar orbiter 1	USA	US lunar orbiter
1967	Cosmos 186/188	USA	Automatic docking
1968	Zond 5	USSR	Animals around the moon
1968	Apollo 8	USA	Manned lunar orbit
1969	Soyuz 4	USSR	Transfer of crews
1969	Soyuz 5	USSR	Transfer of crews
1969	Apollo 11	USA	Manned lunar landing
1970	Oshumi	Japan	Japanese launched satellite
1970	Long March	China	Chinese launched satellite
1970	Venera 7	USSR	Venus soft landing
1970	Luna 16	USSR	Unmanned sample return
1970	Luna 17	USSR	Unmanned Moon rover
1971	Mars 2	USSR	Mars orbit
1971	Mars 3	USSR	Mars soft landing, no data returned
1971	Mariner 9	USA	Mars orbit
1971	Prospero	UK	UK launched satellite
1973	Pioneer 10	USA	Jupiter flyby
1983			Crossed Pluto orbit
1983			Escaped solar system
1974	Pioneer 11	USA	Jupiter flyby
1979			Saturn flyby
1974	Mariner 10	USA	Venus flyby
1974–5			Three Mercury flybys
1975	Venera 9	USSR	Venus orbit
1975	Apollo/Soyuz	USA/USSR	Manned international co-operative mission
1976	Viking 1	USA	Spacecraft operations on Mars surface
1979	Voyager 2	USA	Jupiter flyby
1981			Saturn flyby
1986			Uranus flyby
1989			Neptune flyby
1979	Voyager 1	USA	Jupiter flyby
1980			Saturn flyby
1985	ISEE-C	USA	Comet intercept
1979	Ariane/CAT	ESA	European launcher
1980	Rohini	India	Indian launched satellite
1981	STS1	USA	Space shuttle flight
1981	STS2	USA	Launch vehicle re-use
1983	Soyuz T9	USSR	Construction in space
1984	STS 51A	USA	Satellite retrieval
1985	Vega 1	USSR	Halley flyby

MAJOR SPACE 'FIRSTS' (cont.)

Date	Mission	Nation/Agency	Event description
1986	Giotto	ESA	Close up of comet Halley
1986	Soyuz T15	USSR	Ferry between space stations
1988	Soyuz TM4/6	USSR	Year-long flight
1989	Phobos 2	USSR	Phobos rendezvous
1988	Buran	USSR	Unmanned space shuttle
1990	Muses-A	Japan	Moon orbiter
1990	HST	USA/ESA	Large space telescope
1990	Soyuz TM-11	USSR	Paying passenger flight
1991	Galileo	USA	Close-up photographs of an asteroid
1992	Endeavour	USA	Married couple travelling together
1992	COBE	USA	Big Bang theory strengthened
1993	Ulysses	USA	Grains of interstellar dust detected

MEASUREMENT

ELECTROMAGNETIC SPECTRUM

Radiation	Approximate wavelengths	Uses
Radio waves	>10cm	communications; radio and TV broadcasting
Microwaves	1mm–10cm	communications; radar; microwave ovens
Infrared	10^{-3}–7.8×10^{-7}m	night and smoke vision systems; intruder alarms; weather forecasting; missile guidance systems
Visible	7.8×10^{-7}–3×10^{-7}m	human eyesight
Ultraviolet	3×10^{-7}–10^{-8}m	forensic science; medical treatment
X-rays	10^{-8}–3×10^{-11}m	medical X-ray photographs; material structure analysis
Gamma rays	$<3 \times 10^{-11}$m	medical diagnosis

CONVERSION TABLES

To convert	To	Equation
°Fahrenheit	°Celsius	$-32 \times 5, \div 9$
°Fahrenheit	°Rankine	$+459.67$
°Fahrenheit	°Réaumur	$-32 \times 4, \div 9$
°Celsius	°Fahrenheit	$\times 9, \div 5, + 32$
°Celsius	Kelvin	$+273.15$
°Celsius	°Réaumur	$\times 4, \div 5$
Kelvin	°Celsius	-273.15
°Rankine	°Fahrenheit	-459.67
°Réaumur	°Fahrenheit	$\times 9, \div 4, + 32$
°Réaumur	°Celsius	$\times 5, \div 4$

Carry out operations in sequence.

TEMPERATURE CONVERSION

Degrees Fahrenheit (F) converted to Degrees Celsius (Centigrade) (C)

Degrees Celsius (Centigrade) (C) converted to Degrees Fahrenheit (F)

°F	°C	°F	°C	°C	°F	°C	°F
1	-17.2	43	6.1	1	33.8	43	109.4
2	-16.7	44	6.7	2	35.6	44	111.2
3	-16.1	45	7.2	3	37.4	45	113.0
4	-15.5	46	7.8	4	39.2	46	114.8
5	-15.0	47	8.3	5	41.0	47	116.6
6	-14.4	48	8.9	6	42.8	48	118.4
7	-13.9	49	9.4	7	44.6	49	120.2
8	-13.3	50	10.0	8	46.4	50	122.0
9	-12.8	51	10.5	9	48.2	51	123.8
10	-12.2	52	11.1	10	50.0	52	125.6
11	-11.6	53	11.7	11	51.8	53	127.4
12	11.1	54	12.2	12	53.6	54	129.2
13	-10.5	55	12.8	13	55.4	55	131.0
14	-10.0	56	13.3	14	57.2	56	132.8
15	-9.4	57	13.9	15	59.0	57	134.6
16	-8.9	58	14.4	16	60.8	58	136.4
17	-8.3	59	15.0	17	62.6	59	138.2
18	-7.8	60	15.5	18	64.4	60	140.0
19	-7.2	61	16.1	19	66.2	61	141.8
20	-6.7	62	16.7	20	68.0	62	143.6
21	-6.1	63	17.2	21	69.8	63	145.4
22	-5.5	64	17.8	22	71.6	64	147.2
23	-5.0	65	18.3	23	73.4	65	149.0
24	-4.4	66	18.9	24	75.2	66	150.8
25	-3.9	67	19.4	25	77.0	67	152.6
26	-3.3	68	20.0	26	78.8	68	154.4
27	-2.8	69	20.5	27	80.6	69	156.2
28	-2.2	70	21.1	28	82.4	70	158.0
29	-1.7	71	21.7	29	84.2	71	159.8
30	-1.1	72	22.2	30	86.0	72	161.6
31	-0.5	73	22.8	31	87.8	73	163.4
32	0	74	23.3	32	89.6	74	165.2
33	0.5	75	23.9	33	91.4	75	167.0
34	1.1	76	24.4	34	93.2	76	168.8
35	1.7	77	25.0	35	95.0	77	170.6
36	2.2	78	25.5	36	96.8	78	172.4
37	2.8	79	26.1	37	98.6	79	174.2
38	3.3	80	26.7	38	100.4	80	176.0
39	3.9	81	27.2	39	102.2	81	177.8
40	4.4	82	27.8	40	104.0	82	179.6
41	5.0	83	28.3	41	105.8	83	181.4
42	5.5	84	28.9	42	107.6	84	183.2

TEMPERATURE CONVERSION (cont.)

Degrees Fahrenheit (F) converted to Degrees Celsius (Centigrade) (C)						Degrees Celsius (Centigrade) (C) converted to Degrees Fahrenheit (F)	
°F	°C	°F	°C	°F	°C	°C	°F
85	29.4	128	53.3	171	77.2	85	185.0
86	30.0	129	53.9	172	77.8	86	186.8
87	30.5	130	54.4	173	78.3	87	188.6
88	31.1	131	55.0	174	78.9	88	190.4
89	31.7	132	55.5	175	79.4	89	192.2
90	32.2	133	56.1	176	80.0	90	194.0
91	32.8	134	56.7	177	80.5	91	195.8
92	33.3	135	57.2	178	81.1	92	197.6
93	33.9	136	57.8	179	81.7	93	199.4
94	34.4	137	58.3	180	82.2	94	201.2
95	35.0	138	58.9	181	82.8	95	203.0
96	35.5	139	59.4	182	83.3	96	204.8
97	36.1	140	60.0	183	83.9	97	206.6
98	36.7	141	60.5	184	84.4	98	208.4
99	37.2	142	61.1	185	85.0	99	210.2
100	37.8	143	61.7	186	85.5	100	212.0
101	38.3	144	62.2	187	86.1		
102	38.9	145	62.8	188	86.7		
103	39.4	146	63.3	189	87.2		
104	40.0	147	63.9	190	87.8		
105	40.5	148	64.4	191	88.3		
106	41.1	149	65.0	192	88.8		
107	41.7	150	65.5	193	89.4		
108	42.2	151	66.1	194	90.0		
109	42.8	152	66.7	195	90.5		
110	43.3	153	67.2	196	91.1		
111	43.9	154	67.8	197	91.7		
112	44.4	155	68.3	198	92.2		
113	45.0	156	68.9	199	92.8		
114	45.5	157	69.4	200	93.3		
115	46.1	158	70.0	201	93.9		
116	46.7	159	70.5	202	94.4		
117	47.2	160	71.1	203	95.0		
118	47.8	161	71.7	204	95.5		
119	48.3	162	72.2	205	96.1		
120	48.9	163	72.8	206	96.7		
121	49.4	164	73.3	207	97.2		
122	50.0	165	73.9	208	97.8		
123	50.5	166	74.4	209	98.3		
124	51.1	167	75.0	210	98.9		
125	51.7	168	75.5	211	99.4		
126	52.2	169	76.1	212	100.0		
127	52.8	170	76.7				

NUMERICAL EQUIVALENTS

Arabic	Roman	Greek	Binary numbers
1	I	α'	1
2	II	β'	10
3	III	γ'	11
4	IV	δ'	100
5	V	ε'	101
6	VI	ς'	110
7	VII	ζ'	111
8	VIII	η'	1000
9	IX	θ'	1001
10	X	ι'	1010
11	XI	$\iota\alpha'$	1011
12	XII	$\iota\beta'$	1100
13	XIII	$\iota\gamma'$	1101
14	XIV	$\iota\delta'$	1110
15	XV	$\iota\varepsilon'$	1111
16	XVI	$\iota\varsigma'$	10000
17	XVII	$\iota\zeta'$	10001
18	XVIII	$\iota\eta'$	10010
19	XIX	$\iota\theta'$	10011
20	XX	κ'	10100
30	XXX	λ'	11110
40	XL	μ'	101000
50	L	ν'	110010
60	LX	ξ'	111100
70	LXX	o'	1000110
80	LXXX	π'	1010000
90	XC	$,o'$	1011010
100	C	ρ'	1100100
200	CC	σ'	11001000
300	CCC	τ'	100101100
400	CD	υ'	110010000
500	D	ϕ'	111110100
1 000	M	$,\alpha$	1111101000
5 000		$,\varepsilon$	1001110001000
10 000		$,\iota$	10011100010000
100 000		$,\rho$	11000011010100000

NUMERICAL EQUIVALENTS

Fraction	Decimal	Fraction	Decimal	Fraction	Decimal
1/2	0.5000	8/9	0.8889	15/16	0.9375
1/3	0.3333	1/10	0.1000	1/20	0.0500
2/3	0.6667	3/10	0.3000	3/20	0.1500
1/4	0.2500	7/10	0.7000	7/20	0.3500
3/4	0.7500	9/10	0.9000	9/20	0.4500
1/5	0.2000	1/11	0.0909	11/20	0.5500
2/5	0.4000	2/11	0.1818	13/20	0.6500
3/5	0.6000	3/11	0.2727	17/20	0.8500
4/5	0.8000	4/11	0.3636	19/20	0.9500
1/6	0.1667	5/11	0.4545	1/32	0.0312
5/6	0.8333	6/11	0.5454	3/32	0.0937
1/7	0.1429	7/11	0.6363	5/32	0.1562
2/7	0.2857	8/11	0.7272	7/32	0.2187
3/7	0.4286	9/11	0.8181	9/32	0.2812
4/7	0.5714	10/11	0.9090	11/32	0.3437
5/7	0.7143	1/12	0.0833	13/32	0.4062
6/7	0.8571	5/12	0.4167	15/32	0.4687
1/8	0.1250	7/12	0.5833	17/32	0.5312
3/8	0.3750	11/12	0.9167	19/32	0.5937
5/8	0.6250	1/16	0.0625	21/32	0.6562
7/8	0.8750	3/16	0.1875	23/32	0.7187
1/9	0.1111	5/16	0.3125	25/32	0.7812
2/9	0.2222	7/16	0.4375	27/32	0.8437
4/9	0.4444	9/16	0.5625	29/32	0.9062
5/9	0.5556	11/16	0.6875	31/32	0.9687
7/9	0.7778	13/16	0.8125		

NUMERICAL EQUIVALENTS

%	Decimal	Fraction	%	Decimal	Fraction
1	0.01	1/100	12	0.12	3/25
2	0.02	1/50	12½	0.125	1/8
3	0.03	3/100	13	0.13	13/100
4	0.04	1/25	14	0.14	7/50
5	0.05	1/20	15	0.15	3/20
6	0.06	3/50	16	0.16	4/25
7	0.07	7/100	16⅔	0.167	1/6
8	0.08	2/25	17	0.17	17/100
8⅓	0.083	1/12	18	0.18	9/50
9	0.09	9/100	19	0.19	19/100
10	0.10	1/10	20	0.20	1/5
11	0.11	11/100	21	0.21	21/100

%	Decimal	Fraction	%	Decimal	Fraction
22	0.22	11/50	41	0.41	41/100
23	0.23	23/100	42	0.42	21/50
24	0.24	6/25	43	0.43	43/100
25	0.25	1/4	44	0.44	11/25
26	0.26	13/50	45	0.45	9/20
27	0.27	27/100	46	0.46	23/50
28	0.28	7/25	47	0.47	47/100
29	0.29	29/100	48	0.48	12/25
30	0.30	3/10	49	0.49	49/100
31	0.31	31/100	50	0.50	1/2
32	0.32	8/25	55	0.55	11/20
33	0.33	33/100	60	0.60	3/5
$33\frac{1}{3}$	0.333	1/3	65	0.65	13/20
34	0.34	17/50	70	0.70	7/10
35	0.35	7/20	75	0.75	3/4
36	0.36	9/25	80	0.80	4/5
37	0.37	37/100	85	0.85	17/20
38	0.38	19/50	90	0.90	9/10
39	0.39	39/100	95	0.95	19/20
40	0.40	2/5	100	1.00	1

MULTIPLICATION TABLES

	2	3	4	5	6	7	8	9	10	11	12	13	
2	4	6	8	10	12	14	16	18	20	22	24	26	2
3	6	9	12	15	18	21	24	27	30	33	36	39	3
4	8	12	16	20	24	28	32	36	40	44	48	52	4
5	10	15	20	25	30	35	40	45	50	55	60	65	5
6	12	18	24	30	36	42	48	54	60	66	72	78	6
7	14	21	28	35	42	49	56	63	70	77	84	91	7
8	16	24	32	40	48	56	64	72	80	88	96	104	8
9	18	27	36	45	54	63	72	81	90	99	108	117	9
10	20	30	40	50	60	70	80	90	100	110	120	130	10
11	22	33	44	55	66	77	88	99	110	121	132	143	11
12	24	36	48	60	72	84	96	108	120	132	144	156	12
13	26	39	52	65	78	91	104	117	130	143	156	169	13
14	28	42	56	70	84	98	112	126	140	154	168	182	14
15	30	45	60	75	90	105	120	135	150	165	180	195	15
16	32	48	64	80	96	112	128	144	160	176	192	208	16
17	34	51	68	85	102	119	136	153	170	187	204	221	17
18	36	54	72	90	108	126	144	162	180	198	216	234	18
19	38	57	76	95	114	133	152	171	190	209	228	247	19
20	40	60	80	100	120	140	160	180	200	220	240	260	20

MULTIPLICATION TABLES (cont.)

	2	3	4	5	6	7	8	9	10	11	12	13	
21	42	63	84	105	126	147	168	189	210	231	252	273	21
22	44	66	88	110	132	154	176	198	220	242	264	286	22
23	46	69	92	115	138	161	184	207	230	253	276	299	23
24	48	72	96	120	144	168	192	216	240	264	288	312	24
25	50	75	100	125	150	175	200	225	250	275	300	325	25

	14	15	16	17	18	19	20	21	22	23	24	25	
2	28	30	32	34	36	38	40	42	44	46	48	50	2
3	42	45	48	51	54	57	60	63	66	69	72	75	3
4	56	60	64	68	72	76	80	84	88	92	96	100	4
5	70	75	80	85	90	95	100	105	110	115	120	125	5
6	84	90	96	102	108	114	120	126	132	138	144	150	6
7	98	105	112	119	126	133	140	147	154	161	168	175	7
8	112	120	128	136	144	152	160	168	176	184	192	200	8
9	126	135	144	153	162	171	180	189	198	207	216	225	9
10	140	150	160	170	180	190	200	210	220	230	240	250	10
11	154	165	176	187	198	209	220	231	242	253	264	275	11
12	168	180	192	204	216	228	240	252	264	276	288	300	12
13	182	195	208	221	234	247	260	273	286	299	312	325	13
14	196	210	224	238	252	266	280	294	308	322	336	350	14
15	210	225	240	255	270	285	300	315	330	345	360	375	15
16	224	240	256	272	288	304	320	336	352	368	384	400	16
17	238	255	272	289	306	323	340	357	374	391	408	425	17
18	252	270	288	306	324	342	360	378	396	414	432	450	18
19	266	285	304	323	342	361	380	399	418	437	456	475	19
20	280	300	320	340	360	380	400	420	440	460	480	500	20
21	294	315	336	357	378	399	420	441	462	483	504	525	21
22	308	330	352	374	396	418	440	462	484	506	528	550	22
23	322	345	368	391	414	437	460	483	506	529	552	575	23
24	336	360	384	408	432	456	480	501	528	552	576	600	24
25	350	375	400	425	450	475	500	525	550	575	600	625	25

SQUARES AND ROOTS

No.	Square	Cube	Square root	Cube root
1	1	1	1.000	1.000
2	4	8	1.414	1.260
3	9	27	1.732	1.442
4	16	64	2.000	1.587
5	25	125	2.236	1.710

No.	Square	Cube	Square root	Cube root
6	36	216	2.449	1.817
7	49	343	2.646	1.913
8	64	512	2.828	2.000
9	81	729	3.000	2.080
10	100	1 000	3.162	2.154
11	121	1 331	3.317	2.224
12	144	1 728	3.464	2.289
13	169	2 197	3.606	2.351
14	196	2 744	3.742	2.410
15	225	3 375	3.873	2.466
16	256	4 096	4.000	2.520
17	289	4 913	4.123	2.571
18	324	5 832	4.243	2.621
19	361	6 859	4.359	2.668
20	400	8 000	4.472	2.714
25	625	15 625	5.000	2.924
30	900	27 000	5.477	3.107
40	1 600	64 000	6.325	3.420
50	2 500	125 000	7.071	3.684

COMMON MEASURES

Metric units

Length		Imperial equiv.
	1 millimetre	0.03937 in
10 mm	1 centimetre	0.39 in
10 cm	1 decimetre	3.94 in
100 cm	1 metre	39.37 in
1 000 m	1 kilometre	0.62 mile

Area		Imperial equiv.
	1 square millimetre	0.0016 sq in
	1 square centimetre	0.155 sq in
100 sq cm	1 square decimetre	15.5 sq in
10 000 sq cm	1 square metre	10.76 sq ft
10 000 sq m	1 hectare	2.47 acres

Volume		Imperial equiv.
	1 cubic centimetre	0.016 cu in
1 000 cu cm	1 cubic decimetre	61.024 cu in
1 000 cu dm	1 cubic metre	35.31 cu ft
		1.308 cu yds

COMMON MEASURES (cont.)

Metric units

Volume

		Imperial equiv.
Liquid volume		
	1 litre	1.76 pints
100 litres	1 hectolitre	22 gallons

Weight

		Imperial equiv.
	1 gram	0.035 oz
1 000 g	1 kilogram	2.2046 lb
1 000 kg	1 tonne	0.9842 ton

Imperial units

Length

		Metric equiv.
	1 inch	2.54 cm
12 in	1 foot	30.48 cm
3 ft	1 yard	0.9144 m
1 760 yd	1 mile	1.6093 km

Area

		Metric equiv.
	1 square inch	6.45 sq cm
144 sq in	1 square foot	0.0929 m^2
9 sq ft	1 square yard	0.836 m^2
4 840 sq yd	1 acre	0.405 ha
640 acres	1 square mile	259 ha

Volume

		Metric equiv.
	1 cubic inch	16.3871 cm^3
1 728 cu in	1 cubic foot	0.028 m^3
27 cu ft	1 cubic yard	0.765 m^3

Liquid volume

	1 pint	0.57 litre
2 pints	1 quart	1.14 litres
4 quarts	1 gallon	4.55 litres

Weight

		Metric equiv.
	1 ounce	28.3495 g
16 oz	1 pound	0.4536 kg
14 lb	1 stone	6.35 kg
8 stones	1 hundredweight	50.8 kg
20 cwt	1 ton	1.016 tonnes

CONVERSION FACTORS

Imperial to metric

Length			Multiply by
inches	→	millimetres	25.4
inches	→	centimetres	2.54
feet	→	metres	0.3048
yards	→	metres	0.9144
statute miles	→	kilometres	1.6093
nautical miles	→	kilometres	1.852

Area			Multiply by
square inches	→	square centimetres	6.4516
square feet	→	square metres	0.0929
square yards	→	square metres	0.8361
acres	→	hectares	0.4047
square miles	→	square kilometres	2.5899

Volume			Multiply by
cubic inches	→	cubic centimetres	16.3871
cubic feet	→	cubic metres	0.0283
cubic yards	→	cubic metres	0.7646

Capacity			Multiply by
UK fluid ounces	→	litres	0.0284
US fluid ounces	→	litres	0.0296
UK pints	→	litres	0.5682
US pints	→	litres	0.4732
UK gallons	→	litres	4.546
US gallons	→	litres	3.7854

Weight			Multiply by
ounces (avoirdupois)	→	grams	28.3495
ounces (troy)	→	grams	31.1035
pounds	→	kilograms	0.4536
tons (long)	→	tonnes	1.016

CONVERSION FACTORS (cont.)

Metric to imperial

Length			Multiply by
millimetres	→	inches	0.0394
centimetres	→	inches	0.3937
metres	→	feet	3.2808
metres	→	yards	1.0936
kilometres	→	statute miles	0.6214
kilometres	→	nautical miles	0.54

Area			Multiply by
square centimetres	→	square inches	0.155
square metres	→	square feet	10.764
square metres	→	square yards	1.196
hectares	→	acres	2.471
square kilometres	→	square miles	0.386

Volume			Multiply by
cubic centimetres	→	cubic inches	0.061
cubic metres	→	cubic feet	35.315
cubic metres	→	cubic yards	1.308

Capacity			Multiply by
litres	→	UK fluid ounces	35.1961
litres	→	US fluid ounces	33.8150
litres	→	UK pints	1.7598
litres	→	US pints	2.1134
litres	→	UK gallons	0.2199
litres	→	US gallons	0.2642

Weight			Multiply by
grams	→	ounces (avoirdupois)	0.0353
grams	→	ounces (troy)	0.0322
kilograms	→	pounds	2.2046
tonnes	→	tons (long)	0.9842

CONVERSION TABLES: LENGTH

in	cm	in	cm	cm	in	cm	in	in	mm	mm	in
⅛	0.3	16	40.6	1	0.39	24	9.45	⅛	3.2	1	0.04
¼	0.6	17	43.2	2	0.79	25	9.84	¼	6.4	2	0.08
⅜	1	18	45.7	3	1.18	26	10.24	⅜	9.5	3	0.12
½	1.3	19	48.3	4	1.57	27	10.63	½	12.7	4	0.16
⅝	1.6	20	50.8	5	1.97	28	11.02	⅝	15.9	5	0.2
¾	1.9	21	53.3	6	2.36	29	11.42	¾	19	6	0.24
⅞	2.2	22	55.9	7	2.76	30	11.81	⅞	22.2	7	0.28
1	2.5	23	58.4	8	3.15	31	12.2	1	25.4	8	0.31
2	5.1	24	61	9	3.54	32	12.6	2	50.8	9	0.35
3	7.6	25	63.5	10	3.94	33	12.99	3	76.2	10	0.39
4	10.2	26	66	11	4.33	34	13.39	4	101.6	11	0.43
5	12.7	27	68.6	12	4.72	35	13.78	5	127	12	0.47
6	15.2	28	71.1	13	5.12	36	14.17	6	152.4	13	0.51
7	17.8	29	73.7	14	5.51	37	14.57	7	177.8	14	0.55
8	20.3	30	76.2	15	5.91	38	14.96	8	203.2	15	0.59
9	22.9	40	101.6	16	6.3	39	15.35	9	228.6	16	0.63
10	25.4	50	127	17	6.69	40	15.75	10	254	17	0.67

Exact conversions
1 in = 2.540 cm   1 cm = 0.3937 in   1 in = 25.40 mm   1 mm = 0.0394 in

CONVERSION TABLES: LENGTH

ft	m	m	ft	yd	m	m	yd
1	0.3	1	3.3	1	0.9	1	1.1
2	0.6	2	6.6	2	1.8	2	2.2
3	0.9	3	9.8	3	2.7	3	3.3
4	1.2	4	13.1	4	3.7	4	4.4
5	1.5	5	16.4	5	4.6	5	5.5
6	1.8	6	19.7	6	5.5	6	6.6
7	2.1	7	23.0	7	6.4	7	7.7
8	2.4	8	26.2	8	7.3	8	8.7
9	2.7	9	29.5	9	8.2	9	9.8
10	3.0	10	32.8	10	9.1	10	10.9
15	4.6	15	49.2	15	13.7	15	16.4
20	6.1	20	65.5	20	18.3	20	21.9
25	7.6	25	82.0	25	22.9	25	27.3
30	9.1	30	98.4	30	27.4	30	32.8
35	10.7	35	114.8	35	32.0	35	38.3
40	12.2	40	131.2	40	36.6	40	43.7
45	13.7	45	147.6	45	41.1	45	49.2
50	15.2	50	164.0	50	45.7	50	54.7

CONVERSION TABLES: LENGTH (cont.)

ft	m	m	ft	yd	m	yd	m
75	22.9	75	246.1	75	68.6	75	82.0
100	30.5	100	328.1	100	91.4	100	109.4
200	61.0	200	656.2	200	182.9	200	218.7
300	91.4	300	984.3	220	201.2	220	240.6
400	121.9	400	1 312.3	300	274.3	300	328.1
500	152.4	500	1 640.4	400	365.8	400	437.4
600	182.9	600	1 968.5	440	402.3	440	481.2
700	213.4	700	2 296.6	500	457.2	500	546.8
800	243.8	800	2 624.7	600	548.6	600	656.2
900	274.3	900	2 952.8	700	640.1	700	765.5
1 000	304.8	1 000	3 280.8	800	731.5	800	874.9
1 500	457.2	1 500	4 921.3	880	804.7	880	962.4
2 000	609.6	2 000	6 561.7	900	823.0	900	984.2
2 500	762.0	2 500	8 202.1	1 000	914.4	1 000	1 093.6
3 000	914.4	3 000	9 842.5	1 500	1 371.6	1 500	1 640.4
3 500	1 066.8	3 500	11 482.9	2 000	1 828.8	2 000	2 187.2
4 000	1 219.2	4 000	13 123.4	2 500	2 286.0	2 500	2 734.0
5 000	1 524.0	5 000	16 404.2	5 000	4 572.0	5 000	5 468.1

ml*	km	ml*	km	kl	ml*	kl	ml*
1	1.6	55	88.5	1	0.6	55	34.2
2	3.2	60	96.6	2	1.2	60	37.3
3	4.8	65	104.6	3	1.9	65	40.4
4	6.4	70	112.7	4	2.5	70	43.5
5	8.0	75	120.7	5	3.1	75	46.6
6	9.7	80	128.7	6	3.7	80	49.7
7	11.3	85	136.8	7	4.3	85	52.8
8	12.9	90	144.8	8	5.0	90	55.9
9	14.5	95	152.9	9	5.6	95	59.0
10	16.1	100	160.9	10	6.2	100	62.1
15	24.1	200	321.9	15	9.3	200	124.3
20	32.2	300	482.8	20	12.4	300	186.4
25	40.2	400	643.7	25	15.5	400	248.5
30	48.3	500	804.7	30	18.6	500	310.7
35	56.3	750	1 207.0	35	21.7	750	466.0
40	64.4	1 000	1 609.3	40	24.9	1 000	621.4
45	72.4	2 500	4 023.4	45	28.0	2 500	1 553.4
50	80.5	5 000	8 046.7	50	31.1	5 000	3 106.9

* Statute miles

Exact conversions

1 ft = 0.3048 m	1 m = 3.2808 ft	1 yd = 0.9144 m
1 m = 1.0936 yd	1 ml = 1.6093 km	1 km = 0.6214 ml

CONVERSION TABLES: AREA

sq in	sq cm	sq cm	sq in	sq ft	sq m	sq m	sq ft
1	6.45	1	0.16	1	0.09	1	10.8
2	12.90	2	0.31	2	0.19	2	21.5
3	19.35	3	0.47	3	0.28	3	32.3
4	25.81	4	0.62	4	0.37	4	43.1
5	32.26	5	0.78	5	0.46	5	53.8
6	38.71	6	0.93	6	0.56	6	64.6
7	45.16	7	1.09	7	0.65	7	75.3
8	51.61	8	1.24	8	0.74	8	86.1
9	58.06	9	1.40	9	0.84	9	96.9
10	64.52	10	1.55	10	0.93	10	107.6
11	70.97	11	1.71	11	1.02	11	118.4
12	77.42	12	1.86	12	1.11	12	129.2
13	83.87	13	2.02	13	1.21	13	139.9
14	90.32	14	2.17	14	1.30	14	150.7
15	96.77	15	2.33	15	1.39	15	161.5
16	103.23	16	2.48	16	1.49	16	172.2
17	109.68	17	2.64	17	1.58	17	183
18	116.13	18	2.79	18	1.67	18	193.8
19	122.58	19	2.95	19	1.77	19	204.5
20	129.03	20	3.10	20	1.86	20	215.3
25	161.29	25	3.88	25	2.32	25	269.1
50	322.58	50	7.75	50	4.65	50	538.2
75	483.87	75	11.63	75	6.97	75	807.3
100	645.16	100	15.50	100	9.29	100	1 076.4
125	806.45	125	19.38	250	23.23	250	2 691
150	967.74	150	23.25	500	46.45	500	5 382
				750	69.68	750	8 072.9
				1 000	92.90	1 000	10 763.9

CONVERSION TABLES: AREA

acres	hectares	hectares	acres	sq ml*	sq km	sq km	sq ml*
1	0.40	1	2.5	1	2.6	1	0.39
2	0.81	2	4.9	2	5.2	2	0.77
3	1.21	3	7.4	3	7.8	3	1.16
4	1.62	4	9.9	4	10.4	4	1.54
5	2.02	5	12.4	5	12.9	5	1.93
6	2.43	6	14.8	6	15.5	6	2.32
7	2.83	7	17.3	7	18.1	7	2.70
8	3.24	8	19.8	8	20.7	8	3.09
9	3.64	9	22.2	9	23.3	9	3.47
10	4.05	10	24.7	10	25.9	10	3.86

CONVERSION TABLES: AREA (cont.)

acres	hectares	hectares	acres	sq ml*	sq km	sq km	sq ml*
11	4.45	11	27.2	18	46.6	18	6.95
12	4.86	12	29.7	19	49.2	19	7.34
13	5.26	13	32.1	20	51.8	20	7.72
14	5.67	14	34.6	21	54.4	21	8.11
15	6.07	15	37.1	22	57.0	22	8.49
16	6.47	16	39.5	23	59.6	23	8.88
17	6.88	17	42	24	62.2	24	9.27
18	7.28	18	44.5	25	64.7	25	9.65
19	7.69	19	46.9	30	77.7	30	11.58
20	8.09	20	49.4	40	103.6	40	15.44
25	10.12	25	61.8	300	777.0	300	115.83
50	20.23	50	123.6	400	1 036.0	400	154.44
75	30.35	75	185.3	500	1 295.0	500	193.05
100	40.47	100	247.1	600	1 554.0	600	231.66
250	101.17	250	617.8	700	1 813.0	700	270.27
500	202.34	500	1 235.5	800	2 072.0	800	308.88
750	303.51	750	1 853.3	900	2 331.0	900	347.49
1 000	404.69	1 000	2 471.1	1 000	2 590.0	1 000	386.1
1 500	607.03	1 500	3 706.6	1 500	3 885.0	1 500	579.2
				2 000	5 180.0	2 000	772.2

* Statute miles

Exact conversions

$1 in^2 = 6.4516 cm^2$	$1 cm^2 = 0.155 in^2$	$1 ft^2 = 0.929 m^2$	$1 m^2 = 10.7639 ft^2$
$1 acre = 0.4047 hectare$	$1 hectare = 2.471 acres$	$1 sq ml = 2.589999 sq km$	$1 sq km = 0.3861 sq ml$

CONVERSION TABLES: VOLUME

cu in	cu cm	cu cm	cu in	cu ft	cu m	cu m	cu ft	cu yd	cu m	cu m	cu yd
1	16.39	1	0.61	1	0.03	1	35.3	1	0.76	1	1.31
2	32.77	2	1.22	2	0.06	2	70.6	2	1.53	2	2.62
3	49.16	3	1.83	3	0.08	3	105.9	3	2.29	3	3.92
4	65.55	4	2.44	4	0.11	4	141.3	4	3.06	4	5.23
5	81.93	5	3.05	5	0.14	5	176.6	5	3.82	5	6.54
6	93.32	6	3.66	6	0.17	6	211.9	6	4.59	6	7.85
7	114.71	7	4.27	7	0.20	7	247.2	7	5.35	7	9.16
8	131.10	8	4.88	8	0.23	8	282.5	8	6.12	8	10.46
9	147.48	9	5.49	9	0.25	9	317.8	9	6.88	9	11.77
10	163.87	10	6.10	10	0.28	10	353.1	10	7.65	10	13.08
15	245.81	15	9.15	15	0.42	15	529.7	15	11.47	15	19.62
20	327.74	20	12.20	20	0.57	20	706.3	20	15.29	20	26.16
50	819.35	50	30.50	50	1.41	50	1 765.7	50	38.23	50	65.40
100	1 638.71	100	61.00	100	2.83	100	3 531.5	100	76.46	100	130.80

Exact conversions

$1 in^3 = 16.3871 cm^3$	$1 cm^3 = 0.0610 in^3$	$1 ft^3 = 0.0283 m^3$
$1 m^3 = 35.3147 ft^3$	$1 yd^3 = 0.7646 m^3$	$1 m^3 = 1.3080 yd^3$

CONVERSION TABLES: CAPACITY

Liquid measure

UK fluid ounces	litres	US fluid ounces	litres	litres	UK fluid ounces	US fluid ounces
1	0.0284	1	0.0296	1	35.2	33.8
2	0.0568	2	0.0592	2	70.4	67.6
3	0.0852	3	0.0888	3	105.6	101.4
4	0.114	4	0.118	4	140.8	135.3
5	0.142	5	0.148	5	176.0	169.1
6	0.170	6	0.178	6	211.2	202.9
7	0.199	7	0.207	7	246.4	236.7
8	0.227	8	0.237	8	281.6	270.5
9	0.256	9	0.266	9	316.8	304.3
10	0.284	10	0.296	10	352.0	338.1
11	0.312	11	0.326	11	387.2	372.0
12	0.341	12	0.355	12	422.4	405.8
13	0.369	13	0.385	13	457.5	439.6
14	0.397	14	0.414	14	492.7	473.4
15	0.426	15	0.444	15	527.9	507.2
20	0.568	20	0.592	20	703.9	676.3
50	1.42	50	1.48	50	1 759.8	1 690.7
100	2.84	100	2.96	100	3 519.6	3 381.5

Exact conversions
1 UK fl oz = 0.0284 l　　1 US fl oz = 0.0296 l
1 l = 35.1961 UK fl oz　　1 l = 33.8140 US fl oz

CONVERSION TABLES: CAPACITY

UK pints	litres	US pints	litres	litres	UK pints	US pints
1	0.57	1	0.47	1	1.76	2.11
2	1.14	2	0.95	2	3.52	4.23
3	1.70	3	1.42	3	5.28	6.34
4	2.27	4	1.89	4	7.04	8.45
5	2.84	5	2.37	5	8.80	10.57
6	3.41	6	2.84	6	10.56	12.68
7	3.98	7	3.31	7	12.32	14.79
8	4.55	8	3.78	8	14.08	16.91
9	5.11	9	4.26	9	15.84	19.02
10	5.68	10	4.73	10	17.60	21.13
11	6.25	11	5.20	11	19.36	23.25
12	6.82	12	5.68	12	21.12	25.36
13	7.38	13	6.15	13	22.88	27.47
14	7.95	14	6.62	14	24.64	29.59
15	8.52	15	7.10	15	26.40	31.70

CONVERSION TABLES: CAPACITY (cont.)

UK pints	litres	US pints	litres	litres	UK pints	US pints
20	11.36	20	9.46	20	35.20	105.67
50	28.41	50	23.66	50	87.99	211.34
100	56.82	100	47.32	100	175.98	422.68

Exact conversions
1 UK pt = 0.5682 l   1 UK pt = 1.20 US pt   1 US pt = 0.4732 l
1 US pt = 0.83 UK pt   1 l = 1.7598 UK pt, 2.1134 US pt   1 US cup = 8 fl oz

CONVERSION TABLES: CAPACITY

UK gallons	litres	US gallons	litres	litres	UK gallons	US gallons
1	4.55	1	3.78	1	0.22	0.26
2	9.09	2	7.57	2	0.44	0.53
3	13.64	3	11.36	3	0.66	0.79
4	18.18	4	15.14	4	0.88	1.06
5	22.73	5	18.93	5	1.10	1.32
6	27.28	6	22.71	6	1.32	1.58
7	31.82	7	26.50	7	1.54	1.85
8	36.37	8	30.28	8	1.76	2.11
9	40.91	9	34.07	9	1.98	2.38
10	45.46	10	37.85	10	2.20	2.64
11	50.01	11	41.64	11	2.42	2.91
12	54.55	12	45.42	12	2.64	3.17
13	59.10	13	49.21	13	2.86	3.43
14	63.64	14	52.99	14	3.08	3.70
15	68.19	15	56.78	15	3.30	3.96
16	72.74	16	60.57	16	3.52	4.23
17	77.28	17	64.35	17	3.74	4.49
18	81.83	18	68.14	18	3.96	4.76
19	86.37	19	71.92	19	4.18	5.02
20	90.92	20	75.71	20	4.40	5.28
25	113.65	25	94.63	25	5.50	6.60
50	227.30	50	189.27	50	11.00	13.20
75	340.96	75	283.90	75	16.50	19.81
100	454.61	100	378.54	100	22.00	26.42

Exact conversions
1 UK gall = 4.546 l   1 US gall = 3.7854 l   1 l = 0.220 UK gall, 0.2642 US gall

CONVERSION TABLES: CAPACITY

UK gall	US gall	UK gall	US gall	UK gall	US gall
1	1.2	7	8.4	13	15.6
2	2.4	8	9.6	14	16.8
3	3.6	9	10.8	15	18
4	4.8	10	12	20	24
5	6	11	13.2	25	30
6	7.2	12	14.4	50	60

CONVERSION TABLES: CAPACITY

US gall	UK gall	US gall	UK gall	US gall	UK gall
1	0.8	7	5.8	13	10.8
2	1.7	8	6.7	14	11.7
3	2.5	9	7.5	15	12.5
4	3.3	10	8.3	20	16.6
5	4.2	11	9.2	25	20.8
6	5	12	10	50	41.6

Exact conversions
1 UK gall = 1.200929 US gall   1 US gall = 0.832688 UK gall

CONVERSION TABLES: CAPACITY

Dry capacity measures

UK bushels	cu m	litres	US bushels	cu m	litres
1	0.037	36.4	1	0.035	35.2
2	0.074	72.7	2	0.071	70.5
3	0.111	109.1	3	0.106	105.7
4	0.148	145.5	4	0.141	140.9
5	0.184	181.8	5	0.175	176.2
10	0.369	363.7	10	0.353	352.4

Exact conversions
1 UK bushel = 0.0369 m^3 1 US bushel = 0.9353 m^3
1 UK bushel = 36.3677 l   1 US bushel = 35.2381 l

CONVERSION TABLES: CAPACITY

Dry capacity measures

cu m	UK bushels	US bushels		litres	UK bushels	US bushels
1	27.5	28.4		1	0.027	0.028
2	55.0	56.7		2	0.055	0.057
3	82.5	85.1		3	0.082	0.085
4	110	113		4	0.110	0.114
5	137	142		5	0.137	0.142
10	275	284		10	0.275	0.284

Exact conversions
$1\,m^3 = 27.4962$ UK bu $1\,m^3 = 28.3776$ US bu
$1\,l = 0.0275$ UK bu $1\,l = 0.0284$ US bu

CONVERSION TABLES: CAPACITY

Dry capacity measures

UK pecks	litres		US pecks	litres		litres	UK pecks	US pecks
1	9.1		1	8.8		1	0.110	0.113
2	18.2		2	17.6		2	0.220	0.226
3	27.3		3	26.4		3	0.330	0.339
4	36.4		4	35.2		4	0.440	0.454
5	45.5		5	44		5	0.550	0.567
10	90.9		10	88.1		10	1.100	1.135

Exact conversions
1 UK pk = 9.0919 l   1 US pk = 8.8095 l   1 l = 0.1100 UK pk, 0.1135 US pk

CONVERSION TABLES: CAPACITY

Dry capacity measures

US quarts	cu m	litres		US pints	cu m	litres
1	1 101	1.1		1	551	0.55
2	2 202	2.2		2	1 101	1.10
3	3 304	3.3		3	1 652	1.65
4	4 405	4.4		4	2 202	2.20
5	5 506	5.5		5	2 753	2.75
10	11 012	11		10	5 506	5.51

Exact conversions
1 US qt = 1 101.2209 cm^3 1 US qt = 1.1012 l   1 US pt = 550.6105 cm^3
1 US pt = 0.5506 l

CONVERSION TABLES: WEIGHT

ounces*	grams	ounces*	grams	grams	ounces*	grams	ounces*
1	28.3	9	255.1	1	0.04	20	0.71
2	56.7	10	283.5	2	0.07	30	1.06
3	85	11	311.7	3	0.11	40	1.41
4	113.4	12	340.2	4	0.14	50	1.76
5	141.7	13	368.5	5	0.18	60	2.12
6	170.1	14	396.9	6	0.21	70	2.47
7	198.4	15	425.2	7	0.25	80	2.82
8	226.8	16	453.6	8	0.28	90	3.18
				9	0.32	100	3.53
				10	0.35		

* avoirdupois

CONVERSION TABLES: WEIGHT

pounds	kilograms	pounds	kilograms	kilograms	pounds	kilograms	pounds
1	0.45	19	8.62	1	2.2	19	41.9
2	0.91	20	9.07	2	4.4	20	44.1
3	1.36	25	11.34	3	6.6	25	55.1
4	1.81	30	13.61	4	8.8	30	66.1
5	2.27	35	15.88	5	11	35	77.2
6	2.72	40	18.14	6	13.2	40	88.2
7	3.18	45	20.41	7	15.4	45	99.2
8	3.63	50	22.68	8	17.6	50	110.2
9	4.08	60	27.24	9	19.8	60	132.3
10	4.54	70	31.78	10	22	70	154.4
11	4.99	80	36.32	11	24.3	80	176.4
12	5.44	90	40.86	12	26.5	90	198.5
13	5.90	100	45.36	13	28.7	100	220.5
14	6.35	200	90.72	14	30.9	200	440.9
15	6.80	250	113.40	15	33.1	250	551.2
16	7.26	500	226.80	16	35.3	500	1 102.3
17	7.71	750	340.19	17	37.5	750	1 653.5
18	8.16	1 000	453.59	18	39.7	1 000	2 204.6

Exact conversions
1 oz (avdp) = 28.3495 g   1 g = 0.0353 oz (avdp)   1 lb = 0.454 kg   1 kg = 2.205 lb

CONVERSION TABLES: WEIGHT

Tons: long, UK 2 240 lb; short, US 2 000 lb

UK tons	tonnes	US tons	tonnes	UK tons	US tons
1	1.02	1	0.91	1	1.12
2	2.03	2	1.81	2	2.24
3	3.05	3	2.72	3	3.36
4	4.06	4	3.63	4	4.48
5	5.08	5	4.54	5	5.6
10	10.16	10	9.07	10	11.2
15	15.24	15	13.61	15	16.8
20	20.32	20	18.14	20	22.4
50	50.80	50	45.36	50	56
75	76.20	75	68.04	75	84
100	101.60	100	90.72	100	102

CONVERSION TABLES: WEIGHT

tonnes	UK tons	US tons	US tons	UK tons
1	0.98	1.10	1	0.89
2	1.97	2.20	2	1.79
3	2.95	3.30	3	2.68
4	3.94	4.40	4	3.57
5	4.92	5.50	5	4.46
10	9.84	11.02	10	8.93
15	14.76	16.53	15	13.39
20	19.68	22.05	20	17.86
50	49.21	55.11	50	44.64
75	73.82	82.67	75	66.96
100	98.42	110.23	100	89.29

Exact conversions
1 UK ton = 1.0160 tonnes   1 US ton = 0.9072 tonne   1 UK ton = 1.1199 US tons
1 tonne = 0.9842   UK ton = 1.1023 US tons   1 US ton = 0.8929 UK ton

CONVERSION TABLES: WEIGHT·

Hundredweights: long, UK 112 lb; short, US 100 lb

UK cwt	kilograms	US cwt	kilograms	UK cwt	US cwt
1	50.8	1	45.4	1	1.12
2	102	2	90.7	2	2.24

UK cwt	kilograms	US cwt	kilograms	UK cwt	US cwt
3	152	3	136	3	3.36
4	203	4	181	4	4.48
5	254	5	227	5	5.6
10	508	10	454	10	11.2
15	762	15	680	15	16.8
20	1 016	20	907	20	22.4
50	2 540	50	2 268	50	56
75	3 810	75	3 402	75	84
100	5 080	100	4 536	100	102

CONVERSION TABLES: WEIGHT

kilograms	UK cwt	US cwt	US cwt	UK cwt
1	0.0197	0.022	1	0.89
2	0.039	0.044	2	1.79
3	0.059	0.066	3	2.68
4	0.079	0.088	4	3.57
5	0.098	0.11	5	4.46
10	0.197	0.22	10	8.93
15	0.295	0.33	15	13.39
20	0.394	1.44	20	17.86
50	0.985	1.10	50	44.64
75	1.477	1.65	75	66.96
100	1.970	2.20	100	89.29

Exact conversions
1 UK cwt = 50.8023 kg   1 US cwt = 45.3592 kg   1 UK cwt = 1.1199 US cwt
1 kg = 0.0197 UK cwt = 0.0220 US cwt   1 US cwt = 0.8929 UK cwt

CONVERSION TABLES: WEIGHT

stones	pounds	kilograms	stones	pounds	kilograms
1	14	6.35	11	154	69.85
2	28	12.70	12	168	76.2
3	42	19.05	13	182	82.55
4	56	25.40	14	196	88.9
5	70	31.75	15	210	95.25
6	84	38.10	16	224	101.6
7	98	44.45	17	238	107.95
8	112	50.80	18	252	114.3
9	126	57.15	19	266	120.65
10	140	63.50	20	280	127

Exact conversions
1 st = 14 lb   1 lb = 0.07 st   1 st = 6.350 kg   1 kg = 0.1575 st

ENGINEERING: BRIDGES

Name	Location	Length (m[1])	Type
Akashi-Kaikyo	Honshu–Shikoku, Japan	4 000 (main span 1990)	suspension
Ambassador	Detroit, Michigan, USA	564	suspension
Annacis (renamed Alex Fraser)	Fraser River, Vancouver, Canada	465	(longest) cable stay
Arthur Kill	Staten Island–New Jersey, USA	170	movable
Astoria	Astoria, Oregon	376	truss
Bayonne (Kill van Kull)	New Jersey–Staten Island, USA	504	arch
Bendorf	R Rhine, Coblenz, Germany	1 030	cement girder
Benjamin Franklin	Philadelphia–Camden, USA	534	suspension
Bosporus	Istanbul, Turkey	1 074	suspension
Bosporus II	Istanbul, Turkey	1 090	suspension
Bridge of Sighs	Doge's Palace–Pozzi prison, Venice, Italy	c.5	enclosed arch
Britannia tubular rail	Menai Strait, Wales	420	plate girder
Brooklyn	Brooklyn–Manhattan Island, New York City, USA	486	suspension
Chao Phraya	Bangkok, Thailand	450	(longest single-plane) cable stay
Cincinnati	Cincinnati, Ohio, USA	332	suspension
Commodore Barry	Chester, Pennsylvania, USA	501	cantilever
Cooper River	Charleston, S Carolina, USA	488	truss
Delaware River	Chester, Pennsylvania, USA	501	cantilever
Duisburg-Neuenkamp	Duisburg, Germany	350	cable braced
East Bridge of Store Bælt	Copenhagen, Denmark	6 600 (spans 1 624)	suspension
Erskine	Glasgow, Scotland	305	cable braced
Evergreen	Seattle, Washington, USA	longest span 2 293	floating pontoon
Firth of Forth (rail)	South Queensferry, Scotland	1 658 (spans 521)	cantilever
Firth of Forth (road)	South Queensferry, Scotland	1 006	suspension
George Washington	Hudson River, New York City, USA	1 067	suspension
Gladesville	Sydney, Australia	305	(longest) concrete arch

Name	Location	Length (m[1])	Type
Golden Gate	San Francisco, California, USA	1 280	suspension
Grand Trunk rail-road	Niagara Falls, New York, USA		suspension
Greater New Orleans	Mississippi River, Louisiana, USA	480	cantilever
Howrah (railroad)	Hooghly River, Calcutta, India	457	cantilever
Humber Estuary	Hull–Grimsby, England	1 410	(longest) suspension
Kincardine	R Forth, Scotland	822 (swing span 111)	movable
Kniebrücke	Düsseldorf, Germany	320	cable braced
Lake Pontchartrain Causeway	Maudeville–Jefferson, Louisiana, USA	38 km[2]	twin concrete trestle
Lower Yarra	Melbourne, Australia	336	cable braced
Lions Gate	Vancouver, Canada	473	suspension
London	Southwark–City of London	centre span 46	concrete arch
Mackinac	Michigan, USA	1 158	suspension
McCall's Ferry	USA	110	wooden covered
Menai Strait	Menai Strait, N Wales	177	suspension
Minami Bisan–Seto	Honshu–Shikoku, Japan	1723	suspension
New River Gorge	Fayetteville, West Virginia, USA	518	(longest) arch
Nord Sundet	Norway	223	lattice
Plauen	Plauen, Germany	a span of 90	(longest) masonry arch
Pont d'Avignon	R Rhône, France	c.60	arch
Pontypridd	S Wales	43	single span arch
Port Mann	Fraser River, British Columbia, Canada	366	arch
Quebec (railroad)	St Lawrence, Canada	549	(largest-span) cantilever
Rainbow	Canada–USA, Niagara Falls	300	steel arch
Rialto	Grand Canal, Venice, Italy	25	single span arch
Rio-Niteroi	Guanabara Bay, Brazil	centre span 300, length 14 km	box and plate girder
Salazar	Tagus River, Lisbon, Portugal	1 014	suspension
Severn	Beachley, England	988	suspension
Severn	Ironbridge, Shropshire, England	31	(first) cast-iron arch
Sky Train Bridge (rail)	Vancouver, Canada	340	cable stay
Sydney Harbour	Sydney, Australia	503	(widest) arch
Tacoma Narrows II	Puget Sound, Washington, USA	854	suspension

[1] To convert m to ft, multiply by 3.2808.
[2] To convert km to ml, multiply by 1.6092.

ENGINEERING: BRIDGES (cont.)

Name	Location	Length (m[1])	Type
Tay (road)	Dundee, Scotland	2 246	box girder
Thatcher Ferry	Panama Canal, C America	344	arch
Tower	R Thames, London	76	movable
Transbay	San Francisco, USA	705	suspension
Trois-Rivières	St Lawrence River, Quebec, Canada	336	steel arch
Tsing Ma Bridge	Hong Kong	1 377	two-level suspension
Verrazano Narrows	Brooklyn–Staten Island, New York Harbour, USA	1 298	suspension
Victoria Jubilee	St Lawrence River, Montreal, Canada		open steel
Wheeling	Wheeling, Virginia, USA	308	suspension
Yangpu Bridge	Shanghai, China	main span 602	cable-stay
Yokohama Bay (road)	Japan	855	suspension
Zoo	Cologne, Germany	259	steel box girder

[1]To convert m to ft, multiply by 3.2808.

ENGINEERING: TUNNELS

Name	Use	Location	Length (km*)
Aki	rail	Japan	13
Baltimore Harbour	road	Baltimore, Maryland, USA	2
Box	rail	Wiltshire, England	3
Cascade	rail	Washington, USA	13
Channel	rail	Cheriton, England–Sargette, France	50
Chesapeake Bay Bridge-Tunnel	road	USA	28
Chesbrough	water supply	Chicago, USA	3
Dai-shimizu	rail	Honshu, Japan	22
Delaware Aqueduct		Catskill Mt, New York City, USA	169
Detroit River	rail	Detroit, Michigan, USA–Windsor, Ontario, Canada	2
Eupalinus	water supply	Samos	1
Flathead	rail	Washington, USA	13
Fréjus	rail	Modane, France–Bardonecchia, Italy	13
Fucino	drainage	Lake Fucino, Italy	6

Name	Use	Location	Length (km*)
Great Apennine	rail	Vernio, Italy	19
Hokuriku	rail	Japan	15
Holland	road	Hudson River, New York City–Jersey City, New Jersey, USA	3
Hoosac	rail	Massachusetts	8
Hyperion	sewer	Los Angeles, California, USA	8
Kanmon	rail	Kanmon Strait, Japan	19
Keijo	rail	Japan	11
Kemano	hydro-power	British Columbia, Canada	0.43
Kilsby Ridge	rail	London–Birmingham line	2
Languedoc	Canal du Midi	Malpas, France	0.157
Lierasen	rail	Norway	11
London and Southwark Subway	rail	London, England	11
Lötschberg	rail	Switzerland	15
Mersey	road	Mersey River, Birkenhead–Liverpool, England	4
Moffat	rail	Colorado, USA	10
Mont Blanc	road	France–Italy	12
Mt MacDonald	rail	Canada	15
Orange-Fish River	irrigation	South Africa	(longest irrigation tunnel) 82
Owingsburg Landing	canal	Pennsylvania, USA	0.137
Posilipo	road	Naples–Pozzuoli, Italy	6
Rogers Pass	rail	Calgary–Vancouver	15
Rogers Pass	road	British Columbia, Canada	35
Rokko	rail	Ōsaka–Kōbe, Japan	16
Scheldt River	road–rail	Antwerp, Belgium	0.686
Seikan	rail	Tsugaru Strait, Honshu–Hokkaido, Japan	(longest undersea rail) 54
Shin-shimizu	rail	Japan	13
Simplon I and II	rail	Brigue, Switzerland–Iselle, Italy	20
St Gotthard	rail	Switzerland	15
St Gotthard	road	Göschenen, Switzerland–Airolo, Italy	16
(First) Thames	pedestrian, rail after 1865	Wapping–Rotherhithe, London, England	0.366
Tower Subway	rail	London, England	0.411
Tronquoy	canal	France	1.1

* To convert km to ml, multiply by 1.6092.

ENGINEERING: MAJOR DAMS

Name	River, country	Height (m[1])
Afsluitdijk Sea	Zuider Zee, Netherlands	20 (largest sea dam, length 32 km*)
Aswan High	Nile, Egypt	111
Ataturk	Euphrates, Turkey	184
Bhakra	India	226
Bakun	Rajang, Malaysia	204
Boguchany	Angara, Russia	79
Bratsk	Angara, Russia	125
Chapeton	Paraná, Argentina	35
Chicoasen	Grijalva, Mexico	263
Chirkey	Ukraine	233
Chivor	Colombia	237
Contra	Switzerland	220
Grand Coulee	Columbia (Franklin D Roosevelt Lake), USA	168
Grand Dixence	Dixence, Switzerland	285
Guavio	Guaviare, Colombia	245
Hoover	Colorado (Lake Mead), USA	221
Haipu	Parana, Paraguay/Brazil border	189
Inguri	Inguri, Georgia	272
Kariba	Zambezi (L Kariba), Zambia/Zimbabwe border	128
Kiev	Dneiper, Ukraine	256 (longest dam, length 412 km*)
Kinshau	India	253
LaGrande 2A	LaGrande, Canada	168
Mauvoisin	Drance de Bagnes, Switzerland	237
Mica	Columbia, Canada	244
Mihoesti	Romania	242
Nurek	Vakhsh, Tadzhikistan	310
Oroville	California, USA (Feather River)	230
Poti	Paraná, Argentina	109 (length 150 km*, most massive: volume 238 180 000 m^3)
Rogun	Vakhsh, Tadzhikistan	335 (tallest)
Sayansk	Yenisey, Russia	236
Sera de Mesa	Tocantins, Brazil	144
Thames Barrier	Thames, UK	spans 520 (largest tidal barrier)
Vaiont	Vaiont, Italy	262

* To convert km to ml, multiply by 1.6092.

ENGINEERING: TALLEST BUILDINGS

Name	Location	Height (m[1])	Date of construction
Sears Tower	Chicago, USA	443	1973–4
World Trade Centre	New York City, USA	417	1972
Empire State Building	New York City, USA	381	1931
Bank of China	Hong Kong	368	1988–9
Standard Oil Building	Chicago, USA	346	1971
John Hancock Center	Chicago, USA	344	1967
Chrysler Building	New York City, USA	319	1930
Library Tower	Los Angeles, USA	310	1989
Texas Commercial Plaza	Houston, USA	305	1981
Allied Bank Plaza	Houston, USA	302	1983

[1] To convert m to ft, multiply by 3.2808.

INVENTIONS

Name	Date	Inventor (nationality*)
adding machine	1642	Blaise Pascal (Fr)
adhesive (rubber-based glue)	1850	anon
adhesive (epoxy resin)	1958	Certas Co.
aeroplane (steam powered)	1886	Clement Ader (Fr)
aeroplane	1903	Orville and Wilbur Wright (US)
aeroplane (swing-wing)	1954	Grumman Co. (US)
aerosol	1926	Erik Rotheim (Nor)
airship (non-rigid)	1851	Henri Giffard (Fr)
airship (rigid)	1900	Graf Ferdinand von Zeppelin (Ger)
ambulance	1792	Jean Dominique Larrey (Fr)
aspirin (synthesization)	1859	Heinrich Kolbe (Ger)
aspirin (introduction into medicine)	1899	Heinrich Dreser (Ger)
atomic bomb	1939–45	Otto Frisch (Aus), Niels Bohr (D) and Rudolf Peierls (Ger)
balloon (experimental)	1709	Bartolomeu Lourenço (Braz)
balloon	1783	Jacques and Joseph Montgolfier (Fr)
barbed wire (first patent)	1867	Lucien B Smith (US)
barbed wire (manufacture)	1874	Joseph Glidden (US)
barbiturates (preparation of barbituric acid)	1863	Adolf von Baeyer (Ger)
	1903	Emil Herman von Fischer and Emil von Behring (Ger)

INVENTIONS (cont.)

Name	Date	Inventor (nationality*)
barometer	1643	Evanglelista Torricelli (Ital)
battery (electric)	1800	Alessandro Volta (Ital)
bicycle (self-propelled)	1839–40	Kirkpatrick MacMillan (UK)
bifocal lens	1780	Benjamin Franklin (US)
blood (artificial)	1966	Clark and Gollan (US)
bronze (copper with tin)	c.3700 BC	Pre-dynastic Egypt
bunsen burner	1855	Robert Wilhelm Bunsen (Pruss)
burglar alarm	1858	Edwin T Holmes (US)
cable-car	1866	W Ritter (Ger) or anon (US)
calendar (modern)	525	Dionysius Exiguus (Scythian)
canning	1810	Nicolas Appert (Fr)
cannon	2nd-c BC	Archimedes (Gr)
car (three-wheeled steam tractor)	1769	Nicolas Cugnot (Fr)
car (internal combustion)	1884	Gottlieb Daimler (Ger)
car (petrol)	1886	Karl Benz (Ger)
car (air-conditioning)	1902	J Wilkinson (US)
car (disc brakes)	1902	Frederick W Lanchester (UK)
car (speedometer)	1902	Thorpe & Salter (UK)
carbon fibres	1964	Courtaulds Ltd (UK)
carburettor	1876	Gottlieb Daimler (Ger)
carpet sweeper	1876	Melville Bissell (US)
cash register	1892	William Burroughs (US)
celluloid	1870	John W Hyatt (US)
cement (Portland)	1824	Joseph Aspdin (UK)
chocolate (solid)	1819	François-Louis Cailler (Swiss)
chocolate (solid, milk)	1875	Daniel Peter (Swiss)
chronometer	1735	John Harrison (UK)
cinema	1895	Auguste and Louis Lumière (Fr)
cinema (wide screen)	1900	Raoul Grimoin-Sanson (Fr)
clock (mechanical)	725	I-Hsing (Chinese)
clock (pendulum)	1656	Christiaan Huygens (NL)
clock (quartz)	1929	Warren Alvin Marrison (US)
coffee (instant)	1937	Nestlé (Swiss)
compact disc	1979	Philips (NL) and Sony (Japanese)
compass (discovery of magnetite)	1st-c	China
compass (first record of mariner's compass)	1187	Alexander Neckam (UK)
computer	1835	Charles Babbage (UK)
computer (electronic, digital)	1946	J Presper Eckert and John W Mauchly (US)
concrete	1st-c	Rome
concrete (reinforced)	1892	François Hennebique (Fr)
contact lenses	1887	Adolph E Fick (Ger)
contraceptive pill	1950	Gregor Pincus (US)
corrugated iron	1853	Pierre Carpentier (Fr)

Name	Date	Inventor (nationality*)
credit card	1950	Ralph Scheider (US)
crossword	1913	Arthur Wynne in *New York World*
crystal	c.1450	anon, Venice
decompression chamber	1929	Robert H Davis (UK)
dental plate	1817	Anthony A Plantson (US)
dental plate (rubber)	1854	Charles Goodyear (US)
detergents	1916	anon, Germany
diesel engine	1892	Rudolf Diesel (Ger)
dishwasher (automatic)	1889	Mrs W A Cockran (US)
drill (pneumatic)	1861	Germain Sommelier (Fr)
drill (electric, hand)	1895	Wilhelm Fein (Ger)
electric chair	1888	Harold P Brown and E A Kenneally (US)
electric flat iron	1882	Henry W Seeley (US)
electric generator	1831	Michael Faraday (UK)
electric guitar	1931	Adolph Rickenbacker, Barth and Beauchamp (US)
electric heater	1887	W Leigh Burton (US)
electric light bulb	1879	Thomas Alva Edison (US)
electric motor (DC)	1870	Zenobe Gramme (Belg)
electric motor (AC)	1888	Nikola Tesla (US)
electric oven	1889	Bernina Hotel, Switzerland
electrocardiography	1903	Willem Einthoven (NL)
electromagnet	1824	William Sturgeon (UK)
encyclopedia	c.47 BC	Marcus Terentius Varro
endoscope	1827	Pierre Segalas (Fr)
escalator	1892	Jesse W Reno (US)
explosives (nitroglycerine)	1847	Ascanio Sobrero (Ital)
explosives (dynamite)	1866	Alfred Nobel (Swed)
extinguisher	1866	François Carlier (Fr)
facsimile machine (fax)	1907	Arthur Korn (Ger)
ferrofluids	1968	Ronald Rosensweig (US)
film (moving outlines)	1874	Jules Janssen (Fr)
	1888	Louis Le Prince (Fr)
	1891	Thomas Alva Edison (US)
film (with soundtrack)	1896	Lee De Forest (US)
food processor	1947	Kenneth Wood
forceps (obstetric)	c.1630	Peter Chamberlen
freeze-drying	1906	Arsene D'Arsonval and Georges Bordas (Fr)
galvanometer	1834	André Marie Ampère (Fr)
gas lighting	1792	William Murdock (UK)
gearbox (automatic)	1910	Hermann Fottinger (Ger)
glass (heat-resistant)	1884	Carl Zeiss (Ger)
glass (stained)	pre 850	Europe
glass (toughened)	1893	Leon Appert (Fr)
glass fibre	1713	Renée de Reaumur (Fr)

INVENTIONS (cont.)

Name	Date	Inventor (nationality*)
glass fibre (industrial)	1931	Owens Illinois Glass Co. (US)
glassware	c.2600 BC	
glider	1853	George Cayley (UK)
gramophone	1877	Thomas Alva Edison (US)
gun	245 BC	Ctesibius (Gr)
gyro-compass	1911	Elmer A Sperry (US)
heart (artificial)	1937	Vladimir P Demikhov (USSR)
heat pump	1851	William Thompson, Lord Kelvin (UK)
helicopter (first-manned)	1907	Louis and Jacques Breguet (Fr)
helicopter (forward and vertical control)	1939	Igor Sikorsky
holography	1948	Denis Gabor (Hung/UK)
hovercraft	1955	Christopher Cockerell (UK)
integrated circuit (concept)	1952	Geoffrey Dummer (UK)
interferometry	1802	Thomas Young (UK)
interferometer	1856	J-C Jamin (Fr)
iron (working of)	c.1323 BC	Hittites (Anatolia)
jeans	1872	Levi-Strauss (US)
kidney (artificial)	1945	Willem Kolff (NL)
laser	1960	Theodore Maiman (US)
launderette	1934	J F Cantrell (US)
lawnmower	1902	James Edward Ransome (UK)
lift (mechanical)	1851	Elisha G Otis (US)
lightning conductor	1752	Benjamin Franklin (US)
linoleum	1860	Frederick Walton (UK)
lithography	1796	Aloys Senefelder (Bav)
locomotive (railed)	1804	Richard Trevithick (UK)
lock	c.4000 BC	Mesopotamia
loom (power)	1785	Edmund Cartwright (UK)
loudspeaker	1900	Horace Short (UK)
machine gun	1718	James Puckle (UK)
maps	c.2250 BC	Mesopotamia
margarine	1868	Hippolyte Mergé-Mouriès (Fr)
match	1680	Robert Boyle (UK)
match (safety)	1845	Anton von Schrotter (Ger)
microchip	1958	Jack Saint Clair Kilby (US)
microphone	1876	Alexander Graham Bell (US) and Thomas Alva Edison (US)
microprocessor	1971	Marcian E Hoff (US)
microscope	1590	Zacharias Janssen (NL)
microscope (electron)	1933	Max Knoll and Ernst Ruska (Ger)
microscope (scanning tunnelling)	1982	Gerd Binnig and Heinrich Rohrer (Swiss)
microscope (atomic force)	1985	Gerd Binnig and Heinrich Rohrer (Swiss)

Name	Date	Inventor (nationality*)
microwave oven	1945	Percy Le Baron Spencer (US)
missile (air-to-air)	1943	Herbert Wagner (Ger)
motorcycle	1885	Gottlieb Daimler (Ger)
neon lamp	1910	Georges Claude (Fr)
newspaper	59 BC	Julius Caesar (Roman)
non-stick pan	1954	Marc Grégoir (Fr)
novel (serialized)	1836	Charles Dickens, Chapman and Hall publishers (UK)
nylon	1938	Wallace H Carothers (US)
optical fibres	c.1955	Navinder S Kapany (Ind)
optical sound recording	1920	Lee De Forest (US)
pacemaker (implantable)	1956	Wilson Greatbach (US)
paint (fluorescent)	1933	Joe and Bob Switzer (US)
paint (acrylic)	1964	Reeves Ltd (UK)
paper	AD 105	Ts'ai Lun (Chinese)
paper clip	1900	Johann Vaaler (Nor)
parachute	c.2nd-c BC	China
parachute (jump)	1797	André-Jacques Garnerin (Fr)
parachute (patent)	1802	André-Jacques Garnerin (Fr)
parchment	2nd-c BC	Eumenes II of Pargamum (reigned 197–159 BC)
parking meter	1932	Carlton C Magee (US)
pasteurization	1863	Louis Pasteur (Fr)
pen (fountain)	1884	Lewis Waterman (US)
pen (ball-point)	1938	Laszlo Biro (Hung)
pencil	1795	Nicholas Jacques Conté (Fr)
photoelectric cell	1896	Julius Elster and Hans F Geitel (Ger)
phototypesetting	1894	Eugene Porzolt (Hung)
photographic lens (for camera obscura)	1812	William H Wollaston (UK)
photographic film	1889	Georges Eastman (US)
photography (on metal)	1816	Joseph Nicéphore Niepce (Fr)
photography (on paper)	1838	William Henry Fox Talbot (UK)
photography (colour)	1861	James Clerk Maxwell (UK)
pianoforte	1720	Bartolomeo Cristofori (Ital)
plastics	1868	John W Hyatt (US)
pocket calculator	1972	Jack Saint Clair Kilby, James Van Tassell and Jerry D Merryman (US)
porcelain	c.960	China
pressure cooker	1679	Denis Papin
printing press (wooden)	c.1450	Johannes Gutenberg (Ger)
printing press (rotary)	1845	Richard Hoe (US)
propeller (boat, hand-operated)	1775	David Bushnell (US)
propeller (ship)	1844	Isambard Kingdom Brunel (UK)
radar (theory)	1900	Nikola Tesla (Croat)
radar (theory)	1922	Guglielmo Marconi (Ital)
radar (application)	c.1930	A Hoyt Taylor and Leo C Young (US)

INVENTIONS (cont.)

Name	Date	Inventor (nationality*)
radio telegraphy (discovery and production of sound waves)	1888	Heinrich Hertz (Ger)
radio (transatlantic)	1901	Guglielmo Marconi (Ital)
rails (iron)	1738	Abraham Barby (UK)
railway (underground)	1843	Charles Pearson (UK)
railway (electric)	1878	Ernst Werner von Siemens (Ger)
rayon	1883	Joseph Swan (UK)
razor (safety)	1895	King Camp Gillette (US)
razor (electric)	1928	Jacob Schick (US)
record (flat disc)	1888	Emil Berliner (Ger)
record (long-playing microgroove)	1948	Peter Goldmark (US)
refrigerator (compressed ether)	1855	James Harrison (UK)
refrigerator (absorption)	1857	Ferdinand Carré (Fr)
revolver	1835	Samuel Colt (US)
Richter seismographic scale	1935	Charles Francis Richter (US)
rocket (missile)	1232	Mongols (China)
rubber (latex foam)	1929	E A Murphy, W H Chapman and John Dunlop (US)
rubber (butyl)	1937	Robert Thomas and William Sparks, Exxon (US)
rubber (vulcanized)	1939	Charles Goodyear (US)
Rubik cube	1975	Erno Rubik (Hung)
safety-pin	1849	Walter Hunt (US)
satellite (artificial)	1957	USSR
saw	c.4000 BC	Egypt
scanner	1973	Godfrey N Hounsfield (UK)
scotch tape	1930	Richard Drew (US)
screw	3rd-c BC	Archimedes (Gr)
serotherapy	1890	Emil von Behring (Ger)
sewing machine	1830	Barthelemy Thimonnier (Fr)
ship (steam)	1775	Jacques C Perier (Fr)
ship (turbine)	1884	Charles Parsons (UK)
ship (metal hull and propeller)	1844	Isambard Kingdom Brunel (UK)
silk (reeling)	c.2640 BC	Hsi Ling Shi (Chinese)
skin (artificial)	c.1980	John Tanner (US), Bell (US), Neveu (Fr), Ioannis Yannas (Gr), Howard Green (US) and Jacques Thivolet (Fr)
skyscraper	1882	William Le Baron Jenney (US)
slide rule	1621	William Oughtred (UK)
soap	2500 BC	Sumer, Babylonia
soda (extraction of)	c.16th-c BC	Egypt
spectacles	c.1280	Alessandro della Spina, Salvino degli Armati (Ital)
spinning frame	1768	Richard Arkwright (UK)

Name	Date	Inventor (nationality*)
spinning jenny	c.1764	James Hargreaves (UK)
spinning-mule	1779	Samuel Crompton (UK)
stapler	1868	Charles Henry Gould (UK)
starter motor	1912	Charles F Kettering (US)
steam engine	1698	Thomas Savery (UK)
steam engine (condenser)	1769	James Watt (UK)
steam engine (piston)	1705	Thomas Newcomen (UK)
steel (production)	1854	Henry Bessemer (UK), William Kelly (US)
steel (stainless)	1913	Henry Brearley (UK)
stethoscope	1816	René Théophile Hyacinthe Laënnec (Fr)
stereotype	1725	William Ged (UK)
submarine	c.1620	Cornelis Brebbel or Van Drebbel (NL)
sun-tan cream	1936	Eugene Schueller (Fr)
suspension bridge	25 BC	China
syringe (scientific)	1646	Blaise Pascal (Fr)
syringe (hypodermic)	c.1835	Charles Gabriel Pravaz (Fr)
table tennis	1890	James Gibb (UK)
tampon	1930	Earl Hass (US)
tank	1916	Ernest Swinton (UK)
telegraph (electric)	1774	Georges Louis Lesage (Swiss)
telegraph (transatlantic cable)	1866	William Thompson, Lord Kelvin (UK)
telegraph code	1837	Samuel F B Morse (US)
telephone (first practical)	1876	Alexander Graham Bell (US)
telephone (automatic exchange)	1889	Alman B Strowger (US)
telescope (refractor)	1608	Hans Lippershey (NL)
television (mechanical)	1926	John Logie Baird (UK)
television (colour)	1940	Peter Goldmark (US)
tennis	1873	Walter G Wingfield (UK)
thermometer	3rd-c BC	Ctesibius (Gr)
thermometer (mercury)	1714	Gabriel Fahrenheit (Ger)
timeclock	1894	Daniel M Cooper (US)
toaster	1927	Charles Strite (US)
traffic lights	1868	J P Knight (UK)
traffic lights (automatic)	1914	Alfred Benesch (US)
transformer	1831	Michael Faraday (UK)
tranquillizers	1952	Henri Laborit (Fr)
transistor	1948	John Bardeen (US), Walter Brattain (US), William Shockley (US)
travel agency	1841	Thomas Cook (UK)
traveller's cheques	1891	American Express Travel Agency
turbojet	1928	Frank Whittle (UK)
typewriter	1829	William Burt (US)
typewriter (electric)	1872	Thomas Edison (US)
tyre (pneumatic, coach)	1845	Robert William Thomson (UK)
tyre (pneumatic, bicycle)	1888	John Boyd Dunlop (UK)

INVENTIONS (cont.)

Name	Date	Inventor (nationality*)
ultrasonography (obstetric)	1979	Ian Donald (UK)
universal joint	c.140 BC	Fang Feng (Chinese)
vacuum cleaner (steam powered)	1871	Ives W McGaffrey (US)
vacuum cleaner (electric)	1901	Hubert Cecil Booth (UK)
vending machine	1883	Percival Everitt (UK)
ventilator	1858	Theophile Guibal (Fr)
videophone	1927	American Telegraph & Telephone Co.
video recorder	1956	Ampex Co. (US)
washing machine (electric)	1907	Hurley Machine Co. (US)
watch	1462	Bartholomew Manfredi (Ital)
watch (waterproof)	1927	Rolex (Swiss)
wheel	c.3500 BC	Mesopotamia
windmill	c.600	Syria
writing (pictography)	c.3000 BC	Egypt
xerography	1938	Chester Carbon (US)
zip-fastener	1893	Whitcomb L Judson (US)

*Aus: Austrian	Bav: Bavarian	Belg: Belgian	Braz: Brazilian	Croat: Croatian
D: Danish	Fr: French	Ger: German	Gr: Greek	Hung: Hungarian
Ind: Indian	Ital: Italian	NL: Dutch	Nor: Norwegian	Pruss: Prussian
Swed: Swedish				

SCIENTISTS

Airy, Sir George Biddell (1802–92)
English astronomer and geophysicist. Astronomer Royal (1835–81) who reorganized the Greenwich Observatory. Initiated measurement of Greenwich Mean Time, determined the mass of the Earth from gravity experiments in mines, and carried out extensive work in optics.

Alzheimer, Alois (1864–1915)
German psychiatrist and neuropathologist. Gave full clinical and pathological description of pre-senile dementia (Alzheimer's disease) (1907).

Ampère, André Marie (1775–1836)
French mathematician and physicist. Laid the foundations of the science of electrodynamics. His name is given to the basic SI unit of electric current (ampere, amp).

Archimedes (c.287–212 BC)
Greek mathematician. Discovered formulae for the areas and volumes of plane and solid geometrical figures using methods which anticipated theories of integration to be developed 1 800 years later. Also founded the science of hydrostatics; in popular tradition remembered for the cry of 'Eureka' when he discovered the principle of upthrust on a floating body.

Aristotle (384–322 BC)
Greek philosopher and scientist. One of the most influential figures in the history of Western thought and scientific tradition. Wrote enormous amounts on biology, zoology, physics and psychology.

Avogadro, Amedeo (1776–1856)
Italian physicist. Formulated the hypothesis (Avogadro's Law) that equal volumes of gas contain equal numbers of molecules, when at the same temperature and pressure.

Babbage, Charles (1791–1871)
English mathematician. Attempted to build two calculating machines — the 'difference engine', to calculate logarithms and similar functions by repeated addition performed by trains of gear wheels, and the 'analytical engine', to perform much more varied calculations. Babbage is regarded as the pioneer of modern computers.

Bacon, Francis, Baron Verulam of Verulam, Viscount St Albans (1561–1626)
English statesman and natural philosopher. Creator of scientific induction; stressed the importance of experiment in interpreting nature, giving significant impetus to future scientific investigation.

Baird, John Logie (1888–1946)
Scottish engineer. Gave first demonstration of a television image in 1926. Also researched radar and infrared television, and succeeded in producing 3-D and colour images (1944), as well as projection onto a screen and stereophonic sound.

Barnard, Christiaan Neethling (1922–   )
South African surgeon. Performed first successful heart transplant in December 1967 at Groote Schuur Hospital. Although the recipient died 18 days later from pneumonia, a second patient operated on in January 1968 survived for 594 days.

Bell, Alexander Graham (1847–1922)
Scottish-American inventor, born Edinburgh. After researching and teaching methods in speech therapy and experimenting with various acoustical devices, produced the first intelligible telephonic transmission on 5 June 1875, and patented the telephone in 1876. Founded the Bell Telephone Company in 1877.

Bohr, Niels Henrik David (1885–1962)
Danish physicist. Greatly extended the theory of atomic structure by explaining the spectrum of hydrogen by means of an atomic model and the quantum theory (1913). Awarded the Nobel prize for physics in 1922. Assisted in atom bomb research in America during World War II.

Boyle, The Hon Robert (1627–91)
Irish physicist and chemist. One of the first members of the Royal Society. Carried out experiments on air, vacuum, combustion and respiration and in 1662 arrived at Boyle's law, which states that the pressure and volume of a gas are inversely proportional at constant temperature.

Brahe, Tycho or **Tyge** (1546–1601)
Danish astronomer. After seeing the partial solar eclipse of 1569 became obsessed about astronomy. Accurately measured and compiled catalogues of the positions of stars, providing vital information for later astronomers and recorded unique observations of a new star in Cassiopeia in 1572 (a nova now known as Tycho's star).

Brunel, Isambard Kingdom (1806–59)
English engineer and inventor. Helped to plan the Thames Tunnel and later planned the Clifton suspension bridge. Designed the first steamship to cross the Atlantic, the first ocean

SCIENTISTS (cont.)

screw-steamer. In 1833 appointed engineer to the Great Western Railway and constructed all tunnels, bridges and viaducts on that line; also constructed and improved many docks.

Chandrasekhar, Subrahmanyan (1910–95)
American astrophysicist, born Lahore (then in India). He showed that at the end of their lives, stars of less than a certain critical mass will collapse to form white dwarfs, small hot stars in which material is compressed to densities of millions of times of that of ordinary matter. He shared the 1983 Nobel Prize for Physics with William Fowler.

Copernicus, Nicolaus (1473–1543)
Polish astronomer. Studied mathematics, optics, perspective and canon law before a varied career involving law, medicine and astronomy. Published theory in 1543 that the Sun is at the centre of the Universe; this was not initially accepted due to opposition from the Church in Rome which held that the Universe is Earth-centred.

Crick, Francis Harry Compton (1916–   )
English biologist. Constructed a molecular model of the complex genetic material deoxyribonucleic acid (DNA). Later research on nucleic acids led to far-reaching discoveries concerning the genetic code. Joint winner of the Nobel prize for medicine and physiology in 1962.

Curie, Marie (originally Manya) née Sklodowska (1867–1934)
Polish–French physicist. After graduating from the Sorbonne worked on magnetism and radioactivity, isolating radium and polonium. Shared the Nobel prize for physics in 1903 with her husband Pierre Curie and Antoine Henri Becquerel. Became professor of physics at the Sorbonne in 1906; awarded the Nobel prize for chemistry in 1911.

Cuvier, Georges (Léopold Chrétien Frédéric Dagobert) (1769–1832)
French anatomist. Known as the father of comparative anatomy and palaeontology. Opponent of the Theory of Descent, and originated the natural system of animal classification. Linked comparative anatomy and palaeontology through studies of animal and fish fossils.

Dalton, John (1766–1844)
English chemist. Researched mixed gases, the force of steam, the elasticity of vapours and deduced the law of partial pressures, or Dalton's law. Also made important contributions in atomic theory.

Darwin, Charles Robert (1809–82)
English naturalist. Recommended as naturalist for a scientific survey of South American waters (1831–36) on HMS *Beagle* during which he made many geological and zoological discoveries which led him to speculate on the origin of species. In 1859 published theory of evolution in *The Origin of Species by Means of Natural Selection*.

Davy, Sir Humphry (1778–1829)
English chemist. Experimented with newly-discovered gases, and discovered the anaesthetic effect of laughing gas. Discovered the new metals potassium, sodium, barium, strontium, calcium and magnesium. Also investigated volcanic action, devised safety lamps for use in mining and was important in promoting science within industry.

Descartes, René (1596–1650)
French philosopher and mathematician. Creator of analytical or coordinate geometry, also named after him as Cartesian geometry. Also theorized extensively in physics and physiology, and is regarded as the father of modern philosophy.

Doppler, Christian Johann (1803–53)
Austrian physicist. The Doppler effect, described in a paper in 1842, explains the increase and decrease of wave frequency observed when a wave source and the observer respectively approach or recede from one another.

Edison, Thomas Alva (1847–1931)
American inventor and physicist. Took out more than 1 000 patents, including the gramophone (1877), the incandescent light bulb (1879) and an improved microphone for Bell's telephone. Also discovered thermionic emission, formerly called the Edison effect.

Ehrlich, Paul (1854–1915)
German bacteriologist, born Strehlen. Pioneer in haematology and chemotherapy, synthesized salvarsan as a treatment for syphilis and propounded the side-chain theory in immunology. Joint winner of the 1908 Nobel prize for physiology or medicine.

Einstein, Albert (1879–1955)
German–Swiss–American mathematical physicist. Achieved world fame through his special and general theories of relativity; also studied gases and discovered the photoelectric effect, for which he was awarded the Nobel prize in 1921.

Euler, Leonhard (1707–83)
Swiss mathematician. Published over 800 different books and papers on mathematics, physics and astronomy, introducing many new functions and carrying out important work in calculus. Introduced the notations e and gp, still used today. Also studied motion and celestial mechanics.

Fahrenheit, Gabriel Daniel (1686–1736)
German physicist. Devised alcohol thermometer (1709) and later invented the mercury thermometer (1714). Also devised the temperature scale named after him, and was the first to show that the boiling point of liquids varies at different atmospheric pressures.

Faraday, Michael (1791–1867)
English chemist and physicist. Discovered electro-magnetic induction (1831), the laws of electrolysis (1833) and the rotation of polarized light by magnetism (1845). First to isolate benzene and to synthesize chlorocarbons.

Fermi, Enrico (1901–54)
Italian–American nuclear physicist, born Rome. Published method of calculating atomic particles, and in 1943 succeeded in splitting the nuclei of uranium atoms, producing artificial radioactive substances. Awarded the 1938 Nobel prize for physics, and constructed the first American nuclear reactor at Chicago (1942). The element fermium was named after him.

Feynman, Richard Phillips (1918–88)
American physicist. Made considerable theoretical advances in quantum electrodynamics, for which he was joint winner of the Nobel prize for physics in 1965. Involved in building the first atomic bomb during World War II.

SCIENTISTS (cont.)

Fleming, Sir Alexander (1881–1955)
Scottish bacteriologist. First to use anti-typhoid vaccines on humans and pioneered the use of salvarsan to treat syphilis. In 1928 discovered penicillin by chance, for which he was joint winner of the 1945 Nobel prize for physiology or medicine.

Galilei, Galileo, known as **Galileo** (1564–1642)
Italian astronomer, mathematician and natural philosopher. Deduced the value of a pendulum for exact measurement of time, proved that all falling bodies, great or small, descend due to gravity at the same rate. Perfected the refracting telescope and made astronomical observations which revealed mountains and valleys on the Moon, four satellites of Jupiter and sunspots, and convinced him of the correctness of the Copernican theory. His support for the Copernican theory led to his imprisonment by the Inquisition; he remained under house arrest until his death.

Geiger, Hans Wilhelm (1882–1945)
German physicist. Investigated beta-ray radioactivity and, with Walther Müller, devised a counter to measure it.

Halley, Edmond (1656–1742)
English astronomer and mathematician. Studied the Solar System and correctly predicted the return (in 1758, 1835 and 1910) of a comet that had been observed in 1583, and is now named after him.

Harvey, William (1578–1657)
English physician. Discovered the circulation of the blood.

Henle, Friedrich Gustav Jakob (1809–85)
German anatomist. Discovered the tubules in the kidney which are named after him and wrote treatises on systematic anatomy.

Hertz, Heinrich Rudolph (1857–94)
German physicist. Confirmed James Clerk Maxwell's predictions in 1887 by his discovery of invisible electromagnetic waves, of the same fundamental form as light waves.

Hubble, Edwin Powell (1889–1953)
American astronomer. Demonstrated that some nebulae are independent galaxies, and in 1929 discovered galaxy 'redshift', that distant galaxies are receding from us and that the apparent speed of recession of a galaxy is proportional to its distance from us.

Huygens, Christiaan (1629–93)
Dutch physicist. Made pendulum clock (1657) on Galileo's suggestion, and developed the doctrine of accelerated motion under gravity. Discovered the rings and fourth satellite of Saturn and the laws of collision of elastic bodies.

Jansky, Karl Guthe (1905–50)
American radio engineer. Discovered astronomical radio sources by chance while investigating interference on short-wave radio telephone transmissions, initiating the science of radio astronomy. The SI unit of radio emission strength, the jansky, is named after him.

Jeans, Sir James Hopwood (1877–1946)
English physicist and astronomer. Made important contributions to the dynamical theory of gases, radiation, quantum theory and stellar evolution; best known for his role in popularizing physics and astronomy.

Joule, James Prescott (1818–89)
English physicist. Showed experimentally that heat is a form of energy and established the mechanical equivalent of heat; this became the basis for the theory of conservation of energy. With Lord Kelvin studied temperatures of gases and formulated the absolute scale of temperature.

Kant, Immanuel (1724–1804)
German philosopher. Researched astronomy and geophysics, and predicted the existence of the planet Uranus before its discovery. Philosophical works had enormous influence.

Kelvin, William Thomson, 1st Baron (1824–1907)
Irish–Scottish physicist and mathematician, born Belfast. Solved important problems in electrostatics, proposed the absolute, or Kelvin, temperature scale and established the second law of thermodynamics simultaneously with Rudolf Clausius. Also investigated geomagnetism and hydrodynamics, and invented innumerable instruments.

Kepler, Johannes (1571–1630)
German astronomer. Formulated laws of planetary motion, describing elliptical orbits and forming the starting point of modern astronomy. Also made discoveries in optics, general physics and geometry.

Kirchhoff, Gustav Robert (1824–87)
German physicist. Carried out important research in electricity, heat, optics and spectrum analysis, his work leading to the discovery of caesium and rubidium (1859).

Lamarck, Jean (Baptiste Pierre Antoine de Monet) Chevalier de (1744–1829)
French naturalist. Made the basic distinction between vertebrates and invertebrates. On evolution he postulated that acquired characters can be inherited by later generations, preparing the way for the Darwinian theory of evolution.

Langmuir, Irving (1881–1959)
American physical chemist. He worked at the General Electric Company for 41 years, and his many inventions include the gas-filled tungsten lamp and an improved vacuum pump. He was awarded the 1932 Nobel Prize for Chemistry for his work on solid and liquid services.

Leibniz, Gottfried Wilhelm (1646–1716)
German mathematician and philosopher. Discovered calculus around the same time as Isaac Newton; also made original contribution in the fields of optics, mechanics, statistics, logic and probability, and laid the foundations of 18th-century philosophy.

Leishman, Sir William Boog (1865–1926)
Scottish bacteriologist. Discovered an effective vaccine for inoculation against typhoid and was first to discover the parasite of the disease kala-azar.

Linnaeus, Carolus (Carl von Linné) (1707–78)
Swedish naturalist and physician. Founder of modern scientific nomenclature for plants and animals.

SCIENTISTS (cont.)

Lorentz, Hendrik Antoon (1853–1928)
Dutch physicist. Carried out important work in electromagnetism; joint winner of the Nobel prize for physics in 1902 for explaining the effect whereby atomic spectral lines are split in the presence of magnetic fields.

Lorenz, Konrad Zacharias (1903–89)
Austrian zoologist and ethologist. Regarded as the father of ethology, favouring the study of the instinctive behaviour of animals in the wild. In 1935 published observations on imprinting in young birds by which hatchlings 'learn' to recognize substitute parents, and argued that while aggressive behaviour in man is inborn, it may be channelled into other forms of activity, whereas in other animals it is purely survival-motivated.

Lyell, Sir Charles (1797–1875)
Scottish geologist. Established the principle of uniformitarianism in geology, that geological changes have been gradual and produced by forces still at work, instead of including catastrophic changes as previously believed. His work significantly influenced Charles Darwin, although Lyell never accepted the theory of evolution by natural selection.

Mach, Ernst (1838–1916)
Austrian physicist and philosopher. Carried out experimental work on projectiles and the flow of gases. His name has been given to the ratio of the speed of flow of a gas to the speed of sound (Mach number) and to the angle of a shock wave to the direction of motion (Mach angle).

Marconi, (Marquis) Guglielmo (1874–1937)
Italian physicist and inventor. Experimented in converting electromagnetic waves into electricity and achieved wireless telegraphy in 1895. In 1898 transmitted signals across the English Channel and in 1901 succeeded in sending Morse code signals across the Atlantic. Joint winner of the 1909 Nobel prize for physics. Later developed short-wave radio equipment and established a worldwide radio telegraph network for the British government.

Maxwell, James Clerk (1831–79)
Scottish physicist. Produced mathematical theory of electromagnetism and identified light as electromagnetic radiation. Also suggested that invisible electromagnetic waves could be generated in a laboratory, as later carried out by Hertz. Other research included the kinetic theory of gases, the nature of Saturn's rings, colour perception and colour photography.

Medawar, Sir Peter Brian (1915–87)
British zoologist and immunologist. Pioneered experiments in skin grafting and the prevention of rejection in transplant operations. Joint winner of Nobel prize for physiology or medicine in 1960.

Mendel, Gregor Johann (1822–84)
Austrian biologist and botanist. Became abbot in 1868. Researched inheritance characters in plants leading to the formulation of Mendel's law of segregation and the law of independent assortment; his principles became the basis of modern genetics.

Mendeleyev, Dmitri Ivanovich (1834–1907)
Russian chemist. Formulated the periodic law from which he predicted the existence of

several elements which were subsequently discovered. Element 101 is named mendelevium after him.

Michelson, Albert Abraham (1852–1931)

German–American physicist, born Strelno (now Strzelno, Poland). Carried out famous Michelson–Morley experiment which confirmed the non-existence of the 'ether', a result which set Einstein on the road to the theory of relativity. First American scientist to win a Nobel prize in 1907.

Napier, John (1550–1619)

Scottish mathematician. He is famous for the invention of logarithms to simplify computation, and he also devised a calculating machine using a set of rods, known as *Napier's Bones*.

Newton, Sir Isaac (1642–1727)

English scientist and mathematician. Formulated complete theory of gravitation by 1684; also carried out important work in optics, concluding that the different colours of light making up white light have different refrangibility, developed the reflecting telescope, and invented calculus around the same time as Leibniz.

Pascal, Blaise (1623–62)

French mathematician and physicist. Carried out important work in geometry, invented a calculating machine, demonstrated that air pressure decreases with altitude as previously predicted and developed probability theory. The SI unit of pressure (pascal) and the modern computer programming language, Pascal, are named after him.

Pasteur, Louis (1822–95)

French chemist. Father of modern bacteriology. Discovered possibility of reducing the virulence of injurious micro-organisms by exposure to air, by variety of culture, or by transmission through various animals, and demonstrated that the diluted organisms could be used for immunization. From this he developed vaccinations against anthrax and rabies. Also introduced pasteurization (moderate heating) to kill disease-producing organisms in wine, milk and other foods.

Pauli, Wolfgang (1900–58)

Austrian–American theoretical physicist. Formulated the exclusion principle (1924), that no two electrons can be in the same energy state, producing important advances in the application of quantum theory to the periodic table of elements; for this he was awarded the Nobel prize for physics in 1945.

Pauling, Linus (1901–94)

American chemist. He made important discoveries concerning chemical bonding and complex molecular structures; this led him into work on the chemistry of biological molecules and the chemical basis of hereditary disease. He was awarded the 1954 Nobel Prize for Chemistry, and also the 1962 Nobel Peace Prize.

Pavlov, Ivan Petrovich (1849–1936)

Russian physiologist. Studied physiology of circulation, digestion and 'conditioned' or acquired reflexes, believing the brain's only function to be to couple neurones to produce reflexes. Awarded the Nobel prize for physiology or medicine in 1904.

SCIENTISTS (cont.)

Planck, Max Karl Ernst (1858–1947)
German theoretical physicist. Researched thermodynamics and black-body radiation, leading him to formulate quantum theory (1900), which assumes energy changes take place in abrupt instalments or quanta. Awarded Nobel prize for physics in 1918.

Ptolemy, or **Claudius Ptolemaeus** (c.90–168)
Egyptian astronomer and geographer. Corrected and improved the astronomical work of his predecessors to form the Ptolemaic System, described by Plato and Aristotle, with the Earth at the centre of the Universe and heavenly bodies revolving round it; beyond this lay the sphere of the fixed stars. Also compiled geographical catalogues and maps.

Pythagoras (6th century BC)
Greek mathematician and philosopher. Associated with mathematical discoveries involving the chief musical intervals, the relations of numbers and the relations between the lengths of sides of right-angled triangles (Pythagoras's theorem). Profoundly influenced Plato and later astronomers and mathematicians.

Ramón y Cajal, Santiago (1852–1934)
Spanish physician and histologist. Carried out important work on the brain and nerves, isolated the neuron and discovered how nerve impulses are transmitted to brain cells. Joint winner of the 1906 Nobel prize for physiology or medicine.

Rayleigh, John William Strutt, 3rd Baron (1842–1919)
English physicist. Carried out valuable research on vibratory motion, the theory of sound and the wave theory of light. With Sir William Ramsay discovered argon (1894). Awarded Nobel prize for physics in 1904.

Richter, Charles Francis (1900–85)
American seismologist. Devised the scale of earthquake strength which bears his name (1927–35).

Röntgen, Wilhelm Konrad von (1845–1923)
German physicist. Discovered the electromagnetic rays which he called X-rays (also known as Röntgen rays) in 1895. For his work on X-rays he was joint winner of the Rumford medal in 1896 and winner of the 1901 Nobel prize for physics.

Rutherford, Ernest Rutherford, 1st Baron Rutherford of Nelson (1871–1937)
New Zealand–British physicist. Made first successful wireless transmissions over two miles, discovered the three types of uranium radiations, formulated a theory of atomic disintegration and determined the nature of alpha particles; this led to a new atomic model in which the mass is concentrated in the nucleus. Also discovered that alpha-ray bombardment could produce atomic transformation and predicted the existence of the neutron. Awarded Nobel prize for chemistry in 1908.

Schrödinger, Erwin (1887–1961)
Austrian physicist. Originated the study of wave mechanics as part of the quantum theory with the celebrated Schrödinger wave equation, for which he was joint winner of the 1933 Nobel prize for physics.

Szent-Györgyi, Albert von Nagyrapolt (1893–1986)
Hungarian–American biochemist. Discovered actin, isolated vitamin C and was awarded the Nobel prize for physiology or medicine in 1937.

Thomson, Sir Joseph John (1856–1940)
English physicist. Studied gaseous conductors of electricity and the nature of cathode rays; this led to his discovery of the electron. Also pioneered mass spectrometry and discovered the existence of isotopes of elements. Awarded the Nobel prize for physics in 1906.

Thomson, Sir William *see* **Kelvin, Lord**

Tinbergen, Nikolaas (1907–88)
Dutch ethologist. Co-founder with Konrad Lorenz of the science of ethology (study of animal behaviour in natural surroundings). Analyzed social behaviour of certain animals and insects as an evolutionary process with considerable relevance to human behaviour, especially courtship and aggression. Joint winner of the 1973 Nobel prize for physiology or medicine.

Van der Waals, Johannes Dederik (1837–1923)
Dutch physicist. Discovered van der Waal's equation, defining the physical state of a gas or liquid and investigated the weak attractive forces (van der Waal's forces) between molecules. Awarded the Nobel prize for physics in 1910.

Volta, Alessandro Giuseppe Anastasio, Count (1745–1827)
Italian physicist. Developed the theory of current electricity, discovered the electric composition of water, invented an electric battery, the electrophorus, an electroscope and made investigations into heat an gases. His name is given to the SI unit of electric potential difference, the volt.

Watt, James (1736–1819)
Scottish engineer and inventor. Developed and improved early models of the steam engine, and manufactured it from 1774. The watt, a unit of power, is named after him, and the term horsepower was first used by him.

Young, Thomas (1773–1829)
English physicist and physician. Expounded the phenomenon of interference, which established the wave theory of light. Also made valuable contributions in insurance, haemodynamics and deciphering the inscriptions on the Rosetta Stone.

NOBEL PRIZES (1970–96)

Year	Chemistry	Physics	Physiology/Medicine
1970	Luis Federico Leloir	Louis Eugène Néel Hannes Olof Alfvén	Julius Axelrod Bernard Katz Ulf von Euler
1971	Gerhard Herzberg	Dennis Gabor	Earl W Sutherland

NOBEL PRIZES (1970–96) (cont.)

Year	Chemistry	Physics	Physiology/Medicine
1972	Stanford Moore William H Stein Christian B Anfinsen	John Bardeen Leon N Cooper John R Schrieffer	Gerald M Edelman Rodney M Porter
1973	Ernst Otto Fischer Geoffrey Wilkinson	Leo Esaki Ivar Giaever Brian D Josephson	Konrad Lorenz Nikolaas Tinbergen Karl von Frisch
1974	Paul J Flory	Martin Ryle Antony Hewish	Albert Claude Geoge Emil Palade Christian de Duve
1975	John W Cornforth Vladimir Prelog	Aage N Bohr Ben R Mottelson L James Rainwater	David Baltimore Renato Dulbecco Howard M Temin
1976	William N Lipscomb	Burton Richter Samuel Chao Chung Ting	Baruch S Blumberg Daniel C Gajdusek
1977	Ilya Prigogine	Philip W Anderson Neville F Mott John H van Vleck	Rosalyn S Yalow Roger C L Guillemin Andrew V Schally
1978	Peter Mitchell	Pjotr L Kapitza Arno A Penzias Robert W Wilson	Werner Arber Daniel Nathans Hamilton O Smith
1979	Herbert C Brown Georg Wittig	Steven Weinberg Sheldon L Glashow Abdus Salam	Allan M Cormack Godfrey N Hounsfield
1980	Paul Berg Walter Gilbert Frederick Sanger	James W Cronin Val L Fitch	Baruj Benacerraf George D Snell Jean Dausset
1981	Kenichi Fukui Roald Hoffman	Nicolaas Bloembergen Arthur L Schawlow Kai M Siegbahn	Roger W Sperry David H Hubel Torsten N Wiesel
1982	Aaron Klug	Kenneth G Wilson	Sune K Bergström Bengt I Samuelsson John R Vane
1983	Henry Taube	Subrahmanyan Chandrasekhar William A Fowler	Barbara McClintock

Year	Chemistry	Physics	Physiology/Medicine
1984	Robert B Merrifield	Carlo Rubbia Simon van der Meer	Niels K Jerne Georges J F Köhler César Milstein
1985	Herbert Hauptman Jerome Karle	Klaus von Klitzing	Joseph L Goldstein Michael S Brown
1986	Dudley R Herschbach Yuan Tseh Lee John C Polanyi	Gerd Binnig Heinrich Rohrer Ernst Ruska	Stanley Cohen Rita Levi-Montalcini
1987	Charles Pedersen Donald Cram Jean-Marie Lehn	Georg Bednorz Alex Müller	Susumu Tonegawa
1988	Johann Deisenhofer Robert Huber Hartmut Michel	Leon Lederman Melvin Schwartz Jack Steinberger	James Black Gertrude Elion George Hitchings
1989	Sydney Altman Thomas Cech	Hans Dehmelt Wolfgang Paul Norman Ramsay	J Michael Bishop Harold E Varmus
1990	Elias James Corey	Jerome Friedman Henry Kendall Richard Taylor	Joseph E Murray E Donnall Thomas
1991	Richard R Ernst	Pierre-Gilles de Gennes	Erwin Neher Bert Sakmann
1992	Rudolph A Marcus	George Charpak	Edmond H Fisher Edwin G Krebs
1993	Kary Banks Mullis Michael Smith	Russell Hulse Joseph Hooton Taylor Jr	Richard Roberts Phillip Allen Sharp
1994	George Olah	Clifford Shull Bertram Brockhouse	Martin Rodbell Alfred G Gilman
1995	F Sherwood Roland Mario Molina Paul Crutzen	Martin L Perl Frederick Reines	Edward B Lewis Eric F Wieschaus Christine Nüsslein-Volhard
1996	Harold Kroto Robert Curl Richard Smalley	David Lee Douglas Osheroff Robert Richardson	Peter Doherty Rolf Zinkernagel

COMMUNICATION

LANGUAGE FAMILIES

Estimates of the numbers of speakers in the main language families of the world in the early 1980s. The list includes Japanese and Korean, which are not clearly related to any other languages.

Main language families

Indo-European	2 000 000 000
Sino-Tibetan	1 040 000 000
Niger-Congo	260 000 000
Afro-Asiatic	230 000 000
Austronesian	200 000 000
Dravidian	140 000 000
Japanese	120 000 000
Altaic	90 000 000
Austro-Asiatic	60 000 000
Korean	60 000 000
Tai	50 000 000
Nilo-Saharan	30 000 000
Amerindian (North, Central, South America)	25 000 000
Uralic	23 000 000
Miao-Yao	7 000 000
Caucasian	6 000 000
Indo-Pacific	3 000 000
Khoisan	50 000
Australian aborigine	50 000
Palaeosiberian	25 000

SPECIFIC LANGUAGES

The first column gives estimates (in millions) for mother-tongue speakers of the 20 most widely used languages. The second coloumn gives estimates of the total population of all countries where the language has official or semi-official status; these totals are often over-estimates, as only a minority of people in countries where a second language is recognized may actually be fluent in it.

Mother-tongue speakers		Official language populations	
1 Chinese	1 000	1 English	1 400
2 English	350	2 Chinese	1 000
3 Spanish	250	3 Hindi	700
4 Hindi	200	4 Spanish	280

Mother-tongue speakers		Official language populations	
5 Arabic	150	5 Russian	270
6 Bengali	150	6 French	220
7 Russian	150	7 Arabic	170
8 Portuguese	135	8 Portuguese	160
9 Japanese	120	9 Malay	160
10 German	100	10 Bengali	150
11 French	70	11 Japanese	120
12 Panjabi	70	12 German	100
13 Javanese	65	13 Urdu	85
14 Bihari	65	14 Italian	60
15 Italian	60	15 Korean	60
16 Korean	60	16 Vietnamese	60
17 Telugu	55	17 Persian	55
18 Tamil	55	18 Tagalog	50
19 Marathi	50	19 Thai	50
20 Vietnamese	50	20 Turkish	50

SPEAKERS OF ENGLISH

The first column gives figures for countries where English is used as a mother-tongue or first language; for countries where no figure is given, English is not the first language of a significant number of people. (A question-mark indicates that no agreed estimates are available.) The second column gives total population figures (mainly 1990 figures) for countries where English has official or semi-official status as a medium of communication. These totals are likely to bear little correlation with the real use of English in the area.

Country	First language speakers of English	Country population	Country	First language speakers of English	Country population
Anguilla	8 000 –	8 000	Ghana		15 020 000
Antigua and Barbuda	80 600 –	80 600	Gibraltar		30 689+
			Grenada	101 000+	101 000+
Australia	14 000 000	17 073 000	Guyana	700 000+	756 000
Bahamas	253 000 –	253 000	Hong Kong	?	5 841 000 –
Bangladesh	?	113 005 000+	India	?	853 373 000+
Barbados	257 000+	257 000+	Irish Republic	3 515 000	3 515 000
Belize	100 000+	189 000+	Jamaica	2 300 000+	2 391 000
Bermuda	59 300+	59 300+	Kenya		24 872 000
Bhutan	?	1 442 000+	Kiribati		71 100+
Botswana		1 295 000 –	Lesotho		1 760 000
Brunei		259 000+	Liberia		2 595 000
Cameroon		11 900 000+	Malawi		8 831 000
Canada	17 000 000+	26 620 000+	Malaysia (East)		14 300 000
Dominica	50 000+	82 200 –	Malta		353 000
Fiji		740 000+	Mauritius		1 080 000

SPEAKERS OF ENGLISH (cont.)

Country	First language speakers of English	Country population	Country	First language speakers of English	Country population
Montserrat	12 000	12 000	South Africa	2 000 000+	30 797 000
Namibia		1 302 000	Sri Lanka	?	17 103 000+
Nauru		9 000+	Suriname		411 000
Nepal	?	18 910 000+	Swaziland		770 000
New Zealand	3 000 000	3 389 000	Tanzania		24 403 000
Nigeria	?	119 812 000+	Tonga		96 000+
Pakistan	?	122 666 000+	Trinidad and Tobago	1 233 000	1 233 000
Papua New Guinea		3 671 000	Tuvalu		9 100+
Philippines		61 480 000	Uganda		16 928 000
St Christopher and Nevis	44 100	44 100	UK	57 000 000+	57 384 000
St Lucia	?	151 000+	USA	215 000 000	249 246 000+
St Vincent and the Grenadines	100 000+	115 000+	US territories in Pacific		300 000 –
Senegambia		600 000	Vanuatu		150 000
Seychelles		68 700	Western Samoa		165 000+
Sierra Leone		4 151 00	Zambia		8 456 000
Singapore	?	2 718 000	Zimbabwe	200 000+	9 369 000
Solomon Islands		319 000+	Other British territories	30 000+	30 000+
			TOTALS	317 043 000+	1 895 079 100+

FOREIGN WORDS AND PHRASES USED IN ENGLISH

à bon marché   (Fr) 'good market'; at a good bargain, cheap.

a cappella   (Ital) 'in the style of the chapel'; sung without instrumental accompaniment.

addendum *plural* **addenda**   (Lat) 'that which is to be added'; supplementary material for a book.

à deux   (Fr) 'for two'; often denotes a dinner or conversation of a romantic nature.

ad hoc   (Lat) 'towards this'; for this special purpose.

ad infinitum   (Lat) 'to infinity'; denotes endless repetition.

ad nauseam   (Lat) 'to the point of sickness'; disgustingly endless or repetitive.

ad referendum   (Lat) 'for reference'; to be further considered.

affaire   (Fr) liaison, intrigue; an incident arousing speculation and scandal.

aficionado   (Span) 'amateur'; an ardent follower; a 'fan'.

a fortiori   (Lat) 'from the stronger' (argument); denotes the validity and stronger reason of a proposition.

agent provocateur   (Fr) 'provocative agent'; someone who incites others, by pretended sympathy to commit crimes.

aide-de-camp　(Fr) 'assistant on the field'; an officer who acts as a confidential personal assistant for an officer of higher rank.

aide-mémoire　(Fr) 'help-memory'; a reminder; memorandum-book; a written summary of a diplomatic agreement.

à la carte　(Fr) 'from the menu'; each dish individually priced.

à la mode　(Fr) 'in fashion, fashionable'.

al dente　(Ital) 'to the tooth'; culinary term denoting (usually) pasta fully cooked but still firm.

al fresco　(Ital) 'fresh'; painting on fresh or moist plaster; in the fresh, cool or open air.

aloha　(Hawaiian) 'love'; a salutation, 'hello' or 'goodbye'.

ambiance　(Fr) surroundings, atmosphere.

amende honorable　(Fr) a public apology satisfying the honour of the injured party.

amour-propre　(Fr) 'own love, self-love'; self-esteem.

ancien régime　(Fr) 'old regime'; a superseded and outdated political system or ruling elite.

angst　(Ger) 'anxiety'; an unsettling feeling produced by awareness of the uncertainties and paradoxes inherent in the state of being human.

anno Domini　(Lat) 'in the year of the Lord'; used in giving dates of the Christian era, counting forward from the year of Christ's birth.

anschluss　(Ger) 'joining together'; union, especially the political union of Germany and Austria in 1938.

ante meridiem　(Lat) 'before midday'; between midnight and noon, abbreviated to am.

a posteriori　(Lat) 'from the later'; applied to reasoning from experience, from effect to cause.

appellation contrôlée　(Fr) 'certified name'; used in the labelling of French wines, a guarantee of specified conditions of origin, strength, etc.

a priori　(Lat) 'from the previous'; denotes argument from the cause to the effect; deductive reasoning.

atelier　(Fr) a workshop, an artist's studio.

au contraire　(Fr) 'on the contrary'.

au fait　(Fr) 'to the point'; highly skilled; knowledgeable or familiar with something.

au fond　(Fr) 'at the bottom'; fundamentally.

au naturel　(Fr) 'in the natural state'; naked; cooked plainly, raw, or without dressing.

au pair　(Fr) 'on an equal basis'; a young person from abroad who lives with a family and helps with housework, looking after children, etc, in return for board and lodging.

avant-garde　(Fr) 'front guard'; using or supporting the most modern and advanced ideas in literature, art, music, etc.

babushka　(Russ) 'grandmother'; granny; a triangular headscarf worn under the chin.

bain-marie　(Fr) 'bath of Mary'; a pan of hot water in which a container of food can be cooked gently or kept warm.

banzai　(Jap) a Japanese battle cry, salute to the emperor, or exclamation of joy.

barrio　(Span) 'district, suburb'; a (usually poor) community of Spanish-speaking immigrants (esp American English).

FOREIGN WORDS AND PHRASES USED IN ENGLISH (cont.)

batik   (Javanese) 'painted'; method of producing patterns on fabric by drawing with wax before dyeing.

beau geste   (Fr) 'beautiful gesture'; a magnanimous action.

belle époque   (Fr) 'fine period'; the time of gracious living for the well-to-do immediately preceding World War I.

belles-lettres   beautiful letters; works of literature valued for their style rather than their content.

bête noire   (Fr) 'black beast'; a bugbear; something one especially dislikes.

blasé   (Fr) 'cloyed'; dulled to enjoyment.

blitzkrieg   (Ger) 'lightning war'; a sudden overwhelming attack by ground and air forces; a burst of intense activity.

bodega   (Span) a wine shop that usually sells food as well; a building for wine storage.

bona fides   (Lat) 'good faith'; genuineness.

bonsai   (Jap) art of growing miniature trees in pots; a dwarf tree grown by this method.

bonvivant   (Fr) 'good living (person)'; one who lives well, particularly enjoying good food and wine; a jovial companion.

bon voyage   (Fr) have a safe and pleasant journey.

bourgeois   (Fr) 'citizen'; a member of the middle class; a merchant; conventional, conservative.

canard   (Fr) 'duck'; an untrue report; a false rumour.

carpe diem   (Lat) 'seize the day'; enjoy the pleasures of the present moment while they last.

carte blanche   (Fr) 'blank sheet of paper'; freedom of action.

casus belli   (Lat) 'occasion of war'; whatever sparks off or justifies a war or quarrel.

cause célèbre   (Fr) a very notable or famous trial; a notorious controversy.

caveat emptor   (Lat) 'let the buyer beware'; warns the buyer to examine carefully the article he is about to purchase.

c'est la vie   (Fr) 'that's life'; denotes fatalistic resignation.

chacun à son goût   (Fr) 'each to his own taste'; implies surprise at another's choice.

chef d'oeuvre   (Fr) an artist's or writer's masterpiece.

chicano   (Span) *mejicano* 'Mexican'; or an American of Mexican descent.

chutzpah   (Yiddish) effrontery, nerve to do or say outrageous things.

cinéma-vérité   (Fr) 'cinema truth'; realism in films usually sought by photographic scenes of real life.

cliché   (Fr) 'stereotype printing block'; a phrase that has become stale and feeble through repitition.

comme il faut   (Fr) 'as it is necessary'; correct; genteel.

compos mentis   (Lat) 'having control of one's mind'; sane.

cordon bleu   (Fr) 'blue ribbon'; denotes food cooked to a very high standard; a dish made with ham and cheese and a white sauce.

coup de foudre   (Fr) 'flash of lightning'; a sudden and astonishing happening; love at first sight.

coup de grâce (Fr) 'blow of mercy'; a final decisive blow.
coup d'état (Fr) 'blow of state'; the sudden, usually violent, overthrow of a government.
coupé (Fr) 'cut'; (usually) two-door motor-car with sloping roof.
crème de la crème (Fr) 'cream of the cream'; the very best.
cuisine minceur (Fr) 'slenderness cooking'; a style of cooking characterized by imaginative use of light, simple, low-fat ingredients.
cul-de-sac (Fr) 'bottom of the bag'; a road closed at one end.
curriculum vitae (Lat) 'course of life'; denotes a summary of someone's educational qualifications and work experience for presenting to a prospective employer.

décolleté (Fr) 'with bared neck and shoulders'; with neck uncovered; (of dress) low cut.
de facto (Lat) 'from the fact'; in fact, actually, irrespective of what is legally recognized.
déjà vu (Fr) 'already seen'; the feeling or illusion of having experienced something before.
deo volente (Lat) 'God willing'; a sort of good-luck talisman.
de rigueur (Fr) 'of strictness'; compulsory; required by strict etiquette.
derrière (Fr) 'behind'; the buttocks.
déshabillé (Fr) 'undressed', state of being only partially dressed, or of being casually dressed.
de trop (Fr) 'of too much'; superfluous; in the way.
distingué (Fr) 'distinguished'; having an aristocratic or refined demeanour; striking.
dolce far niente (Ital) 'sweet doing nothing'; denotes the pleasure of idleness.
doppelgänger (Ger) 'double goer'; a ghostly duplicate of a living person, a wraith; someone who looks exactly like someone else.
double entendre (Fr) 'double meaning'; ambiguity (normally with indecent connotations).
doyen (Fr) 'dean'; most distinguished member or representative by virtue of seniority, experience, and often also excellence.
droit de seigneur (Fr) 'the lord's right'; originally the alleged right of a feudal superior to take the virginity of a vassal's bride; any excessive claim imposed on a subordinate.
dummkopf (Ger) 'dumb-head'; blockhead; idiot.

élan (Fr) 'dash, rush, bound'; flair, flamboyance.
el dorado (Span) 'the gilded man'; the golden land (or city) imagined by the Spanish conquerors of America; any place which offers the opportunity of acquiring fabulous wealth.
embarras de richesse (Fr) 'embarrassment of wealth'; a perplexing amount of wealth or an abundance of any kind.
embonpoint (Fr) *en bon point* 'in fine form'; well-fed, stout, plump.
éminence grise (Fr) someone exerting power through their influence over a superior.
enfant terrible (Fr) 'terrible child'; a precocious child whose sayings embarrass its parents; a person whose behaviour is indiscreet, embarrassing to his associates.
ennui (Fr) world-weary listlessness, boredom.
en passant (Fr) 'in passing'; by the way, incidentally; chess term.
en route (Fr) on the way, on the road; let us go.
entente (Fr) 'understanding'; a friendly agreement between nations.
ersatz (Ger) 'replacement, substitute'; connotes a second-rate substitute; a supplementary reserve from which waste can be made good.

FOREIGN WORDS AND PHRASES USED IN ENGLISH (cont.)

et al (Lat) *et alli* 'and other things'; used to avoid giving a complete and possibly over-lengthy list of all items eg of authors.

eureka (Gr) *heureka* 'I have found!'; cry of triumph at a discovery.

ex cathedra (Lat) 'from the seat'; from the chair of office; authoritatively, judicially.

ex gratia (Lat) 'from favour'; as a favour; given as a favour

ex officio (Lat) 'from office, by virtue of office'; used as a reason for membership of a body.

ex parte (Lat) 'from (one) part'; 'from (one) side'; on behalf of one side only in legal proceedings; partial, prejudiced.

fait accompli (Fr) 'accomplished fact'; already done or settled, and therefore irreversible.

fata Morgana (Ital) a striking kind of mirage, attributed to witchcraft.

fatwa (Arabic) 'the statement of a formal legal opinion'; a formal legal opinion delivered by an Islamic religious leader.

faute de mieux (Fr) 'for lack of anything better'.

faux pas (Fr) 'false step'; a social blunder.

femme fatale (Fr) 'fatal woman'; an irresistibly attractive woman who brings difficulties or disasters on men; a siren.

film noir (Fr) 'black film'; a bleak and pessimistic film.

fin de siècle (Fr) 'end of the century'; of the end of the 19th-c in Western culture or of an era; decadent.

force de frappe (Fr) 'strike force'; equivalent of the 'independent nuclear deterrent'.

force majeure (Fr) 'superior force'; an unforeseeable or uncontrollable course of events, excusing one from fulfilling a contract, a legal term.

führer (Ger) 'leader, guide'; an insulting term for anyone bossily asserting authority.

gastarbeiter (Ger) 'guest-worker'; an immigrant worker, especially one who does menial work.

gemütlich (Ger) amiable, comfortable, cosy.

gestalt (Ger) 'form, shape'; original whole or unit, more than the sum of its parts.

gesundheit (Ger) 'health'; 'your health', said to someone who has just sneezed.

glasnost (Russ) 'publicity'; the policy of openness and forthrightness followed by the Soviet government, initiated by Mikhail Gorbachev.

götterdämmerung (Ger) 'twilight of the gods'; the downfall of any once powerful system.

grand mal (Fr) 'large illness'; a violently convulsive form of epilepsy.

grand prix (Fr) 'great prize'; any of several international motor races; any competition of similar importance in other sports.

gran turismo (Ital) 'great touring, touring on a grand scale'; a motor car designed for high speed touring in luxury (abbreviation GT).

gringo (Mexican-Spanish) 'foreigner'.

guru (Hindi) a spiritual leader; a revered instructor or mentor.

habeas corpus (Lat) 'you should have the body'; a writ to a jailer to produce a prisoner in person, and to state the reasons for detention; maintains the right of the subject to protection from unlawful imprisonment.

hajj   (Arabic) 'pilgrimage'; the Muslim pilgrimage to Mecca.

haka   (Maori) a Maori ceremonial war dance; a similar dance performed by New Zealanders eg before a rugby game.

haute couture   (Fr) 'higher tailoring'; fashionable, expensive dress designing and tailoring.

haut monde   (Fr) 'high world'; high society, fashionable society, composed of the aristocracy and the wealthy.

hoi polloi   (Gr) 'the many'; the rabble, the vulgar.

hombre   (Span) 'man'.

hors concours   (Fr) 'out of the competition'; not entered for a contest; unequalled.

idée fixe   (Fr) 'a fixed idea'; an obsession.

ikebana   (Jap) 'living flowers'; the Japanese art of flower arrangement.

in absentia   (Lat) 'in absence'; used for occasions, such as the receiving of a degree award, when the recipient would normally be present.

in camera   (Lat) 'in the room'; in a private room, in secret.

incommunicado   (Span) 'unable to communicate'; deprived of the right to communicate with others.

in extremis   (Lat) 'in the last'; at the point of death; in desperate circumstances.

in flagrante delicto   (Lat) 'with the crime blazing'; in the very act of committing the crime.

infra dig   (Lat) 'below dignity'; below one's dignity.

in loco parentis   (Lat) 'in place of a parent'.

in shallah   (Arabic) 'if God wills'; *see* **deo volente**

inter alia   (Lat) 'among other things'.

in vitro   (Lat) 'in glass'; in the test tube.

ipso facto   (Lat) 'by the fact itself'; thereby.

jihad   'struggle'; a holy war undertaken by Muslims against unbelievers.

kamikaze   (Jap) 'divine wind'; Japanese pilots making a suicide attack; any reckless, potentially self-destructive act.

karaoke   (Jap) 'empty orchestra'; in bars, clubs, etc members of the public sing a solo to a recorded backing.

karma   (Sanskrit) 'act'; the concept that the actions in a life determine the future condition of an individual.

kibbutz   (Hewbrew) A Jewish communal agricultural settlement in Israel.

kitsch   (Ger) 'rubbish'; work in any of the arts that is pretentious and inferior or in bad taste.

la dolce vita   (Ital) 'the sweet life'; the name of a film made by Federico Fellini in 1960 showing a life of wealth, pleasure and self-indulgence.

laissez-faire   (Fr) 'let do'; a general principle of non-interference.

lebensraum   (Ger) 'life space'; room to live; used by Hitler to justify his acquisition of land for Germany.

leitmotiv   (Ger) 'leading motive'; a recurrent theme.

FOREIGN WORDS AND PHRASES USED IN ENGLISH (cont.)

lèse majesté   (Fr) 'injured majesty'; offence against the sovereign power; treason.
lingua franca   (Ital) 'Frankish language'; originally a mixed Italian trading language used in the Levant, subsequently any language chosen as a means of communication among speakers of different languages.

macho   (Mexican/Spanish) 'male'; originally a positive term denoting masculinity or virility, it has come in English to describe an ostentatious virility.
maharishi   (Sanskrit) a Hindu sage or spiritual leader, a guru.
mañana   (Span) 'tomorrow'; an unspecified time in the future.
mea culpa   (Lat) 'through my fault'; originally part of the Latin mass; an admission of fault and an expression of repentance.
ménage à trois   (Fr) 'household of three'; a household comprised of a husband and wife and the lover of one of them.
mens sana in corpore sano   (Lat) 'a sound mind in a sound body' (Juvenal X, 356); the guiding rule of the 19th-c English educational system.
mot juste   (Fr) 'exact word'; the word which fits the context exactly.
mutatis mutandis   (Lat) 'with the necessary changes made'.

négociant   (Fr) 'merchant, trader'.
ne plus ultra   (Lat) 'not more beyond'; extreme perfection.
netsuke   (Jap) a small Japanese carved ornament used to fasten small objects, eg a purse, tobacco pouch, or medicine box, to the sash of a kimono. They are now collectors' pieces.
noblesse oblige   (Fr) 'nobility obliges'; rank imposes obligations.
non sequitur   (Lat) 'it does not follow'; an illogical step in an argument.
nostalgie de la boue   (Fr) 'hankering for mud'; a craving for a debased physical life without civilized refinements.
nota bene   (Lat) 'observe well, note well'; often abbreviated NB.
nouveau riche   (Fr) 'new rich'; one who has recently acquired wealth but lacks the good taste or social graces to go with it.
nouvelle cuisine   (Fr) 'new cooking'; a simple style of cookery characterized by much use of fresh produce and elegant presentation.
nouvelle vague   (Fr) 'new wave'; a movement in French cinema aiming at imaginative quality films.

origami   (Jap) 'paper-folding'; Japanese art of folding paper to make shapes suggesting birds, boats, etc.
outré   (Fr) 'gone to excess'; beyond what is customary or proper; eccentric.

per capita   (Lat) 'by heads'; per head of the population in statistical contexts.
perestroika   (Russ) 'reconstruction'; restructuring of an organization.
pied à terre   (Fr) 'foot to the ground'; a flat, small house, etc kept for temporary or occasional accommodation.

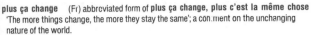

plus ça change   (Fr) abbreviated form of **plus ça change, plus c'est la même chose** 'The more things change, the more they stay the same'; a comment on the unchanging nature of the world.

post meridiem   (Lat) 'after midday, after noon'.

poule de luxe   (Fr) 'luxurious hen'; a sexually attractive promiscuous young woman; a prostitute.

pour encourager les autres   (Fr) 'to encourage the others' (Voltaire *Candide*, on the execution of Admiral Byng); exemplary punishment.

premier cru   (Fr) 'first growth'; wine of the highest quality in a system of classification.

prêt-à-porter   (Fr) 'ready to wear'; refers to 'designer' clothes that are made in standard sizes as opposed to made-to-measure clothes.

prima donna   (Ital) 'first lady'; leading female singer in an opera; a person who is temperamental and hard to please.

prima facie   (Lat) 'at first sight'; on the evidence available

primus inter pares   (Lat) 'first among equals'.

prix fixe   (Fr) 'fixed price'; used of a meal in a restaurant offered at a set price for a restricted choice.

pro bono publico   (Lat) 'for the public good'; something done for no fee.

quid pro quo   (Lat) 'something for something'; something given or taken as equivalent to another, often as retaliation.

quod erat demonstrandum   (Lat) 'which was to be shown'; often used in its abbreviated form **qed**

raison d'être   (Fr) 'reason for existence'.

realpolitik   (Ger) 'politics of realism'; practical politics based on the realities and necessities of life, rather than moral or ethical ideas.

recherché   (Fr) 'sought out'; particularly choice; rare or exotic

reductio ad absurdum   (Lat) 'reduction to absurdity'; originally used in logic to mean the proof of a proposition by proving the falsity of its contradictory; the application of a principle so strictly that it is carried to absurd lengths.

répondez, s'il vous plaît   (Fr) 'reply, please'; in English mainly in its abbreviated form, **RSVP**, on invitations.

rijsttafel   (Dutch) 'rice table'; an Indonesian rice dish served with a variety of foods.

risqué   (Fr) 'risky, hazardous'; audaciously bordering on the unseemly.

rus in urbe   (Lat) 'the country in the town' (Martial XII, 57 21); the idea of country charm in the centre of a city.

samizdat   (Russ) 'self-publisher'; the secret printing and distribution of banned literature in the USSR and other Eastern European countries under Communist rule.

sang froid   (Fr) 'cold blood'; self possession; coolness under stress.

savoir faire   (Fr) 'knowing what to do'; expertise; tact.

schadenfreude   (Ger) 'hurt joy'; pleasure in others' misfortunes.

shlock   (Yiddish) 'broken or damaged goods'; inferior, shoddy.

FOREIGN WORDS AND PHRASES USED IN ENGLISH (cont.)

shmaltz   (Yiddish) 'melted fat, grease'; showy sentimentality, particularly in writing, music, art, etc.

shmuck   (Yiddish) 'penis'; a (male) stupid person.

shogun   (Jap) 'leader of the army'; ruler of feudal Japan.

sic transit gloria mundi   (Lat) 'so passes away earthly glory'.

sine qua non   (Lat) 'without which not'; an indispensable condition.

sotto voce   (Ital) 'below the voice'; in an undertone; aside.

sub judice   (Lat) 'under a judge'; under consideration by a judge or a court of law.

sub rosa   (Lat) 'under the rose'; in secret, privately.

succès de scandale   (Fr) 'success of scandal'; the success of a book, film, etc due not to merit but to its connection with, or reference to, a scandal.

summa cum laude   (Lat) 'with the highest praise'; with great distinction; the highest class of degree award that can be gained by a US college student.

table d'hôte   (Fr) 'host's table'; a set meal at a fixed price.

tai chi   (Chin) 'great art of boxing'; a system of exercise, and self-defence in which good use of balance and co-ordination allows effort to be minimized.

tempus fugit   (Lat) 'time flies'; delay cannot be tolerated.

touché   (Fr) 'touched'; claiming or acknowledging a hit made in fencing; claiming or acknowledging a point scored in an argument.

tour de force   (Fr) 'turning movement'; feat of strength or skill.

trompe l'oeil   (Fr) 'deceives the eye'; an appearance of reality achieved by the use of perspective and detail in painting, architecture, etc.

tsunami   (Jap) 'wave in harbour'; a wave generated by movement of the earth's surface underwater; commonly (and erroneously) called a 'tidal wave'.

übermensch   (Ger) 'over-person'; superman.

ultra vires   (Lat) 'beyond strength, beyond powers'; beyond one's power or authority.

urbi et orbi   (Lat) 'to the city and the world'; used of the Pope's pronouncements; to everyone.

vade-mecum   (Lat) 'go with me'; a handbook, pocket companion.

vin du pays   (Fr) 'wine of the country'; a locally produced wine for everyday consumption.

vis-à-vis   (Fr) 'face to face'; one who faces or is opposite another; in relation to.

volte-face   (Fr) 'turn-face'; a sudden and complete change in opinion or in views expressed.

wunderkind   (Ger) 'wonder-child'; a 'child prodigy'; one who shows great talent and/or achieves great success at an early (or comparatively early) age.

FIRST NAME MEANINGS IN THE UK AND USA

The meanings of the most popular first names in the UK and USA are given below, along with a few other well-known names.

Name   Original meaning

Aaron   high mountain (*Hebrew*)
Adam   redness (*Hebrew*)
Alan   harmony (*Celtic*)
Albert   nobly bright (*Germanic*)
Alexander   defender of men (*Greek*)
Alison   *French diminutive of* Alice; of noble kind
Amanda   fit to be loved (*Latin*)
Amy   loved (*French*)
Andrea   *female form of* Andrew
Andrew   manly (*Greek*)
Angela   messenger, angel (*Greek*)
Ann(e)   *English form of* Hannah
Anthony   *Roman family name*
April   name of the month
Arthur   ?bear, stone (*Celtic*)
Barbara   strange, foreign (*Greek*)
Barry   spear, javelin (*Celtic*)
Beatrice   bringer of joy (*Latin*)
Benjamin   son of my right hand (*Hebrew*)
Bernard   bear + brave (*Germanic*)
Beth   *pet form of* Elizabeth
Betty   *pet form of* Elizabeth
Bill/Billy   *pet form of* William
Bob   *pet form of* Robert
Brandi   *variant of* Brandy, *from the common noun*
Brandon   *place name;* broom-covered hill (*Germanic*)
Brian   ?hill (*?Celtic*)
Candice   *meaning unknown*
Carl   man, husbandman (*Germanic*)
Carol(e)   *forms of* Caroline, *Italian female form of* Charles
Catherine   pure (*Greek*)
Charles   man, husbandman (*Germanic*)
Christine   *French form of* Christina *ultimately from* Christian; anointed
Christopher   carrier of Christ (*Greek*)
Claire   bright, shining (*Latin*)
Colin   *form of* Nicholas
Craig   rock (*Celtic*)

Crystal   *female use of the common noun*
Daniel   God is my judge (*Hebrew*)
Danielle   *female form of* Daniel
Darren   *Irish surname*
Darryl   *surname; uncertain origin*
David   beloved, friend (*Hebrew*)
Dawn   *female use of the common noun*
Dean   *surname;* valley *or* leader
Deborah   bee (*Hebrew*)
Dennis   of Dionysus (*Greek*), *the god of wine*
Derek   *form of* Theodoric; ruler of the people (*Germanic*)
Diane   *French form of* Diana; divine (*Latin*)
Donald   world mighty (*Gaelic*)
Donna   lady (*Latin*)
Doreen   *from* Dora, *a short form of* Dorothy; gift of God
Doris   woman from Doris (*Greek*)
Dorothy   gift of God (*Greek*)
Ebony   *female use of the common noun*
Edward   property guardian (*Germanic*)
Eileen   *Irish form of* ?Helen
Elizabeth   oath/perfection of God (*Hebrew*)
Emily   *Roman family name*
Emma   all-embracing (*Germanic*)
Eric   ruler of all (*Norse*)
Erica   *female form of* Eric
Eugenie   *French form of* Eugene; well-born (*Greek*)
Frank   *pet form of* Francis; Frenchman
Frederick   peaceful ruler (*Germanic*)
Gail   *pet form of* Abigail; father rejoices (*Hebrew*)
Gareth   gentle (*Welsh*)
Gary   *US place name*
Gavin   *Scottish form of* Gawain; hawk + white (*Welsh*)
Gemma   gem (*Italian*)
Geoffrey   ?peace (*Germanic*)
George   husbandman, farmer (*Greek*)
Graham   *Germanic place name*
Hannah   grace, favour (*Hebrew*)

FIRST NAME MEANINGS IN THE UK AND USA (cont.)

Name   Original meaning

Harold   army power/ruler (*Germanic*)
Harry   *pet form of* Henry; home ruler (*Germanic*)
Hayley   *English place name;* hay-meadow
Heather   *plant name*
Helen   bright/shining one (*Greek*)
Ian   *modern Scottish form of* John
Irene   peace (*Greek*)
Jacqueline   *French female form of* Jacques (James)
James   *Latin form of* Jacob; one who takes by the heel (*Hebrew*)
Jane   *from Latin* Johanna, *female form of* John
Janet   *diminutive form of* Jane
Jason   *form of* Joshua; Jehovah is salvation (*Hebrew*)
Jeffrey   *US spelling of* Geoffrey
Jean   *French form of* Johanna, *from* John
Jennifer   fair/white + yielding/smooth (*Celtic*)
Jeremy   *English form of* Jeremiah; Jehova exalts (*Hebrew*)
Jessica   he beholds (*Hebrew*)
Joan   *contracted form of* Johanna, *from* John
Joanne   *French form of* Johanna, *from* John
John   Jehovah has been gracious (*Hebrew*)
Jonathan   Jehovah's gift (*Hebrew*)
Joseph   Jehovah adds (*Hebrew*)
Joyce   ?joyful (*?Latin*)
Julie   *French female form of Latin* Julius; descended from Jove
Karen   *Danish form of* Katarina (Catherine)
Katherine   *US spelling of* Catherine
Kathleen   *English form of Irish* Caitlin (*from* Catharine)
Kelly   *Irish surname;* warlike one
Kenneth   *English form of Gaelic;* fair one *or* fire-sprung
Kerry   *Irish place name*
Kevin   handsome at birth (*Irish*)
Kimberly   *South African place name*
Lakisha   La + ?Aisha; woman (*Arabic*)
Latoya   La + *form of* Tonya (Antonia)
Laura   bay, laurel (*Latin*)
Lauren   *diminutive of* Laura
Lee   *Germanic place name;* wood, clearing
Leslie   *Scottish place name*
Lilian   lily (*Italian*)

Name   Original meaning

Linda   serpent (symbol of wisdom) (*Germanic*)
Lindsay   *Scottish place name*
Lisa   *pet form of* Elizabeth
Margaret   pearl (*Greek*)
Marjorie   *from* Marguerite, *French form of* Margaret
Mark   *English form of* Marcus, *from* Mars, *god of war*
Martin   *from* Mars, *god of war* (*Latin*)
Mary   *Greek form of* Miriam (*Hebrew*); unknown meaning
Matthew   gift of the Lord (*Hebrew*)
Melissa   bee (*Greek*)
Michael   like the Lord (*Hebrew*)
Michelle   *English spelling of French* Michèle, *from* Michael
Nancy   *pet form of* Ann
Natalie   birthday of the Lord (*Latin*)
Neil   champion (*Irish*)
Nicholas   victory people (*Greek*)
Nicola   *Italian female form of* Nicholas
Nicole   *French female form of* Nicholas
Pamela   ?all honey (*Greek*)
Patricia   noble (*Latin*)
Paul   small (*Latin*)
Pauline   *French female form of* Paul
Peter   stone, rock (*Greek*)
Philip   fond of horses (*Greek*)
Rachel   ewe (*Hebrew*)
Rebecca   ?noose (*Hebrew*)
Richard   strong ruler (*Germanic*)
Robert   fame bright (*Germanic*)
Ronald   counsel + power (*Germanic*)
Ruth   ?vision of beauty (*Hebrew*)
Ryan   *Irish surname*
Sally   *pet form of* Sarah
Samantha   *female form of* Samuel; heard/ name of God (*Hebrew*)
Sandra   *pet form from* Alexandra
Sarah   princess (*Hebrew*)
Scott   *surname;* from Scotland
Sharon   the plain (*Hebrew*)
Shaun   *English spelling of Irish* Sean, *from* John
Shirley   bright clearing (*Germanic*)
Simon   *form of* Simeon; listening attentively (*Hebrew*)

Name	Original meaning
Stephanie	*French female form of* Stephen
Stephen	crown (*Greek*)
Stuart	steward (*Germanic*)
Susan	*short form of* Susannah; lily (*Hebrew*)
Teresa	woman of Theresia (*Greek*)
Thomas	twin (*Hebrew*)
Tiffany	manifestation of God (*Greek*)
Timothy	honouring God (*Greek*)
Trac(e)y	?pet form of Teresa

Name	Original meaning
Vera	faith (*Slavic*)
Victoria	victory (*Latin*)
Vincent	conquer (*Latin*)
Virginia	maiden (*Latin*)
Walter	ruling people (*Germanic*)
Wayne	*surname*; wagon-maker
William	will + helmet (*Germanic*)
Zoë	life (*Greek*)

NATIONAL NEWSPAPERS: EUROPE

Name	Location	Circulation[1]	Date founded
ABC	Madrid	350 000	1905
Algemeen Dagblad	Rotterdam	405 100	1946
Apogevmatini	Athens	67 300	1956
Auriani	Athens	42 100	1980
B.T.	Copenhagen	202 600	1916
Berliner Zeitung	Berlin	424 000	1877
Berlingske Tidende	Copenhagen	132 200	1749
Bild am Sonntag (s)	Hamburg	2 649 900	1956
Bild Zeitung	Hamburg	4 404 900	1952
Correio do Manha	Lisbon	90 000	1979
Corriere della Sera	Milan	684 900	1876
De Standaard/Het Nieuwsblad/De Gentenaar	Brussels	331 000	N/A
De Telegraaf	Amsterdam	730 300	1893
De Volkskrant	Amsterdam	342 900	1919
Diario de Noticias	Lisbon	65 000	1864
Diario Popular	Lisbon	29 300	1942
Die Welt	Bonn	225 000[2]	1946
Die Zeit (weekly)	Hamburg	494 100	1946
Ekstra Bladet	Copenhagen	190 600	1904
El Pais	Madrid	375 800	1976
El Periodico	Barcelona	160 000	1978
Ethnos	Athens	70 000	1981
Evening Herald	Dublin	95 300	1891
Evening Press	Dublin	66 300	1954
France-Dimanche (s)	Paris	721 000[2]	N/A
France-Soir	Paris	257 100	1944
Frankfurter Allgemeine Zeitung	Frankfurt	394 800	1949
Het Laatste Nieuws	Brussels	301 306	1888
Il Giornale	Milan	160 100	1974
Il Giorno	Milan	185 000	1965

(s) published on Sundays only
[1] 1994 figures (rounded to nearest 100)
[2] 1991 figures (rounded to nearest 100)

NATIONAL NEWSPAPERS: EUROPE (cont.)

Name	Location	Circulation[1]	Date founded
Il Messaggero	Rome	320 000	1878
International Herald Tribune	Paris	174 200	1887
Irish Independent	Dublin	144 300	1905
Irish Times	Dublin	92 300	1859
La Libre Belgique	Brussels	85 000	1884
La Dernière Heure	Brussels	170 000	1906
La Lanterne	Brussels	132 800[2]	1944
La Republica	Rome	787 000	1976
La Stampa	Turin	571 500	1867
La Vanguardia	Barcelona	218 500	1881
Le Figaro	Paris	424 000	1828
Le Monde	Paris	362 400	1944
Le Parisien Libère	Paris	339 300[2]	1944
Le Soir	Brussels	158 000	1887
L'Humanité	Paris	117 000[2]	1904
L'Humanité Dimanche (s)	Paris	360 000[2]	1946
Luxemburger Wort/La Voix du Luxembourg	Luxembourg	82 400	1848
Politiken	Copenhagen	165 600	1884
Suddeutsche Zeitung	Munich	378 400	1945
Sunday Independent (s)	Dublin	252 600	1905
Sunday Press (s)	Dublin	173 945	1949
Sunday World (s)	Dublin	214 100	1973
Ta Nea	Athens	135 000	1944
Welt am Sonntag (s)	Hamburg	423 400	N/A
Ya	Madrid	380 000[2]	1935

(s) published on Sundays only
[1] 1994 figures (rounded to nearest 100)   [2] 1991 figures (rounded to nearest 100)

NATIONAL NEWSPAPERS: UK

Name	Location	Circulation[1]	Date founded
Daily Express	London	1 339 000	1900
Daily Mail	London	1 789 700	1896
Daily Mirror	London	2 512 300	1903
Daily Telegraph	London	1 039 300	1855
Financial Times	London	290 000	1880
The Guardian	London	398 600	1821
The Herald	Glasgow	113 300	1783
The Independent on Sunday (s)	London	318 700	1990
The Independent	London	276 300	1986
The Mail on Sunday (s)	London	1 952 600	1982
News of the World (s)	London	4 803 700	1843
Observer (s)	London	487 800	1791

Name	Location	Circulation[1]	Date founded
The People (s)	London	2 017 200	1881
Scotland on Sunday (s)	Edinburgh	89 700	1988
The Scotsman	Edinburgh	83 600	1817
The Sun	London	4 160 300	1964
The Sunday Mirror (s)	London	2 566 100	1963
The Sunday Post (s)	Dundee	996 500	1920
The Sunday Telegraph (s)	London	656 200	1961
The Sunday Times (s)	London	1 196 700	1822
The Times	London	549 800	1785
Today	London	612 800	1986

(s) published on Sundays only   [1] 1994 figures (rounded to nearest 100)

MAJOR NEWSPAPERS: USA

Includes national newspapers and local newspapers having an all-day, morning, or evening circulation of 250 000 or more.

Name	Location	Circulation[1]	Date founded
Atlanta Constitution	Atlanta, Ga	302 600	1868
Arizona Republic	Phoenix, Ariz	350 000	1890
Baltimore Sun	Baltimore, Md	388 600	1837
Boston Globe	Boston, Mass	508 900	1872
Boston Herald	Boston, Mass	330 600	1892
Buffalo News	Buffalo, NY	305 500	1880
Chicago Sun-Times	Chicago, Ill	357 100	1948
Chicago Tribune	Chicago, Ill	724 300	1847
Christian Science Monitor[2]	Boston, Mass	106 000	1908
Cleveland Plain Dealer	Cleveland, Ohio	446 300	1842
Columbus Dispatch	Columbus, Ohio	264 600	1871
Dallas Morning News	Dallas, Texas	520 400	1885
Denver Rocky Mountain News	Denver, Colo	356 600	1859
Detroit Free Press	Detroit, Mich	580 400	1831
Detroit News	Detroit, Mich	398 600	1873
Forth Worth Star-Telegram	Fort Worth, Texas	256 200	1906
Houston Chronicle	Houston, Texas	439 600	1901
Houston Post	Houston, Texas	300 100	1885
Kansas City Star	Kansas City, Mo	287 100	1880
Los Angeles Times	Los Angeles, Cal	1 146 600	1881
Miami Herald	Miami, Fla	388 900	1910
Milwaukee Sentinel	Milwaukee, Wisc	170 000	1837
Minneapolis Star Tribune	Minneapolis, Minn	408 400	1867
New Orleans Times-Picayune	New Orleans, La	269 600	1837
New York Daily News	New York, NY	762 100	1919
New York Post	New York, NY	731 700	1801

[1] 1994 figures (rounded to nearest 100)   [2] National newspapers

MAJOR NEWSPAPERS: USA (cont.)

Name	Location	Circulation[1]	Date founded
New York Times[2]	New York, NY	1 209 200	1851
Newark Star-Ledger	Newark, NJ	470 700	1832
Newsday	Melville, NY	699 000	1940
Orange County Register	Santa Ana, Cal	332 200	1905
Orlando Sentinel	Orlando, Fla	271 400	1876
Philadelphia Inquirer	Philadelphia, Pa	741 500	1829
Portland Oregonian	Portland, Ore	336 100	1850
Sacramento Bee	Sacramento, Cal	264 300	1857
San Diego Union	San Diego, Cal	373 400	1868
San Francisco Chronicle	San Francisco, Cal	556 800	1865
San Jose Mercury News	San Jose, Cal	270 200	1851
St Louis Post-Dispatch	St Louis, Mo	339 500	1878
St Petersburg Times	St Petersburg, Fla	326 100	1884
Tampa Tribune	Tampa, Fla	275 600	1893
USA Today[2]	Arlington, Va	1 506 700	1982
Wall Street Journal[2]	New York, NY	1 795 200	1889
Washington Post	Washington, DC	802 100	1877

[1] 1994 figures (rounded to nearest 100)   [2] National newspapers

SYMBOLS IN GENERAL USE

&	ampersand (*and*)	☎	telephone number follows
&c.	et cetera	☜ ☞	this way
@	at; per (in costs)	✂ ✂·····	cut here
×	by (measuring dimensions, eg 3 × 4)		
£	pound	**In astronomy**	
$	dollar (also peso, escudo, etc in certain countries)	●	new moon
		☽	moon, first quarter
¢	cent (also centavo, etc in certain countries)	○	full moon
		☾	moon, last quarter
©	copyright		
®	registered	**In meteorology**	
¶	new paragraph	▲▲▲	cold front (in meteorology)
§	new section	▬▬▬	warm front
"	ditto	▀▼▀▼	stationary front
*	born (in genealogy)	▲▲▼	occluded front
†	died		
*	hypothetical or unacceptable form (in linguistics)	**In cards**	
		♥	hearts
☠	poison; danger	♦	diamonds
♂, □	male	♠	spades
♀, ○	female	♣	clubs
✠	bishop's name follows		

CLOTHES CARE SYMBOLS

⌧	Do not iron
⌁	Can be ironed with *cool* iron (up to 110°C)
⌁	Can be ironed with *warm* iron (up to 150°C)
⌁	Can be ironed with *hot* iron (up to 200°C)
⌫	Hand wash only
⬚	Can be washed in a washing machine. The number shows the most effective washing temperature (in °C)
⬚	Reduced (medium) washing conditions
⬚	Much reduced (minimum) washing conditions (for wool products)
⌧	Do not wash
⊙	Can be tumble dried (one dot within the circle means a low temperature setting; two dots for higher temperatures)
⊠	Do not tumble dry
⊗	Do not dry clean
Ⓐ	Dry cleanable (letter indicates which solvents can be used) A: all solvents Dry cleanable
Ⓕ	F: white spirit and solvent 11 can be used Dry cleanable
Ⓟ	P: perchloroethylene (tetrachloroethylene), white spirit, solvent 113 and solvent 11 can be used
Ⓟ	Dry cleanable, if special care taken
⚠	Chlorine bleach may be used with care
⌧	Do not use chlorine bleach

CAR INDEX MARKS: INTERNATIONAL

A	Austria	BRN	Bahrain	CY	Cyprus*
ADN	Yemen PDR	BRU	Brunei*	D	German Federal Republic
AFG	Afghanistan	BS	Bahamas*		
AL	Albania	BUR	Burma	DK	Denmark
AND	Andorra	C	Cuba	DOM	Dominican Republic
AUS	Australia*	CDN	Canada	DY	Benin
B	Belgium	CH	Switzerland	DZ	Algeria
BD	Bangladesh*	CI	Côte d'Ivoire	E	Spain
BDS	Barbados*	CL	Sri Lanka*	EAK	Kenya*
BG	Bulgaria	CO	Colombia	EAT	Tanzania*
BH	Belize	CR	Costa Rica	EAU	Uganda*
BR	Brazil	CS	Czechoslovakia	EAZ	Tanzania*

* In countries so marked, the rule of the road is to drive on the left; in other countries, drive on the right.

CAR INDEX MARKS: INTERNATIONAL (cont.)

EC	Ecuador	M	Malta*	RSM	San Marino
ES	El Salvador	MA	Morocco	RU	Burundi
ET	Egypt	MAL	Malaysia*	RWA	Rwanda
ETH	Ethiopia	MC	Monaco	S	Sweden
F	France	MEX	Mexico	SD	Swaziland*
FJI	Fiji*	MS	Mauritius*	SF	Finland
FL	Liechtenstein	MW	Malawi*	SGP	Singapore*
FR	Faroe Is	N	Norway	SME	Suriname*
GB	UK*	NA	Netherlands Antilles	SN	Senegal
GBA	Alderney*	NIC	Nicaragua	SU	CIS
GBG	Guernsey*	NL	Netherlands	SWA	Namibia*
GBJ	Jersey*	NZ	New Zealand	SY	Seychelles*
GBM	Isle of Man*	P	Portugal	SYR	Syria
GBZ	Gibraltar	PA	Panama	T	Thailand*
GCA	Guatemala	PK	Pakistan*	TG	Togo
GH	Ghana	PE	Peru	TN	Tunisia
GR	Greece	PL	Poland	TR	Turkey
GUY	Guyana*	PNG	Papua New Guinea*	TT	Trinidad and
H	Hungary	PY	Paraguay		Tobago*
HK	Hong Kong*	RA	Argentina	USA	USA
HKJ	Jordan	RB	Botswana*	V	Vatican City
I	Italy	RC	Taiwan	VN	Vietnam
IL	Israel	RCA	Central African	WAG	Gambia
IND	India*		Republic	WAL	Sierra Leone
IR	Iran	RCB	Congo	WAN	Nigeria
IRL	Ireland*	RCH	Chile	WD	Dominica*
IRQ	Iraq	RH	Haiti	WG	Grenada*
IS	Iceland	RI	Indonesia*	WL	St Lucia*
J	Japan*	RIM	Mauritania	WS	W Somoa
JA	Jamaica*	RL	Lebanon	WV	St Vincent and the
K	Kampuchea	RM	Madagascar		Grenadines*
KWT	Kuwait	RMM	Mali	YU	Yugoslavia
L	Luxembourg	RN	Niger	YV	Venezuela
LAO	Laos	RO	Romania	Z	Zambia*
LAR	Libya	ROK	Korea, Republic of	ZA	South Africa*
LB	Liberia	ROU	Uruguay	ZRE	Zaire
LS	Lesotho*	RP	Philippines	ZW	Zimbabwe*

* In countries so marked, the rule of the road is to drive on the left; in other countries, drive on the right.

UK AIRPORTS

Alderney Channel Islands	**Biggin Hill** Kent	**Cardiff**
Baltasound Unst, Shetlands	**Blackpool** Lancashire	**Coventry** West Midlands
Belfast City	**Bournemouth** Dorset	**Dundee**
Belfast International	**Bristol** Avon	**Dyce** Aberdeen
Benbecula Hebrides	**Cambridge**	**East Midlands** Derbyshire

Exeter Devon
Fair Isle Shetlands
Gatwick London
Glenegedale Islay
Glasgow
Grimsetter Orkney
Guernsey Channel Islands
Heathrow London
Humberside
Inverness
Jersey Channel Islands
Kirkwall Orkney
Leeds-Bradford
Liverpool
London City

Luton Bedfordshire
Lydd Kent
Manchester
Newcastle
North Bay Barra, Hebrides
Norwich Norfolk
Penzance Cornwall
Plymouth
  (Roborough) Devon
Prestwick Ayrshire
Ronaldsway Isle of Man
Saint Mary's Scilly Isles
Sandown Isle of Wight
Scatsa Shetlands
Southampton Hampshire

Southend Essex
Standsted London
Stornoway Hebrides
Sumburgh Shetlands
Swansea
Teeside Cleveland
Tingwall Lerwick, Shetlands
Tiree Hebrides
Tresco Scilly Isles
Turnhouse Edinburgh
West Midlands Birmingham
Westray Orkney
Wick Caithness

MAJOR US AIRPORTS

Albany County New York
Albuquerque New Mexico
Amarillo Texas
Anchorage Alaska
Birmingham Alabama
Bradley Hartford
Buffalo New York
Canton Akron
Charleston West Virginia
Charlotte North Carolina
Columbus Ohio
Dallas/Fort Worth Texas
Des Moines Iowa
Detroit-Wayne County Detroit
Dulles Washington
El Paso Texas
Eppley Airfield Nebraska
Erie Pennsylvania
Fort Lauderdale Florida
Fort Myers Florida
Gen Mitchell Milwaukee
Greater Cincinatti Ohio
Greater Pittsburgh
  Pennsylvania
Hancock Field Syracuse
Harrisburg Pennsylvania
Hartsfield Atlanta
Hopkins Cleveland
Houston Texas
Indianapolis Indiana

J F Kennedy New York
Jacksonville Florida
James M Cox Dayton
Kansas City Missouri
Kent County Grand Rapids
Key West Florida
La Guardia New York
Lincoln Nebraska
Lindbergh San Diego
Little Rock Arkansas
Logan Boston
Long Beach California
Los Angeles California
Louisville Kentucky
Lubbock Texas
McCarran Las Vegas
McCoy Orlando
Manchester New
  Hampshire
Memphis Tennessee
Miami Florida
Midway Chicago
Minneapolis/St
  Paul Minneapolis
Monroe County Rochester
Nashville Tennessee
New Orleans Louisiana
Newark New Jersey
Norfolk Virginia
Oakland California

O'Hare Chicago
Orlando Florida
Peninsula Monterey
Peterson Field Colorado
  Springs
Philadelphia Pennsylvania
Portland Maine
Portland Oregon
Raleigh/Durham North
  Carolina
Richmond Virginia
Robert Mueller
  Municipal Texas
St Louis Missouri
Salt Lake City Utah
San Antonio Texas
San Diego California
San Francisco California
San José California
Sky Harbour Phoenix
Spokane Washington
Stapleton Denver
Tacoma Washington
Tallahasse Florida
Tampa Florida
Theodore Francis Providence
Truax Field Madison
Tucson Arizona
Washington Baltimore
Will Rodgers Oklahoma

INTERNATIONAL AIRPORTS

Alborg Roedslet   Norresundbyr, Denmark
Abadan International   Iran
Abu Dhabi   United Arab Emirates
Adana   Turkey
Adelaide   Australia
Agno   Lugano, Switzerland
Ain el Bay   Constantine, Algeria
Albany County   New York, USA
Albuquerque   New Mexico, USA
Alexandria   Egypt
Alfonso Bonilla Aragon   Cali, Colombia
Alicante   Spain
Almeria   Spain
Amarillo   Texas, USA
Amborovy   Majunga, Madagascar
Amilcar Cabral International   Sal I, Cape
Verde
Aminu International   Kano, Nigeria
Anchorage   Alaska, USA
Archangel   Russia
Arlanda   Stockholm, Sweden
Arnos Vale   St Vincent
Arrecife   Lanzarote, Canary Is
Arturo Marino Benitez   Santiago, Chile
Asturias   Spain
Ataturk   Istanbul, Turkey
Auckland   New Zealand
Augusto C Sandino   Managua, Nicaragua
Baghdad International   Iraq
Bahrain International   Bahrain
Bali International/Ngurah Rai   Denpasar,
Indonesia
Balice   Kracow, Poland
Bandar Seri Begawan   Brunei
Baneasa   Bucharest, Romania
Bangkok International   Thailand
Barajas   Madrid, Spain
Barcelona   Spain
Basle-Mulhouse   Basle, Spain
Beijing (Peking)   China
Beira   Mozambique
Beirut International   Khaldeh, Lebanon
Belfast International   UK
Belgrade   Yugoslavia
Belize City International   Belize
Ben Gurion   Tel Aviv, Israel

Benina   Benghazi, Libya
Benito Juarez   Mexico City, Mexico
Berlin-Schonefeld   Berlin, Germany
Berlin-Tegel   Berlin, Germany
Berne   Switzerland
Billund   Denmark
Birmingham   Alabama, USA
Blackburne/Plymouth   Montserrat (Leeward I)
Blagnac   Toulouse, France
Bole   Addis Ababa, Ethiopia
Bombay   India
Borispol   Kiev, Ukraine
Boukhalef   Tangier, Morocco
Boulogne   France
Bourgas   Bulgaria
Bradley International   Hartford, Connecticut,
USA
Brasilia International   Brazil
Bremen   Germany
Brisbane   Australia
Brnik   Ljubjana, Yugoslavia
Bromma   Stockholm, Sweden
Brussels National   Belgium
Buffalo   New York, USA
Bujumbura   Burindi
Bulawayo   Zimbabwe
Butmir   Sarajevo, Yugoslavia
Cairns   Queensland, Australia
Cairo International   Egypt
Calabar   Nigeria
Calcutta   India
Calgary International   Canada
Cancun   Mexico
Cannon International   Reno, Nevada, USA
Canton   Akron, Ohio, USA
Capodichino   Naples, Italy
Carrasco   Montevideo, Uruguay
Carthage   Tunis, Tunisia
Cebu   Philippines
Chang Kai Shek   Taipei, Taiwan
Changi   Singapore
Charleroi (Gossilies)   Belgium
Charles de Gaulle   Paris, France
Charleston   South Carolina, USA
Charleston   West Virginia, USA
Charlotte   North Carolina, USA

Château Bougon   Nantes, France
Christchurch   New Zealand
Ciampino   Rome, Italy
Cologne-Bonn   Cologne, Germany
Columbus   Ohio, USA
Congonhas   Sao Paulo, Brazil
Copenhagen International   Kastrup, Denmark
Cork   Republic of Ireland
Costa Smeralda   Olbia, Sardinia
Côte d'Azure   Nice, France
Cotonou   Benin
Cristoforo Colombo   Genoa, Italy
Crown Point   Scarborough, Tobago
Cuscatlan   Comalapa, El Salvador
D F Malan   Cape Town, South Africa
Dalaman   Turkey
Dallas/Fort Worth   Dallas, Texas, USA
Damascus   Syria
Dar-es-Salaam   Tanzania
Darwin   Australia
Des Moines   Iowa, USA
Detroit-Wayne County   Detroit, Michigan, USA
Deurne   Antwerp, Belgium
Dhahran International   Al Khobar, Saudi Arabia
Djibouti   Djibouti
Doha   Qatar
Dois de Julho International   Salvador, Brazil
Domodedovo   Moscow, Russia
Don Miguel Hidalgo y Castilla   Guadalajara, Mexico
Dorval International   Montreal, Canada
Douala   Cameroon
Dresden   Germany
Dubai   United Arab Emirates
Dublin   Republic of Ireland
Dubrovnik   Yugoslavia
Dulles International   Washington DC, USA
Dusseldorf   Germany
Edmonton International   Canada
Eduardo Gomes   Manaus, Brazil
Eindhoven   Netherlands
El Alto   La Paz, Bolivia
El Dorado   Bogata, Colombia
El Paso   Texas, USA
Elat   Israel
Elmas   Cagliari, Italy
Entebbe   Uganda
Entzheim   Strasbourg, France

Eppley Airfield   Omaha, Nebraska, USA
Erie   Pennsylvania, USA
Ernesto Cortissoz   Barranquilla, Colombia
Esbjerg   Denmark
Esenboga   Ankara, Turkey
Faleolo   Apia, Samoa
Faro   Portugal
Ferihegy   Budapest, Hungary
Findel   Luxembourg
Fiumicino (Leonardo da Vinci)   Rome, Italy
Flesland   Bergen, Norway
Fontanarossa   Catonia, Sicily
Fornebu   Oslo, Norway
Fort de France   Lamentin, Martinique
Fort Lauderdale   Florida, USA
Fort Myers   Florida, USA
Frankfurt am Main   Germany
Freeport International   Bahamas
Frejorgues   Montpellier, France
Fuenterrabia   San Sebastian, Spain
Fuerteventura   Canary Is
Fuhlsbuttel   Hamburg, Germany
G Marconi   Bologna, Italy
Galileo Galilei   Pisa, Italy
Gatwick   London, UK
G'Bessia   Conakry, Guinea Republic
General Abelard L Rodriguez   Tijuana, Mexico
General Juan N Alvarez   Acapulco, Mexico
General Manuel Marquez de Leon   La Paz, Mexico
General Mariano Escobedo   Monterrey, Mexico
General Mitchell   Milwaukee, Wisconsin, USA
General Rafael Buelna   Mazatlan, Mexico
Geneva   Switzerland
Gerona/Costa Brava   Gerona, Spain
Gillot   St Denis de la Réunion, Indian Ocean
Golden Rock   St Kitts
Goleniow   Szczecin, Poland
Glasgow   UK
Granada   Spain
Grantley Adams International   Bridgetown, Barbados
Greater Cincinnati   Ohio, USA
Greater Pittsburgh   Pennsylvania, USA
Guam   Guam
Guararapes International   Recife, Brazil
Guarulhos International   São Paulo, Brazil
Halifax   Canada

INTERNATIONAL AIRPORTS (cont.)

Halim Perdanakusama   Jakarta, Indonesia
Hamilton Kindley Field   Hamilton, Bermuda
Hancock Field   Syracuse, New York State, USA
Hanover-Langenhagen   Hanover, Germany
Hanoi   Vietnam
Harare   Zimbabwe
Harrisburg   Pennsylvania, USA
Hartsfield   Atlanta, Georgia, USA
Hassan   Laayoune, Morocco
Hato   Curaao, Netherlands Antilles
Hahaya International   Moroni, Comoros
Hanedi   Tokyo, Japan
Heathrow   London, UK
Hellenikon   Athens, Greece
Henderson Field   Honiari, Solomon Is
Heraklion   Crete, Greece
Hewanorra International   St Lucia
Ho Chi Minh City   Vietnam
Hong Kong International   Hong Kong
Hongqiao   Shanghai, China
Honolulu   Hawaii, USA
Hopkins   Cleveland, Ohio, USA
Houari Boumedienne International   Dar-el-Beida, Algeria
Houston   Texas, USA
Ibiza   Balearics, Spain
Indianapolis   Indiana, USA
Indira Ghandi International   Delhi, India
Inezgane   Agadir, Morocco
Islamabad   Pakistan
Isle Verde   San Juan, Puerto Rico
Izmir   Turkey
Itazuke   Fukuoka, Japan
Ivanka   Bratislava, Czechoslovakia
Ivato   Antananarivo, Madagascar
J F Kennedy   New York, USA
Jackson Field   Port Moresby, Papua New Guinea
Jacksonville   Florida, USA
James M Cox   Dayton, Ohio, USA
Jan Smuts   Johannesburg, South Africa
Jomo Kenyatta   Nairobi, Kenya
Jorge Chavez International   Lima, Peru
Jose Marti International   Havana, Cuba
Juan Santa Maria International   Alajuela, Costa Rica

Kagoshima   Japan
Kalmar   Sweden
Kamazu   Lilongwe, Malawi
Kansas City   Missouri, USA
Kaohsiung   Taiwan
Karachi   Pakistan
Karpathos   Karpathos, Greece
Katunayake   Colombo, Sri Lanka
Keflavik   Reykjavik, Iceland
Kent County   Grand Rapids, Michigan, USA
Kerkyra   Corfo, Greece
Key West   Florida, USA
Khartoum   Sudan
Khoramaksar   Aden, Yemen Arab Republic
Khwaja Rawash   Kabul, Afghanistan
Kigali   Rwanda
Kimpo International   Seoul, South Korea
King Abdul Aziz   Jeddah, Saudi Arabia
King Khaled   Riyadh, Saudi Arabia
Kingsford Smith   Sydney, Australia
Kjevik   Kristiansand, Norway
Klagenfurt   Austria
Komaki   Nagoya, Japan
Kos   Greece
Kota Kinabulu   Sabah, Malaysia
Kotoka   Accra, Ghana
Kranebitten   Innsbruck, Austria
Kuching   Sarawak, Malaysia
Kungsangen   Norrkoping, Sweden
Kuwait International   Kuwait
La Aurora   Guatemala City, Guatemala
La Coruna   Spain
La Guardia   New York, USA
La Mesa   San Pedro Sula, Honduras
La Parra   Jerez de la Frontera, Spain
Lahore   Pakistan
Landvetter   Gothenburg, Sweden
Larnaca International   Cyprus
Las Americas International   Santo Domingo, Dominican Republic
Las Palmas   Gran Canaria, Canary Is
Le Raizet   Point-à-Pitre, Guadeloupe
Leipzig   Germany
Les Angades   Oujda, Morocco
Lesquin   Lille, France
Lester B Pearson International   Toronto, Canada

Libreville Gabon
Lic Gustavo Diaz Ordaz Puerto Vallarta, Mexico
Lic Manuel Crecencio Rejon Merida, Mexico
Liège (Bierset) Belgium
Linate Milan, Italy
Lincoln Nebraska, USA
Lindbergh International San Diego, USA
Linz Austria
Lisbon Portugal
Little Rock Arkansas, USA
Llabanère Perpignan, France
Logan International Boston, Massachusetts, USA
Lomé Togo
London City UK
Long Beach California, USA
Los Angeles California, USA
Loshitsa Minsk, Byelorussia
Louis Botha Durban, South Africa
Louisville Kentucky, USA
Lourdes/Tarbes Juillan, France
Luanda Angola
Luano Lubumashi, Zaire
Lubbock Texas, USA
Luis Munoz Marin International San Juan, Puerto Rica
Lungi Freetown, Sierra Leone
Luqa Malta
Lusaka Zambia
Luxor Egypt
Maastricht Netherlands
McCarran International Las Vegas, Nevada, USA
McCoy International Orlando, Florida, USA
Mactan International Cebu, Philippines
Mahon Menorca
Mais Gate Port au Prince, Haiti
Malaga Spain
Male' Maldives
Malpensa Milan, Italy
Managua Nicaragua
Manchester New Hampshire, USA
Manchester UK
Maputo Mozambique
Marco Polo Venice, Italy
Mariscal Sucre Quito, Ecuador
Maseru Lesotho
Matsapha Manzini, Swaziland

Maupertus Cherbourg, France
Maxglan Salzburg, Austria
Maya Maya Brazaville, Congo
Medina Saudi Arabia
Meenambakkam International Madras, India
Mehrabad International Teheran, Iran
Melita Djerba, Tunisia
Memphis Tennessee, USA
Menara Marrakech, Morocco
Merignac Bordeaux, France
Miami Florida, USA
Midway Chicago, Illinois, USA
Mingaladon, Yangon Myanmar, Malaysia
Ministro Pistarini Buenos Aires, Argentina
Minneapolis/St Paul Minneapolis, USA
Mirabel Montreal, Canada
Mogadishu Somalia
Mohamed V Casablanca, Morocco
Moi International Mombasa, Kenya
Monroe County Rochester, New York State, USA
Morelos Mexico City, Mexico
Münster/Osnabrück Germany
Murmansk Russia
Murtala Muhammed Lagos, Nigeria
Nadi International Fiji
Nagasaki Japan
Narita Tokyo, Japan
Narssarsuaq Greenland
Nashville Tennessee, USA
Nassau International Bahamas
Nauru Nauru
N'djamena Chad
N'Djili Kinshasa, Zaire
Nejrab Aleppo, Syria
Newcastle UK
New Orleans Louisiana, USA
Newark New York, USA
Niamey Niger
Ninoy Aquino International Manila, Philippines
Nis Yugoslavia
Norfolk International Virginia, USA
Norman Manley International Kingston, Jamaica
North Front Gibraltar
Nouadhibou Mauritania
Nouakchott Mauritania
Novo-Alexeyevka Tblisi, Georgia

INTERNATIONAL AIRPORTS (cont.)

Nuremberg Germany
Oakland International California, USA
Octeville Le Havrets, France
Odense Denmark
O'Hare Chicago, Illinois, USA
Okecie Warsaw, Poland
Okinawa Naha, Japan
Oran Algeria
Orebro Sweden
Orlando Florida, USA
Orly Paris, France
Osaka Japan
Osvaldo Veira Bissau, Guinea Bissau
Otopeni Bucharest, Romania
Ouagadougou Burkino Faso
Owen Roberts Grand Cayman, West Indies
Pago Pago Samoa
Palese Bari, Italy
Palma Majorca
Pamplona Spain
Panama City Panama
Paphos Cyprus
Papola Casale Brindisi, Italy
Paradisi Rhodes, Greece
Patenga Chittagong, Bangladesh
Penang Malaysia
Peninsula Monterey, California, USA
Peretola Florence, Italy
Perth Australia
Peshawar Pakistan
Peterson Field Colorado Springs, Colorado, USA
Philadelphia Pennsylvania, USA
Piarco Port of Spain, Trinidad
Pleso Zagreb, Yugoslavia
Pochentong Phnom Penh, Cambodia
Point Salines Grenada
Pointe Noire Congo
Polonia Medan, Indonesia
Ponta Delgado São Miguel, Azores
Port Bouet Abidjan, Ivory Coast
Port Harcourt Nigeria
Portland Maine, USA
Portland Oregon, USA
Port Sudan Sudan
Porto Pedra Rubras Oporto, Portugal
Praia Cape Verde

Prestwick UK
Princess Beatrix Aruba, Netherlands Antilles
Provence Marseille, France
Pula Yugoslavia
Pulkovo St Petersburg, Russia
Punta Arenas International Chile
Punta Raisi Palermo, Sicily
Queen Alia Amman, Jordan
Releigh/Durham North Carolina, USA
Ras al Khaimah United Arab Emirates
Rabiechowo Gdańsk, Poland
Regina Canada
Reina Sofia Tenerife
Rejon Merida, Mexico
Richmond Virginia, USA
Riem Munich, Germany
Rio de Janeiro International Brazil
Riyadh International Saudi Arabia
Roberts International Monrovia, Liberia
Rochambau Cayenne, French Guiana
Robert Mueller Municipal Airport Austin, Texas, USA
Ronchi dei Legionari Trieste, Italy
Rotterdam Netherlands
Ruzyne Prague, Czechoslovakia
Saab Linkoping, Sweden
Saint Eufemia Lamezia Terma, Italy
Saint Louis Missouri, USA
Saint Thomas Virgin Is
Sainte Foy Quebec, Canada
Sale Rabat, Morocco
Salgado Filho International Porto Alegre, Brazil
Salt Lake City Utah, USA
San Antonio Texas, USA
San Diego California, USA
San Francisco California, USA
San Giusto Pisa, Italy
San Javier Murcia, Spain
San José California, USA
San Pablo Seville, Spain
San Salvador El Salvador
Sanaa International Yemen
Sangster International Montego Bay, Jamaica
Santa Caterina Funchal, Madeira
Santa Cruz La Palma, Canary Is
Santa Isabel Malabo, Guinea

Santander Spain
Santiago Spain
Santos Dumont Rio de Janeiro, Brazil
São Tomé São Tomé
Satolas Lyon, France
Schipol Amsterdam, Netherlands
Schwechat Vienna, Austria
Seeb Muscat, Oman
Senou Bamako, Mali
Seychelles International Mahé, Seychelles
Sfax Tunisia
Shannon Republic of Ireland
Sharjah United Arab Emirates
Sheremetyevo Moscow, Russia
Silvio Pettirossi Asuncion, Paraguay
Simon Bolivar Caracas, Venezuela
Simon Bolivar Guayaquil, Ecuador
Sir Seewoosagur Ramgoolam Plaisance, Mauritius
Sir Seretse Khama Gaborone, Botswana
Skanes Monastir, Morocco
Skopje Yugoslavia
Sky Harbour Phoenix, Arizona, USA
Snilow Lwow, Ukraine
Sofia International Bulgaria
Sola Stavanger, Norway
Sondica Bilbao, Spain
Søndre Strømfjord Greenland
Spilve Riga, Latvia
Split Yugoslavia
Spokane Washington, USA
Standsted UK
Stapleton International Denver, Colorado, USA
Sturup Malmö, Sweden
Subang International Kuala Lumpur, Malaysia
Sunan Pyongyang, North Korea
Stuttgart-Echterdingen Stuttgart, Germany
Tacoma Seattle, USA
Tallahassee Florida, USA
Tamatve Madagascar
Tampa Florida, USA
Tegucigalpa Toncontin, Honduras
Thalerhof Graz, Austria
Theodore Francis Providence, Rhode I, USA
Thessalonika Greece

Timehri International Georgetown, Guyana
Timişoara Romania
Tirana Albania
Tito Menniti Reggio Calabria, Italy
Tontouta Noumea, New Caledonia
Townsville Australia
Tribhuyan Kathmandu, Nepal
Tripoli Libya
Trivandrum India
Truax Field Madison, Wisconsin, USA
Tucson Arizona, USA
Tullamarine Melbourne, Australia
Turin Italy
Turku Finland
Turnhouse Edinburgh, UK
Ulemiste Tallinn, Estonia
Unokovo Moscow, Russia
Uplands Ottawa, Canada
V C Bird International Antigua
Vaasa Finland
Vagar Faeroe Is
Valencia Spain
Vancouver International Canada
Vantaa Helsinki, Finland
Varna International Bulgaria
Verona Italy
Victoria British Columbia, Canada
Vigie St Lucia
Vigo Spain
Vilnius Lithuania
Vilo de Porto Santa Maria, Azores
Viracopos Sao Paulo, Brazil
Vitoria Spain
Washington International Baltimore, Maryland, USA
Wattay Vientiane, Laos
Wellington New Zealand
Wichita Kansas, USA
Will Rogers Oklahoma City, Oklahoma, USA
Winnipeg International Manitoba, Canada
Yoff Dakar, Senegal
Yundum Banjul, Gambia
Zakynthos Greece
Zia International Dhaka, Bangladesh
Zürich Switzerland

UK ROAD DISTANCES

Road distances between British centres are given in statute miles, using routes recommended by the Automobile Association based on the quickest travelling time. To convert to kilometres, multiply number given by 1.6093.

From	Birmingham	Bristol	Cambridge	Cardiff	Dover	Edinburgh	Exeter	Glasgow	Holyhead	Hull	Leeds	Liverpool	Manchester	Newcastle	Norwich	Nottingham	Oxford	Penzance	Plymouth	Shrewsbury	Southampton	Stranraer	York	London
York																								209
Stranraer																							228	419
Southampton																						447	252	76
Shrewsbury																					190	287	144	162
Plymouth																				242	155	502	340	215
Penzance																			78	315	227	572	406	283
Oxford																		265	193	113	67	371	185	56
Nottingham																	104	336	265	85	171	295	86	128
Norwich																123	144	407	336	205	192	393	185	115
Newcastle															258	156	253	477	410	216	319	164	83	280
Manchester														141	183	71	153	355	281	69	227	226	71	199
Liverpool													34	170	232	107	164	366	294	64	241	234	100	210
Leeds												72	43	91	173	73	171	401	328	116	235	232	24	196
Hull											59	126	97	121	153	92	188	411	341	164	253	259	38	215
Holyhead											215	163	104	123	260	174	218	419	347	104	296	332	190	263
Glasgow									319	245	215	220	214	150	379	281	354	559	486	272	436	88	208	402
Exeter								444	305	297	288	250	239	361	295	222	152	112	45	201	114	457	291	170
Edinburgh							446	45	325	229	205	222	218	107	365	268	361	561	488	276	437	130	191	405
Dover						457	248	490	347					348	167	202	148	362	290	243	155	503	274	77
Cardiff					234	395	119	393	209	246	236	200	188	311	252	170	109	232	164	110	123	406	241	155
Cambridge				191	121	337	233	349	246	157	143	195	153	224	62	82	82	346	275	142	133	361	153	60
Bristol			156	45	198	373	81	372	232	216	178	167	161	217	151	74	195	128	75	386	199	221	118	119
Birmingham		85	101	107	198	293	157	291	151	136	115	98	88	207	161	50	63	290	199	48	128	272	128	118
Aberdeen	430	511	468	532	591	130	584	149	457	361	336	361	354	239	501	402	497	624		412	571	199	325	543
London	119	118	60	155	77	405	170	402	263	215	196	210	199	280	115	128	56	283	215	162	76	419	209	

THE WORLD

NATIONS OF THE WORLD

Where more than one language is shown within a country, the status of the languages may not be equal. Some languages have a 'semi-official' status, or are used for a restricted set of purposes, such as trade or tourism.

English name	Capital	Official language(s)	Population[1]
Afghanistan	Kabul	Dari, Pushtøu	19 062 000
Albania	Tirana	Albanian	3 363 000
Algeria	Algiers	Arabic	26 346 000
Andorra	Andorra-la-Vella	Catalan, French	47 000
Angola	Luanda	Portuguese	10 609 000
Antigua and Barbuda	St John's	English	66 000
Argentina	Buenos Aires	Spanish	33 101 000
Armenia	Yerevan	Armenian	3 677 000
Australia	Canberra	English	17 581 000
Austria	Vienna	German	7 898 000
Azerbaijan	Baku	Azeri (Azerbaijan)	7 398 000
Bahamas	Nassau	English	262 000
Bahrain	Manama	Arabic	533 000
Bangladesh	Dhaka	Bengali	119 288 000
Barbados	Bridgetown	English	259 000
Belgium	Brussels	Flemish, French, German	9 998 000
Belize	Belmopan	English	198 000
Belorussia	Minsk	Belorussian, Russian	10 297 000
Benin	Porto-Novo/Cotonou	French	4 918 000
Bhutan	Thimphu	Dzongkha	1 612 000
Bolivia	La Paz/Sucre	Spanish	6 344 000
Bosnia-Herzegovina	Sarajevo	Serbo-Croat	4 366 000
Botswana	Gaborone	English, Setswana	1 373 000
Brazil	Brasilia	Portuguese	156 275 000
Brunei	Bandar Seri Begawan	Malay, English	270 000
Bulgaria	Sofia	Bulgarian	8 473 000
Burkina	Ouagadougou	French	9 490 000
Burma (Myanmar)	Rangoon (Yangon)	Burmese	43 668 000
Burundi	Bujumbura	French, Kirundi	5 786 000
Cambodia	Phnom Penh	Khmer	9 054 000
Cameroon	Yaoundé	English, French	12 198 000
Canada	Ottawa	English, French	27 562 000
Cape Verde	Praia	Portuguese	384 000
Central African Republic	Bangui	French	3 173 000
Chad	Ndjamena	French	5 961 000
Chile	Santiago	Spanish	13 599 000
China	Beijing (Peking)	Chinese	1 187 997 000

[1] 1991 population census figures or later

NATIONS OF THE WORLD (cont.)

English name	Capital	Official language(s)	Population[1]
Colombia	Bogotá	Spanish	33 424 000
Comoros	Moroni	French	585 000
Congo	Brazzaville	French	2 368 000
Costa Rica	San José	Spanish	3 099 000
Croatia	Zagreb	Serbo-Croat	4 784 000
Cuba	Havana	Spanish	10 822 000
Cyprus	Nicosia	Greek, Turkish	716 000
Czech Republic	Prague	Czech	10 310 000
Denmark	Copenhagen	Danish	5 181 000
Djibouti	Djibouti	Arabic, French	467 000
Dominica	Roseau	English	109 000
Dominican Republic	Santo Domingo	Spanish	7 471 000
Ecuador	Quito	Spanish	10 741 000
Egypt	Cairo	Arabic	55 163 000
El Salvador	San Salvador	Spanish	5 047 000
Equatorial Guinea	Malabo	Spanish	369 000
Eritrea	Asmara	Arabic, English	505 000
Estonia	Tallinn	Estonian	1 527 000
Ethiopia	Addis Ababa	Amharic	55 117 000
Fiji	Suva	English	747 000
Finland	Helsinki	Finnish, Swedish	5 056 000
France	Paris	French	57 372 000
Gabon	Libreville	French	1 237 000
Gambia, The	Banjul	English	878 000
Georgia	Tbilisi	Georgian, Russian	5 471 000
Germany	Berlin	German	80 569 000
Ghana	Accra	English	15 959 000
Greece	Athens	Greek	10 300 000
Greenland	Nuuk	Danish, Greenlandic	56 000
Grenada	St George's	English	91 000
Guatemala	Guatemala City	Spanish	9 745 000
Guinea	Conakry	French	6 116 000
Guinea-Bissau	Bissau	Portuguese	1 006 000
Guyana	Georgetown	English	808 000
Haiti	Port-au-Prince	French	6 764 000
Honduras	Tegucigalpa	Spanish	5 462 000
Hong Kong	Hong Kong	English, Chinese	5 800 000
Hungary	Budapest	Hungarian	10 304 000
Iceland	Reykjavík	Icelandic	260 000
India	New Delhi	Hindi, English	879 548 000
Indonesia	Jakarta	Bahasa Indonesia	191 170 000
Iran	Tehran	Farsi	59 964 000
Iraq	Baghdad	Arabic	19 290 000
Ireland	Dublin	Irish, English	3 547 000
Israel	Jerusalem	Hebrew, Arabic	5 191 000

English name	Capital	Official language(s)	Population[1]
Italy	Rome	Italian	57 782 000
Ivory Coast	Yamoussoukro	French	12 910 000
Jamaica	Kingston	English	2 469 000
Japan	Tokyo	Japanese	123 463 000
Jordan	Amman	Arabic	4 291 000
Kazakhstan	Alma-Ata	Kazakh	17 038 000
Kenya	Nairobi	Swahili, English	26 985 000
Kirghizia	Bishkek	Kirghiz	4 472 000
Kiribati	Bairiki	English	74 000
Kuwait	Kuwait City	Arabic	1 970 000
Laos	Vientiane	Lao	4 469 000
Latvia	Rīga	Latvian	2 591 000
Lebanon	Beirut	Arabic	2 838 000
Lesotho	Maseru	English, Sesotho	1 836 000
Liberia	Monrovia	English	2 580 000
Libya	Tripoli	Arabic	4 875 000
Liechtenstein	Vaduz	German	29 000
Lithuania	Vilnius	Lithuanian	3 570 000
Luxembourg	Luxembourg	French, German, Letzebuergesch	370 000
Macedonia	Skopje	Macedonian	2 034 000
Madagascar	Antananarivo	Malagasy, French	12 827 000
Malawi	Lilongwe	Chichewa, English	8 823 000
Malaysia	Kuala Lumpur	Malay	18 181 000
Maldives	Malé	Divehi	231 000
Mali	Bamako	French	9 818 000
Malta	Valletta	English, Maltese	360 000
Marshall Islands	Dalap-Uliga-Darrit (on Majuro)	English, Marshallese	46 000
Mauritania	Nouakchott	Arabic, French	2 143 000
Mauritius	Port Louis	English	1 084 000
Mexico	Mexico City	Spanish	89 538 000
Micronesia, Federated states of	Palikir (on Pohnpei)	English	101 000
Moldavia	Kishinev	Moldavian	4 359 000
Monaco	Monaco-Ville	French	30 000
Mongolia	Ulan Bator	Khalka	2 310 000
Morocco	Rabat	Arabic	26 318 000
Mozambique	Maputo	Portuguese	14 872 000
Namibia	Windhoek	Afrikaans, English	1 534 000
Nauru	Yaren District (Admin centre)	Nauruan, English	10 000
Nepal	Kathmandu	Napali	20 577 000
Netherlands, The	Amsterdam	Dutch	15 238 000
New Zealand	Wellington	English	3 414 000
Nicaragua	Managua	Spanish	4 130 000
Niger	Niamey	French	8 252 000

[1] 1991 population census figures or later

NATIONS OF THE WORLD (cont.)

English name	Capital	Official language(s)	Population[1]
Nigeria	Abuja	English	88 515 000
North Korea	Pyongyang	Korean	22 618 000
Norway	Oslo	Norwegian	4 286 000
Oman	Muscat	Arabic	1 637 000
Pakistan	Islamabad	Urdu, English	115 520 000
Panama	Panama City	Spanish	2 515 000
Papua New Guinea	Port Moresby	English, Tok Písin, Hi-i Motu	4 056 900
Paraguay	Asunción	Spanish	4 124 000
Peru	Lima	Spanish	22 454 000
Philippines	Manila	English, Pilipino	64 259 000
Poland	Warsaw	Polish	38 365 000
Portugal	Lisbon	Portuguese	9 846 000
Puerto Rico	San Juan	Spanish, English	3 580 000
Qatar	Doha	Arabic	453 000
Romania	Bucharest	Romanian	22 760 000
Russia	Moscow	Russian	148 673 000
Rwanda	Kigali	Kinyarwanda, French	7 526 000
St Christopher-Nevis	Basseterre	English	42 000
St Lucia	Castries	English	153 000
St Vincent and the Grenadines	Kingstown	English	108 000
San Marino	San Marino	Italian	23 000
São Tomé and Principe	São Tomé	Portuguese	124 000
Saudi Arabia	Riyadh	Arabic	15 922 000
Senegal	Dakar	French	7 736 000
Seychelles	Victoria	Creole French, English, French	72 000
Sierra Leone	Freetown	English	4 376 000
Singapore	Singapore	Chinese, English, Malay, Tamil	2 812 000
Slovakia	Bratislava	Slovak	5 297 000
Slovenia	Ljubljana	Slovene	1 993 000
Solomon Islands	Honiara	English	326 000
Somalia	Mogadishu	Arabic, Somali	9 204 000
South Africa	Pretoria/Cape Town/ Bloemfontein	Afrikaans, English	39 818 000
South Korea	Seoul	Korean	43 924 000
Spain	Madrid	Spanish	39 116 000
Sri Lanka	Colombo	Sinhala, Tamil	17 405 000
Sudan	Khartoum	Arabic	26 656 000
Suriname	Paramaribo	Dutch	438 000
Swaziland	Mbabane	English, Siswati	792 000
Sweden	Stockholm	Swedish	8 697 000
Switzerland	Bern	French, German, Italian, Romansch	6 936 000
Syria	Damascus	Arabic	12 958 000
Taiwan	Taipei	Chinese	20 592 000
Tajikistan	Dushanbe	Tajik	5 465 000

English name	Capital	Official language(s)	Population[1]
Tanzania	Dodoma	Swahili, English	27 829 000
Thailand	Bangkok	Thai	57 760 000
Togo	Lomé	French	3 763 000
Tonga	Nuku'alofa	English, Tongan	103 000
Trinidad and Tobago	Port of Spain	English	1 265 000
Tunisia	Tunis	Arabic	8 401 000
Turkey	Ankara	Turkish	58 775 000
Turkmenistan	Ashkhabad	Turkmen	3 714 000
Tuvalu	Fongafale (on Funafuti)	English	12 000
Uganda	Kampala	English	18 674 000
Ukraine	Kiev	Ukrainian, Russian	52 200 000
United Arab Emirates	Abu Dhabi	Arabic	1 629 000
United Kingdom	London	English	58 430 000
Uruguay	Montevideo	Spanish	3 131 000
USA	Washington, DC	English	255 020 000
Uzbekistan	Tashkent	Uzbek	20 708 000
Vanuatu	Port-Vila	English, French	154 000
Vatican City	—	Latin, Italian widely spoken	1 000
Venezuela	Caracas	Spanish	20 249 000
Vietnam	Hanoi	Vietnamese	69 306 000
Western Sahara	Laâyoune	Arabic	250 000
Western Samoa	Apia	English, Samoan	158 000
Yemen	San'a	Arabic	13 000 000
Yugoslavia	Belgrade	Serbo-Croat	10 469 000
Zaire	Kinshasa	French	39 882 000
Zambia	Lusaka	English	8 638 000
Zimbabwe	Harare	English	10 402 000

[1] 1991 population census figures or later

CAPITAL CITIES OF THE WORLD

Capital	Country	Population
Abu Dhabi	United Arab Emirates	64 318 (1985e)
Abuja	Nigeria	379 000 (1991)
Accra	Ghana	949 000 (1988e)
Addis Ababa	Ethiopia	1 891 000 (1990e)
Algiers	Algeria	3 033 000 (1990e)
Alma-Ata	Kazakhstan	1 200 000 (1990e)
Amman	Jordan	1 300 000 (1989e)
Amsterdam	Netherlands, The	1 100 000 (1991e)
Andorra-la-Vella	Andorra	20 000 (1990e)
Ankara	Turkey	3 000 000 (1990)
Antananarivo	Madagascar	802 000 (1990e)
Apia	Western Samoa	33 000 (1991)
Ashkhabad	Turkmenistan	412 000 (1991e)

CAPITAL CITIES OF THE WORLD (cont.)

Capital	Country	Population
Asmara	Eritrea	343 000 (1989e)
Asunción	Paraguay	608 000 (1990e)
Athens	Greece	862 133 (1991)
Baghdad	Iraq	4 000 000 (1990e)
Bairiki	Kiribati	25 000 (1990)
Baku	Azerbaijan	1 800 000 (1990e)
Bamako	Mali	746 000 (1992e)
Bandar Seri Begawan	Brunei	46 000 (1991)
Bangkok	Thailand	5 900 000 (1990)
Bangui	Central African Republic	452 000 (1988)
Banjul	Gambia, The	44 000 (1986e)
Basseterre	St Christopher-Nevis	19 000 (1985e)
Beijing (Peking)	China	10 800 000 (1990)
Beirut	Lebanon	1 500 000 (1991e)
Belgrade	Yugoslavia	1 600 000 (1991)
Belmopan	Belize	5 000 (1990e)
Berlin	Germany	3 400 000 (1991e)
Bern	Switzerland	300 000 (1991e)
Bishkek	Kirghizia	641 000 (1991e)
Bissau	Guinea-Bissau	966 000 (1990e)
Bogotá	Colombia	4 900 000 (1992e)
Brasília	Brazil	1 600 000 (1991)
Bratislava	Slovakia	442 000 (1991)
Brazzaville	Congo	938 000 (1992e)
Bridgetown	Barbados	6 000 (1990)
Brussels	Belgium	951 000 (1992e)
Bucharest	Romania	2 100 000 (1992)
Budapest	Hungary	2 000 000 (1991e)
Buenos Aires	Argentina	12 200 000 (1991e)
Bujumbura	Burundi	227 000 (1990e)
Cairo	Egypt	15 000 000 (1991e)
Canberra	Australia	310 000 (1990e)
Caracas	Venezuela	4 100 000 (1990e)
Castries	St Lucia	53 000 (1991e)
Colombo	Sri Lanka	615 000 (1990e)
Conakry	Guinea	705 000 (1983)
Copenhagen	Denmark	1 300 000 (1992e)
Dalap-Uliga-Darrit	Marshall Islands	20 000 (1990e)
Dhaka	Bangladesh	6 600 000 (1990e)
Dakar	Senegal	1 700 000 (1992e)
Damascus	Syria	2 700 000 (1990e)
Djibouti	Djibouti	180 000 (1984e)
Dodoma	Tanzania	204 000 (1988)
Doha	Qatar	217 000 (1986)

Capital	Country	Population
Dublin	Ireland	916 000 (1991)
Dushanbe	Tajikistan	582 000 (1991e)
Fongafale (on Funafuti)	Tuvalu	3 000 (1985)
Freetown	Sierra Leone	470 000 (1985)
Gaborone	Gaborone	134 000 (1991)
Georgetown	Guyana	150 000 (1986e)
Guatemala City	Guatemala	9 800 000 (1992e)
Hanoi	Vietnam	3 100 000 (1989)
Harare	Zimbabwe	863 000 (1987e)
Havana	Cuba	2 100 000 (1990e)
Helsinki	Finland	496 000 (1992e)
Hong Kong	Hong Kong	5 800 000 (1992e)
Honiara	Solomon Islands	35 000 (1990e)
Islamabad	Pakistan	537 000 (1990e)
Jakarta	Indonesia	9 300 000 (1990e)
Jerusalem	Israel	508 000 (1990e)
Kabul	Afghanistan	1 300 000 (1992e)
Kampala	Uganda	774 000 (1991)
Kathmandu	Nepal	235 000 (1981)
Khartoum	Sudan	2 000 000 (1990e)
Kiev	Ukraine	2 600 000 (1990e)
Kigali	Rwanda	233 000 (1991)
Kingston	Jamaica	644 000 (1991)
Kingstown	St Vincent and the Grenadines	27 000 (1991)
Kinshasa	Zaire	3 800 000 (1991e)
Kishinev	Moldavia	677 000 (1991e)
Kuala Lumpur	Malaysia	1 800 000 (1990e)
Kuwait City	Kuwait	400 000 (1993e)
Laâyoune	Western Sahara	94 000 (1982)
La Paz/Sucre	Bolivia	1 200 000 (1990e)
Libreville	Gabon	352 000 (1988e)
Lilongwe	Malawi	223 000 (1987)
Lima	Peru	6 400 000 (1990e)
Lisbon	Portugal	1 900 000 (1991)
Ljubljana	Slovenia	323 000 (1991)
Lomé	Togo	500 000 (1987e)
London	United Kingdom	6 900 000 (1992e)
Luanda	Angola	1 800 000 (1990e)
Lusaka	Zambia	982 000 (1990)
Luxembourg	Luxembourg	75 000 (1991e)
Madrid	Spain	3 000 000 (1991)
Malabo	Equatorial Guinea	10 000 (1986e)
Malé	Maldives	55 000 (1990)
Managua	Nicaragua	682 000 (1985e)
Manama	Bahrain	152 000 (1988e)
Manila	Philippines	7 900 000 (1990)

CAPITAL CITIES OF THE WORLD (cont.)

Capital	Country	Population
Maputo	Mozambique	1 200 000 (1991e)
Maseru	Lesotho	109 000 (1986)
Mbabane	Swaziland	38 000 (1986)
Mexico City	Mexico	13 600 000 (1990)
Minsk	Belorussia	1 600 000 (1990e)
Mogadishu	Somalia	1 000 000 (1987e)
Monaco-Ville	Monaco	1 200 (1990)
Monrovia	Liberia	421 000 (1984)
Montevideo	Uruguay	1 200 000 (1990e)
Moroni	Comoros	22 000 (1988)
Moscow	Russia	8 800 000 (1991e)
Muscat	Oman	380 000(1990e)
Nairobi	Kenya	1 500 000 (1990e)
Nassau	Bahamas	172 000 (1990)
Ndjamena	Chad	688 000 (1992e)
New Delhi	India	8 400 000 (1991)
Niamey	Niger	398 000 (1988)
Nicosia	Cyprus	167 000 (1991e)
Nouakchott	Mauritania	393 000 (1988)
Nuku'alofa	Tonga	29 000 (1986)
Nuuk	Greenland	12 000 (1990)
Oslo	Norway	467 000 (1992e)
Ottawa	Canada	921 000 (1991e)
Ouagadougou	Burkina	442 000 (1985)
Palikir (on Pohnpei)	Micronesia, Federated states of	6 000 (1980e)
Panama City	Panama	585 000 (1990)
Paramaribo	Surinam	200 000 (1990e)
Paris	France	9 100 000 (1990)
Phnom Penh	Cambodia	1 000 000 (1990e)
Port Louis	Mauritius	143 000 (1991e)
Port Moresby	Papua New Guinea	193 000 (1990)
Port of Spain	Trinidad and Tobago	51 000 (1990)
Port-au-Prince	Haiti	1 300 000 (1992e)
Porto-Novo/Cotonou	Benin	208 000 (1982e)
Port-Vila	Vanuatu	19 000 (1989)
Prague	Czech Republic	1 200 000 (1991)
Praia	Cape Verde	62 000 (1990)
Pretoria/Cape Town/ Bloemfontein	South Africa	823 000 (1985e)
Pyongyang	North Korea	2 200 000 (1990e)
Quito	Ecuador	1 400 000 (1990)
Rabat	Morocco	1 500 000 (1990e)
Rangoon (Yangon)	Burma (Myanma)	3 300 000 (1990e)
Reykjavík	Iceland	100 000 (1991e)

Capital	Country	Population
Rīga	Latvia	910 000 (1991e)
Riyadh	Saudi Arabia	1 500 000 (1991e)
Rom	Italy	3 800 000 (1990e)
Roseau	Dominica	21 000 (1991)
St George's	Grenada	4 000 (1991e)
St John's	Antigua and Barbuda	36 000 (1986e)
San José	Costa Rica	300 000 (1991e)
San Juan	Puerto Rico	1 400 000 (1990e)
San Marino	San Marino	23 000 (1991e)
San Salvador	El Salvador	1 500 000 (1992)
San'a	Yemen	500 000 (1990e)
Santiago	Chile	5 300 000 (1991e)
Santo Domingo	Dominican Republic	2 200 000 (1990e)
São Tomé	São Tomé and Principe	35 000 (1984e)
Sarajevo	Bosnia-Herzegovina	526 000 (1991)
Seoul	South Korea	10 600 000 (1990)
Singapore	Singapore	2 800 000 (1992e)
Skopje	Macedonia	563 000 (1991)
Sofia	Bulgaria	1 200 000 (1991e)
Stockholm	Sweden	679 000 (1992e)
Suva	Fiji	70 000 (1986)
Taipei	Taiwan	2 700 000 (1992e)
Tallinn	Estonia	484 000 (1990e)
Tashkent	Uzbekistan	2 100 000 (1990e)
Tbilisi	Georgia	1 300 000 (1991e)
Tegucigalpa	Honduras	608 000 (1989)
Tehran	Iran	6 800 000 (1990e)
Thimphu	Bhutan	9 301 (1980e)
Tirana	Albania	239 000 (1989)
Tokyo	Japan	8 200 000 (1991e)
Tripoli	Libya	1 500 000 (1990e)
Tunis	Tunisia	1 600 000 (1990e)
Ulan Bator	Mongolia	575 000 (1991e)
Vaduz	Liechtenstein	5 000 (1991e)
Valletta	Malta	9 000 (1990)
Victoria	Seychelles	24 000 (1987)
Vienna	Austria	1 500 000 (1991)
Vientiane	Laos	178 000 (1985)
Vilnius	Lithuania	593 000 (1990e)
Warsaw	Poland	1 700 000 (1991e)
Washington, DC	USA	3 900 000 (1990)
Wellington	New Zealand	326 000 (1991)
Windhoek	Namibia	159 000 (1991)
Yamoussoukro	Ivory Coast	120 000 (1984)
Yaoundé	Cameroon	776 000 (1988e)
Yerevan	Armenia	1 200 000 (1990e)
Zagreb	Croatia	704 000 (1991e)

WORLD POPULATION ESTIMATES

Date (AD)	Millions	Date (AD)	Millions	Date (AD)	Millions
1	200	1900	1 625	1970	3 700
1000	275	1920	1 860	1980	4 450
1250	375	1930	2 070	1985	4 845
1500	420	1940	2 295	1990	5 246
1700	615	1950	2 500	2000	6 100
1800	900	1960	3 050	2050	11 000

Estimates for 2000 and 2050 are United Nations 'medium' estimates. They should be compared with the 'low' estimates for these years of 5 400 and 8 500, and 'high' estimates of 7 000 and 13 500, respectively.

UNITED NATIONS SECRETARY GENERALS

Secretary General		Secretary General	
1946–53	Trygve Lie *Norway*	1982–91	Javier Pérez de Cuéllar *Peru*
1953–61	Dag Hammarskjöld *Sweden*	1991–96	Boutros Boutros-Ghali *Egypt*
1962–71	U Thant *Burma*	1996–	Kofi Annan *Ghana*
1971–81	Kurt Waldheim *Austria*		

UNITED NATIONS MEMBERSHIP

Grouped according to year of entry

1945	Argentina, Australia, Belgium, Belorussian SSR, Bolivia, Brazil, Canada, Chile, China (Taiwan) (to 1971), Colombia, Costa Rica, Cuba, Czechoslovakia[1], Denmark, Dominican Republic, Ecuador, Egypt, El Salvador, Ethiopia, France, Greece, Guatemala, Haiti, Honduras, India, Iran, Iraq, Lebanon, Liberia, Luxembourg, Mexico, Netherlands, New Zealand, Nicaragua, Norway, Panama, Paraguay, Peru, Philippines, Poland, Saudi Arabia, South Africa, Syria, Turkey, Ukranian SSR, USSR[2], UK, USA, Uruguay, Venezuela, Yugoslavia
1946	Afghanistan, Iceland, Sweden, Thailand
1947	Pakistan, Yemen
1948	Burma
1949	Israel
1950	Indonesia

1955	Albania, Austria, Bulgaria, Kampuchea (formerly Cambodia), Sri Lanka (formerly Ceylon), Finland, Hungary, Ireland, Italy, Jordan, Laos, Libya, Nepal, Portugal, Romania, Spain
1956	Japan, Morocco, Sudan, Tunisia
1957	Ghana, Malaya (Malaysia, 1963)
1958	Guinea
1960	Benin (formerly Dahomey), Burkina Faso (formerly Upper Volta), Cameroon, Central African Republic, Chad, Congo, Ivory Coast (Côte d'Ivoire), Cyprus, Gabon, Madagascar, Mali, Niger, Nigeria, Senegal, Somalia, Togo, Zaire
1961	Mauritania, Mongolia, Sierra Leone, Tanganyika (within Tanzania, 1964)
1962	Algeria, Burundi, Jamaica, Rwanda, Trinidad and Tobago, Uganda
1963	Kenya, Kuwait, Zanzibar (within Tanzania, 1964)

1964	Malawi, Malta, Zambia, Tanzania	1979	St Lucia
1965	Gambia, Maldives, Singapore	1980	St Vincent and the Grenadines,
1966	Barbados, Botswana, Guyana, Lesotho		Zimbabwe
1968	Equatorial Guinea, Mauritius, Swaziland	1981	Antigua and Barbuda, Belize, Vanuatu
1970	Fiji	1983	St Christopher and Nevis
1971	Bahrain, Bhutan, China (People's	1984	Brunei
	Republic), Oman, Qatar, United Arab	1990	Namibia, Yemen (formerly N Yemen
	Emirates		and S Yemen) (Germany replaced
1973	Bahamas, German Democratic		GDR and GFR)
	Republic, German Federal Republic	1991	Estonia, Latvia, Lithuania, Marshall
1974	Bangladesh, Grenada, Guinea-Bissau		Islands, Micronesia, N Korea, Russia,
1975	Cape Verde, Comoros, Mozambique,		S Korea
	Papua New Guinea, São Tomé and	1992	Armenia, Azerbaijan, Kazakhstan,
	Principe, Suriname		Kirgizia, Moldavia, San Marino,
1976	Angola, Seychelles, Western Samoa		Tadzhikistan, Turkmenistan,
1977	Djibouti, Vietnam		Uzbekistan
1978	Dominica, Solomon Islands	1993	Czech Republic, Slovakia

[1] Ceased to be a member in 1992

[2] Membership assumed by Russian Federation in 1991.

UNITED NATIONS SPECIALIZED AGENCIES

Abbreviated form	Full title	Area of concern
ILO	International Labour Organization	Social justice
FAO	Food and Agriculture	Improvement of the production and distrubution of agricultural products
UNESCO	United Nations Educational, Scientific and Cultural Organization	Stimulation of popular education and the spread of culture
ICAO	International Civil Aviation Organization	Encouragement of safety measures in international flight
IBRD	International Bank for Reconstruction and Development	Aid of development through investment
IMF	International Monetary Fund	Promotion of international monetary co-operation
UPU	Universal Postal Union	Uniting members within a single postal territory
WHO	World Health Organization	Promotion of the highest standards of health for all people
ITU	International Telecommunication Union	Allocation of frequencies and regulation of procedures
WMO	World Meteorological Organization	Standardization and utilization of meteorological observations
IFC	International Finance Corporation	Promotion of the international flow of private capital

UNITED NATIONS SPECIALIZED AGENCIES (cont.)

Abbreviated form	Full title	Area of concern
IMCO	Inter-governmental Maritime Consultative Organization	The co-ordination of safety at sea
IDA	International Development Association	Credit on special terms to provide assistance for less developed countries
WIPO	World Intellectual Property Organization	Protection of copyright, designs, inventions, etc
IFAD	International Fund for Agricultural Development	Increase of food production in developing countries by the generation of grants or loans

COMMONWEALTH SECRETARY GENERALS

Secretary General

1965–75	Arnold Smith
1975–90	Shridath S Ramphal
1990–	Emeka Anyaoku

COMMONWEALTH MEMBERSHIP

The Commonwealth is an informal association of sovereign states.
Member countries are grouped by year of entry.

1931	Australia, Canada, New Zealand, South Africa (left 1961; rejoined 1994), United Kingdom
1941	Irish Free State (Ireland left 1949)
1947	India, Pakistan (left 1972, rejoined 1989)
1948	Sri Lanka
1957	Ghana, Malaysia
1960	Nigeria
1961	Cyprus, Sierra Leone, Tanzania
1962	Jamaica, Trinidad and Tobago, Uganda
1963	Kenya, Malawi
1964	Malawi, Malta, Zambia
1965	the Gambia, Singapore
1966	Barbados, Botswana, Guyana, Lesotho
1968	Mauritius, Nauru, Swaziland
1970	Tonga, Western Samoa, Fiji (British Colony until 1970 then became independent within the Commonwealth; membership lapsed in 1987)
1972	Bangladesh
1973	Bahamas
1974	Grenada
1975	Papua New Guinea
1976	Seychelles
1978	Dominica, Solomon Islands, Tuvalu
1979	Kiribati, St Lucia, St Vincent and the Grenadines
1980	Vanuatu, Zimbabwe
1981	Antigua and Barbuda, Belize
1982	Maldives
1983	St Christopher and Nevis
1984	Brunei
1990	Namibia
1995	Cameroon, Mozambique

EUROPEAN COMMISSION PRESIDENTS

President	
1967–70	Jean Rey
1970–2	Franco M Malfatti
1972–3	Sicco L Mansholt
1973–7	Francois-Xavier Ortoli

President	
1977–81	Roy Jenkins
1981–5	Gaston Thorn
1985–1995	Jacques Delors
1995–	Jacques Santer

EUROPEAN UNION MEMBERSHIP

On 1 November 1993 the European Union came into effect—the European Community is a component part. Member countries are listed by year of entry.

1958	Belgium		1973	Republic of Ireland
1958	France		1973	United Kingdom
1958	Germany (Federal Republic of)		1981	Greece
1958	Italy		1986	Portugal
1958	Luxembourg		1986	Spain
1958	The Netherlands		1995	Austria, Finland, Sweden
1973	Denmark			

Applications for Hungary, Poland, Switzerland and the Czech Republic are under consideration. Slovenia gained associate membership in 1996.

EUROPEAN COMMUNITY ORGANIZATIONS

Abbreviation	Full title	Area of concern
	European Court of Justice	Adjudication of disputes arising from application of the Treaties
CAP	Common Agricultural Policy	Aiming to ensure reasonable standards of living for farmers; its policies have led to supluses in the past
EMS	European Monetary System	Assistance of trading relations between member
EIB	European Investment Bank	Financing of capital investment projects to assist development of the Community
ECSC	European Coal and Steel Community	Regulation of prices and trade in these commodities
EURATOM	European Atomic Energy Community	Creation of technical and industrial conditions to produce nuclear energy on a large scale

COUNTIES OF ENGLAND

County	Area sq km	sq ml	Population[1]	Admin centre
Avon[2]	1 346	520	973 300	Bristol
Bedfordshire	1 235	477	539 400	Bedford
Berkshire	1 259	486	763 700	Reading
Buckinghamshire	1 883	727	651 700	Aylesbury
Cambridgeshire	3 409	1 316	682 600	Cambridge
Cheshire	2 328	899	971 900	Chester
Cleveland[2]	583	225	559 500	Middlesbrough
Cornwall	3 564	1 376	477 000	Truro
Cumbria[2]	6 810	2 629	490 200	Carlisle
Derbyshire	2 631	1 016	950 900	Matlock
Devon	6 711	2 591	1 049 200	Exeter
Dorset	2 654	1 025	667 500	Dorchester
Durham	2 436	941	607 500	Durham
Essex	3 672	1 418	1 560 300	Chelmsford
Gloucestershire	2 643	1 020	543 900	Gloucester
Greater London[2]	1 579	610	6 933 000	—
Greater Manchester[2]	1 287	497	2 578 900	—
Hampshire	3 777	1 458	1 593 700	Winchester
Hereford and Worcester[2]	3 926	1 516	694 800	Worcester
Hertfordshire	1 634	631	999 700	Hertford
Humberside[2]	3 512	1 356	884 400	Hull
Isle of Wight	381	147	124 800	Newport
Kent	3 731	1 441	1 539 700	Maidstone
Lancashire	3 063	1 183	1 420 700	Preston
Leicestershire	2 553	986	910 300	Leicester
Lincolnshire	5 915	2 284	601 400	Lincoln
Merseyside[2]	652	252	1 440 900	Liverpool
Norfolk	5 368	2 073	765 100	Norwich
Northamptonshire	2 367	914	591 900	Northampton
Northumberland	5 032	1 943	307 200	Newcastle upon Tyne
Nottinghamshire	2 164	836	1 028 400	Nottingham
Oxfordshire	2 608	1 007	585 800	Oxford
Shropshire	3 490	1 347	413 900	Shrewsbury
Somerset	3 451	1 332	474 100	Taunton
Staffordshire	2 716	1 049	1 053 600	Stafford
Suffolk	3 797	1 466	646 200	Ipswich
Surrey	1 679	648	1 037 700	Kingston upon Thames
Sussex, East	1 795	693	722 200	Lewes
Sussex, West	1 989	768	717 700	Chichester
Tyne and Wear[2]	540	208	1 137 900	Newcastle
Warwickshire	1 981	765	493 600	Warwick
West Midlands[2]	899	347	2 633 700	Birmingham
Wiltshire	3 481	1 344	583 000	Trowbridge

| County | Area | | Population[1] | Admin centre |
	sq km	sq ml		
Yorkshire, North	8 309	3 208	721 800	Northallerton
Yorkshire, South	1 560	602	1 306 200	Barnsley
Yorkshire, West	2 039	787	2 101 600	Wakefield

[1] Mid-1993 population estimates
[2] New counties in 1974 were formed as follows:
Avon: parts of Somerset and Gloucestershire
Cleveland: parts of Durham and Yorkshire
Cumbria: Cumberland, Westmoreland, parts of Lancashire and Yorkshire
Greater London: London and most of Middlesex
Greater Manchester: parts of Lancashire, Cheshire and Yorkshire
Hereford and Worcester: Hereford, most of Worcestershire
Humberside: parts of Yorkshire and Lincolnshire
Merseyside: parts of Lancashire and Cheshire
Tyne and Wear: parts of Northumberland and Durham
West Midlands: parts of Staffordshire, Warwickshire and Worcestershire

REGIONS OF SCOTLAND

| Region | Area | | Population[1] | Admin centre |
	sq km	sq ml		
Borders	4 672	1 804	105 300	Newton St Boswells
Central	2 631	1 016	272 900	Stirling
Dumfries & Galloway	6 370	2 459	147 900	Dumfries
Fife	1 307	505	351 200	Glenrothes
Grampian	8 704	3 361	528 100	Aberdeen
Highland	25 391	9 804	206 900	Inverness
Lothian	1 755	678	753 900	Edinburgh
Strathclyde	13 537	5 227	2 286 800	Glasgow
Tayside	7 493	2 893	395 200	Dundee
Orkney Is	976	377	19 760	Kirkwall
Shetland Is	1 433	553	22 830	Lerwick
Western Is	2 898	1 119	29 410	Stornoway

[1] Mid-1993 population estimates

COUNTIES OF WALES

| County | Area | | Population[1] | Admin centre |
	sq km	sq ml		
Clwyd	2 426	937	415 900	Mold
Dyfed	5 768	2 227	351 500	Carmarthen
Gwent	1 376	531	450 300	Cwmbrån

[1] Mid-1993 population estimates

COUNTIES OF WALES (cont.)

County	Area sq km	sq ml	Population[1]	Admin centre
Gwynedd	3 869	1 494	240 200	Caernarvon
Powys	5 077	1 960	119 900	Llandrindod Wells
Mid Glamorgan	1 018	393	544 300	Cardiff
S Glamorgan	416	161	413 200	Cardiff
W Glamorgan	817	315	371 200	Swansea

[1] Mid-1993 population estimates

UK ISLANDS

Name	Area sq km	sq ml	Population[1]	Admin centre
Channel Is				
Alderney	8	3	2 297	St Anne's
Guernsey	63	24	58 867	St Peter Port
Jersey	116	45	84 082	St Helier
Sark	4	2	550	—
Isle of Man	572	221	70 600[2]	Douglas

[1] 1991 population census figures
[2] 1993 population estimate

DISTRICTS OF NORTHERN IRELAND

Districts	Area sq km	sq ml	Population[1]	Admin centre
Antrim	563	217	47 500	Antrim
Ards	369	142	66 200	Newtownards
Armagh	672	259	52 400	Armagh
Ballymena	638	246	57 000	Ballymena
Ballymoney	419	162	24 400	Ballymoney
Banbridge	444	171	36 600	Banbridge
Belfast	140	54	296 700	—
Carrickfergus	87	34	34 500	Carrickfergus
Castlereagh	85	33	63 000	Belfast
Coleraine	485	187	53 600	Coleraine
Cookstown	623	240	30 900	Cookstown
Craigavon	382	147	76 800	Craigavon
Down	646	249	60 500	Downpatrick
Dungannon	779	301	46 200	Dungannon
Fermanagh	1 876	715	54 800	Enniskillen

Districts	Area sq km	sq ml	Population[1]	Admin centre
Larne	338	131	29 800	Larne
Limavady	587	227	30 300	Limavady
Lisburn	444	171	104 100	Lisburn
Londonderry	382	147	100 500	—
Magherafelt	573	221	36 300	Magherafelt
Moyle	495	191	14 700	Ballycastle
Newry & Mourne	895	346	81 700	Newry
Newtownabbey	152	59	77 700	Newtownabbey
North Down	73	28	73 600	Bangor
Omagh	1 129	436	46 300	Omagh
Strabane	870	336	35 700	Strabane

[1] Mid-1993 population estimates

COUNTIES OF IRELAND

County	Area sq km	sq ml	Population[1]	Admin centre
Carlow	896	346	14 027	Carlow
Cavan	1 891	730	52 796	Cavan
Clare	3 188	1 231	90 918	Ennis
Cork	7 459	2 880	410 369	Cork
Donegal	4 830	1 865	128 117	Lifford
Dublin	922	356	1 025 304	Dublin
Galway	5 939	2 293	180 364	Galway
Kerry	4 701	1 815	121 894	Tralee
Kildare	1 694	654	122 656	Naas
Kilkenny	2 062	796	17 669	Kilkenny
Laoighis (Leix)	1 720	664	52 314	Portlaoise
Leitrim	1 526	589	25 301	Carrick
Limerick	2 686	1 037	161 956	Limerick
Longford	1 044	403	30 296	Longford
Louth	821	317	90 724	Dundalk
Mayo	5 398	2 084	110 713	Castlebar
Meath	2 339	903	105 370	Trim
Monaghan	1 290	498	51 293	Monaghan
Offaly	1 997	771	58 494	Tullamore
Roscommon	2 463	951	51 897	Roscommon
Sligo	1 795	693	54 756	Sligo
Tipperary	4 254	1 642	132 772	Clonmel
Waterford	1 839	710	41 853	Waterford
Westmeath	1 764	681	61 880	Mullingar
Wexford	2 352	908	15 393	Wexford
Wicklow	2 025	782	97 265	Wicklow

[1] 1991 population census figures

STATES OF THE USA

Population: figures from the 1990 population census
Abbreviations are given after each state name: the first is the common abbreviation, the second the ZIP (postal) code.

Alabama (Ala; AL)
Entry to Union   1819 (22nd)
Pop   4 136 000
Nickname   Camellia State, Heart of Dixie
Area   133 911 sq km/51 705 sq ml
Capital   Montgomery
Alaska (Alaska; AK)
Entry to Union   1959 (49th)
Pop   587 000
Nickname   Mainland State, The Last Frontier
Area   1 518 748 sq km/586 412 sq ml
Capital   Juneau
Arizona (Ariz; AZ)
Entry to Union   1912 (48th)
Pop   3 832 000
Nickname   Apache State,
  Grand Canyon State
Area   295 249 sq km/114 000 sq ml
Capital   Phoenix
Arkansas (Ark; AR)
Entry to Union   1836 (25th)
Pop   2 399 000
Nickname   Bear State, Land of Opportunity
Area   137 403 sq km/53 187 sq ml
Capital   Little Rock
California (Calif; CA)
Entry to Union   1850 (31st)
Pop   30 867 000
Nickname   Golden State
Area   411 033 sq km/158 706 sq ml
Capital   Sacramento
Colorado (Colo; CO)
Entry to Union   1876 (38th)
Pop   3 470 000
Nickname   Centennial State
Area   269 585 sq km/104 091 sq ml
Capital   Denver
Connecticut (Conn; CT)
Entry to Union   1788 (5th)
Pop   3 281 000
Nickname   Nutmeg State, Constitution State
Area   12 996 sq km/5 018 sq ml
Capital   Hartford

Delaware (Del; DE)
Entry to Union   1787 (1st)
Pop   689 000
Nickname   Diamond State, First State
Area   5 296 sq km/2 045 sq ml
Capital   Dover
District of Columbia (DC; DC)
Pop   589 000
Area   173.5 sq km/67 sq ml
Capital   Washington
Florida (Fla; FL)
Entry to Union   1845 (27th)
Pop   13 488 000
Nickname   Everglade State, Sunshine State
Area   151 934 sq km/58 664 sq ml
Capital   Tallahassee
Georgia (Ga; GA)
Entry to Union   1788 (4th)
Pop   6 751 000
Nickname   Empire State of the South,
  Peach State
Area   152 571 sq km/58 910 sq ml
Capital   Atlanta
Hawaii (Hawaii; HI)
Entry to Union   1959 (50th)
Pop   1 160 000
Nickname   Aloha State
Area   16 759 sq km/6 471 sq ml
Capital   Honolulu
Idaho (Idaho; ID)
Entry to Union   1890 (43rd)
Pop   1 067 000
Nickname   Gem State
Area   216 422 sq km/83 564 sq ml
Capital   Boise
Illinois (Ill; IL)
Entry to Union   1818 (21st)
Pop   11 631 000
Nickname   Prairie State, Land of Lincoln
Area   145 928 sq km/56 345 sq ml
Capital   Springfield
Indiana (Ind; IN)
Entry to Union   1816 (19th)

Pop 5 662 000
Nickname Hoosier State
Area 93 715.5 sq km/36 185 sq ml
Capital Indianapolis

Iowa (Iowa; IA)
Entry to Union 1846 (29th)
Pop 2 812 000
Nickname Hawkeye State, Corn State
Area 145 747 sq km/56 275 sq ml
Capital Des Moines

Kansas (Kans; KS)
Entry to Union 1861 (34th)
Pop 2 523 000
Nickname Sunflower State, Jayhawker State
Area 213 089 sq km/82 277 sq ml
Capital Topeka

Kentucky (Ky; KY)
Entry to Union 1792 (15th)
Pop 3 755 000
Nickname Bluegrass State
Area 104 658 sq km/40 410 sq ml
Capital Frankfort

Louisiana (La; LA)
Entry to Union 1812 (18th)
Pop 4 287 000
Nickname Pelican State, Sugar State, Creole State
Area 123 673 sq km/47 752 sq ml
Capital Baton Rouge

Maine (Maine; ME)
Entry to Union 1820 (23rd)
Pop 1 235 000
Nickname Pine Tree State
Area 86 153 sq km/33 265 sq ml
Capital Augusta

Maryland (Md; MD)
Entry to Union 1788 (7th)
Pop 4 908 000
Nickname Old Line State, Free State
Area 27 090 sq km/10 460 sq ml
Capital Annapolis

Massachusetts (Mass; MA)
Entry to Union 1788 (6th)
Pop 5 998 000
Nickname Bay State, Old Colony
Area 21 455 sq km/8 284 sq ml
Capital Boston

Michigan (Mich; MI)
Entry to Union 1837 (26th)

Pop 9 437 000
Nickname Wolverine State, Great Lake State
Area 151 579 sq km/58 527 sq ml
Capital Lansing

Minnesota (Minn; MN)
Entry to Union 1858 (32nd)
Pop 4 480 000
Nickname Gopher State, North Star State
Area 218 593 sq km/84 402 sq ml
Capital St Paul

Mississippi (Miss; MS)
Entry to Union 1817 (20th)
Pop 2 614 000
Nickname Magnolia State
Area 123 510 sq km/47 689 sq ml
Capital Jackson

Missouri (Mo; MO)
Entry to Union 1821 (24th)
Pop 5 193 000
Nickname Bullion State, Show Me State
Area 180 508 sq km/69 697 sq ml
Capital Jefferson City

Montana (Mont; MT)
Entry to Union 1889 (41st)
Pop 824 000
Nickname Treasure State, Big Sky Country
Area 380 834 sq km/147 046 sq ml
Capital Helena

Nebraska (Nebr; NE)
Entry to Union 1867 (37th)
Pop 1 606 000
Nickname Cornhusker State, Beef State
Area 200 342 sq km/77 355 sq ml
Capital Lincoln

Nevada (Nev; NV)
Entry to Union 1864 (36th)
Pop 1 327 000
Nickname Silver State, Sagebrush State
Area 286 341 sq km/110 561 sq ml
Capital Carson City

New Hampshire (NH; NH)
Entry to Union 1788 (9th)
Pop 1 111 000
Nickname Granite State
Area 24 032 sq km/9 279 sq ml
Capital Concord

New Jersey (NJ; NJ)
Entry to Union 1787 (3rd)

Pop 7 789 000
Nickname Garden State
Area 20 167 sq km/7 787 sq ml
Capital Trenton

New Mexico (N Mex; NM)
Entry to Union 1912 (47th)
Pop 1 581 000
Nickname Sunshine State,
Land of Enchantment
Area 314 914 sq km/121 593 sq ml
Capital Santa Fe

New York (NY; NY)
Entry to Union 1788 (11th)
Pop 18 119 000
Nickname Empire State
Area 127 185 sq km/49 108 sq ml
Capital Albany

North Carolina (NC; NC)
Entry to Union 1789 (12th)
Pop 6 843 000
Nickname Old North State, Tar Heel State
Area 136 407 sq km/52 699 sq ml
Capital Raleigh

North Dakota (N Dak; ND)
Entry to Union 1889 (39th)
Pop 638 000
Nickname Flickertail State, Sioux State
Area 180 180 sq km/69 567 sq ml
Capital Bismarck

Ohio (Ohio; OH)
Entry to Union 1803 (17th)
Pop 11 016 000
Nickname Buckeye State
Area 107 040 sq km/41 330 sq ml
Capital Columbus

Oklahoma (Okla; OK)
Entry to Union 1907 (46th)
Pop 3 212 000
Nickname Sooner State
Area 181 083 sq km/69 919 sq ml
Capital Oklahoma City

Oregon (Oreg; OR)
Entry to Union 1859 (33rd)
Pop 2 977 000
Nickname Sunset State, Beaver State
Area 251 409 sq km/97 073 sq ml
Capital Salem

Pennsylvania (Pa; PA)
Entry to Union 1787 (2nd)

Pop 12 009 000
Nickname Keystone State
Area 117 343 sq km/45 308 sq ml
Capital Harrisburg

Rhode Island (RI; RI)
Entry to Union 1790 (13th)
Pop 1 005 000
Nickname Little Rhody, Plantation State
Area 3 139 sq km/1 212 sq ml
Capital Providence

South Carolina (SC; SC)
Entry to Union 1788 (8th)
Pop 3 603 000
Nickname Palmetto State
Area 80 579 sq km/31 113 sq ml
Capital Columbia

South Dakota (S Dak; SD)
Entry to Union 1889 (40th)
Pop 711 000
Nickname Sunshine State, Coyote State
Area 199 723 sq km/77 116 sq ml
Capital Pierre

Tennessee (Tenn; TN)
Entry to Union 1796 (16th)
Pop 5 024 000
Nickname Volunteer State
Area 109 149 sq km/42 144 sq ml
Capital Nashville

Texas (Tex; TX)
Entry to Union 1845 (28th)
Pop 17 656 000
Nickname Lone Star State
Area 691 003 sq km/266 807 sq ml
Capital Austin

Utah (Utah; UT)
Entry to Union 1896 (45th)
Pop 1 813 000
Nickname Mormon State, Beehive State
Area 219 880 sq km/84 899 sq ml
Capital Salt Lake City

Vermont (Vt; VT)
Entry to Union 1791 (14th)
Pop 570 000
Nickname Green Mountain State
Area 24 899 sq km/9 614 sq ml
Capital Montpelier

Virginia (Va; VA)
Entry to Union 1788 (10th)
Pop 6 377 000

Nickname Old Dominion State, Mother of Presidents
Area 105 582 sq km/40 767 sq ml
Capital Richmond
Washington (Wash; WA)
Entry to Union 1889 (42nd)
Pop 5 136 000
Nickname Evergreen State, Chinook State
Area 176 473 sq km/68 139 sq ml
Capital Olympia
West Virginia (W Va; WV)
Entry to Union 1863 (35th)
Pop 1 812 000
Nickname Panhandle State, Mountain State

Area 62 758 sq km/24 232 sq ml
Capital Charleston
Wisconsin (Wis; WI)
Entry to Union 1848 (30th)
Pop 5 007 000
Nickname Badger State, America's Dairyland
Area 145 431 sq km/56 135 sq ml
Capital Madison
Wyoming (Wyo; WY)
Entry to Union 1890 (44th)
Pop 466 000
Nickname Equality State
Area 253 315 sq km/97 809 sq ml
Capital Cheyenne

AUSTRALIAN STATES AND TERRITORIES

Name	Area sq km	sq ml	Population[1]	State Capital
Australian Capital Territory	2 400	930	280 085	Canberra
New South Wales	801 400	309 400	5 731 926	Sydney
Northern Territory	1 346 200	519 800	175 253	Darwin
Queensland	1 727 200	666 900	2 976 617	Brisbane
South Australia	984 000	379 900	1 400 656	Adelaide
Tasmania	67 800	26 200	452 847	Hobart
Victoria	227 600	87 900	4 243 719	Melbourne
Western Australia	2 525 500	975 000	1 586 393	Perth

[1] 1991 population census figures

CANADIAN PROVINCES

Name	Area sq km	sq ml	Population[1]	Provincial Capital
Alberta	661 190	255 285	2 545 553	Edmonton
British Columbia	947 800	365 945	3 282 061	Victoria
Manitoba	649 950	250 945	1 091 942	Winnipeg
New Brunswick	73 440	28 355	723 900	Fredericton
Newfoundland	405 720	156 648	568 474	St John's
Northwest Territories	3 426 320	1 322 902	57 649	Yellowknife
Nova Scotia	55 490	21 424	899 942	Halifax
Ontario	1 068 580	412 578	10 084 885	Toronto
Prince Edward Islands	5 660	2 185	129 765	Charlottetown
Quebec	1 540 680	594 856	6 895 963	Quebec City
Saskatchewan	652 380	251 883	988 928	Regina
Yukon Territory	483 450	186 660	27 797	Whitehorse

[1] 1991 population census figures

HISTORY

JOURNEYS OF EXPLORATION

Date	Name	Exploration
490 BC	Hanno	Makes voyage round part of the coast of Africa
325 BC	Alexander the Great	Leads fleet along the N Indian coast and up the Persian Gulf
84 AD	Agricola	His fleet circumnavigates Britain
1003	Leif Ericsson	Voyages to N America and discovers 'Vinland' (possibly Nova Scotia)
1418	Henry the Navigator	Sends seamen who discover Madeira
1433	Henry the Navigator	Sails round Cape Bojadar
1446	Denis Fernandez	Discovers Cape Verde and the Senegal
1469	Fernao Gomes	Crosses the equator and reaches Cape Catherine
1488	Bartholomew Diaz	Sails round the Cape of Storms (Cape of Good Hope)
1492	Christopher Columbus	Discovers the New World
1493	Christopher Columbus	Discovers Puerto Rico, Antigua and Jamaica
1497	John Cabot	Explores the coast of Newfoundland
1497	Vasco da Gama	Voyages round the Cape of Good Hope
1498	Vasco da Gama	Explores coast of Mozambique and discovers sea route to India
1498	Christopher Columbus	Discovers Trinidad and South America
1499	Amerigo Vespucci	Discovers mouth of the River Amazon
1500	Pedro Alvarez Cabral	Discovers Brazil
1500	Diego Diaz	Discovers Madagascar
1500	Gaspar de Corte Real	Explores east coast of Greenland and Labrador
1501	Amerigo Vespucci	Explores S American coast
1502	Christopher Columbus	Explores Honduras and Panama
1513	Vasco Nunez de Balboa	Crosses the Panama Isthmus to discover the Pacific Ocean
1520	Ferdinand Magellan	Discovers the Straits of Magellan
1521	Ferdinand Magellan	Discovers the Philippines
1524	Giovanni de Verrazano	Discovers New York Bay and the Hudson River
1526	Sebastian Cabot	Explores the Rio de la Plata
1531	Diego de Ordaz	Explores the River Orinoco
1534	Jacques Cartier	Explores the Gulf of St Lawrence
1535	Jacques Cartier	Navigates the St Lawrence River
1536	Pedro de Mendoza	Founds Buenos Aires and explores Parana and Paraguay rivers
1539	Hernando de Soto	Explores Florida
1540	G L de Cardenas	Discovers the Grand Canyon
1580	Francis Drake	Completes circumnavigation of the globe

Date	Name	Exploration
1585	John Davis	Discovers Davis Strait on expedition to Greenland
1595	Walter Raleigh	Explores the River Orinoco
1610	Henry Hudson	Discovers Hudson's Bay
1616	William Baffin	Discovers Baffin Bay during search for the N W Passage
1617	Walter Raleigh	Begins expedition to Guiana
1642	Abel Janszoon Tasman	Discovers Tasmania and New Zealand
1678	Robert Cavelier de Salle	Explores the Great Lakes of Canada
1692	Ijsbrand Iders	Explores the Gobi Desert
1736	Andreas Celsius	Undertakes expedition to Lapland
1761	C Niebuhr	Undertakes expedition to Arabia
1766	Louis de Bougainville	Voyage of discovery in Pacific, names Navigator Is.
1769	James Cook	Names Society Islands; charts coasts of New Zealand and E Australia
1770	James Cook	Lands at Botany Bay, Australia
1774	James Cook	Discoveries and rediscoveries in the Pacific; discovers and names S Georgia and the S Sandwich Is.
1772	James Bruce	Explores Abyssinia and the confluence of the Blue Nile and White Nile
1778	James Cook	Discovers Hawaiian group; surveys coast of Bering Straits
1787	Horace Saussure	Makes first ascent of Mont Blanc
1790	George Vancouver	Explores the coast of N W America
1795	Mungo Park	Explores the course of the Niger
1818	John Ross	Attempts to discover N W Passage
1819	John Barrow	Enters Barrow Straits in the N Arctic
1823	Walter Oudney	Discovers Lake Chad in C Africa
1841	David Livingstone	Discovers Lake Ngami
1845	John Franklin	Attempts to discover N W Passage
1854	Richard Burton and John Speke	Explore interior of Somaliland
1855	David Livingstone	Discovers the Victoria Falls on the Zambesi River
1858	Richard Burton and John Speke	Discover Lake Tanganyika
1875	Henry Morton Stanley	Traces the Congo to the Atlantic
1888	Fridtjof Nansen	Crosses Greenland
1893	Fridtjof Nansen	Attempts to reach North Pole
1909	Robert Edwin Peary	Reaches North Pole
1911	Roald Amundsen	Reaches South Pole
1912	Robert Falcon Scott	Reaches South Pole
1914	Ernest Shackleton	Leads expedition to the Antarctic
1953	Edmund Hilary and Norgay Tensing	Make first ascent of Mt Everest
1961	Yuri Gagarin	Becomes first man in space
1969	Neil Armstrong and Buzz Aldrin	Make first landing on the moon

This table comprises mainly European explorers; 'discovers' is used to indicate the first recorded visit by a European

MONARCHS

AUSTRIA

Name	Dates of reign
Habsburg Dynasty	
Frederick III	1440–93
Maximilian I	1493–1519
Charles V	1519–58
Ferdinand I	1558–64
Maximilian II	1564–76
Rudolf II	1576–1612
Matthias	1611–19
Ferdinand II	1619–37
Ferdinand III	1637–57
Leopold I	1657–1705
Joseph I	1705–11
Charles VI	1711–40
Interregnum	1740–2
Charles VII	1742–5
Francis I	1745–65
Joseph II	1765–90
Leopold II	1790–2
Francis II	1792–1835
Ferdinand I	1835–48
Francis Joseph	1848–1916
Charles I	1916–18

BELGIUM

Belgium became an independent kingdom in 1831. A national congress elected Prince Leopold of Saxe–Coburg as king.

Name	Dates of reign
Leopold I	1831–65
Leopold II	1865–1909
Albert	1909–34
Leopold III	1934–51
Baudouin	1951–93
Albert II	1993–

DENMARK

Name	Dates of reign
Christian I	1448–81
John	1481–1513
Christian II	1513–23
Frederick I	1523–34
Christian III	1534–59
Frederick II	1559–88
Christian IV	1588–1648
Frederick III	1648–70
Christian V	1670–99
Frederick IV	1699–1730
Christian VI	1730–46
Frederick V	1746–66
Christian VII	1766–1808
Frederick VI	1808–39
Christian VIII	1839–48
Frederick VII	1848–63
Christian IX	1863–1906
Frederick VIII	1906–12
Christian X	1912–47
Frederick IX	1947–72
Margaret II	1972–

ENGLAND

Name	Dates of reign
West Saxon Kings	
Egbert	802–39
Æthelwulf	839–58
Æthelbald	858–60
Æthelbert	860–5
Æthelred	866–71
Alfred	871–99
Edward (the Elder)	899–924
Athelstan	924–39
Edmund	939–46
Edred	946–55
Edwy	955–9
Edgar	959–75
Edward (the Martyr)	975–8
Æthelred (the Unready)	978–1016
Edmund (Ironside)	1016
Danish Kings	
Cnut (Canute)	1016–35
Harold *Regent*	1035–7
Harold I (Harefoot)	1037–40
Harthacnut	1040–2
Edward (the Confessor)	1042–66
Harold II	1066
House of Normandy	
William I (the Conqueror)	1066–87
William II (Rufus)	1087–1100
Henry I	1100–35
House of Blois	
Stephen	1135–54
House of Plantagenet	
Henry II	1154–89
Richard I (Cœur de Lion)	1189–99
John	1199–1216
Henry III	1216–72
Edward I	1272–1307
Edward II	1307–27
Edward III	1327–77
Richard II	1377–99
House of Lancaster	
Henry IV	1399–1413
Henry V	1413–22
Henry VI	1422–61
House of York	
Edward IV	1461–70
House of Lancaster	
Henry VI	1470–1

Name	Dates of reign
House of York	
Edward IV	1471–83
Edward V	1483
Richard III	1483–5
House of Tudor	
Henry VII	1485–1509
Henry VIII	1509–47
Edward VI	1547–53
Mary I	1553–8
Elizabeth I	1558–1603

FINLAND

Finland was under Swedish control from the 13c until it was ceded to Russia in 1809 by the Treaty of Friedrichsham. Russian rulers then assumed the title of Grand Duke of Finland. In 1917 it became an independent monarchy. However in November 1918, after initially accepting the throne the previous month, Landgrave Frederick Charles of Hesse, the brother-in-law of the German emperor William II, withdrew his acceptance because of the Armistice and the ensuing abdicaton of William II. The previous regent remained in power until a Republic was declared in July 1919.

Name	Dates of reign
Dr Pehr Evind	
Svinhufvud *Regent*	1918
Landgrave Frederick	
Charles of Hesse	1918
(withdrew acceptance)	
Dr Pehr Evind	
Svinhufvud *Regent*	1918–19

FRANCE

France became a republic in 1793 and an empire in 1804 under Napoleon Bonaparte. The monarchy was restored in 1814 and then once more dissolved in 1848.

Name	Dates of reign
Hugh Capet	987–996
Robert II	996–1031
Henry I	1031–60
Philip I	1060–1108
Louis VI	1108–37
Louis VII	1137–80
Philip II Augustus	1180–1223
Louis VIII	1223–6
Louis IX	1226–70
Philip III	1270–85
Philip IV	1285–1314
Louis X	1314–16
John I	1316
Philip V	1316–22
Charles IV	1322–8
Philip VI	1328–50
John II	1350–64
Charles V	1364–80
Charles VI	1380–1422
Charles VII	1422–61
Louis XI	1461–83
Charles VIII	1483–98
Louis XII	1498–1515
Francis I	1515–47
Henry II	1547–59
Francis II	1559–60
Charles IX	1560–74
Henry III	1574–89
Henry IV (of	
Navarre)	1589–1610
Louis XIII	1610–43
Louis XIV	1643–1715
Louis XV	1715–74
Louis XVI	1774–92
Louis XVIII	1814–24
Charles X	1824–30
Louis-Philippe	1830–48

GERMANY

Modern Germany was united under Prussia in 1871; it became a republic (1919) after World War I and the abdication of William II in 1918.

Name	Dates of reign
William I	1871–88
Frederick	1888
William II	1888–1918

GREAT BRITAIN

Name	Dates of reign
House of Stuart	
James I (VI of	
Scotland)	1603–25
Charles I	1625–49
Commonwealth and	
Protectorate	
Council of State	1649–53
Oliver Cromwell	
Lord Protector	1653–8
Richard Cromwell	
Lord Protector	1658–9
House of Stuart (restored)	
Charles II	1660–85
James II	1685–8
William III (*jointly*	
with Mary II)	1689–94
William III (*alone*)	1694–1702
Anne	1702–14
House of Hanover	
George I	1714–27
George II	1727–60
George III	1760–1820
George IV	1820–30
William IV	1830–7
Victoria	1837–1901

MONARCHS (cont.)

Great Britain (cont.)

Name	Dates of reign
House of Saxe-Coburg	
Edward VII	1901–10
House of Windsor	
George V	1910–36
Edward VIII	1936
George VI	1936–52
Elizabeth II	1952–

GREECE

In 1832 the Greek National Assembly elected Otto of Bavaria as King of modern Greece. In 1917 Constantine I abdicated the throne in favour of his son Alexander. In 1920 a plebiscite voted for his return. In 1922 he again abdicated. A republic was proclaimed in 1924. In 1935 a plebiscite restored the monarchy until in 1967 a military junta staged a coup. The monarchy was formally abolished in 1973; Greece officially became a republic again in 1975.

Name	Dates of reign
Otto of Bavaria	1832–62
George I (of Denmark)	1863–1913
Constantine I	1913–17
Alexander	1917–20
Constantine I	1920–2
George II	1922–3
Republic	1924–35
George II	1935–47
Paul	1947–64
Constantine II	1964–7
Military Junta	1967–73
Republic	1973–

ITALY

Modern Italy became a united kingdom in 1861; it voted by referendum to become a republic in 1946.

Name	Dates of reign
Victor-Emanuel II	1861–78
Humbert I	1878–1900
Victor-Emanuel III	1900–46
Humbert II	1946

LUXEMBOURG

The Duchy of Luxembourg formally separated from the Netherlands in 1890.

Name	Dates of reign
Adolf of Nassau	1890–1905
William	1905–12
Marie-Adelaide	1912–19
Charlotte	1919–64
Jean	1964–

THE NETHERLANDS

Name	Dates of reign
William the Silent	1572–84
Maurice	1584–1625
Frederick Henry	1625–47
William II	1647–50
William III	1672–1702
William IV	1747–51
William V	1751–95
Louis Bonaparte	1806–10
William I	1813–40
William II	1840–9
William III	1849–90
Wilhelmina	1890–1948
Juliana	1948–80
Beatrix	1980–

PORTUGAL

From 1383 to 1385 the Portuguese throne was the subject of a dispute between John of Castile and John of Aviz. In 1826 Peter IV (I of Brazil) renounced his right to the Portuguese throne in order to remain in Brazil. His abdication was contingent upon his successor and daughter, Maria II marrying her uncle, Miguel. In 1828 Miguel usurped the throne on his own behalf. In 1834 Miguel was deposed and Maria II was restored to the throne. In 1910 Manuel II was deposed and Portugal became a republic.

Name	Dates of reign
Henry of Burgandy	1095–1112
Alfonso I	1112–85
Sancho I	1185–1211
Alfonso II	1211–23
Sancho II	1223–45
Alfonso III	1245–79
Diniz	1279–1325
Alfonso IV	1325–57
Peter I	1357–67
Ferdinand	1367–83
John I of Aviz	1385–1433
Edward	1433–8
Alfonso V	1438–81
John II	1481–95
Manuel I	1495–1521
John III	1521–57
Sebastian	1557–78
Henry	1578–80
Philip I (II of Spain)	1580–98
Philip II (III of Spain)	1598–1621
Philip III (IV of Spain)	1621–40
John IV of Braganza	1640–56

Name	Dates of reign
Altonso VI	1656–83
Peter II	1683–1706
John V	1706–50
Joseph	1750–77
Maria I	1777–1816
Peter III (King Consort)	1777–86
John VI	1816–26
Peter IV (I of Brazil)	1826
Maria II	1826–8
Miguel	1828–34
Maria II	1834–53
Peter V	1853–61
Luis	1861–89
Charles	1889–1908
Manuel II	1908–10

SCOTLAND

Name	Dates of reign
Malcolm II	1005–34
Duncan I	1034–40
Macbeth	1040–57
Lulach	1057–8
Malcolm III	1058–93
Donald Bane Deposed	1093–4
1094	
Restored	1094–7
Duncan II	1094
Edgar	1097–1107
Alexander I	1107–24
David I	1124–53
Malcolm IV	1153–65
William I	1165–1214
Alexander II	1214–49
Alexander III	1249–86
Margaret	1286–90
(Interregnum)	1290–2
John Balliol	1292–96
(Interregnum)	1296–1306
Robert I (the Bruce)	1306–29
David II	1329–71
Robert II	1371–90
Robert III	1390–1406

James I	1406–37
James II	1437–60
James III	1460–88
James IV	1488–1513
James V	1513–42
Mary Queen of Scots	1542–67
James VI[1]	1567–1625

[1] In 1603, James VI succeeded Elizabeth I to the English throne (Union of the Crowns) and united the thrones of Scotland and England.

SPAIN

Philip V abdicated in favour of Luis in 1724, but returned to the throne in the same year following Luis' death. After the French invasion of Spain in 1808 Napoleon set up Joseph Bonaparte as king. In 1814 Ferdinand was restored to the crown. In 1868 a revolution deposed Isabella II. In 1870 Amadeus of Savoy was elected as king. In 1873 he resigned the throne and a temporary republic was formed. In 1874 Alfonso XII restored the Bourbon dynasty to the throne. In 1931 Alfonso XIII was deposed and a republican constitution was proclaimed. From 1939 Franco ruled Spain under a dictatorship until his death in 1975 and the restoration of King Juan Carlos.

Name	Dates of reign
Charles I (Emperor Charles V)	1516–56
Philip II	1556–98
Philip III	1598–1621
Philip IV	1621–65
Charles II	1665–1700
Philip V	1700–24
Luis	1724
Philip V	1724–46

Ferdinand VI	1746–59
Charles III	1759–88
Charles IV	1788–1808
Ferdinand VII	1808
Joseph Bonaparte	1808–14
Ferdinand VII	1814–33
Isabella II	1833–68
Amadeus of Savoy	1870–3
Alfonso XII	1874–85
Alfonso XIII	1886–1931
Juan Carlos	1975–

SWEDEN

Name	Dates of reign
Vasa	
Gustav I	1523–60
Eric XIV	1560–8
Johan III	1568–92
Sigismund	1592–9
Karl IX	1599–1611
Gustav II Adolf	1611–32
Christina	1632–54
Zweibrucken	
Karl X Gustav	1654–60
Karl XI	1660–97
Karl XII	1697–1718
Ulrika Elconora	1718–20
Hesse	
Fredrik	1720–51
Oldenburg-Holstein-Gottorp	
Adolf Fredrik	1751–71
Gustav III	1771–92
Gustav IV Adolf	1792–1809
Karl XIII	1809–18
Bernadotte	
Karl XIV Johan	1818–44
Oskar I	1844–59
Karl XV	1859–72
Oskar II	1872–1907
Gustav V	1907–50
Gustav VI Adolf	1950–73
Karl XVI Gustav	1973–

ANCIENT EGYPT: DYNASTIES

Dynasty	Period	Date BC
I	**Early Dynastic Period**	c.3100–2890
II	First use of stone in building	c.2890–2686
III	**Old Kingdom**	c.2686–2613
IV	The age of the great pyramid builders. Longest reign in history: Pepi II, 90 years	c.2613–2494
V		c.2494–2345
VI		c.2345–2181
VII	**First Intermediate Period**	c.2181–2173
VIII	Social order upset; few monuments built	c.2173–2160
IX		c.2160–2130
X		c.2130–2040
XI		c.2133–1991
XII	**Middle Kingdom**	1991–1786
XIII	Golden age of art and craftsmanship	1786–1633
XIV	**Second Intermediate Period**	1786–c.1603
XV	Country divided into principalities	1674–1567
XVI		c.1684–1567
XVII		c.1660–1567
XVIII	**New Kingdom**	1567–1320
XIX	Began with colonial expansion, ended in divided rule	1320–1200
XX		1200–1085
XXI	**Third Intermediate Period**	1085–945
XXII	Revival of prosperity and restoration of cults	945–730
XXIII		817?–730
XXIV		720–715
XXV		751–668
XXVI	**Late Period**	664–525
XXVII	Completion of Nile — Red Sea canal	525–404
XXVIII		404–399
XXIX		399–380
XXX		380–343
XXXI	Alexander the Great reached Alexandria in 332 BC	343–332

ANCIENT CHINA: DYNASTIES

Name	Dates of reign
Hsai Dynasty	22nd–18th-c BC
Shang or Yin Dynasty	18th–12th-c BC
Western (Hsi) Chou Dynasty	1111–770 BC
Eastern (Tung) Chou Dynasty	770–256 BC
Warring States Period	475–221 BC
Ch'in Dynasty (Unified Empire)	221–206 BC
Han Dynasty	206 BC–220 AD
Western (Hsi) Han	206 BC–9 AD
Hsin (Wang Mang, usurper)	9–23 AD
Eastern (Tung) Han	25–220 AD
Three Kingdoms (San-kuo)	220–265 AD
Western (Hsi) Chin Dynasty	265–317 AD
Eastern (Tung) Chin Dynasty	317–420 AD
Southern Dynasties	420–589 AD
Sui Dynasty (Unified China)	581–618 AD
Tang Dynasty	618–907 AD
Five Dynasties and Ten Kingdoms Period	907–960 AD
Sung Dynasty	960–1279 AD
Northern (Pei) Sung	960–1127 AD
Western (Hsi) Sung	990–1227 AD
Chin or Juchen Dynasty (Tartars)	1115–1234 AD
Yuan or Mongol Dynasty	1206–1368 AD
Ming Dynasty (Capital at Nanking (1368–1421), and Peking (1421–1644)	1368–1644 AD
Ching or Manchu Dynasty	1644–1911 AD

MUGHAL EMPERORS

The 2nd Mughal emperor, Humayun lost his throne in 1540, became a fugitive, and did not regain his title until 1555.

Name	Dates of reign
Babur	1526–30
Humayun	1530–56
Akbar	1556–1605
Jahangir	1605–27
Shah Jahan	1627–58
Aurangzeb (Alamgir)	1658–1707
Bahadur Shah I (or Shah Alam I)	1707–12
Jahandar Shah	1712–13
Farruksiyar	1713–19
Rafid-ud-Darajat	1719
Rafi-ud-Daulat	1719
Nekusiyar	1719
Ibrahim	1719
Muhammad Shah	1719–48
Ahmad Shah	1748–54
Alamgir II	1754–9
Shah Alam II	1759–1806
Akbar II	1806–37
Bahadur Shah II	1837–57

JAPANESE EMPERORS

The first 14 emperors (to Chuai) are regarded as legendary, and the dates of reign for the 15th to the 28th emperor (Senka), taken from the early Japanese chronicle, 'Nihon shoki' are not considered to be authentic.

Name	Dates of reign	Name	Dates of reign	Name	Dates of reign
Jimmu	660–585 BC	Korei	290–215 BC	Selmu	131–190 AD
Suizei	581–549 BC	Kogen	214–158 BC	Chuai	192–200 AD
Annei	549–511 BC	Kaika	158–98 BC	Ojin	270–310 AD
Itoku	510–477 BC	Sujin	97–30 BC	Nintoku	313–399 AD
Kosho	475–393 BC	Suinin	29 BC–70 AD	Richu	400–405 AD
Koan	392–291 BC	Keiko	71 AD–130 AD	Hanzel	406–410 AD

JAPANESE EMPERORS (cont.)

Name	Dates of reign	Name	Dates of reign	Name	Dates of reign
Ingyo	412–453 AD	Yozei	876–884 AD	Hanazono	1308–18
Anko	453–456 AD	Koko	884–887 AD	Go-Daigo	1318–39
Yuryaku	456–479 AD	Uda	887–897 AD	Go-Murakami	1339–68
Seinei	480–484 AD	Daigo	897–930 AD	Chokei	1368–83
Kenzo	485–487 AD	Suzaku	930–946 AD	Go-Kameyama	1383–92
Ninken	488–498 AD	Murakami	946–967 AD		
Buretsu	498–506 AD	Reizei	967–969 AD	*Northern Court*	
Keitai	507–531 AD	En'yu	969–984 AD	Kogon	1331–3
Ankan	531–535 AD	Kazan	984–986 AD	Komyo	1336–48
Senka	535–539 AD	Ichijo	986–1011 AD	Suko	1348–51
Kimmei	539–571 AD	Sanjo	1011–16 AD	Go-Kogon	1352–71
Bidatsu	572–585 AD	Go-Ichijo	1016–36	Go-Enyu	1371–82
Yomei	585–587 AD	Go-Suzako	1036–45	Go-Komatsu	1382–1412
Sushun	587–592 AD	Go-Reizei	1045–68	Shoko	1412–28
Suiko	592–628 AD	Go-Sanyo	1068–72	Go-Hanazono	1428–64
Jomei	629–641 AD	Shirakawa	1072–86	Go-Tsuchimikado	1464–1500
Kogyoku	642–645 AD	Horikawa	1086–1107	Go-Kashiwabara	1500–26
Kotuko	645–654 AD	Toba	1107–23	Go-Nara	1526–57
Saimei	655–661 AD	Sutoku	1123–41	Ogimachi	1557–86
Tenji	662–671 AD	Konoe	1141–55	Go-Yozei	1586–1611
Kobun	671–672 AD	Goshirakawa	1155–8	Go-Mizunoo	1611–29
Temmu	673–686 AD	Nijo	1158–65	Meisho	1629–43
Jito	686–697 AD	Rokujo	1165–8	Go-Komyo	1643–54
Mommu	697–707 AD	Takakura	1168–80	Go-Sai	1654–63
Gemmei	707–715 AD	Antoku	1180–3	Reigen	1663–87
Gensho	715–724 AD	Go-Toba	1183–98	Higashiyama	1687–1709
Shomu	724–749 AD	Tsuchimikado	1198–1210	Nakamikado	1709–35
Koken	749–758 AD	Juntoku	1210–21	Sakuramachi	1735–47
Junnin	758–764 AD	Chukyo	1221	Momozono	1747–62
Shotoku	764–770 AD	Goshirakawa	1221–32	Go-Sakuramachi	1762–70
Konin	770–781 AD	Shijo	1232–42	Go-Momozono	1770–9
Kammu	781–806 AD	Go-Saga	1242–6	Kokaku	1779–1817
Heizei	806–809 AD	Go-Fukakusa	1246–59	Ninko	1817–46
Saga	809–823 AD	Kameyama	1259–74	Komei	1846–66
Junna	823–833 AD	Go-Uda	1274–87	Meiji	1867–1912
Nimmyo	833–850 AD	Fushimi	1287–98	Taisho	1912–26
Montoku	850–858 AD	Go-Fushimi	1298–1301	Hirohito	1926–89
Seiwa	858–876 AD	Go-Nijo	1301–8	Akihito	1989–

ROMAN KINGS

The founding of Rome by Romulus is a Roman literary tradition.

Name	Dates of reign
Romulus	753–715 BC
Numa Pompilius	715–673 BC
Tullus Hostilius	673–642 BC
Ancus Marcius	642–616 BC
Tarquinius Priscus	616–578 BC
Servius Tullius	578–534 BC
Tarquinius Superbus	534–509 BC

ROMAN EMPERORS

Dates overlap where there are periods of joint rule (eg Marcus Aurelius and Lucius Verus) and where the government of the empire divides between east and west.

Name	Dates of reign	Name	Dates of reign	Name	Dates of reign
Augustus (Caesar Augustus)	27 BC–14 AD	Alexander Severus	222–235	Constantius I	305–306
Tiberius	14–37	Maximin	235–238	Severus–(West)	306–307
Caligula (Gaius Caesar)	37–41	Gordian I	238	Maxentius–(West)	306–312
Claudius	41–54	Gordian II	238	Constantine I	306–337
Nero	54–68	Maximus	238	Licinius–(East)	308–324
Galba	68–69	Balbinus	238	Constantine II	337–340
Otho	69	Gordian III	238–244	Constans I	337–350
Vitellius	69	Philip	244–249	Constantius II	337–361
Vespasian	69–79	Decius	249–251	Magnentius	350–351
Titus	79–81	Hostilian	251	Julian	360–363
Domitian	81–96	Gallus	251–253	Jovian	363–364
Nerva	96–98	Aemilian	253	Valentinian I–(West)	364–375
Trajan	98–117	Valerian	253–260	Valens–(East)	364–378
Hadrian	117–138	Gallienus	253–268	Procopius–(East)	365–366
Antoninus Pius	138–161	Claudius II (the Goth)	268–269	Gratian–(West)	375–383
Marcus Aurelius	161–180	Quintillus	269–270	Valentinian II– (West)	375–392
Lucius Verus	161–169	Aurelian	270–275	Theodosius I	379–395
Commodus	176–192	Tacitus	275–276	Arcadius–(East)	395–408
Pertinax	193	Florian	276	Honorius–(West)	395–423
Didius Julianus	193	Probus	276–282	Theodosius II–(East)	408–450
Septemius Severus	193–211	Carus	282–283	Constantius III– (West)	421–423
Caracalla	198–217	Carinus	283–285	Valentinian III– (West)	423–455
Geta	209–212	Numerian	283–284		
Macrinus	217–218	Diocletian–(East)	284–305	Marcian–(East)	450–457
Elagabalus	218–222	Maximian–(West)	286–305		
		Galerius–(East)	305–311		

ROMAN EMPERORS (cont.)

Name	Dates of reign	Name	Dates of reign	Name	Dates of reign
Petronius Maximus–(West)	455	Libius Severus–(West)	461–467	Leo II–(East)	474
Avitus–(West)	455–456	Anthemius–(West)	467–472	Zeno–(East)	474–491
Leo I–(East)	457–474	Olybrius–(West)	472–473	Romulus Augustus–(West)	475–476
Majorian–(West)	457–461	Julius Nepos–(West)	474–480		

HOLY ROMAN EMPERORS

Name	Dates of reign	Name	Dates of reign	Name	Dates of reign
Charlemagne (Charles I)	800–814	Rudolf[2]	1077–80	Louis IV	1314–46
Louis I (the Pious)	814–840	Hermann[2]	1081–93	Charles IV	1346–78
Civil War	840–843	Conrad[2]	1093–1101	Wenceslas	1378–1400
Lothair I	843–855	Henry V	1106–25	Rupert	1400–10
Louis II	855–875	Lothair II	1125–37	Sigismund	1410–37
Charles II (the Bald)	875–877	Conrad III	1138–52	Albert II	1438–9
Interregnum	877–881	Frederick I (Barbarossa)	1152–90	Frederick III	1440–93
Charles III (the Fat)	881–887	Henry VI	1190–7	Maximilian I	1493–1519
Interregnum	887–891	Philip[2]	1198–1208	Charles V	1519–56
Guido of Spoleto	891–894	Otto IV	1198–1214	Ferdinand I	1556–64
Lambert of Spoleto[1]	892–898	Frederick II	1215–50	Maximilian II	1564–76
Arnulf[2]	896–899	Henry Raspe[2]	1246–7	Rudolf II	1576–1612
Louis III	901–905	William of Holland[2]	1247–56	Matthias	1612–19
Conrad I[2]	911–918	Conrad IV	1250–4	Ferdinand II	1619–37
Berengar	905–924	*Great Interregnum*	1254–73	Ferdinand III	1637–57
Henry I	919–936	Richard[2]	1257–72	Leopold I	1658–1705
Otto I (the Great)	936–973	Alfonso (Alfonso X of Castile)[2]	1257–75	Joseph I	1705–11
Otto II	973–983			Charles VI	1711–40
Otto III	983–1002	Rudolf I	1273–91	*Interregnum*	1740–42
Henry II (the Saint)	1002–24	Adolf	1292–8	Charles VII	1742–5
Conrad II	1024–39	Albert I	1298–1308	Francis I	1745–65
Henry III (the Black)	1039–56	Henry VII	1308–13	Joseph II	1765–90
Henry IV	1056–1106	Frederick (III)[3]	1314–26	Leopold II	1790–2
				Francis II	1792–1806

[1] Co-emperor
[2] Rival
[3] Co-regent

RUSSIAN RULERS

In 1610 Vasili Shuisky was deposed as Tsar and the throne remained vacant until the election of Michael Romanov in 1613. In 1682 a condition of the succession was that the two step-brothers, Ivan V and Peter I (the Great) should jointly be proclaimed as Tsars. In 1917 the empire was overthrown and Tsar Nicholas II was forced to abdicate.

Name	Dates of reign	Name	Dates of reign	Name	Dates of reign
Daniel	1283–1303	Boris Godunov	1598–1605	Ivan VI	1740–1
Yuri	1303–25	Feodor II	1605	Elizabeth	1741–62
Ivan I	1325–41	Dimitri II	1605–6	Peter III	1762
Semeon	1341–53	Vasili IV Shuisky	1606–10	Catherine II (the	
Ivan II	1353–9	Michael Romanov	1613–45	Great)	1762–96
Dimitri Donskoy	1359–89	Alexei	1645–76	Paul	1796–1801
Vasili I	1389–1425	Feodor III	1676–82	Alexander I	1810–25
Vasili II	1425–62	Ivan V	1682–96	Nicholas I	1825–55
Ivan III (the Great)	1462–1505	Peter I (the Great)	1682–1725	Alexander II	1855–81
Vasili III	1505–33	Catherine I	1725–7	Alexander III	1881–94
Ivan IV (the Terrible)	1533–84	Peter II	1727–30	Nicholas II	1894–1917
Feodor I	1584–98	Anne	1730–40		

POLITICAL LEADERS

Countries and organizations are listed alphabetically. Leaders are named chronologically since 1900. For the major English-speaking nations, relevant details are also given of pre-20th-century leaders, along with a note of any political affiliation.
The list does not distinguish successive terms of office by a single leader.
Listings complete to 2 June 1997.

AUSTRALIA

Chief of State: British monarch, represented by Governor General

Prime Minister

Edmund Barton *Prot*	1901–3
Alfred Deakin *Prot*	1903–4
John Christian Watson *Lab*	1904
George Houston Reid *Free*	1904–5
Alfred Deakin *Prot*	1905–8
Andrew Fisher *Lab*	1908–9
Alfred Deakin *Fusion*	1909–10
Andrew Fisher *Lab*	1910–13
Joseph Cook *Lib*	1913–14

Prime Minister

Andrew Fisher *Lab*	1914–15
William Morris Hughes *Nat Lab*	1915–17
William Morris Hughes *Nat*	1917–23
Stanley Melbourne Bruce *Nat*	1923–9
James Henry Scullin *Lab*	1929–32
Joseph Aloysius Lyons *Un*	1932–9
Earle Christmas Page *Co*	1939
Robert Gordon Menzies *Un*	1939–41
Arthur William Fadden *Co*	1941
John Joseph Curtin *Lab*	1941–5
Francis Michael Forde *Lab*	1945
Joseph Benedict Chifley *Lab*	1945–9
Robert Gordon Menzies *Lib*	1949–66
Harold Edward Holt *Lib*	1966–7
John McEwen *Co*	1967–8

POLITICAL LEADERS (cont.)

Australia (cont.)
Prime Minister

John Grey Gorton *Lib*	1968–71
William McMahon *Lib*	1971–2
Edward Gough Whitlam *Lab*	1972–5
John Malcolm Fraser *Lib*	1975–83
Robert James Lee Hawke *Lab*	1983–91
Paul Keating *Lab*	1991–6
John Howard *Lib*	1996–

Co Country	*Nat Nationalist*
Free Free Trade	*Nat Lab National Labor*
Lab Labor	*Prot Protectionist*
Lib Liberal	*Un United*

AUSTRIA

President

Karl Sätz	1918–20
Michael Hainisch	1920–8
Wilhelm Miklas	1928–38
German rule	1938–45
Karl Renner	1945–50
Theodor Körner	1950–7
Adolf Schärf	1957–65
Franz Jonas	1965–74
Rudolf Kirchsläger	1974–86
Kurt Waldheim	1986–92
Thomas Klestil	1992–

Chancellor

Michael Mayr	1920–1
Johann Schober	1921–2
Walter Breisky	1922
Johann Schober	1922
Ignaz Seipel	1922–4
Rudolph Ramek	1924–6
Ignaz Seipel	1926–9
Ernst Streeruwitz	1929–30
Johann Schober	1930
Carl Vaugoin	1930
Otto Ender	1930–1
Karl Buresch	1931–2
Karl Renner	1918–20

Chancellor

Engelbert Dollfus	1932–4
Kurt von Schuschnigg	1934–8
German rule	1938–45
Karl Renner	1945
Leopold Figl	1945–53
Julius Raab	1953–61
Alfons Gorbach	1961–4
Josef Klaus	1964–70
Bruno Kreisky	1970–83
Fred Sinowetz	1983–6
Franz Vranitzky	1986–

BELGIUM

Prime Minister

Paul de Smet de Nayer	1899–1907
Jules de Trooz	1907–8
Frans Schollaert	1908–11
Charles de Broqueville	1911–18
Gerhard Cooreman	1918
Léon Delacroix	1918–20
Henri Carton de Wiart	1920–1
Georges Theunis	1921–5
Alois van de Vyvere	1925
Prosper Poullet	1925–6
Henri Jaspar	1926–31
Jules Renkin	1931–2
Charles de Broqueville	1932–4
Georges Theunis	1934–5
Paul van Zeeland	1935–7
Paul Émile Janson	1937–8
Paul Henri Spaak	1938–9
Hubert Pierlot	1939–45
Achille van Acker	1945–6
Paul Spaak	1946
Achille van Acker	1946
Camille Huysmans	1946–7
Paul Spaak	1947–9
Gaston Eyskens	1949–50
Jean Pierre Duvieusart	1950
Joseph Pholien	1950–2
Jean van Houtte	1952–4
Achille van Acker	1954–8
Gaston Eyskens	1958–61

Prime Minister

Théodore Lefèvre	1961–5
Pierre Harmel	1965–6
Paul Vanden Boeynants	1966–8
Gaston Eyskens	1968–72
Edmond Leburton	1973–4
Léo Tindemans	1974–8
Paul Vanden Boeynants	1978
Wilfried Martens	1979–81
Marc Eyskens	1981
Wilfried Martens	1981–91
Jean-Luc Dehaene	1992–

CANADA

Chief of State: British monarch, represented by Governor General

Prime Minister

John A MacDonald *Con*	1867–73
Alexander Mackenzie *Lib*	1873–8
John A MacDonald *Con*	1878–91
John J C Abbot *Con*	1891–2
John S D Thompson *Con*	1892–4
Mackenzie Bowell *Con*	1894–6
Charles Tupper *Con*	1896
Wilfrid Laurier *Lib*	1896–1911
Robert Borden *Con*	1911–17
Robert Borden *Con*	1917–20
Arthur Meighen *Con*	1920–1
William Lyon Mackenzie King *Lib*	1921–6
Arthur Meighen *Con*	1926
William Lyon Mackenzie King *Lib*	1926–30
Richard Bedford Bennett *Con*	1930–5
William Lyon Mackenzie King *Lib*	1935–48
Louis St Laurent *Lib*	1948–57
John George Diefenbaker *Con*	1957–63
Lester Bowles Pearson *Lib*	1963–8
Pierre Elliott Trudeau *Lib*	1968–79
Jospeh Clark *Con*	1979–80
Pierre Elliott Trudeau *Lib*	1980–4
John Turner *Lib*	1984
Brian Mulroney *Con*	1984–93
Kim Campbell *Con*	1993
Jean Chrétien *Lib*	1993–
Con Conservative Lib Liberal	

CHINA

Emperor

Kuang-hsü	1875–1908
Hsüan-T'ung	1908–12
Sun Yat-sen	1912
Yüan Shih-k'ai	1912–16
Li Yuan-hung	1916–17
Feng Kuo-chang	1917–18
Hsü Shih-ch'ang	1918–22
Sun Yat-sen *Canton Administration*	1921–5
Li Yuan-hung	1922
Ts'ao K'un	1923–4
Tuan Ch'i-jui	1924–6
Civil Disorder	1926–7
Chang Tso-lin	1927–8
Chiang Kai-shek	1928–31
Ch'eng Ming-hsu *Acting President*	1931–2
Lin Sen	1932–43
Wang Ching-wei *in Japanese-occupied territory*	1940–4
Chiang Kai-shek	1943–9
Civil War	1945–9
Li Tsung-jen	1949

People's Republic of China
President

Mao Zedong (Mao Tse-tung)	1949–59
Liu Shaoqi	1959–68
Dong Biwu	1968–75
Zhu De	1975–6
Sung Qingling	1976–8
Ye Jianying	1978–83
Li Xiannian (Li Hsien-nien)	1983–8
Yang Shangkun	1988–93
Jiang Zemin	1993–

Prime Minister

Jung-lu	1901–3
Prince Ch'ing	1903–11
Lu Cheng-hsiang	1912
Chao Ping-chiin	1912–13
Sun Pao-chi	1913–14
no Prime Minister	1914–16

POLITICAL LEADERS (cont.)

China (cont.)
Prime Minister

Chang-hsün	1916–17
Tuan ch'i-jui	1917
Ch'ien Neng-hsün	1918–19
Kung Hsin-chan	1919
Chin Yün-p'eng	1919–20
Sa Chen-ping	1920
Chin Yün-p'eng	1920–1
Liang Shihi	1921–2
Yen Hui-ching	1922
Chow Tzu-ch'i	1922
Yen Hui-ching	1922
Wang Ch'ung-hui	1922
Wang Ta-hsieh	1922–3
Chang Shao-ts'êng	1923
Kao Ling-wei	1923–4
Jun Pao-ch'i	1924
Ku Wei-chiin	1924
Yen Hui-ch'ing	1924
Huang Fu	1924–5
Tuan Ch'i-jui	1925
Hsu Shih-ying	1925–6
Chia Teh-yao	1926
Hu Wei-te	1926
Yen Hui-ch'ing	1926
Tu Hsi-kuei	1926
Ku Wei-chün	1926–7
Civil Disorder	1927
Executive Council	1927
P'an Fu	1927–9
T'an Yen-kai	1929–30
Sung Tzu-wen *Acting Prime Minister*	1930
Wang Ching-wei	1930
Chiang Kai-shek	1930–1
Sun Fo	1931–2
Wang Ching-wei	1932–5
Chiang Kai-shek	1935–7
Wang Ch'ung-hui *Acting Prime Minister*	1937–8
K'ung Hsiang-hsi	1938–9
Chiang Kai-shek	1939–44
Sung Tzu-wen	1944–7
Civil War	1945–9
Chang Ch'ün	1947–8
Wong Wen-hao	1948

Prime Minister

Sun Fo	1948–9
Ho Ying-ch'in	1949
Yen Hsi-shan	1949
Zhou Enlai (Chou En-lai)	1949–76
Hua Guofeng	1976–80
Zhao Ziyang (Chao Tzu-yang)	1980–7
Li Peng	1987–

Communist Party
Chairman

Mao Zedong (Mao Tse-tung)	1935–76
Hua Guofeng	1976–81
Hu Yaobang	1981–2

General Secretary

Hu Yaobang	1982–7
Zhao Ziyang (Chao Tzu-yang)	1987–9
Jiang Zemin	1989–

DENMARK

Prime Minister

H Sehested	1900–1
J H Deuntzer	1901–5
J C Christensen	1905–8
N Neergaard	1908–9
L Holstein-Ledreborg	1909
C Th Zahle	1909–10
Klaus Berntsen	1910–13
C Th Zahle	1913–20
Otto Liebe	1920
M P Friis	1920
N Neergaard	1920–4
Thorvald Stauning	1924–6
Th Madsen-Mygdal	1926–9
Thorvald Stauning	1929–42
Wilhelm Buhl	1942
Erik Scavenius	1942–3
No government	1943–5
Wilhelm Buhl	1945

Prime Minister

Knud Kristensen	1945–7
Hans Hedtoft	1947–50
Erik Eriksen	1950–3
Hans Hedtoft	1953–5
Hans Christian Hansen	1955–60
Viggo Kampmann	1960–2
Jens Otto Krag	1962–8
Hilmar Baunsgaard	1968–71
Jens Otto Krag	1971–2
Anker Jorgensen	1972–3
Poul Hartling	1973–5
Anker Jorgensen	1975–82
Poul Schlüter	1982–93
Poul Nyrup Rasmussen	1993–

FINLAND

President

Kaarlo Juho Ståhlberg	1919–25
Lauri Kristian Relander	1925–31
Pehr Evind Svinhufvud	1931–7
Kyösti Kallio	1937–40
Risto Ryti	1940–4
Carl Gustaf Mannerheim	1944–6
Juho Kusti Paasikivi	1946–56
Urho Kekkonen	1956–81
Mauno Koivisto	1982–94
Martti Ahtisaari	1994–

Prime Minister

Juho Kusti Pasaikivi	1918
Lauri Johannes Ingman	1918–19
Kaarlo Castrén	1919
Juho Vennola	1919–20
Rafael Erich	1920–1
Juho Vennola	1921–2
Aino Kaarlo Cajander	1922
Kyösti Kallio	1922–4
Aino Kaarlo Cajander	1924
Lauri Johannes Ingman	1924–5
Antti Agaton Tulenheimo	1925
Kyösti Kallio	1925–6
Väinö Tanner	1926–7

Prime Minister

Juho Emil Sunila	1927–8
Oskari Mantere	1928–9
Kyösti Kallio	1929–30
Pehr Evind Svinhufvud	1930–1
Juho Emil Sunila	1931–2
Toivo Kivimäki	1932–6
Kyösti Kallio	1936–7
Aino Kaarlo Cajander	1937–9
Risto Ryti	1939–41
Johann Rangell	1941–3
Edwin Linkomies	1943–4
Andreas Hackzell	1944
Urho Jonas Castrén	1944
Juho Kusti Paasikivi	1944–5
Mauno Pekkala	1946–8
Karl August Fagerholm	1948–50
Urho Kekkonen	1950–3
Sakari Tuomioja	1953–4
Ralf Törngren	1954
Urho Kekkonen	1954–6
Karl August Fagerholm	1956–7
Väinö Johannes Sukselainen	1957
Rainer von Fieandt	1957–8
Reino Lisakki Kuuskoski	1958
Karl August Fagerholm	1958–9
Väinö Johannes Sukselainen	1959–61
Martti Miettunen	1961–2
Ahti Karjalainen	1962–3
Reino Ragnar Lehto	1963–4
Johannes Virolainen	1964–6
Rafael Paasio	1966–8
Mauno Koivisto	1968–70
Teuvo Ensio Aura	1970
Ahti Karjalainen	1970–1
Teuvo Ensio Aura	1971–2
Rafael Paasio	1972
Kalevi Sorsa	1972–5
Keijo Antero Liinamaa	1975
Martti Miettunen	1975–7
Kalevi Sorsa	1977–9
Mauno Koivisto	1979–82
Kalevi Sorsa	1982–87
Harri Holkeri	1987–91
Esko Aho	1991–5
Paavo Lipponen	1995–

FRANCE

President

Third Republic

Emile Loubet	1899–1906
Armand Fallières	1906–13
Raymond Poincaré	1913–20
Paul Deschanel	1920
Alexandre Millerand	1920–4
Gaston Doumergue	1924–31
Paul Doumer	1931–2
Albert Lebrun	1932–40

Fourth Republic

Vincent Auriol	1947–54
René Coty	1954–8

Fifth Republic

Charles de Gaulle	1958–69
George Pompidou	1969–74
Valéry Giscard d'Estaing	1974–81
François Mitterrand	1981–95
Jacques Chirac	1995–

Prime Minister

Third Republic

Pierre Waldeck-Rousseau	1899–1902
Emile Combes	1902–5
Maurice Rouvier	1905–6
Jean Sarrien	1906
Georges Clemenceau	1906–9
Aristide Briand	1909–11
Ernest Monis	1911
Joseph Caillaux	1911–12
Raymond Poincaré	1912–13
Aristide Briand	1913
Louis Barthou	1913
Gaston Doumergue	1913–14
Alexandre Ribot	1914
René Viviani	1914–15
Aristide Briand	1915–17
Alexandre Ribot	1917
Paul Painlevé	1917
Georges Clemenceau	1917–20
Alexandre Millerand	1920
Georges Leygues	1920–1

Prime Minister

Aristide Briand	1921–2
Raymond Poincaré	1922–4
Frédéric François-Marsal	1924
Edouard Herriot	1924–5
Paul Painlevé	1925
Aristide Briand	1925–6
Edouard Herriot	1926
Raymond Poincaré	1926–9
Aristide Briand	1929
André Tardieu	1929–30
Camille Chautemps	1930
André Tardieu	1930
Théodore Steeg	1930–1
Pierre Laval	1931–2
André Tardieu	1932
Edouard Herriot	1932
Joseph Paul-Boncour	1932–3
Edouard Daladier	1933
Albert Sarrault	1933
Camille Chautemps	1933–4
Edouard Daladier	1934
Gaston Doumergue	1934
Pierre-Etienne Flandin	1934–5
Fernand Bouisson	1935
Pierre Laval	1935–6
Albert Sarrault	1936
Léon Blum	1936–7
Camille Chautemps	1937–8
Léon Blum	1938
Edouard Daladier	1938–40
Paul Reynaud	1940
Philippe Pétain	1940

Vichy Government

Philippe Pétain	1940–4

Provisional Government of the French Republic

Charles de Gaulle	1944–6
Félix Gouin	1946
Georges Bidault	1946

Fourth Republic

Léon Blum	1946–7
Paul Ramadier	1947
Robert Schuman	1947–8
André Marie	1948
Robert Schuman	1948

Prime Minister	
Henri Queuille	1948–9
Georges Bidault	1949–50
Henri Queuille	1950
René Pleven	1950–1
Henri Queuille	1951
René Pleven	1951–2
Edgar Faure	1952
Antoine Pinay	1952–3
René Mayer	1953
Joseph Laniel	1953–4
Pierre Mendès-France	1954–5
Edgar Faure	1955–6
Guy Mollet	1956–7
Maurice Bourgès-Maunoury	1957
Félix Gaillard	1957–8
Pierre Pfimlin	1958
Charles de Gaulle	1958–9

Fifth Republic

Michel Debré	1959–62
Georges Pompidou	1962–8
Maurice Couve de Murville	1968–9
Jacques Chaban Delmas	1969–72
Pierre Mesmer	1972–4
Jacques Chirac	1974–6
Raymond Barre	1976–81
Pierre Mauroy	1981–4
Laurent Fabius	1984–6
Jacques Chirac	1986–8
Michel Rocard	1988–91
Édith Cresson	1991–92
Pierre Bérégovoy	1992–93
Edouard Balladur	1993–95
Alain Juppé	1995–7
Lionel Jospin	1997–

GERMANY

German Empire
Emperor

Wilhelm II	1888–1918

Chancellor

Theobald von Bethmann-Hollweg	1909–17

Chancellor	
Georg Michaelis	1917
Georg Graf von Hertling	1917–18
Prince Max of Baden	1918
Friedrich Ebert	1918

German Republic
President

Friedrich Ebert	1919–25
Paul von Hindenburg	1925–34

Reich Chancellor

Philipp Scheidemann	1919
Gustav Bauer	1919–20
Hermann Müller	1920
Konstantin Fehrenbach	1920–1
Karl Joseph Wirth	1921–2
Wilhelm Cuno	1922–3
Gustav Stresemann	1923
Wilhelm Marx	1923–4
Hans Luther	1925–6
Wilhelm Marx	1926–8
Hermann Müller	1928–30
Heinrich Brüning	1930–2
Franz von Papen	1932
Kurt von Sleicher	1932–3
Adolf Hitler	1933

Chancellor and Führer

Adolf Hitler	1934–45
Karl Dönitz	1945

German Democratic Republic (East Germany)
President

Wilhelm Pieck	1949–60

Chairman of the Council of State

Walter Ernst Karl Ulbricht	1960–73
Willi Stoph	1973–6
Erich Honecker	1976–89
Egon Krenz	1989
Gregor Gysi	1989–90

POLITICAL LEADERS (cont.)

German Democratic Republic (East Germany)
(cont.)
General Secretary as Chairman
Premier

Otto Grotewohl	1949–64
Willi Stoph	1964–73
Horst Sindermann	1973–6
Willi Stoph	1976–89
Hans Modrow	1989–90
Lothar de Maizière	1990

German Federal Republic (West Germany)
President

Theodor Heuss	1949–59
Heinrich Lübke	1959–69
Gustav Heinemann	1969–74
Walter Scheel	1974–9
Karl Carstens	1979–84
Richard von Weizsäcker	1984–90

Chancellor

Konrad Adenauer	1949–63
Ludwig Erhard	1963–6
Kurt Georg Kiesinger	1966–9
Willy Brandt	1969–74
Helmut Schmidt	1974–82
Helmut Kohl	1982–90

Germany
President

Richard von Weizsäcker	1990–4
Roman Herzog	1994–

Chancellor

Helmut Kohl	1990–

GREECE

Republic
President

Paul Koundouriotis	1924–6
Theodore Pangalos	1926

President

Paul Koundouriotis	1926–9
Alexander T Zaïmis	1929–35

Republic
President

George Papadopoulos	1973
Phaedon Gizikis	1973–4
Michael Stasinopoulos	1974–5
Constantine Tsatsos	1975–80
Constantine Karamanlis	1980–5
Christos Sartzetakis	1985–90
Constantine Karamanlis	1990–5
Constantine Stephanopoulos	1995–

Prime Minister

George Theotokis	1899–1901
Alexander T Zaïmis	1901–2
Theodore Diligiannis	1902–3
George Theotokis	1903
Demetrius G Rallis	1903
George Theotokis	1903–4
Theodore Deligiannis	1904–5
Demetrius G Rallis	1905
George Theotokis	1905–9
Demetrius G Rallis	1909
Kyriakoulis P Mavromichalis	1909–10
Stephen N Dragoumis	1910
Eleftherios K Venizelos	1910–15
Demetrius P Gounaris	1915
Eleftherios K Venizelos	1915
Alexander T Zaïmis	1915
Stephen Skouloudis	1915–16
Alexander T Zaïmis	1916
Nicholas P Kalogeropoulos	1916
Spyridon Lambros	1916–17
Alexander T Zaïmis	1917
Eleftherios K Venizelos	1917–20
Demetrius G Rallis	1920–1
Nicholas P Kalogeropoulos	1921
Demetrius P Gounaris	1921–2
Nicholas Stratos	1922
Peter E Protopapadakis	1922
Nicholas Triandaphyllakos	1922

Prime Minister

Sortirios Krokidas	1922
Alexander T Zaïmis	1922
Stylianos Gonatas	1922–3
Eleftherios Venizelos	1924
George Kaphandaris	1924
Alexander Papanastasiou	1924
Themistocles Sophoulis	1924
Andreas Michalakopoulos	1924–5
Alexander N Chatzikyriakos	1925–6
Theodore Pangalos	1926
Athanasius Eftaxias	1926
George Kondylis	1926
Alexander T Zaïmis	1926–8
Eleftherios K Venizelos	1928–32
Alexander Papanastasiou	1932
Eleftherios K Venizelos	1932
Panagiotis Tsaldaris	1932–3
Eleftherios K Venizelos	1933
Nicholas Plastiras	1933
Alexander Othonaos	1933
Panagiotis Tsaldaris	1933–5
George Kondylis	1935
Constantine Demertzis	1935–6
John Metaxas	1936–41
Alexander Koryzis	1941

Chairman of Ministers
George II	1941

German Occupation Emmanuel
Tsouderos	1941
George Tsolakoglou	1941–2
Constantine Logothetopoulos	1942–3
John Rallis	1943–4

Government in exile
Emmanuel Tsouderos	1941–4
Sophocles Venizelos	1944
George Papandreou	1944–5

Post-war
Nicholas Plastiras	1945
Peter Voulgaris	1945
Damaskinos, Archbishop of Athens	1945
Panagiotis Kanellopoulos	1945
Themistocles Sophoulis	1945–6
Panagiotis Politzas	1946
Constantine Tsaldaris	1946–7
Demetrius Maximos	1947
Constantine Tsaldaris	1947

Prime Minister

Themistocles Sophoulis	1947–9
Alexander Diomedes	1949–50
John Theotokis	1950
Sophocles Venizelos	1950
Nicholas Plastiras	1950
Sophocles Venizelos	1950–1
Nicholas Plastiras	1951
Demetrius Kiusopoulos	1952
Alexander Papagos	1952–5
Stephen C Stefanopoulos	1955
Constantine Karamanlis	1955–8
Constantine Georgakopoulos	1958
Constantine Karamanlis	1958–61
Constantine Dovas	1961
Constantine Karamanlis	1961–3
Panagiotis Pipinellis	1963
Stylianos Mavromichalis	1963
George Papandreou	1963
John Parskevopoulos	1963–4
George Papandreou	1964–5
George Athanasiadis-Novas	1965
Elias Tsirimokos	1965
Stephen C Stafanopoulos	1965–6
John Paraskevopoulos	1966–7
Panagiotis Kanellopoulos	1967
Military Junta	1967–74
Constantine Kollias	1967
George Papadopoulos	1967–73
Spyridon Markezinis	1973
Adamantios Androutsopoulos	1973–4
Constantine Karamanlis	1974–80
George Rallis	1980–1
Andreas Papandreou	1981–9
Tzannis Tzannetakis	1989
Xenofon Zolotas	1989–90
Constantine Mitsotakis	1990–93
Andreas Papandreou	1993–6
Kostas Simitis	1996–

INDIA

President

Rajendra Prasad	1950–62
Sarvepalli Radhakrishnan	1962–7
Zakir Husain	1967–9

POLITICAL LEADERS (cont.)

India (cont.)
President

Varahagiri Venkatagiri *Acting*	1969
Mohammed Hidayatullah *Acting*	1969
Varahagiri Venkatagiri	1969–74
Fakhruddin Ali Ahmed	1974–7
B D Jatti *Acting*	1977
Neelam Sanjiva Reddy	1977–82
Giani Zail Singh	1982–7
Ramaswami Venkataraman	1987–92
Shankar Dayal Sharma	1992–

Prime Minister

Jawaharlal Nehru	1947–64
Gulzari Lal Nanda *Acting*	1964
Lal Bahadur Shastri	1964–6
Gulzari Lal Nanda *Acting*	1966
Indira Gandhi	1966–77
Morarji Desai	1977–9
Charan Singh	1979–80
Indira Gandhi	1980–4
Rajiv Gandhi	1984–9
Vishwanath Pratap Singh	1989–90
Chandra Shekhar	1990–1
P V Narasimha Rao	1991–6
Atal Behari Vajpayee	1996
H D Deve Gowda	1996–7
Inder Kumar Gujral	1997–

IRELAND

Governor General

Timothy Michael Healy	1922–7
James McNeill	1927–32
Donald Buckley	1932–6

President

Douglas Hyde	1938–45
Sean Thomas O'Kelly	1945–59
Eamon de Valera	1959–73
Erskine H Childers	1973–4
Carroll Daly	1974–6

President

Patrick J Hillery	1976–90
Mary Robinson	1990–7

Prime Minister

Eamon de Valera	1919–21
Arthur Griffiths	1922
William Cosgrave	1922–32
Eamon de Valera	1932–48
John Aloysius Costello	1948–51
Eamon de Valera	1951–4
John Aloysius Costello	1954–7
Eamon de Valera	1957–9
Sean Lemass	1959–66
John Lynch	1966–73
Liam Cosgrave	1973–7
John Lynch	1977–9
Charles Haughey	1979–82
Garrett FitzGerald	1982–7
Charles Haughey	1987–92
Albert Reynolds	1992–94
John Bruton	1994–

ITALY

Italian Republic
President

Enrico de Nicola	1946–8
Luigi Einaudi	1948–55
Giovanni Gronchi	1955–62
Antonio Segni	1962–4
Giuseppe Saragat	1964–71
Giovanni Leone	1971–8
Alessandro Pertini	1978–85
Francesco Cossiga	1985–92
Oscar Luigi Scalfaro	1992–

Kingdom of Italy
Prime Minister

Giuseppe Saracco	1900–1
Giuseppe Zanardelli	1901–3
Giovanni Giolitti	1903–5

Prime Minister

Alessandro Fortis	1905–6
Sydney Sonnino	1906
Giovanni Giolitti	1906–9
Sydney Sonnino	1909–10
Luigi Luzzatti	1910–11
Giovanni Giolitti	1911–14
Antonio Salandra	1914–16
Paolo Boselli	1916–17
Vittorio Emmanuele Orlando	1917–19
Francesco Saveiro Nitti	1919–20
Giovanni Giolitti	1920–1
Ivanoe Bonomi	1921–2
Luigi Facta	1922
Benito Mussolini	1922–43
Pietro Badoglio	1943–4
Ivanoe Bonomi	1944–5
Ferrucio Parri	1945
Alcide de Gasperi	1945

Italian Republic

Alcide De Gasperi	1946–53
Giuseppe Pella	1953–4
Amintore Fanfani	1954
Mario Scelba	1954–5
Antonio Segni	1955–7
Adone Zoli	1957–8
Amintore Fanfani	1958–9
Antonio Segni	1959–60
Fernando Tambroni	1960
Amintore Fanfani	1960–3
Giovanni Leone	1963
Aldo Moro	1963–8
Giovanni Leone	1968
Mariano Rumor	1968–70
Emilio Colombo	1970–2
Giulio Andreotti	1972–4
Aldo Moro	1974–6
Giulio Andreotti	1976–8
Francisco Cossiga	1979–80
Arnaldo Forlani	1980–1
Giovanni Spadolini	1981–2
Amintore Fanfani	1982–3
Bettino Craxi	1983–7
Amintore Fanfani	1987
Giovanni Goria	1987–8
Ciriaco de Mita	1988–9
Giulio Andreotti	1989–92

Prime Minister

Giuliano Amato	1992–93
Carlo Azeglio Ciampi	1993–94
Silvio Berlusconi	1994–95
Lamberto Dini	1995–6
Romano Prodi	1996–

JAPAN

Chief of State (Emperor)

Mutsuhito (Meiji)	1867–1912
Yoshihito (Taishō)	1912–26
Hirohito (Shōwa)	1926–89
Akihito (Heisei)	1989–

Prime Minister

Hirobumi Itō	1900–1
Tarō Katsura	1901–6
Kimmochi Saionji	1906–8
Tarō Katsura	1908–11
Kimmochi Saionji	1911–12
Tarō Katsura	1912–13
Gonnohyōe Yamamoto	1913–14
Shigenobu Ōkuma	1914–16
Masatake Terauchi	1916–18
Takashi Hara	1918–21
Korekiyo Takahashi	1921–2
Tomosaburō Katō	1922–3
Gonnohyōe Yamamoto	1923–4
Keigo Kiyoura	1924
Takaaki Katō	1924–6
Reijirō Wakatsuki	1926–7
Giichi Tanaka	1927–9
Osachi Hamaguchi	1929–31
Reijirō Wakatsuki	1931
Tsuyoshi Inukai	1931–2
Makoto Saitō	1932–4
Keisuke Okada	1934–6
Kōki Hirota	1936–7
Senjūrō Hayashi	1937
Fumimaro Konoe	1937–9
Kiichirō Hiranuma	1939
Nobuyuki Abe	1939–40
Mitsumasa Yonai	1940
Fumimaro Konoe	1940–1

POLITICAL LEADERS (cont.)

Japan (cont.)
Prime Minister

Hideki Tōjō	1941–4
Kuniaki Koiso	1944–5
Kantarō Suzuki	1945
Naruhiko Higashikuni	1945
Kijūrō Shidehara	1945–6
Shigeru Yoshida	1946–7
Tetsu Katayama	1947–8
Hitoshi Ashida	1948
Shigeru Yoshida	1948–54
Ichirō Hatoyama	1954–6
Tanzan Ishibashi	1956–7
Nobusuke Kishi	1957–60
Hayato Ikeda	1960–4
Eisaku Satō	1964–72
Kakuei Tanaka	1972–4
Takeo Miki	1974–6
Takeo Fukuda	1976–8
Masayoshi Ōhira	1978–80
Zenkō Suzuki	1980–2
Yasuhiro Nakasone	1982–7
Noburu Takeshita	1987–9
Sasuke Uno	1989
Toshiki Kaifu	1989–91
Kiichi Miyazawa	1991–93
Morihiro Hosokawa	1993–94
Tsutomu Hata	1994
Tomiichi Murayama	1994–6
Ryutaro Hashimoto	1996–

LUXEMBOURG

Prime Minister

Paul Eyschen	1889–1915
Mathias Mongenast	1915
Hubert Loutsch	1915–16
Victor Thorn	1916–17
Léon Kaufmann	1917–18
Emil Reuter	1918–25
Pierre Prum	1925–6
Joseph Bech	1926–37
Pierre Dupont *in exile 1940–4*	1937–53
Joseph Bech	1953–8

Prime Minister

Pierre Frieden	1958
Pierre Werner	1959–69
Gaston Thorn	1969–79
Pierre Werner	1979–84
Jacques Santer	1984–95
Jean-Claude Juncker	1995–

THE NETHERLANDS

Prime Minister

Nicholas G Pierson	1897–1901
Abraham Kuyper	1901–5
Theodoor H de Meester	1905–8
Theodorus Heemskerk	1908–13
Pieter W A Cort van der Linden	1913–18
Charles J M Ruys de Beerenbrouck	1918–25
Hendrikus Colijn	1925–6
Dirk J de Geer	1926
Charles J M Ruys de Beerenbrouck	1926–33
Hendrikus Colijn	1933–9
Dirk J de Geer	1939–40
Pieter S Gerbrandy *in exile*	1940–5
Willem Schemerhorn/Willem Drees	1945–6
Louis J M Beel	1946–8
Willem Drees/Josephus R H van Schaik	1948–51
Willem Drees	1951–8
Louis J M Beel	1958–9
Jan E de Quay	1959–63
Victor G M Marijnen	1963–5
Joseph M L T Cals	1965–6
Jelle Zijlstra	1966–7
Petrus J S de Jong	1967–71
Barend W Biesheuvel	1971–3
Joop M Den Uyl	1973–7
Andreas A M van Agt	1977–82
Ruud F M Lubbers	1982–94
Wim Kok	1994–

NEW ZEALAND

Chief of State: British monarch, represented by Governor General

Prime Minister

Henry Sewell	1856
William Fox	1856
Edward William Stafford	1856–61
William Fox	1861–2
Alfred Domett	1862–3
Frederick Whitaker	1863–4
Frederick Aloysius Weld	1864–5
Edward William Stafford	1865–9
William Fox	1869–72
Edward William Stafford	1872
William Fox	1873
Julius Vogel	1873–5
Daniel Pollen	1875–6
Julius Vogel	1876
Harry Albert Atkinson	1876–7
George Grey	1877–9
John Hall	1879–82
Frederick Whitaker	1882–3
Harry Albert Atkinson	1883–4
Robert Stout	1884
Harry Albert Atkinson	1884
Robert Stout	1884–7
Harry Albert Atkinson	1887–91
John Ballance	1891–3
Richard John Seddon *Lib*	1893–1906
William Hall-Jones *Lib*	1906
Joseph George Ward *Lib/Nat*	1906–12
Thomas Mackenzie *Nat*	1912
William Ferguson Massey *Ref*	1912–25
Francis Henry Dillon Bell *Ref*	1925
Joseph Gordon Coates *Ref*	1925–8
Joseph George Ward *Lib/Nat*	1928–30
George William Forbes *Un*	1930–5
Michael Joseph Savage *Lab*	1935–40
Peter Fraser *Lab*	1940–9
Sidney George Holland *Nat*	1949–57
Keith Jacka Holyoake *Nat*	1957
Walter Nash *Lab*	1957–60
Keith Jacka Holyoake *Nat*	1960–72
John Ross Marshall *Nat*	1972
Norman Eric Kirk *Lab*	1972–4

Prime Minister

Wallace Edward Rowling *Lab*	1974–5
Robert David Muldoon *Nat*	1975–84
David Russell Lange *Lab*	1984–89
Geoffrey Palmer *Lab*	1989–90
Mike Moore *Lab*	1990
Jim Bolger *Nat*	1990–

Lab Labour		*Ref Reform*
Lib Liberal		*Un United*
Nat National		

PORTUGAL

President

1st Republic

Teófilo Braga	1910–11
Manuel José de Arriaga	1911–15
Teófilo Braga	1915
Bernardino Machado	1915–17
Sidónio Pais	1917–18
João do Canto e Castro	1918–19
António José de Almeida	1919–23
Manuel Teixeira Gomes	1923–5
Bernardino Machado	1925–6

New State

Military Junta (José Mendes Cabeçadas)	1926
Military Junta (Manuel de Oliveira Gomes da Costa)	1926
António Oscar Fragoso Carmona	1926–51
Francisco Craveiro Lopes	1951–8
Américo de Deus Tomás	1958–74

2nd Republic

Military Junta (António Spínola)	1974
Military Junta (Francisco da Costa Gomes)	1974–6

3rd Republic

António dos Santos Ramalho Eanes	1976–86
Mario Soares	1986–96
Jorge Sampaio	1996–

Prime Minister

António de Oliveira Salazar	1932–68
Marcelo Caetano	1968–74

POLITICAL LEADERS (cont.)

Portugal (cont.)
Prime Minister

Adelino da Palma Carlos	1974
Vasco Gonçalves	1974–5
José Pinheiro de Azevedo	1975–6
Mário Soares	1976–8
Alfredo Nobre da Costa	1978
Carlos Alberto de Mota Pinto	1978–9
Maria de Lurdes Pintasilgo	1979
Francisco de Sá Carneiro	1980–1
Francisco Pinto Balsemao	1981–3
Mário Soares	1983–5
Aníbal Cavaço Silva	1985–95
António Guterres	1995–

RUSSIAN FEDERATION

With the disbandment of the USSR in 1991, the Russian Federation became an independent Republic.

President

Boris Yeltsin	1991–

Prime Minister

Viktor Chernomyrdin	1991–

SPAIN

Second Republic
President

Niceto Alcalá Zamora y Torres	1931–6
Diego Martínez Barrio *Acting President*	1936

Civil War

Manuel Azaña y Díez	1936–9
Miguel Cabanellas Ferrer	1936–9

Nationalist Government
Chief of State

Francisco Franco Bahamonde	1936–75

Monarch

Juan Carlos I	1975–

Prime Minister

Marcelo de Azcárraga y Palmero	1900–1
Práxedes Mateo Sagasta	1901–2
Francisco Silvela y Le-Vielleuze	1902–3
Raimundo Fernández Villaverde	1903
Antonio Maura y Montaner	1903–4
Marcelo de Azcárraga y Palmero	1904–5
Raimundo Fernández Villaverde	1905
Eugenio Montero Ríos	1905
Segismundo Moret y Prendergast	1905–6
José López Domínguez	1906
Segismundo Moret y Prendergast	1906
Antonio Aguilar y Correa	1906–7
Antonio Maura y Montaner	1907–9
Segismundo Moret y Prendergast	1909–10
José Canalejas y Méndez	1910–12
Álvaro Figueroa y Torres	1912
Manuel García Prieto	1912–13
Eduardo Dato y Iradier	1913–15
Álvaro Figueroa y Torres	1915–17
Manuel García Prieto	1917
Eduardo Dato y Iradier	1917
Manuel García Prieto	1917–18
Antonio Maura y Montaner	1918
Manuel García Prieto	1918
Álvaro Figueroa y Torres	1918–19
Antonio Maura y Montaner	1919
Joaquín Sánchez de Toca	1919
Manuel Allendesalazar	1919–20
Eduardo Dato y Iradier	1920–1
Gabino Bugallal Araujo *Acting*	1921
Manuel Allendesalazar	1921
Antonio Maura y Montaner	1921–2
José Sánchez Guerra y Martffnez	1922
Manuel García Prieto	1922–3
Miguel Primo de Rivera y Oraneja	1923–30
Dámaso Berenguer y Fusté	1930–1
Juan Bautista Aznar-Cabañas	1931
Niceto Alcalá Zamora y Torres	1931
Manuel Azaña y Díez	1931–3
Alejandro Lerroux y García	1933
Diego Martínez Barrio	1933

Prime Minister	
Alejandro Lerroux y García	1933 4
Ricardo Samper Ibáñez	1934
Alejandro Lerroux y García	1934–5
Joaquín Chapaprieta y Terragosa	1935
Manuel Portela Valladares	1935–6
Manuel Azaña y Diez	1936
Santiago Casares Quiroga	1936
Diego Martínez Barrio	1936
José Giral y Pereyra	1936
Francisco Largo Caballero	1936–7
Juan Negrín	1937–9

Chairman of the Council of Ministers	
Francisco Franco Bahamonde	1939–73

Prime Minister	
Torcuato Fernández Miranda y Hevffa	
Acting Prime Minister	1973
Carlos Arias Navarro	1973–6
Adolfo Suárez	1976–81
Calvo Sotelo	1981–2
Felipe González	1982–96
José María Aznar	1996–

SWEDEN

Prime Minister

Fredrik von Otter	1900–2
Erik Gustaf Boström	1902–5
Johan Ramstedt	1905
Christian Lundeberg	1905
Karl Staaf	1905–6
Arvid Lindman	1906–11
Karl Staaf	1911–14
Hjalmar Hammarskjöld	1914–17
Carl Swartz	1917
Nils Edén	1917–20
Hjalmar Branting	1920
Louis de Geer	1920–1
Oscar von Sydow	1921
Hjalmar Branting	1921–3
Ernst Trygger	1923–4
Hjalmar Branting	1924–5

Prime Minister	
Rickard Sandler	1925–6
Carl Gustaf Ekman	1926–8
Arvid Lindman	1928–30
Carl Gustaf Ekman	1930–2
Felix Hamrin	1932
Per Albin Hansson	1932–6
Axel Pehrsson-Branstorp	1936
Per Albin Hansson	1936–46
Tage Erlander	1946–69
Olof Palme	1969–76
Thorbjörn Fälldin	1976–8
Ola Ullsten	1978–9
Thorbjörn Fälldin	1979–82
Olof Palme	1982–6
Ingvar Carlsson	1986–91
Carl Bildt	1991–94
Ingvar Carlsson	1994–6
Göran Persson	1996–

UNITED KINGDOM

Prime Minister

Robert Walpole *Whig*	1721–42
Earl of Wilmington (Spencer Compton)	
Whig	1742–3
Henry Pelham *Whig*	1743–54
Duke of Newcastle (Thomas	
Pelham-Holles) *Whig*	1754–6
Duke of Devonshire (William Cavendish)	
Whig	1756–7
Duke of Newcastle *Whig*	1757–62
Earl of Bute (John Stuart) *Tory*	1762–3
George Grenville *Whig*	1763–5
Marquess of Rockingham (Charles	
Watson Wentworth) *Whig*	1765–6
Duke of Grafton (Augustus Henry	
Fitzroy) *Whig*	1766–70
Lord North (Frederick North) *Tory*	1770–82
Marquess of Rockingham *Whig*	1782
Earl of Shelburne (William	
Petty-Fitzmaurice) *Whig*	1782–3
Duke of Portland (William Henry	
Cavendish) *Coal*	1783
William Pitt *Tory*	1783–1801
Henry Addington *Tory*	1801–4

♛ POLITICAL LEADERS (cont.)

United Kingdom (cont.)
Prime Minister

William Pitt *Tory*	1804–6
Lord Grenville (William Wyndham) *Whig*	1806–7
Duke of Portland *Tory*	1807–9
Spencer Perceval *Tory*	1809–12
Earl of Liverpool (Robert Banks Jenkinson) *Tory*	1812–27
George Canning *Tory*	1827
Viscount Goderich (Frederick John Robinson) *Tory*	1827–8
Duke of Wellington (Arthur Wellesley) *Tory*	1828–30
Earl Grey (Charles Grey) *Whig*	1830–4
Viscount Melbourne (William Lamb) *Whig*	1834
Robert Peel *Con*	1834–5
Viscount Melbourne *Whig*	1835–41
Robert Peel *Con*	1841–6
Lord John Russell *Lib*	1846–52
Earl of Derby (Edward George Stanley) *Con*	1852
Lord Aberdeen (George Hamilton-Gordon) *Peelite*	1852–5
Viscount Palmerston (Henry John Temple) *Lib*	1855–8
Earl of Derby *Con*	1858–9
Viscount Palmerston *Lib*	1859–65
Lord John Russell *Lib*	1865–6
Earl of Derby *Con*	1866–8
Benjamin Disraeli *Con*	1868
William Ewart Gladstone *Lib*	1868–74
Benjamin Disraeli *Con*	1874–80
William Ewart Gladstone *Lib*	1880–5
Marquess of Salisbury (Robert Gascoyne-Cecil) *Con*	1885–6
William Ewart Gladstone *Lib*	1886
Marquess of Salisbury *Con*	1886–92
William Ewart Gladstone *Lib*	1892–4
Earl of Rosebery (Archibald Philip Primrose) *Lib*	1894–5
Marquess of Salisbury *Con*	1895–1902
Arthur James Balfour *Con*	1902–5
Henry Campbell-Bannerman *Lib*	1905–8
Herbert Henry Asquith *Lib*	1908–15
Herbert Henry Asquith *Coal*	1915–16

Prime Minister

David Lloyd George *Coal*	1916–22
Andrew Bonar Law *Con*	1922–3
Stanley Baldwin *Con*	1923–4
James Ramsay MacDonald *Lab*	1924
Stanley Baldwin *Con*	1924–9
James Ramsay MacDonald *Lab*	1929–31
James Ramsay MacDonald *Nat*	1931–5
Stanley Baldwin *Nat*	1935–7
Arthur Neville Chamberlain *Nat*	1937–40
Winston Churchill *Coal*	1940–5
Clement Attlee *Lab*	1945–51
Winston Churchill *Con*	1951–5
Anthony Eden *Con*	1955–7
Harold Macmillan *Con*	1957–63
Alec Douglas-Home *Con*	1963–4
Harold Wilson *Lab*	1964–70
Edward Heath *Con*	1970–4
Harold Wilson *Lab*	1974–6
James Callaghan *Lab*	1976–9
Margaret Thatcher *Con*	1979–90
John Major *Con*	1990–7
Tony Blair *Lab*	1997–

Coal Coalition	*Lib* Liberal
Con Conservative	*Nat* Nationalist
Lab Labour	

UNITED STATES OF AMERICA

President

Vice President in parentheses

George Washington (1st) (John Adams)	1789–97
John Adams (2nd) *Fed* (Thomas Jefferson)	1797–1801
Thomas Jefferson (3rd) *Dem-Rep* (Aaron Burr, 1801–5) (George Clinton, 1805–9)	1801–9
James Madison (4th) *Dem-Rep* (George Clinton, 1809–12) *no Vice President 1812–13* (Elbridge Gerry, 1813–14) *no Vice President 1814–17*	1809–17

President	
James Monroe (5th) *Dem-Rep* (Daniel D Tompkins)	1817–25
John Quincy Adams (6th) *Dem-Rep* (John C Calhoun)	1825–9
Andrew Jackson (7th) *Dem* (John C Calhoun, 1829–32) *no Vice President 1832–3* (Martin van Buren, 1833–7)	1929–37
Martin van Buren (8th) *Dem* (Richard M Johnson)	1837–41
William Henry Harrison (9th) *Whig* (John Tyler)	1841
John Tyler (10th) *Whig no Vice President*	1841–5
James Knox Polk (11th) *Dem* (George M Dallas)	1845–9
Zachary Taylor (12th) *Whig* (Millard Fillmore)	1849–50
Millard Fillmore (13th) *Whig no Vice President*	1850–3
Franklin Pierce (14th) *Dem* (William R King, 1853) *no Vice President 1853–7*	1853–7
James Buchanan (15th) *Dem* (John C Breckinridge)	1857–61
Abraham Lincoln (16th) *Rep* (Hannibal Hamlin, 1861–5) (Andrew Johnson, 1865)	1861–5
Andrew Johnson (17th) *Dem-Nat no Vice President*	1865–9
Ulysses Simpson Grant (18th) *Rep* (Schuyler Colfax, 1869–73) (Henry Wilson, 1873–5) *no Vice President 1875–7*	1869–77
Rutherford Birchard Hayes (19th) *Rep* (William A Wheeler)	1877–81
James Abram Garfield (20th) *Rep* (Chester A Arthur)	1881
Chester Alan Arthur (21st) *Rep no Vice President*	1881–5
Grover Cleveland (22nd) *Dem* (Thomas A Hendricks, 1885) *no Vice President 1885–9*	1885–9
Benjamine Harrison (23rd) *Rep* (Levi P Morton)	1889–93
Grover Cleveland (24th) *Dem* (Adlai E Stevenson)	1893–7

President	
William McKinley (25th) *Rep* (Garrat A Hobart, 1897–9) *no Vice President 1899–1901* (Theodore Roosevelt, 1901)	1897–1901
Theodore Roosevelt (26th) *Rep no Vice President 1901–5* (Charles W Fairbanks, 1905–9)	1901–9
William Howard Taft (27th) *Rep* (James S Sherman, 1909–12) *no Vice President 1912–13*	1909–13
Woodrow Wilson (28th) *Dem* (Thomas R Marshall)	1913–21
Warren Gamaliel Harding (29th) *Rep* (Calvin Coolidge)	1921–3
Calvin Coolidge (30th) *Rep no Vice President 1923–5* (Charles G Dawes, 1925–9)	1923–9
Herbert Clark Hoover (31st) *Rep* (Charles Curtis)	1929–33
Franklin Delano Roosevelt (32nd) *Dem* (John N Garner, 1933–41) (Henry A Wallace, 1941–5) (Harry S Truman, 1945)	1933–45
Harry S Truman (33rd) *Dem no Vice President 1945–9* (Alben W Barkley, 1949–53)	1945–53
Dwight David Eisenhower (34th) *Rep* (Richard M Nixon)	1953–61
John Fitzgerald Kennedy (35th) *Dem* (Lyndon B Johnson)	1961–3
Lyndon Baines Johnson (36th) *Dem no Vice President 1963–5* (Hubert H Humphrey, 1965–9)	1963–9
Richard Milhous Nixon (37th) *Rep* (Spiro T Agnew, 1969–73) *no Vice President 1973, Oct–Dec* (Gerald R Ford, 1973–4)	1969–74
Gerald Rudolph Ford (38th) *Rep no Vice President 1974, Aug–Dec* (Nelson A Rockefeller, 1974–7)	1974–7
Jimmy Carter (39th) *Dem* (Walter F Mondale)	1977–81
Ronald Wilson Reagan (40th) *Rep* (George H W Bush)	1981–9
George Herbert Walker Bush (41st) *Rep* (J Danforth Quayle)	1989–93

POLITICAL LEADERS (cont.)

United States of America (cont.)
President

Bill Clinton (42nd) *Dem* (Al Gore)		1993–

Dem Democrat
Fed Federalist
Nat National Union
Rep Republican

USSR (Union of Soviet Socialist Republics)

No longer in existence, but included for reference

President

Leo Borisovich Kamenev	1917
Yakov Mikhailovich Sverlov	1917–19
Mikhail Ivanovich Kalinin	1919–46
Nikolai Shvernik	1946–53
Klimentiy Voroshilov	1953–60
Leonid Brezhnev	1960–4
Anastas Mikoyan	1964–5
Nikolai Prodgorny	1965–77
Leonid Brezhnev	1977–82
Vasily Kuznetsov *Acting President*	1982–3
Yuri Andropov	1983–4
Vasily Kuznetsov *Acting President*	1984
Konstantin Chernenko	1984–5
Vasily Kuznetsov *Acting President*	1985
Andrei Gromyko	1985–8
Mikhail Gorbachev	1988–90

Executive President

Mikhail Gorbachev	1990–1

Executive President

Gennady Yanayev *Acting President*	1991
Mikhail Gorbachev	1991

Chairman (Prime Minister)

Council of Ministers

Georgy Evgenyevich Lvov	1917
Aleksandr Fyodorovich Kerensky	1917

Council of People's Commissars

Vladimir Ilyich Lenin	1917–24
Aleksei Ivanovich Rykov	1924–30
Vyacheslav Mikhailovich Molotov	1930–41
Josef Stalin	1941–53

Council of Ministers

Georgiy Malenkov	1953–5
Nikolai Bulganin	1955–8
Nikita Khrushchev	1958–64
Alexei Kosygin	1964–80
Nikolai Tikhonov	1980–5
Nikolai Ryzhkov	1985–91
Valentin Pavlov	1991
Ivan Silayev *Acting*	1991

General Secretary

Josef Stalin	1922–53
Georgiy Malenkov	1953
Nikita Khrushchev	1953–64
Leonid Brezhnev	1964–82
Yuri Andropov	1982–4
Konstantin Chernenko	1984–5
Mikhail Gorbachev	1985–91

POPES

Antipopes (who claimed to be pope in opposition to those canonically chosen) are given in parentheses.

Pope		Pope		Pope	
Peter	until c.64	Clement I	c.90–c.99	Sixtus I	c.117–c.127
Linus	c.64–c.76	Evaristus	c.99–c.105	Telesphorus	c.127–c.137
Anacletus	c.76–c.90	Alexander I	c.105–c.117	Hyginus	c.137–c.140

Pope		Pope		Pope	
Pius I	c.140–c.154	Symmachus	498–514	Stephen II (*not consecrated*)	752
Anicetus	c.154–c.166	[Laurentius	498, 501–5]	Stephen II (III)	752–7
Soter	c.166–c.175	Hormisdas	514–23	Paul I	757–67
Eleutherius	175–89	John I	523–6	[Constantine II	767–9]
Victor I	189–98	Felix IV (III)	526–30	[Philip	768]
Zephyrinus	198–217	Boniface II	530–2	Stephen III (IV)	768–72
Callistus I	217–22	[Dioscorus	530]	Hadrian I	772–95
[Hippolytus	217–c.235]	John II	533–5	Leo III	795–816
Urban I	222–30	Agapetus I	535–6	Stephen IV (V)	816–17
Pontian	230–5	Silverius	536–7	Paschal I	817–24
Anterus	235–6	Vigilius	537–55	Eugenius II	824–7
Fabian	236–50	Pelagius I	556–61	Valentine	827
Cornelius	251–3	John III	561–74	Gregory IV	827–44
[Novatian	251–c.258]	Benedict I	575–9	[John	844]
Lucius I	253–4	Pelagius II	579–90	Sergius II	844–7
Stephen I	254–7	Gregory I	590–604	Leo IV	847–55
Sixtus II	257–8	Sabinianus	604–6	Benedict III	855–8
Dionysius	259–68	Boniface III	607	[Anastasius Bibliothecarius	855]
Felix I	269–74	Boniface IV	608–15		
Eutychianus	275–83	Deusdedit *or* Adeodatus I	615–18	Nicholas I	858–67
Caius	283–96			Hadrian II	867–72
Marcellinus	296–304	Boniface V	619–25	John VIII	872–82
Marcellus I	308–9	Honorius I	625–38	Marinus I	882–4
Eusebius	310	Severinus	640	Hadrian III	884–5
Miltiades	311–14	John IV	640–2	Stephen V (VI)	885–91
Sylvester I	314–35	Theodore I	642–9	Formosus	891–6
Mark	336	Martin I	649–55	Boniface VI	896
Julius I	337–52	Eugenius I[1]	654–7	Stephen VI (VII)	896–7
Liberius	352–66	Vitalian	657–72	Romanus	897
[Felix II	355–65]	Adeodatus II	672–6	Theodore II	897
Damasus I	366–84	Donus	676–8	John IX	898–900
[Ursinus	366–7]	Agatho	678–81	Benedict IV	900–3
Siricius	384–99	Leo II	682–3	Leo V	903
Anastasius I	399–401	Benedict II	684–5	[Christopher	903–4]
Innocent I	402–17	John V	685–6	Sergius III	904–11
Zosimus	417–18	Cono	686–7	Anastasius III	911–13
Boniface I	418–22	[Theodore	687]	Lando	913–14
[Eulalius	418–19]	[Paschal	687–92]	John X	914–28
Celestine I	422–32	Sergius I	687–701	Leo VI	928
Sixtus III	432–40	John VI	701–5	Stephen VII (VIII)	928–31
Leo I	440–61	John VII	705–7	John XI	931–5
Hilarus	461–8	Sisinnius	708	Leo VII	936–9
Simplicius	468–83	Constantine	708–15	Stephen IX	939–42
Felix III (II)	483–92	Gregory II	715–31	Marinus II	942–6
Gelasius I	492–6	Gregory III	731–41	Agapetus II	946–55
Anastasius II	496–8	Zacharias	741–52		

[1] Elected during the banishment of Martin I

POPES (cont.)

Pope		Pope		Pope	
John XII	955–64	Callistus II	1119–24	Innocent VI	1352–62
Leo VIII	963–5	Honorius II	1124–30	Urban V	1362–70
Benedict V	964–6	[Celestine II	1124]	Gregory XI	1370–8
John XIII	965–72	Innocent II	1130–43	Urban VI	1378–89
Benedict VI	973–4	[Anacletus II	1130–8]	[Clement VII	1378–94]
[Boniface VII	974, 984–5]	[Victor IV²	1138]	Boniface IX	1389–1404
Benedict VII	974–83	Celestine II	1143–4	[Benedict XIII	1394–1423]
John XIV	983–4	Lucius II	1144–5	Innocent VII	1404–6
John XV	985–96	Eugenius III	1145–53	Gregory XII	1406–15
Gregory V	996–9	Anastasius IV	1153–4	[Alexander V	1409–10]
[John XVI	997–8]	Hadrian IV	1154–9	[John XXIII	1410–15]
Sylvester II	999–1003	Alexander III	1159–81	Martin V	1417–31
John XVII	1003	[Victor IV²	1159–64]	[Clement VIII	1423–9]
John XVIII	1004–9	[Paschal III	1164–8]	[Benedict XIV	1425–30]
Sergius IV	1009–12	[Callistus III	1168–78]	Eugenius IV	1431–47
Benedict VIII	1012–24	[Innocent III	1179–80]	[Felix V	1439–49]
[Gregory	1012]	Lucius III	1181–5	Nicholas V	1447–55
John XIX	1024–32	Urban III	1185–7	Callistus III	1455–8
Benedict IX	1032–44	Gregory VIII	1187	Pius II	1458–64
Sylvester III	1045	Clement III	1187–91	Paul II	1464–71
Benedict IX		Celestine III	1191–8	Sixtus IV	1471–84
(*second reign*)	1045	Innocent III	1198–1216	Innocent VIII	1484–92
Gregory VI	1045–6	Honorius III	1216–27	Alexander VI	1492–1503
Clement II	1046–7	Gregory IX	1227–41	Pius III	1503
Benedict IX		Celestine IV	1241	Julius II	1503–13
(*third reign*)	1047–8	Innocent IV	1243–54	Leo X	1513–21
Damasus II	1048	Alexander IV	1254–61	Hadrian VI	1522–3
Leo IX	1048–54	Urban IV	1261–4	Clement VII	1523–34
Victor II	1055–7	Clement IV	1265–8	Paul III	1534–49
Stephen IX (X)	1057–8	Gregory X	1271–6	Julius III	1550–5
[Benedict X	1058–9]	Innocent V	1276	Marcellus II	1555
Nicholas II	1059–61	Hadrian V	1276	Paul IV	1555–9
Alexander II	1061–73	John XXI³	1276–7	Pius IV	1559–65
[Honorius II]	1061–72]	Nicholas III	1277–80	Pius V	1566–72
Gregory VII	1073–85	Martin IV	1281–5	Gregory XIII	1572–85
[Clement VII		Honorius IV	1285–7	Sixtus V	1585–90
	1080, 1084–1100]	Nicholas IV	1288–92	Urban VII	1590
Victor III	1086–7	Celestine V	1294	Gregory XIV	1590–1
Urban II	1088–99	Boniface VIII	1294–1303	Innocent IX	1591
Paschal II	1099–1118	Benedict XI	1303–4	Clement VIII	1592–1605
[Theodoric	1100–2]	Clement V	1305–14	Leo XI	1605
[Albert	1102]	John XXII	1316–34	Paul V	1605–21
[Sylvester IV	1105–11]	[Nicholas V	1328–30]	Gregory XV	1621–3
Gelasius II	1118–19	Benedict XII	1334–42	Urban VIII	1623–44
[Gregory VIII	1118–21]	Clement VI	1342–52	Innocent X	1644–55

Pope		Pope		Pope	
Alexander VII	1655–67	Benedict XIV	1740–58	Pius X	1903–14
Clement IX	1667–9	Clement XIII	1758–69	Benedict XV	1914–22
Clement X	1670–6	Clement XIV	1769–74	Pius XI	1922–39
Innocent XI	1676–89	Pius VI	1775–99	Pius XII	1939–58
Alexander VIII	1689–91	Pius VII	1800–23	John XXIII	1958–63
Innocent XII	1691–1700	Leo XII	1823–9	Paul VI	1963–78
Clement XI	1700–21	Pius VIII	1829–30	John Paul I	1978
Innocent XIII	1721–4	Gregory XVI	1831–46	John Paul II	1978–
Benedict XIII	1724–30	Pius IX	1846–78		
Clement XII	1730–40	Leo XIII	1878–1903		

[2] Different individuals
[3] There was no John XX

THOUGHT AND BELIEF

GREEK GODS OF MYTHOLOGY

Adonis	God of vegetation	Hebe	Goddess of youth
Aeolus	God of the winds	Hecate	Goddess of the moon
Alphito	Barley goddess of Argos	Helios	God of the sun
Aphrodite	Goddess of sexual love and beauty	Hephaestus	God of fire and crafts associated with fire
Apollo	God of prophecy, music, youth, archery and healing	Hera	Goddess of marriage and childbirth; queen of heaven
Ares	God of war	Hermes	Messenger to the gods
Arethusa	Goddess of springs and fountains	Hestia	Goddess of the hearth
Artemis	Goddess of childbirth and wild animals	Hypnos	God of sleep
		Iris	Goddess of the rainbow
Asclepius	God of healing	Morpheus	God of dreams
Athene	Goddess of prudence and wise council; protectress of Athens	Nemesis	God of destiny
		Nereus	God of the sea
Atlas	A Titan who bears up the earth	Nike	Goddess of victory
Attis	God of vegetation	Oceanus	God of the river Oceanus
Boreas	God of the north wind	Pan	God of fertility
Cronus	Father of Zeus	Persephone	Goddess of the underworld and of corn
Cybele	Goddess of the earth		
Demeter	Goddess of the harvest	Poseidon	God of the sea
Dionysus	God of wine, vegetation and ecstasy	Rhea	The original mother goddess; wife (and sister) of Cronus
Eos	Goddess of the dawn	Selene	Goddess of the moon
Eros	God of love	Thanatos	God of death
Gaia	Goddess of the earth	Zeus	Overlord of the Olympian gods and goddesses; god of the sky and all its properties
Ganymede	God of rain		
Hades	God of the underworld		

ROMAN GODS OF MYTHOLOGY

Apollo	God of the sun	Faunus	God of crops and herbs
Bacchus	God of wine	Feronia	Goddess of spring flowers
Bellona	Goddess of war	Fides	God of honesty
Ceres	Goddess of corn	Flora	Goddess of flowering plants
Consus	God of seed sowing	Fortuna	Goddess of chance and fate
Cupid	God of love	Genius	Protective god of individuals, groups and the state
Diana	Goddess of fertility and hunting		
Egeria	Goddess of fountains and childbirth	Janus	God of entrances and beginnings
		Juno	Goddess of marriage and childbirth
Epona	Goddess of horses		
Fauna	Goddess of fertility	Jupiter	The chief Roman god; god of the

	sky and the weather	Pales	Goddess of flocks
Lares	Gods of the house	Penates	Household gods of the storeroom
Liber Pater	God of agricultural and human	Picus	God of woods
	fertility	Pluto	God of the underworld
Libitina	Goddess of funeral rites	Pomona	Goddess of fruit trees
Maia	Goddess of fertility	Portunus	God of husbands
Mars	God of war	Prosperina	Goddess of the underworld
Mercury	Messenger to the gods; also god	Rumina	Goddess of nursing mothers
	. of merchants	Saturn	God of fertility and agriculture
Minerva	Goddess of war, craftsmen,	Silvanus	God of agriculture and woods
	education and the arts	Venus	Goddess of vegetation and love
Mithras	The sun god; god of regeneration	Vertumnus	God of fertility
Neptune	God of the sea	Vesta	Goddess of the hearth
Ops	Goddess of the harvest	Victoria	Goddess of victory
Orcus	God of death	Vulcan	God of fire

NORSE GODS OF MYTHOLOGY

Aegir	God of the sea	Mimir	God of wisdom
Aesir	Race of warlike gods, including	Nanna	Goddess wife of Balder
	Odin, Thor, Tyr	Nehallenia	Goddess of plenty
Alcis	Twin gods of the sky	Nerthus	Goddess of earth
Balder	Son of Odin and favourite of the	Njord	God of ships and the sea
	gods	Norns	Goddesses of destiny
Bor	Father of Odin	Odin (Woden,	Chief of the Aesir family of gods,
Bragi	God of poetry	Wotan)	the 'father' god; the god of
Fafnir	Dragon god		battle, death, inspiration
Fjorgynn	Mother of Thor	Otr	Otter god
Freyja	Goddess of libido	Ran	Goddess of the sea
Frey	God of fertility	Sif	Goddess wife of Thor
Frigg	Goddess of fertility; wife of Odin	Sigyn	Goddess wife of Loki
Gefion	Goddess who received virgins	Thor (Donar)	God of thunder and sky; good
	after death		crops
Heimdall	Guardian of the bridge Bifrost	Tyr	God of battle
Hel	Goddess of death; Queen of	Ull	Stepson of Thor, an enchanter
	Niflheim, the land of mists	Valkyries	Female helpers of the gods of
Hermod	Son of Odin		war
Hoenir	Companion to Odin and Loki	Vanir	Race of benevolent gods,
Hoder	Blind god who killed Baldur		including Njrd, Frey, Freyja
Idunn	Guardian goddess of the golden	Vidar	Slayer of the wolf, Fenvir
	apples of youth; wife of Bragi	Weland	Craftsman god
Kvasir	God of wise utterances	(Volundr,	
Logi	Fire god	Weiland,	
Loki	God of mischief	Wayland)	

EGYPTIAN GODS

Amun-Re	Universal god	Khonsou	Son of Amun-Re
Anubis	God of funerals	Maat	Goddess of sterility
Apis	God of fertility	Nephthys	Goddess of funerals
Aten	Unique god	Nut	God of the sky
Geb	God of the earth	Osiris	God of vegetation
Hathor	Goddess of love	Ptah	God of creation
Horus	God of light	Sekmet	Goddess of might
Isis	Goddess of magic	Set	God of evil
Khnum	Goddess of creation	Thoth	Supreme scribe

BAHA'I FAITH

Founded 1863 in Persia.
Founder Mirza Husayn Ali (1817–92), known as Baha Ullah (Glory of God). He declared himself the prophet foretold by Mirza ali Mohammed (1819–50), a direct descendant of Mohammed, who proclaimed himself to be the bab ('gate' or 'door').
Sacred texts Kitab al-Aqdas, Haft Wadi, al-Kalimat al-Maknnah and the Bayan.
Beliefs Baha'i Faith teaches the oneness of God, the unity of all faiths, the inevitable unification of humankind, the harmony of all people, universal education, and obedience to government. It does not predict an end to this world or any intervention by God but believes there will be a change within man and society.
Organization There is virtually no organization and Baha'i Faith has no clergy or sacraments. Although there is little formal ritual (most assemblies are simply gatherings of the faithful), there are ceremonies for marriage, funerals and naming babies and there are shrines and temples.

BUDDHISM

Founded c.500 BC in India.
Founder Prince Siddharta Guatama (c.563–c.483 BC) who became Buddha ('the enlightened') through meditation.
Sacred texts The Pali Canon or Tripitaka made up of the Vinaya Pitaka (Discourses of the Buddha) and the Abhidhamma Pitaka (higher subtleties of law), the Mahayana Sutras, the Milindapanha and Bardo Thodol (the Tibetan Book of the Dead).
Beliefs Buddha's teaching is summarized in the Four Noble Truths; suffering is always present in life; desire is the cause of suffering; freedom from life can be achieved by nirvana (perfect peace and bliss); the Eightfold Path leads to nirvana. Karma, by which good and evil deeds result in appropriate reward or punishment, and the cycle of rebirth can be broken by taking the Eightfold Path. All Buddhas are revered but particularly Guatama.
Organization There is a monastic system which aims to create favourable conditions for spiritual development. This involves meditation, personal discipline and spiritual exercises in the hope of liberation from self. Buddhism has proved very flexible in adapting its organization, ceremony and pattern of belief to different cultural and social conditions. There are numerous festivals and ceremonies and pilgrimage is of great spiritual value.
Divisions There are two main traditions in Buddhism. Theravada Buddhism is closest to Buddha's teaching; salvation can be attained only by the few who accept the severe discipline and effort necessary to achieve it. Mahayana Buddhism developed later and is more flexible and creative, embracing popular piety. It teaches

that salvation is possible for everyone and introduced the doctrine of the bodhisattva (a personal sa-viour). As Buddhism spread other schools sprang up including Zen, Lamaism, Tendai, Nichiven and Soka Gakkai.

MAJOR BUDDHIST FESTIVALS

Weekly Uposatha Days Buddha's Birth Enlightenment, First Sermon and Death are observed in the different countries where Buddhism is practised but often on different dates. In some of these countries there are additional festivals in honour of Buddha.

CHRISTIANITY

Founded 1st-c AD.

Founder Jesus Christ 'the Son of God' (c.4 BC–c.30 AD).

Sacred texts The Bible consisting of the Old and New Testaments. The New Testament written between AD 30 and 150 consists of the Gospels, the Acts of the Apostles, the Epistles, and the Apocalypse.

Beliefs A world religion, centred on the life and works of Jesus of Nazareth in Judaea; he proclaimed the most important rule of life to be love of God and love of one's neighbour. Unselfishness and compassion are central themes in Christianity. Belief in Jesus's divinity and his resurrection from the dead after his crucifixion promises victory over death. The earliest followers of Jesus were Jews who believed him to be the messiah 'Saviour' promised by the prophets in the Old Testament. Christians believe he will come again to inaugurate the 'Kingdom of God'.

Organization Jesus Christ appointed 12 men to be his disciples:

1 Peter (brother of Andrew)
2 Andrew (brother of Peter)
3 James, son of Zebedee (brother of John)
4 John (brother of James)
5 Philip
6 Bartholomew
7 Thomas
8 Matthew
9 James of Alphaeus
10 Simon the Canaanite (in Matthew and Mark) or Simon 'the Zealot' (in Luke and the Acts)
11 Judas Iscariot

(Thaddeus in the book of Matthew and Mark is the twelfth disciple, while in Luke and the Acts the twelfth is Judas or James. Matthias succeeded to Judas's place.) Soon after the resurrection the disciples gathered for the festival of Pentecost and received special signs of the power of God, the Holy Spirit. The disciples became a defined new body, the Church. Through the witness of the Apostles and their successors, the Christian faith quickly spread and in AD 315 became the official religion of the Roman Empire. It survived the 'Dark Ages' to become the basis of civilization in the Middle Ages in Europe.

Divisions Major divisions, separated as a result of differences of doctrine and practice, are the Orthodox or Eastern Church, the Roman Catholic Church, acknowledging the Bishop of Rome as head, and the Protestant Churches stemming from the split with the Roman Church in the 16th-c. All Christians recognize the authority of the Bible, read at public worship, which takes place at least every Sunday, to celebrate the resurrection of Jesus Christ. Most Churches recognize at least two sacraments (Baptism and the Eucharist, Mass, or Lord's Supper) as essential.

MAJOR IMMOVABLE CHRISTIAN FEASTS

For Saints' Days, *see* opposite.

Jan 1	Solemnity of Mary, Mother of God	Aug 22	Queenship of Mary
Jan 6	Epiphany	Sep 8	Birthday of the Virgin Mary
Jan 7	Christmas Day (*Eastern Orthodox*)[1]	Sep 14	Exaltation of the Holy Cross
Jan 11	Baptism of Jesus	Oct 2	Guardian Angels
Jan 25	Conversion of Apostle Paul	Nov 1	All Saints
Feb 2	Presentation of Jesus (*Candelmas Day*)	Nov 2	All Souls
Feb 22	The Chair of Peter, Apostle	Nov 9	Dedication of the Lateran Basilica
Mar 25	Annunciation of the Virgin Mary	Nov 21	Presentation of the Virgin Mary
Jun 24	Birth of John the Baptist	Dec 8	Immaculate Conception
Aug 6	Transfiguration	Dec 25	Christmas Day
Aug 15	Assumption of the Virgin Mary	Dec 28	Holy Innocents

[1] Fixed feasts in the Julian Calendar fall 13 days later than the Gregorian Calendar date.

MOVABLE CHRISTIAN FEASTS, 1994–2000

Ash Wednesday, the first day of Lent, can fall at the earliest on 4 February and at the latest on 10 March.

Palm (Passion) Sunday is the Sunday before Easter; Good Friday is the Friday before Easter; Holy Saturday (often referred to as Easter Saturday) is the Saturday before Easter; Easter Saturday, in traditional usage, is the Saturday following Easter.

Easter Day can fall at the earliest on 22 March and at the latest on 25 April. Ascension Day can fall at the earliest on 30 April and at the latest on 3 June. Whit Sunday can fall at the earliest on 10 May and at the latest on 13 June.

There are not less than 22 and not more than 27 Sundays after Trinity.

The first Sunday of Advent is the Sunday nearest to 30 November.

Year	Ash Wednesday	Easter	Ascension	Whit Sunday	Sundays after Trinity	Advent	Trinity Sunday	Corpus Christi
1994	16 Feb	3 Apr	12 May	22 May	25	27 Nov	29 May	2 Jun
1995	1 Mar	16 Apr	25 May	4 Jun	24	3 Dec	11 Jun	15 Jun
1996	21 Feb	7 Apr	16 May	26 May	25	1 Dec	2 Jun	6 Jun
1997	12 Feb	30 Mar	8 May	18 May	26	30 Nov	25 May	29 May
1998	25 Feb	12 Apr	21 May	31 May	24	29 Nov	7 Jun	11 Jun
1999	17 Feb	4 Apr	13 May	23 May	25	28 Nov	30 May	3 Jun
2000	8 Mar	23 Apr	1 Jun	11 Jun	23	3 Dec	18 Jun	22 Jun

SAINTS' DAYS

The official recognition of Saints, and the choice of a Saint's Day, varies greatly between different branches of Christianity, calendars and localities. Only major variations are included below, using the following abbreviations:

C Coptic   *E* Eastern   *G* Greek   *W* Western

January
1 Basil (*E*), Fulgentius, Telemachus
2 Basil and Gregory of Nazianzus (*W*), Macarius of Alexandria, Seraphim of Sarov
3 Geneviève
4 Angela of Foligno
5 Simeon Stylites (*W*)
7 Cedda, Lucian of Antioch (*W*), Raymond of Penyafort
8 Atticus (*E*), Gudule, Severinus
9 Hadrian the African
10 Agatho, Marcian
12 Ailred, Benedict Biscop
13 Hilary of Poitiers
14 Kentigern
15 Macarius of Egypt, Maurus, Paul of Thebes
16 Honoratus
17 Antony of Egypt
19 Wulfstan
20 Euthymius, Favian, Sebastian
21 Agnes, Fructuosus, Maximus (*E*), Meinrad
22 Timothy (*G*), Vincent
23 Ildefonsus
24 Babylas (*W*), Francis de Sales
25 Gregory of Nazianzus (*E*)
26 Paula, Timothy and Titus, Xenophon (*E*)
27 Angela Merici
28 Ephraem Syrus (*E*), Paulinus of Nola, Thomas Aquinas
29 Gildas
31 John Bosco, Marcella

February
1 Bride, Pionius
3 Anskar, Blaise (*W*), Werburga, Simeon (*E*)
4 Gilbert of Sempringham, Isidore of Pelusium, Phileas
5 Agatha, Avitus
6 Dorothy, Paul Miki and companions, Vedast
8 Theodore (*G*), Jerome Emiliani
9 Teilo
10 Scholastica
11 Benedict of Aniane, Blaise (*E*), Caedmon, Gregory II
12 Meletius
13 Agabus (*W*), Catherine dei Ricci, Priscilla (*E*)
14 Cyril and Methodius (*W*), Valentine (*W*)
16 Flavian (*E*), Pamphilus (*E*), Valentine (*G*)
18 Bernadette (*France*), Colman, Flavian (*W*), Leo I (*E*)
20 Wulfric
21 Peter Damian
23 Polycarp
25 Ethelbert, Tarasius, Walburga
26 Alexander (*W*), Porphyrius
27 Leander
28 Oswald of York

March
1 David
2 Chad, Simplicius
3 Ailred
4 Casimir
6 Chrodegang
7 Perpetua and Felicity
8 Felix, John of God, Pontius
9 Frances of Rome, Gregory of Nyssa, Pacian
10 John Ogilvie, Macarius of Jerusalem, Simplicius
11 Constantine, Oengus, Sophronius
12 Gregory (the Great)
13 Nicephorus
14 Benedict (*E*)
15 Clement Hofbauer
17 Gertrude, Joseph of Arimathea (*W*), Patrick
18 Anselm of Lucca, Cyril of Jerusalem, Edward
19 Joseph
20 Cuthbert, John of Parma, Martin of Braga
21 Serapion of Thmuis
22 Catherine of Sweden, Nicholas of Flüe
23 Turibius de Mongrovejo
30 John Climacus

SAINTS' DAYS (cont.)

April

1 Hugh of Grenoble, Mary of Egypt (*E*), Melito
2 Francis of Paola, Mary of Egypt (*W*)
3 Richard of Chichester
4 Isidore of Seville
5 Juliana of Liège, Vincent Ferrer
7 Hegesippus, John Baptist de la Salle
8 Agabus (*E*)
10 Fulbert
11 Gemma Galgani, Guthlac, Stanislaus
12 Julius I, Zeno
13 Martin I
15 Aristarchus, Pudus (*E*), Trophimus of Ephesus
17 Agapetus (*E*), Stephen Harding
18 Mme Acarie
19 Alphege, Leo IX
21 Anastasius (*E*), Anselm, Beuno, Januarius (*E*)
22 Alexander (*C*)
23 George
24 Egbert, Fidelis of Sigmaringen, Mellitus
25 Mark, Phaebadius
27 Zita
28 Peter Chanel, Vitalis and Valeria
29 Catherine of Siena, Hugh of Cluny, Peter Martyr, Robert
30 James (the Great) (*E*), Pius V

May

1 Asaph, Joseph the Worker, Walburga
2 Athanasius
3 Philip and James (the Less) (*W*)
4 Gotthard
5 Hilary of Arles
7 John of Beverley
8 John (*E*), Peter of Tarantaise
10 Antoninus, Comgall, John of Avila, Simon (*E*)
11 Cyril and Methodius (*E*), Mamertus
12 Epiphanius, Nereus and Achilleus, Pancras
14 Matthias (*W*)
16 Brendan, John of Nepomuk, Simon Stock
17 Robert Bellarmine, Paschal Baylon
18 John I
19 Dunstan, Ivo, Pudens (*W*), Pudentiana (*W*)
20 Bernardino of Siena
21 Helena (*E*)
22 Rita of Cascia

23 Ivo of Chartres
24 Vincent of Lérins
25 Aldhelm, Bede, Gregory VII, Mary Magdalene de Pazzi
26 Philip Neri, Quadratus
27 Augustine of Canterbury
30 Joan of Arc

June

1 Justin Martyr, Pamphilus
2 Erasmus, Marcellinus and Peter, Nicephorus (*G*), Pothinus
3 Charles Lwanga and companions, Clotilde, Kevin
4 Optatus, Petrock
5 Boniface
6 Martha (*E*), Norbert
7 Paul of Constantinople (*W*), Willibald
8 William of York
9 Columba, Cyril of Alexandria (*E*), Ephraem (*W*)
11 Barnabas, Bartholomew (*E*)
12 Leo III
13 Anthony of Padua
15 Orsisius, Vitus
17 Alban, Botulph
19 Gervasius and Protasius, Jude (*E*), Romuald
20 Alban
21 Alban of Mainz, Aloysius Gonzaga
22 John Fisher and Thomas More, Niceta, Pantaenus (*C*), Paulinus of Nola
23 Etheldreda
24 Birth of John the Baptist
25 Prosper of Aquitaine
27 Cyril of Alexandria (*W*), Ladislaus
28 Irenaeus
29 Peter and Paul
30 First Martyrs of the Church of Rome

July

1 Cosmas and Damian (*E*), Oliver Plunket
3 Anatolius, Thomas
4 Andrew of Crete (*E*), Elizabeth of Portugal, Ulrich
5 Anthony Zaccaria
6 Maria Goretti
7 Palladius, Pantaenus
8 Kilian, Aquila and Prisca (*W*)

11 Benedict (*W*), Pius I
12 John Gualbert, Veronica
13 Henry II, Mildred, Silas
14 Camillus of Lellis, Deusdedit, Nicholas of the Holy Mountain (*E*)
15 Bonaventure, Jacob of Nisibis, Swithin, Vladimir
16 Eustathius, Our Lady of Mt Carmel
17 Ennodius, Leo IV, Marcellina, Margaret (*E*), Scillitan Martyrs
18 Arnulf, Philastrius
19 Macrina, Symmachus
20 Aurelius, Margaret (*W*)
21 Lawrence of Brindisi, Praxedes
22 Mary Magdalene
23 Apollinaris, Bridget of Sweden
25 Anne and Joachim (*E*), Christopher, James (the Great) (*W*)
26 Anne and Joachim (*W*)
27 Pantaleon
28 Innocent I, Samson, Victor I
29 Lupus, Martha (*W*), Olave
30 Peter Chrysologus, Silas (*G*)
31 Giovanni Colombini, Germanus, Joseph of Arimathea (*E*), Ignatius of Loyola

August

1 Alphonsus Liguori, Ethelwold
2 Eusebius of Vercelli, Stephen I
4 Jean-Baptiste Vianney
6 Hormisdas
7 Cajetan, Sixtus II and companions
8 Dominic
9 Matthias (*G*)
10 Laurence, Oswald of Northumbria
11 Clare, Susanna
13 Maximus (*W*), Pontian and Hippolytus, Radegunde
14 Maximilian Kolbe
15 Arnulf, Tarsicius
16 Roch, Simplicianus, Stephen of Hungary
17 Hyacinth
19 John Eudes, Sebaldus
20 Bernard, Oswin, Philibert
21 Jane Frances de Chantal, Pius X
23 Rose of Lima, Sidonius Apollinaris
24 Bartholomew (*W*), Ouen
25 Joseph Calasanctius, Louis IX, Menas of Constantinople

26 Blessed Dominic of the Mother of God, Zephyrinus
27 Caesarius, Monica
28 Augustine of Hippo
29 Beheading of John the Baptist, Sabina
30 Pammachius
31 Aidan, Paulinus of Trier

September

1 Giles, Simeon Stylites (*E*)
2 John the Faster (*E*)
3 Gregory (the Great)
4 Babylas (*E*), Boniface I
5 Zacharias (*E*)
9 Peter Claver, Sergius of Antioch
10 Finnian, Nicholas of Tolentino, Pulcheria
11 Deiniol, Ethelburga, Paphnutius
13 John Chrysostom (*W*)
15 Catherine of Genoa, Our Lady of Sorrows
16 Cornelius, Cyprian of Carthage, Euphemia, Ninian
17 Robert Bellarmine, Hildegard, Lambert, Satyrus
19 Januarius (*W*), Theodore of Tarsus
20 Agapetus or Eustace (*W*)
21 Matthew (*W*)
23 Adamnan, Linus
25 Sergius of Rostov
26 Cosmas and Damian (*W*), Cyprian of Carthage, John (*E*)
27 Frumentius (*W*), Vincent de Paul
28 Exuperius, Wenceslaus
29 Michael (*Michaelmas Day*), Gabriel and Raphael
30 Jerome, Otto

October

1 Remigius, Romanos, Teresa of the Child Jesus
2 Leodegar (Leger)
3 Teresa of Lisieux, Thomas de Cantilupe
4 Ammon, Francis of Assisi, Petronius
6 Bruno, Thomas (*G*)
9 Demetrius (*W*), Denis and companions, Dionysius of Paris, James (the Less) (*E*), John Leonardi
10 Francis Borgia, Paulinus of York
11 Atticus (*E*), Bruno, Nectarius
12 Wilfrid

SAINTS' DAYS (cont.)

13 Edward the Confessor
14 Callistus I, Cosmas Melodus (*E*)
15 Lucian of Antioch (*E*), Teresa of Avila
16 Gall, Hedwig, Lullus, Margaret Mary Alacoque
17 Ignatius of Antioch, Victor
18 Luke
19 John de Bréboeuf and Isaac Jogues and companions, Paul of the Cross, Peter of Alcántara
21 Hilarion, Ursula
22 Abercius
23 John of Capistrano, James
24 Anthony Claret
25 Crispin and Crispinian, Forty Martyrs of England and Wales, Gaudentius
26 Demetrius (*E*)
28 Firmilian (*E*), Simon and Jude
30 Serapion of Antioch
31 Wolfgang

November
1 All Saints, Cosmas and Damian (*E*)
2 Eustace (*E*), Victorinus
3 Hubert, Malachy, Martin de Porres, Pirminius, Winifred
4 Charles Borromeo, Vitalis and Agricola
5 Elizabeth (*W*)
6 Illtyd, Leonard, Paul of Constantinople (*E*)
7 Willibrord
8 Elizabeth (*E*), Willehad
9 Simeon Metaphrastes (*E*)
10 Justus, Leo I (*W*)
11 Martin of Tours (*W*), Menas of Egypt, Theodore of Studios
12 Josaphat, Martin of Tours (*E*), Nilus the Ascetic
13 Abbo, John Chrysostom (*E*), Nicholas I
14 Dubricius, Gregory Palamas (*E*)
15 Albert the Great, Machutus
16 Edmund of Abingdon, Eucherius, Gertrude (the Great), Margaret of Scotland, Matthew (*E*)

17 Elizabeth of Hungary, Gregory Thaumaturgus, Gregory of Tours, Hugh of Lincoln
18 Odo, Romanus
19 Mechthild, Nerses
20 Edmund the Martyr
21 Gelasius
22 Cecilia
23 Amphilochius, Clement I (*W*), Columban, Felicity, Gregory of Agrigentum
25 Clement I (*E*), Mercurius, Mesrob
26 Siricius
27 Barlam and Josaphat
28 Simeon Metaphrastes
29 Cuthbert Mayne
30 Andrew, Frumentius (*G*)

December
1 Eligius
2 Chromatius
3 Francis Xavier
4 Barbara, John Damascene, Osmund
5 Clement of Alexandria, Sabas
6 Nicholas
7 Ambrose
10 Miltiades
11 Damasus, Daniel
12 Jane Frances de Chantal, Spyridon (*E*), Vicelin
13 Lucy, Odilia
14 John of the Cross, Spyridon (*W*)
16 Eusebius
18 Frumentiús (*C*)
20 Ignatius of Antioch (*G*)
21 Peter Canisius, Thomas
22 Anastasia (*E*), Chrysogonus (*E*)
23 John of Kanty
26 Stephen (*W*)
27 John (*W*), Fabiola, Stephen (*E*)
29 Thomas Becket, Trophimus of Arles
31 Sylvester

CONFUCIANISM

Founded 6th-c BC in China.
Founder K'ung Fu-tse (Confucius) (c.551–479 BC).
Sacred texts Shih Ching, Li Ching, Chu'un Ch'iu, I Ching.
Beliefs The oldest school of Chinese thought, Confucianism did not begin as a religion. Confucius was con-

cerned with the best way to behave and live in this world and was not concerned with the afterlife. He emerges as a great moral teacher who tried to replace the old religious observances with moral values as the basis of social and political order. He laid particular emphasis on the family as the basic unit in society and the foundation of the whole community. He believed that government was a matter of moral responsibility, not just manipulation of power.

Organization Confucianism is not an institution and has no church or clergy. However ancestor-worship and veneration of the sky have their sources in Confucian texts. Weddings and funerals follow a tradition handed down by Confucian scholars. Social life is ritualized and colour and patterns of clothes have a sacred meaning.

Divisions There are two ethical strands in Confucianism. One, associated with Confucius and Hsun Tzu (c.298–238 BC), is conventionalistic: we ought to follow the traditional codes of behaviour for their own sake. The other, associated with Mencius and medieval neo-Confucians, is intuitionistic: we ought to do as our moral natures dictate.

MAJOR CHINESE FESTIVALS

January/February	Chinese New Year
February/March	Lantern Festival
March/April	Festival of Pure Brightness
May/June	Dragon Boat Festival
July/August	Herd Boy and Weaving Maid
August	All Souls' Festival
September	Mid-Autumn Festival
September/October	Double Ninth Festival
November/December	Winter Solstice

HINDUISM

Founded c.1500 BC by Aryan invaders of India with their Vedic religion.

Sacred texts Vedas ('knowledge'), including the Upanishads which are spiritual truths and the epic poems the Ramayana and the Mahabharata. Best known of all is the Bhagavadgita, part of the Mahabharata.

Beliefs Hinduism emphasizes the right way of living (dharma) and embraces many diverse religious beliefs and practices rather than a set of doctrines. It acknowledges many gods who are seen as manifestations of an underlying reality. Devout Hindus aim to become one with the 'absolute reality' or Brahman. Only after a completely pure life will the soul be released from the cycle of rebirth. Until then the soul will be repeatedly reborn. Samsara refers to the cycle of birth and rebirth. Karma is the law by which consequences of actions within one life are carried over into the next.

Organization There is very little formal structure. Hinduism is concerned with the realization of religious values in every part of life yet there is a great emphasis on the performance of complex demanding rituals under the supervision of a Brahman priest and teacher. There are three categories of worship: temple, domestic and congregational. The most common ceremony is prayer (puja). Many pilgrimages take place and there is an annual cycle of festivals.

Divisions As there is no concept of orthodoxy in Hinduism, there are many different sects worshipping different gods. The three most important gods are Brahman, the primeval god, Vishnu, the preserver, and Shiva, both destroyer and creator of life. The three major living traditions are those devoted to Vishnu, Shiva and the goddess Shakti. Folk beliefs and practices exist together with sophisticated philosophical schools.

MAJOR HINDU FESTIVALS

S = Sukla 'waxing fortnight' K = Krishna 'waning fortnight'

Chaitra	S 9	Ramanavami (Birthday of Lord Rama)
Asadha	S 2	Rathayatra (Pilgrimage of the Chariot at Jagannath)
Sravana	S 11–15	Jhulanayatra ('Swinging the Lord Krishna')
Sravana	S 15	Rakshabandhana ('Tying on lucky threads')
Bhadrapada	K 8	Janamashtami (Birthday of Lord Krishna)
Asvina	S 7–10	Durga-puja (Homage to Goddess Durga) (*Bengal*)
Asvina	S 1–10	Navaratri (Festival of 'nine nights')
Asvina	S 15	Lakshmi-puja (Homage to Goddess Lakshmi)
Asvina	K 15	Diwali, Dipavali ('String of Lights')
Kartikka	S 15	Guru Nanak Jananti (Birthday of Guru Nanak)
Magha	K 5	Sarasvati-puja (Homage to Goddess Sarasvati)
Magha	K 13	Maha-sivaratri (Great Night of Lord Shiva)
Phalguna	S 14	Holi (Festival of Fire)
Phalguna	S 15	Dolayatra (Swing Festival) (*Bengal*)

ISLAM

Founded 7th-c AD.
Founder Mohammed (c.570–c.632).
Sacred texts The Koran, the word of God as revealed to Mohammed and the Hadith, a collection of the prophet's sayings.
Beliefs A monotheistic religion, God is the creator of all things and holds absolute power over man. All persons should devote themselves to lives of grateful and praise-giving obedience to God as they will be judged on the Day of Resurrection. It is acknowledged that Satan often misleads humankind but those who have obeyed God or have repented of their sins will dwell in paradise. Those sinners who are unrepentant will go to hell. Muslims accept the Old Testament and acknowledge Jesus Christ as an important prophet, but they believe the perfect word of God was revealed to Mohammed. Islam imposes five pillars of faith on its followers: belief in one God and his prophet, Mohammed; salat, formal prayer preceded by ritual cleansing five times a day, facing Mecca; saum, fasting during the month of Ramadan; Hajj, pilgrimage to Mecca at least once; zakat, a religious tax on the rich to provide for the poor.
Organization There is no organized priesthood but great respect is accorded to descendants of Mohammed and holymen, scholars and teachers such as mullahs and ayatollahs. The Shari'a is the Islamic law and applies to all aspects of life, not just religious practices.
Divisions There are two main groups within Islam. The Sunni are the majority and the more orthodox. They recognize the succession from Mohammed to Abu Bahkr, his father-in-law, and to the next three caliphs. The Shiites are followers of Ali, Mohammed's nephew and son-in-law. They believe in 12 imams, perfect teachers, who still guide the faithful from paradise. Shi'ah practice tends towards the ecstatic. There are many other subsects including the Sufis, the Ismailis and the Wahhabis.

MAJOR ISLAMIC FESTIVALS

1 Muharram	New Year's Day; starts on the day which celebrates Mohammed's departure from Mecca to Medina in AD 622.

12 Rabi I	Birthday of Mohammed (Mawlid al-Nabi) AD 572; celebrated throughout month of Rabi I.
27 Rajab	'Night of Ascent' (Laylat al-Miraj) of Mohammed to Heaven.
1 Ramadan	Beginning of month of fasting during daylight hours.
27 Ramadan	'Night of Power' (Laylat al-Qadr); sending down of the Koran to Mohammed.
1 Shawwal	'Feast of breaking the Fast' (Id al-Fitr); marks the end of Ramadan.
8–13 Dhu-I-Hijja	Annual pilgrimage ceremonies at and around Mecca; month during which the great pilgrimage (Hajj) should be made.
10 Dhu-I-Hijja	Feast of the Sacrifice (Id al-Adha).

JAINISM

Founded 6th-c BC in India.
Founder Vardhamana Mahavira (599–527 BC).
Sacred Texts Svetambara canon of scripture and Digambara texts.
Beliefs Jainism is derived from the ancient jinas ('those who overcome'). They believe that salvation consists in conquering material existence through adhering to a strict ascetic discipline, thus freeing the 'soul' from the working of karma for eternal, all-knowing bliss. Liberation requires detachment from worldly existence, an essential part of which is Ahimsa, non-injury to living beings. Jains are also strict vegetarians.
Organization Like Buddhists, the Jains are dedicated to the quest for liberation and the life of the ascetic. However, rather than congregating in monastic centres, Jainist monks and nuns have developed a strong relationship with lay people. There are temple rituals resembling Hindu puja. There is also a series of lesser vows and specific religious practices that give the lay person an identifiable religious career.
Divisions There are two categories of religious and philosophical literature. The Svetambara have a canon of scripture consisting of 45 texts, including a group of 11 texts in which the sermons and dialogues of Mahavira himself are collected. The Digambara hold that the original teachings of Mahavira have been lost but that their texts preserve accurately the substance of the original message. This disagreement over scriptures has not led to fundamental doctrinal differences.

JUDAISM

Founded c.2000 BC.
Founder Abraham (c.2000–1650 BC) with whom god made a covenant and Moses (15th–13th-c BC) who gave the Israelites the law.
Sacred texts The Hebrew bible consisting of 24 books, the most important of which are the Torah or Pentateuch — the first five books. Also the Talmud made up of the Mishna, the oral law, and the Gemara, an extensive commentary.
Beliefs A monotheistic religion, the Jews believe God is the creator of the world who delivered the Israelites out of bondage in Egypt, revealed his law to them, and chose them to be a light to all humankind. However varied their communities, Jews see themselves as members of a community whose origins lie in the patriarchal period. Ritual is very important and the family is the basic unit of ritual.
Organization Originally a theocracy, the basic institution is now the synagogue, operated by the congregation and led by a rabbi of their choice. The chief rabbis in France and Britain have authority over those who accept it; in Israel the two chief rabbis have civil authority in family law. The synagogue is the centre for communal worship and study. Its main feature is the 'ark' (a cupboard) containing the handwritten scrolls of the Pentateuch. Daily life is governed by a number of practices and observances: male children are circumcised, the Sabbath is observed, and food has to be correctly prepared. The most important festival is the Passover which celebrates the liberation of the Israelites from Egypt.

JUDAISM (cont.)

Divisions Today most Jews are descendants of either the Ashkenazim or the Sephardim, each with marked cultural differences. There are also several religious branches of Judaism from ultra liberal to ultra conservative, reflecting different points of view regarding the binding character of the prohibitions and duties prescribed for Jews.

MAJOR JEWISH FESTIVALS

For Gregorian calendar equivalents, *see* p 319.

1–2 Tishri	Rosh Hashana (New Year)
3 Tishri	Tzom Gedaliahu (Fast of Gedaliah)
10 Tishri	Yom Kippur (Day of Atonement)
15–21 Tishri	Sukkot (Feast of Tabernacles)
22 Tishri	Shemini Atzeret (8th Day of the Solemn Assembly)
23 Tishri	Simchat Torah (Rejoicing of the Law)
25 Kislev–2–3 Tevet	Hanukkah (Feast of Dedication)
10 Tevet	Asara be-Tevet (Fast of 10th Tevet)
13 Adar	Taanit Esther (Fast of Esther)
14–15 Adar	Purim (Feast of Lots)
15–22 Nisan	Pesach (Passover)
5 Iyar	Israel Independence Day
6–7 Sivan	Shavuot (Feast of Weeks)
17 Tammuz	Shiva Asar be-Tammuz (Fast of 17th Tammuz)
9 Av	Tisha be-Av (Fast of 9th Av)

SHINTOISM

Founded 8th-c AD in Japan.
Sacred texts Kojiki and Nihon Shoki.
Beliefs Shinto 'the teaching' or 'way of the gods', came into existence independently from Buddhism which was coming to the mainland of Japan at that time. It subsequently incorporated many features of Buddhism. Founded on the nature-worship of Japanese folk religions, it is made up of many elements; animism, veneration of nature and ancestor-worship. Its gods are known as kami and there are many ceremonies appealing to these kami for benevolent treatment and protection. Great stress is laid on the harmony between humans, their kami and nature. Moral and physical purity is a basic law. Death and other pollutions are to be avoided. Shinto is primarily concerned with life and this world and the good of the group. Followers must show devotion and sincerity but aberrations can be erased by purification procedures.
Organization As a set of prehistoric agricultural ceremonies Shinto was never supported by a body of philosophical or moralistic literature. Shamans originally performed the ceremonies and tended the shrines, then gradually a particular tribe took over the ceremonies. In the 8th-c Shinto became political with the imperial family ascribed divine origins and state Shintoism was established.
Divisions In the 19th-c Shinto was divided into Shrine (jinga) Shinto and Sectarian (kyoko) Shinto. Jinga became a state cult and it remained the national religion until 1945.

MAJOR JAPANESE FESTIVALS

1–3 Jan	Oshogatsu (New Year)
3 Mar	Ohinamatsuri (Doll's or Girls' Festival)
5 May	Tango no Sekku (Boys' Festival)
7 Jul	Hoshi matsuri or Tanabata (Star Festival)
13–31 Jul	Obon (Buddhist All Souls)

SIKHISM

Founded 15th-c in India.

Founder Guru Nanak (1469–1539).

Sacred text Adi Granth.

Beliefs Nanak preached tolerance and devotion to one God before whom everyone is equal. Sikh is the Sanskrit word for disciple. Nanak's doctrine sought a fusion of Brahmanism and Islam on the grounds that both were monotheistic. God is the true Guru and his divine word has come to humanity through the ten historical gurus. The line ended in 1708 since when the Sikh community is called guru.

Organization There is no priestly caste and all Sikhs are empowered to perform rituals connected with births, marriages, and deaths. Sikhs worship in their own temples but they evolved distinct features like the langar, 'kitchen', a communal meal where people of any religion or caste could eat. Rest houses for travellers were also provided. The tenth guru instituted an initiation ceremony, the Khalsa. Initiates wear the Five Ks (uncut hair, steel bangle, comb, shorts, ceremonial sword) and a turban. Members of the Khalsa add the name singh (lion) to their name and have to lead pure lives and follow a code of discipline. Sikhs generally rise before dawn, bathe and recite the japji, a morning prayer. Hindu festivals from northern India are observed.

Divisions There are several religious orders of Sikhs based either on disputes over the succession of gurus or points of ritual and tradition. The most important current issue is the number of Khalsa Sikhs cutting off their hair and beards and relapsing into Hinduism.

TAOISM

Founded 600 BC in China.

Founder Lao-tzu (6th-c BC).

Sacred texts Chuang-tzu, Lao-tzu (Tao-te ching).

Beliefs Taoism is Chinese for 'the school of the tao' and the 'Taoist religion'. Tao ('the way') is central in both Confucianism and Taoism. The former stresses the tao of humanity, the latter the tao of nature, harmony with which ensures appropriate conduct. Taoist religion developed later and was probably influenced by Buddhist beliefs. The doctrine emphasizes that good and evil action decide the fate of the soul. The Taoists believe that the sky, the earth and water are deities; that Lao-tzu is supreme master; that the disciple masters his body and puts evil spirits to flight with charms; that body and spirit are purified through meditation and by taking the pill of immortality to gain eternal life; and that the way is handed down from master to disciple. Religious Taoism incorporated ideas and images from philosophical Taoist texts, especially the Tao-te-ching but also the theory of Yin-yang, the quest for immortality, mental and physical discipline, interior hygiene, internal alchemy, healing and exorcism, a pantheon of gods and spirits, and ideals of theocratic states. The Immortals are meant to live in the mountains far from the tumult of the world.

Organization This is similar to Buddhism in the matter of clergy and temple. The jiao is a ceremony to purify the ground. Zhon-gyual is the only important religious festival, when the hungry dead appear to the living and Taoist priests free the souls of the dead from suffering.

TAOISM (cont.)

Divisions Religious Taoism emerged from many sects. These sects proliferated between 618 and 1126 AD and were described collectively as Spirit Cloud Taoists. They form the majority of Taoist priests in Taiwan, where they are called 'Masters of Methods' or Red-headed Taoists. The more orthodox priests are called 'Tao Masters' or Black-headed Taoists.

SACRED TEXTS OF WORLD RELIGIONS

Religion	Texts
Baha'i Faith	Kitab al-Aqdas, Haft Wadi, al-Kalimat al-Maknnah, Bayan
Buddhism	Tripitaka, Mahayana Sutra, Milindapanha, Bardo Thodol
Christianity	Old Testament: Genesis, Exodus, Leviticus, Numbers, Deuteronomy, Joshua, Judges, Ruth, 1 Samuel, 2 Samuel, 1 Kings, 2 Kings, 1 Chronicles, 2 Chronicles, Ezra, Nehemiah, Esther, Job, Psalms, Proverbs, Ecclesiastes, Song of Solomon, Isaiah, Jeremiah, Lamentations, Ezekiel, Daniel, Hosea, Joel, Amos, Obadiah, Jonah, Micah, Nahum, Habakkuk, Zephaniah, Haggai, Zechariah, Malachi. New Testament: Matthew, Mark, Luke, John, Acts of the Apostles, Romans, 1 Corinthians, 2 Corinthians, Galatians, Ephesians, Philippians, Colossians, 1 Thessalonians, 2 Thessalonians, 1 Timothy, 2 Timothy, Titus, Philemon, Hebrews, James, 1 Peter, 2 Peter, 1 John, 2 John, 3 John, Jude, Revelation. Apocrypha (Revised standard version 1957): 1 Esdras, 2 Esdras, Tobit, Judith, Additions to Esther, Wisdom of Solomon, Ecclesiasticus, Epistle of Jeremiah, Baruch, Prayer of Azariah and the Song of the Three Young Men, (History of) Susanna, Bel and the Dragon, Prayer of Manasseh, 1 Maccabees, 2 Maccabbees. (The Authorized version incorporates Jeremiah into Baruch; The prayer of Azariah is simply called the Song of the Three Holy Children. The Roman Catholic Church includes Tobit, Judith, all of Esther, Maccabees 1 and 2, Wisdom of Solomon, Ecclesiasticus, and Baruch in its canon.)
Confucianism	Shih ching, Li ching, Shu ching, Chu'un Ch'iu, I Ching
Hinduism	Vedas (Upanishads), Ramayana, Mahabharata and the Bhagavad Gita
Islam	The Koran, the Hadith
Jainism	Svetambara canon, Digambara texts
Judaism	The Hebrew Bible: Torah (Pentateuch): Genesis, Exodus, Leviticus, Numbers, Deuteronomy. Also the books of the Prophets, Psalms, Chronicles and Proverbs. The Talmud including the Mishna and Gemara. The Zohar (Book of Splendour) is a famous Cabalistic book.
Shintoism	Kojiki, Nohon Shoki
Sikhism	Adi Granth
Taoism	Chuang-tzu, Lao-tzu (Tao-te-ching)

ARTS AND CULTURE

NOVELISTS AND WRITERS

Selected works are listed.

Achebe, Chinua (Albert Chinualumogu) (1930–)
Nigerian novelist, born Ogidi; *Things Fall Apart* (1959), *Anthills of the Savannah* (1988).

Adams, Douglas (Noel) (1952–)
English novelist, short-story writer; *The Hitch Hiker's Guide to the Galaxy* (1979), *Dirk Gently's Holistic Detective Agency* (1987).

Adams, Richard (George) (1920–)
English novelist, short-story writer, born Newbury, Berkshire; *Watership Down* (1972), *Shardik* (1974), *The Girl in a Swing* (1980).

Aldiss, Brian (1925–)
British novelist, poet, short-story writer, playwright, born East Dereham, Norfolk; *The Helliconia Trilogy* (1985), *Forgotten Life* (1988), *Dracula Unbound* (1991).

Ambler, Eric (1909–)
British novelist, playwright, born London; *The Mask of Dimitrios* (1939), *A King of Anger* (1964), *The Care of Time* (1981).

Amis, Kingsley (William) (1922–95)
English novelist, poet, born London; *Lucky Jim* (1954), *That Uncertain Feeling* (1955), *Jake's Thing* (1978), *The Old Devils* (1986) Booker Prize.

Amis, Martin (Louis) (1949–)
English novelist, short-story writer, born Oxford; *The Rachel Papers* (1973), *Money* (1984), *London Fields* (1990), *Time's Arrow* (1991).

Angelou, Maya (Marguerita Johnson) (1928–)
American novelist, poet, playwright, born St Louis, Missouri; *I Know Why The Caged Bird Sings* (1969), *All God's Children Need Travelling Shoes* (1986).

Archer, Jeffrey (Howard) (1940–)
English novelist, short-story writer, born Somerset; *Not a Penny More, Not a Penny Less* (1975), *Kane and Abel* (1979), *First Among Equals* (1984), *A Twist in the Tale* (1989), *Honour Among Thieves* (1993), *Twelve Red Herrings* (1994).

Asimov, Isaac (1920–92)
American novelist, short-story writer, born Petrovichi, USSR; *I Robot* (1950), *Foundation* (1951), *The Disappearing Man and other stories* (1985), *Nightfall* (1990).

Atwood, Margaret (Eleanor) (1939–)
Canadian novelist, poet, short-story writer, born Ottowa; *Bluebeards' Egg* (1983), *The Handmaid's Tale* (1986), *Cat's Eye* (1989).

Austen, Jane (1775–1817)
English novelist, born Steventon, Hampshire; *Sense and Sensibility* (1811), *Pride and Prejudice* (1813), *Mansfield Park* (1814), *Emma* (1816), *Persuasion* (1818).

Bainbridge, Beryl (1934–)
English novelist, born Liverpool; *The Dressmaker* (1973), *Injury Time* (1977).

NOVELISTS AND WRITERS (cont.)

Ballantyne, R(obert) M(ichael) (1825–94)
Scottish novelist, born Edinburgh; *The Coral Island* (1857), *The Gorilla Hunters* (1862).

Balzac, Honoré de (1799–1850)
French novelist, born Tours; *Comédie humaine* (1827–47), *Illusions perdues* (1837–43).

Bates, H(erbert) E(rnest) (1905–74)
English novelist and short-story writer, born Rushden, Northamptonshire; *Fair Stood the Wind for France* (1944), *The Jacaranda Tree* (1949), *Love for Lydia* (1952), *The Darling Buds of May* (1958).

Bellow, Saul (1915–   )
Canadian novelist, born Lachine, Quebec; *Henderson the Rain King* (1959), *Herzog* (1964), *Humboldt's Gift* (1974); Nobel Prize for Literature 1976.

Bennett, (Enoch) Arnold (1867–1931)
English novelist, born Hanley, Staffordshire; *Anna of the Five Towns* (1902), The Old Wives' Tale (1908), *Clayhanger* series (1910–18).

Berger, Thomas (Louis) (1924–   )
American novelist, born Cincinnati, Ohio; *Reinhart in Love* (1962), *Arthur Rex* (1978), *The Houseguest* (1988).

Binchy, Maeve (1940–   )
Irish novelist, short-story writer, born Dublin; *Light a Penny Candle* (1982), *Echoes* (1985), *Firefly Summer* (1987), *Circle of Friends* (1990), *The Copper Beech* (1992).

Blackmore, R(ichard) D(odderidge) (1825–1900)
English novelist, born Longworth, Berkshire; *Lorna Doone* (1869).

Böll, Heinrich (1917–85)
German novelist, born Cologne; *And Never Said a Solitary Word* (1953), *The Unguarded House* (1954), *The Bread of Our Early Years* (1955); Nobel Prize for Literature 1972.

Bradbury, Malcolm (Stanley) (1932–   )
English novelist, born Sheffield; *Eating People is Wrong* (1959), *The History Man* (1975), *Dr Criminale* (1992).

Bradbury, Ray(mond) (Douglas) (1920–   )
American novelist, short-story writer, born Waukegan, Illinois; *The Martian Chronicles* (1950), *Fahrenheit 451* (1954), *Something Wicked this Way Comes* (1962).

Bradford, Barbara Taylor (1933–   )
English novelist; *A Woman of Substance* (1979), *Hold the Dream* (1985).

Brontë, Anne (1820–49)
English novelist, poet, born Thornton, Yorkshire; *Agnes Grey* (1847), *The Tenant of Wildfell Hall* (1848).

Brontë, Charlotte (1816–55)
English novelist, poet, born Thornton, Yorkshire; *Jane Eyre* (1847), *Shirley* (1849), *Villette* (1853).

Brontë, Emily (1818–48)
English novelist, poet, born Thornton, Yorkshire; *Wuthering Heights* (1847).

Brookner, Anita (1938–   )
English novelist, born London; *Hotel du Lac* (1984) Booker Prize, *Family and Friends* (1985), *Brief Lives* (1991).

Buchan, John (1875–1940)
Scottish novelist, poet, born Perth; *The Thirty-Nine Steps* (1915), *Greenmantle* (1916), *Sir Walter Scott* (biography) (1932).

Buck, Pearl (née **Sydenstricker**) (1892–1973)
American novelist, born Hillsboro, W Virginia; *The Good Earth* (1913), *Pavilion of Women* (1946); Nobel Prize for Literature 1938.

Bunyan, John (1628–88)
English writer, born Elstow, near Bedford; *Pilgrim's Progress* (1678).

Burgess, Anthony (John Anthony Burgess Wilson) (1917–93)
English novelist, born Manchester; *A Clockwork Orange* (1962), *The Malayan Trilogy* (1972), *Earthly Powers* (1980), *Kingdom of the Wicked* (1985), *Any Old Iron* (1989).

Burney, Fanny (Frances, Mme d'Arblay) (1752–1840)
English novelist, born King's Lynn; *Evelina* (1778), *Cecilia* (1782).

Burroughs, Edgar Rice (1875–1950)
American novelist, born Chicago; *Tarzan of the Apes* (1914), *The Land that Time Forgot* (1924).

Burroughs, William S(eward) (1914–)
American novelist, born St Louis, Missouri; *The Naked Lunch* (1959), *The Soft Machine* (1961), *The Wild Boys* (1971), *Exterminator!* (1974).

Byatt, A(ntonia) S(usan) (1936–)
English novelist, born Sheffield; *The Shadow of a Sun* (1964), *The Virgin in the Garden* (1978), *Possession* (1990) Booker Prize.

Camus, Albert (1913–60)
French novelist, playwright, born Mondovi, Algeria; *The Outsider* (1942), *The Plague* (1948), *The Fall* (1957); Nobel Prize for Literature 1957.

Canetti, Elias (1905–94)
Bulgarian novelist, born Russe, Bulgaria; *Auto da Fé* (1935, trans 1946), *Crowds and Power* (1960, trans 1962); Nobel Prize for Literature 1981.

Capote, Truman (1924–84)
American playwright, novelist, short-story writer, born New Orleans; *Other Voices, Other Rooms* (1948), *Breakfast at Tiffany's* (1958).

Carey, Peter (1943–)
Australian novelist, short-story writer, born Bacchus Marsh, Victoria; *Bliss* (1981), *Illywhacker* (1985), *Oscar and Lucinda* (1989) Booker Prize.

Carter, Angela (1940–92)
English novelist, poet, playwright, born London; *The Magic Toyshop* (1967), *The Infernal Desire Machines of Dr Hoffman* (1972), *Nights at the Circus* (1984), *Wise Children* (1991).

Cartland, (Mary) Barbara (Hamilton) (1901–)
English novelist, born Birmingham; prolific writer, over 400 titles, eg *The Husband Hunters* (1976), *Wings on My Heart* (1954), *The Castle Made for Love* (1985).

Cather, Willa (Silbert) (1876–1947)
American novelist, poet, born near Winchester, Virginia; *O Pioneers!* (1913), *My Antonia* (1918), *One of Ours* (1922), *The Professor's House* (1925), *My Mortal Enemy* (1926), *Death Comes for the Archbishop* (1927), *Sapphira and the Slave Girl* (1940).

Cervantes, Saavedra, Miguel de (1547–1616)
Spanish novelist and poet, born Alcala de Henares; *La Galatea* (1585), *Don Quixote* (1605–15).

Chandler, Raymond (1888–1959)
American novelist, born Chicago; *The Big Sleep* (1939), *Farewell, My Lovely* (1940), *The High Window* (1942), *The Lady in the Lake* (1943), *The Long Goodbye* (1953).

Chesterton, G(ilbert) K(eith) (1874–1936)
English novelist, poet, born London; *The Napoleon of Notting Hill* (1904), *The Innocence of Father Brown* (1911).

Christie, Dame Agatha (Mary Clarissa) (1890–1976)
English novelist, born Torquay, Devon; *Murder on the Orient Express* (1934), *Death on the Nile* (1937), *And Then There Were None* (1941), *Curtain* (1975).

NOVELISTS AND WRITERS (cont.)

Clarke, Arthur C(harles) (1917–)
 English novelist, short-story writer, born Minehead, Somerset; *Childhood's End* (1953),
 The Fountains of Paradise (1979), *The Garden of Rama* (1991).
Clavell, James (du Maresq) (1922–94)
 American novelist, playwright, born England; *King Rat* (1962), *Tai-Pan* (1966), *Shogun* (1975).
Coetzee, J(ohn) M(ichael) (1940–)
 South African novelist, born Cape Town; *Life and Times of Michael K* (1983) Booker Prize.
Collins, (William) Wilkie (1824–89)
 English novelist, born London; *The Woman in White* (1860), *No Name* (1862), *Armadale* (1866),
 The Moonstone (1868).
Conrad, Joseph (originally **Jozef Teodor Konrad Nalecz Korzeniowski**) (1857–1924)
 Polish/British novelist, short-story writer, born Berdichev, Ukraine; *Lord Jim* (1900), *Heart of
 Darkness* (1902), *Nostromo* (1904), *The Secret Agent* (1907), *Chance* (1914).
Cookson, Catherine Ann (1906–)
 English novelist, born Tyne Dock, County Durham; prolific author, over 40 titles eg *Tilly Trotter*
 (1956), *The Glass Virgin* (1969).

de Beauvoir, Simone (1908–86)
 French novelist, born Paris; *The Second Sex* (1949, trans 1953). *Les Mandarins* (1954), *Memoirs of
 a Dutiful Daughter* (1959).
Defoe, Daniel (1660–1731)
 English novelist, born Stoke Newington, London; *Robinson Crusoe* (1719), *Moll Flanders* (1722),
 A Journal of the Plague Year (1722).
Deighton, Len (Leonard Cyril) (1929–)
 English novelist, born London; *The Ipcress File* (1962), *Spy Hook* (1988), *Spy Line* (1989), *Spy
 Sinker* (1990).
de Quincey, Thomas (1785–1859)
 English novelist, born Manchester; *Confessions of an English Opium Eater* (1822).
Dickens, Charles (1812–70)
 English novelist, born Landport, Portsmouth; *Oliver Twist* (1837–9), *David Copperfield* (1849–50),
 Bleak House (1852–3), *Great Expectations* (1860–1).
Disraeli, Benjamin (1804–81)
 English novelist, born London; *Coningsby* (1844), *Sybil* (1846), *Tancred* (1847).
Dos Passos, John Roderigo (1896–1970)
 American novelist, born Chicago; *Manhattan Transfer* (1925), *USA* (1930–6).
Dostoevsky, Fyodor Mikhailovich (1821–81)
 Russian novelist, born Moscow; *Notes from Underground* (1864), *Crime and Punishment* (1866),
 The Brothers Karamazov (1880).
Doyle, Sir Arthur Conan (1859–1930)
 Scottish novelist, short-story writer, born Edinburgh; *The Memoirs of Sherlock Holmes* (1894),
 The Hound of the Baskervilles (1902), *The Lost World* (1912).
Doyle, Roddy (1958–)
 Irish novelist, born Dublin; *Your Granny's a Hunger Striker* (1982), *The Commitments* (1988),
 The Snapper (1990), *The Van* (1991), *Paddy Clarke Ha Ha Ha* (1993) Booker Prize.
Drabble, Margaret (1939–)
 English novelist, short-story writer, born Sheffield; *The Millstone* (1965), *Jerusalem the Golden*
 (1967), *The Ice Age* (1977).

Duffy, Maureen (Patricia) (1933–)
English novelist, playwright, born Worthing, Sussex; *That's How It Was* (1962), *The Paradox Players* (1967), *The Microcosm* (1966).
Dumas, Alexandre (père) (Alexandre Dumas Davy de la Pailleterie) (1802–70)
French novelist and playwright, born Villers-Cotterets, Aisne; *The Three Musketeers* (1844–5).
Dumas, Alexandre (fils) (1824–95)
French novelist, playwright, born Paris; *La Dame aux camélias* (1848).
du Maurier, Dame Daphne (1907–89)
English novelist, born London; *Rececca* (1938), *My Cousin Rachel* (1951).
Durrell, Gerald Malcolm (1925–95)
English writer, born Jamshedpur, India; *The Overloaded Ark* (1953), *My Family and Other Animals* (1956).
Durrell, Lawrence George (1912–90)
English novelist, poet, born Julundur, India; *'Alexandria Quartet'* (1957–60).

Eco, Umberto (1932–)
Italian novelist, born Alessandria, Piedmont; *The Name of the Rose* (1980), *Foucault's Pendulum* (1989).
Eliot, George (originally **Mary Ann,** later **Marian Evans**) (1819–80)
English novelist, born Arbury, Warwickshire; *Adam Bede* (1858), *The Mill on the Floss* (1860), *Middlemarch* (1871–2), *Daniel Deronda* (1874–6).

Faulkner, William Harrison (1897–1962)
American novelist, born near Oxford, Mississippi; *Sartoris* (1929), *The Sound and the Fury* (1929), *Absalom, Absalom!* (1936); Nobel Prize for Literature 1949.
Fielding, Henry (1707–54)
English novelist, born Sharpham Park, near Glastonbury, Somerset; *Joseph Andrews* (1742), *Tom Jones* (1749).
Fitzgerald, F(rancis) Scott (Key) (1896–1940)
American novelist, short-story writer, born St Paul, Minnesota; *The Great Gatsby* (1925), *Tender is the Night* (1934).
Fitzgerald, Penelope (Mary) (née **Knox**) (1916–)
English novelist, born Lincoln; *The Bookshop* (1978), *Offshore* (1979) Booker Prize, *The Gate of Angels* (1990).
Flaubert, Gustave (1821–80)
French novelist, born Rouen; *Madame Bovary* (1857), *Salammbô* (1862).
Fleming, Ian (Lancaster) (1908–64)
English novelist; author of the 'James Bond' novels eg *Casino Royale* (1953), *From Russia with Love* (1957), *Dr No* (1958), *Goldfinger* (1959), *The Man with the Golden Gun* (1965).
Forester, C(ecil) S(cott) (1899–1966)
British novelist, born Cairo, Egypt; *Payment Deferred* (1926), *The African Queen* (1935), *The Happy Return* (1937).
Forster, E(dward) M(organ) (1879–1970)
English novelist, short-story writer, born London; *A Room with a View* (1908), *Howards End* (1910), *A Passage to India* (1922–4).
Forsyth, Frederick (1938–)
English novelist, short-story writer, born Ashford, Kent; *The Day of the Jackal* (1971), *The Odessa File* (1972), *The Fourth Protocol* (1984).

NOVELISTS AND WRITERS (cont.)

Fowles, John (Robert) (1926–   )
  English novelist, born Leigh-on-Sea; *The Magus* (1965, revised 1977), *The French Lieutenant's Woman* (1969).

Francis, Dick (Richard Stanley) (1920–   )
  English novelist, born Tenby, Pembrokeshire; *Dead Cert* (1962), *Slay-Ride* (1973), *The Edge* (1988), *Comeback* (1991).

French, Marilyn (1929–   )
  American novelist, born New York City; *The Women's Room* (1977), *The Bleeding Heart* (1980), *Her Mother's Daughter* (1987), *The War Against Women* (1992).

Fuller, Roy (Broadbent) (1912–91)
  English novelist, poet, born Failsworth, Lancashire; *The Second Curtain* (1953), *The Ruined Boys* (1959), *My Child, My Sister* (1965).

Galsworthy, John (1867–1933)
  English novelist, playwright, born Coombe, Surrey; *The Man of Property* (1906), *The Forsyte Saga* (1906–31); Nobel Prize for Literature 1932.

García Márquez, Gabriel (1928–   )
  Colombian novelist, born Aracataca; *One Hundred Years of Solitude* (1970), *Chronicle of a Death Foretold* (1982); Nobel Prize for Literature 1982.

Gaskell, Mrs Elizabeth (Cleghorn) (1810–65)
  English novelist, born Cheyne Row, Chelsea, London; *Mary Barton* (1848), *Cranford* (1853), *North and South* (1855), *Sylvia's Lovers* (1863).

Gibbon, Lewis Grassic (James Leslie Mitchell) (1901–35)
  Scottish novelist, born near Auchterless, Aberdeenshire; *Sunset Song* (1932), *Cloud Howe* (1933), *Grey Granite* (1934).

Gide, André (Paul Guillaume) (1860–1951)
  French novelist, born Paris; *The Immoralist* (1902), *The Vatican Cellars* (1914).

Godden, (Margaret) Rumer (1907–   )
  English, born Sussex; *Black Narcissus* (1939), *Breakfast with the Nikolides* (1942), *The Greengage Summer* (1958), *Coromandel Sea Change* (1991).

Godwin, William (1756–1836)
  English novelist, born Wisbech; *Caleb Williams* (1794), *Mandeville* (1817).

Goethe, Johann Wolfgang von (1749–1832)
  German novelist, poet, born Frankfurt-am-Main; *The Sorrows of Young Werther* (1774).

Gogol, Nikolai Vasilievich (1809–52)
  Russian novelist, short-story writer, playwright, born Sorochinstsi, Poltava; *The Overcoat* (1835), *Diary of a Madman* (1835), *Dead Souls* (1842), *The Odd Women* (1893).

Golding, (Sir) William (Gerald) (1911–93)
  English novelist, born St Columb Minor, Cornwall; *The Lord of the Flies* (1954), *The Inheritors* (1955), *Pincher Martin* (1956), *The Spire* (1964), *Darkness Visible* (1979), *Rites of Passage* (1980) Booker Prize, *The Paper Men* (1984), *Close Quarter* (1987), *Fire Down Below* (1989); Nobel Prize for Literature 1983.

Goldsmith, Oliver (1728–74)
  Anglo-Irish playwright, novelist, poet, born Pallasmore, County Longford; *The Vicar of Wakefield* (1766).

Gordimer, Nadine (1923–   )
  South African novelist, short-story writer, born Springs, Transvaal; *Occasion for Loving* (1963),

A Guest of Honour (1970), *The Conservationist* (1974) Booker Prize, *A Sport of Nature* (1987); Nobel Prize for Literature 1991.

Gorky, Maxim (Aleksei Maksimovich Peshkov) (1868–1936)
Russian novelist, short-story writer, born Nizhni Novgorod (New Gorky); *The Mother* (1906–7), *Childhood* (1913), *The Life of Klim Samgin* (1925–36).

Grass, Günter (Wilhelm) (1927–)
German novelist, born Danzig; *The Tin Drum* (1959), *The Meeting at Telgte* (1979).

Graves, Robert von Ranke (1895–1985)
English novelist, poet, born London; *I Claudius* (1934), *Claudius the God* (1934).

Gray, Alasdair (1934–)
Scottish novelist, short-story writer, poet, born Glasgow; *Lanark* (1981), *Unlikely Stories, Mostly* (1983), *1982 Janine* (1984).

Greene, (Henry) Graham (1904–91)
English novelist, playwright, born Berkhamstead, Hertfordshire; *Brighton Rock* (1938), *The Power and the Glory* (1940), *The Third Man* (1950), *The Honorary Consul* (1973).

Haggard, Sir (Henry) Rider (1856–1925)
British novelist, born Bradenham Hall, Norfolk; *King Solomon's Mines* (1885), *She* (1887), *Allan Quatermain* (1887).

Hailey, Arthur (1920–)
Anglo-Canadian novelist, playwright, born Luton, Bedfordshire; *Flight into Danger* (1958), *Airport* (1968), *The Evening News* (1990).

Hardy, Thomas (1840–1928)
English novelist, poet, born Higher Bockhampton, Dorset; *Far from the Madding Crowd* (1874), *The Mayor of Casterbridge* (1886), *Tess of the D'Urbervilles* (1891), *Jude the Obscure* (1895).

Hartley, L(eslie) P(oles) (1895–1972)
English novelist, short-story writer, born near Peterborough; *The Shrimp and the Anemone* (1944), *The Go-Between* (1953), *The Hireling* (1957).

Hawthorne, Nathaniel (1804–64)
American novelist, short-story writer, born Salem, Massachusetts; *The Scarlet Letter* (1850), *The House of the Seven Gables* (1851).

Heller, Joseph (1923–)
American novelist, born Brooklyn, New York; *Catch-22* (1961), *Something Happened* (1974), *Picture This* (1988) *Closing Time* (1994).

Hemingway, Ernest (Millar) (1899–1961)
American novelist, short-story writer, born Oak Park (Chicago), Illinois; *A Farewell to Arms* (1929), *For Whom the Bell Tolls* (1940), *The Old Man and the Sea* (1952); Nobel Prize for Literature 1954.

Hesse, Herman (1877–1962)
German novelist, born Calw in Württemberg; *Rosshalde* (1914), *Steppenwolf* (1927), *The Glass Bead Game* (1943); Nobel Prize for Literature 1946.

Heyer, Georgette (1902–74)
English novelist, born London; 56 novels eg *The Black Moth* (1929), *Footsteps in the Dark* (1932), *Regency Buck* (1935), *The Corinthian* (1940), *Friday's Child* (1944), *The Grand Sophy* (1950), *Bath Tangle* (1955), *Venetia* (1958), *The Nonesuch* (1962), *Frederica* (1965).

Highsmith, Patricia (Mary Patricia Plangman) (1921–95)
American novelist, short-story writer, born Fort Worth, Texas; *This Sweet Sickness* (1960), *The Cry of the Owl* (1962), *The Boy Who Followed Ripley* (1980).

NOVELISTS AND WRITERS (cont.)

Holt, Victoria (Eleanor Alice Burford Hibbert) (1906–93)
English novelist, prolific output, also wrote as Philippa Carr, Jean Plaidy; *Catherine de 'Medici* (1969 — as JP), *Will You Love Me in September* (1981 — as PC), *The Captive* (1989 — as VH).

Hughes, Thomas (1822–96)
English novelist, born Uffington, Berkshire; *Tom Brown's Schooldays* (1857).

Hugo, Victor (Marie) (1802–85)
French novelist, dramatist, poet, born Besançon; *Notre Dame de Paris* (1831), *Les Misérables* (1862).

Hunter, Evan (Salvatore A Lombino) (1926–   )
American novelist, playwright, short-story writer, born New York City; *The Blackboard Jungle* (1954), *Strangers When We Meet* (1958), *The Paper Dragon* (1966), *Last Summer* (1968).

Huxley, Aldous (Leonard) (1894–1963)
English novelist, born Godalming, Surrey; *Brave New World* (1932), *Eyeless in Gaza* (1936), *Island* (1962).

Innes, (Ralph) Hammond (1913–   )
English novelist, playwright, born Horsham, Sussex; *The Trojan Horse* (1940), *Atlantic Fury* (1962), *Isvik* (1991).

Irving, John (1942–   )
American novelist, short-story writer; *The World According to Garp* (1978), *The Hotel New Hampshire* (1981), *A Prayer for Owen Meany* (1989).

Isherwood, Christopher (William Bradshaw) (1904–86)
English/American novelist, born Disley, Cheshire; *Mr Norris Changes Trains* (1935), *Goodbye to Berlin* (1939), *Down there on a Visit* (1962).

Ishiguro, Kazuo (1954–   )
British novelist, short-story writer, born Japan; *The Remains of the Day* (1989) Booker Prize.

James, Henry (1843–1916)
American novelist, born New York; *Portrait of a Lady* (1881), *The Bostonians* (1886), *The Turn of the Screw* (1889), *The Awkward Age* (1899), *The Ambassadors* (1903), *The Golden Bowl* (1904).

James, P(hyliss) D(orothy) (1920–   )
English novelist, born Oxford; *Cover Her Face* (1966), *Taste for Death* (1986).

Jhabvala, Ruth Prawer (1927–   )
British/Polish novelist, born Cologne, Germany; *Heat and Dust* (1975), *In Search of Love and Beauty* (1983).

Jong, Erica (née Mann) (1942–   )
American novelist, poet, born New York City; *Fear of Flying* (1973), *Fanny, Being the True History of the Adventures of Fanny Hackabout-Jones* (1980), *Serenissima* (1987).

Joyce, James (Augustine Aloysius) (1882–1941)
Irish novelist, poet, born Dublin; *Dubliners* (1914), *A Portrait of the Artist as a Young Man* (1914–15), *Ulysses* (1922), *Finnegan's Wake* (1939).

Kafka, Franz (1883–1924)
Austrian novelist, short-story writer, born Prague; *The Metamorphosis* (1916), *The Trial* (1925), *The Castle* (1926), *America* (1972).

Kelman, James (Alexander) (1946–   )
Scottish novelist, short-story writer, playwright, born Glasgow; *The Busconductor Hines* (1984),

A Chancer (1985), *Greyhound for Breakfast* (1987), *A Disaffection* (1989), *How late it was, how late* (1994) Booker Prize.

Keneally, Thomas (Michael) (1935–)
Australian novelist, short-story writer, playwright, born Sydney; *Bring Larks and Heroes* (1967), *Three Cheers for a Paraclete* (1968), *The Survivor* (1969), *Schindler's Ark* (1982) Booker Prize.

Kerouac, Jack (Jean-Louis) (1922–69)
American novelist, born Lowell, Massachusetts; *On the Road* (1957), *The Dharma Bums* (1958).

Kesey, Ken (Elton) (1935–)
American novelist, short-story writer, born La Junta, Colorado; *One Flew Over the Cuckoo's Nest* (1962).

King, Stephen (Edwin) (1947–)
American novelist, short-story writer; *Carrie* (1974), *The Shining* (1977), *Christine* (1983).

Kingsley, Charles (1819–75)
English novelist, born Holne vicarage, Dartmoor; *Westward Ho!* (1855), *The Water-Babies* (1863), *Hereward the Wake* (1866).

Kipling, Rudyard (1865–1936)
English novelist, poet, short-story writer, born Bombay, India; *Barrack-room Ballads* (1892), *The Jungle Book* (1894), *Kim* (1901), *Just So Stories* (1902); Nobel Prize for Literature 1907.

Kundera, Milan (1929–)
French/Czech novelist, born Brno; *Life is Elsewhere* (1973), *The Farewell Party* (1976), *The Unbearable Lightness of Being* (1984), *Immortality* (1991).

La Fayette, Marie Madeleine Pioche de Lavergne, Comtesse de (1634–93)
French novelist, born Paris; *Zaïde* (1670), *La Princesse de Clèves* (1678).

Lampedusa Giuseppe Tomasi di (1896–1957)
Italian novelist, born Palermo, Sicily; *Il Gattopardo* (The Leopard) (1958).

Lawrence, D(avid) H(erbert) (1885–1930)
English novelist, poet, short-story writer, born Eastwood, Nottinghamshire; *Sons and Lovers* (1913), *The Rainbow* (1915), *Women in Love* (1920), *Lady Chatterley's Lover* (1928).

Le Carré, John (David John Moore Cornwell) (1931–)
English novelist, born Poole, Dorset; *Tinker, Tailor, Soldier, Spy* (1974), *Smiley's People* (1980), *The Little Drummer Girl* (1983), *The Secret Pilgrim* (1992), *The Night Manager* (1993).

Lee, (Nelle) Harper (1926–)
American novelist, born Monroeville, Alabama; *To Kill a Mockingbird* (1960).

Lee, Laurie (1914–97)
English novelist, poet, born Slad, Gloucestershire; *Cider with Rosie* (1959), *As I Walked Out One Midsummer Morning* (1969), *A Moment of War* (1991).

Lessing, Doris (1919–)
British novelist, short-story writer, born Kermanshah, Iran; *The Grass is Singing* (1950), *The Golden Notebook* (1962), *Canopus in Argus Archives* (1979–83).

Levi, Primo (1919–87)
Italian novelist, born Turin; *If this is a Man* (1947), *The Periodic Table* (1984).

Lewis, C(live) S(taples) (1898–1963)
British novelist, religious writer, born Belfast; *Out of the Silent Planet* (1938), *Perelandra* (1939), *That Hideous Strength* (1945), *The Chronicles of Narnia*—a series of seven books beginning with *The Lion, The Witch and The Wardrobe* (1950) and ending with *The Last Battle* (1956).

Lewis, (Harry) Sinclair (1885–1951)
American novelist, born Sauk Center, Minnesota; *Main Street* (1920), *Babbitt* (1922), *Martin Arrowsmith* (1925), *Elmer Gantry* (1927); Nobel Prize for Literature 1930.

NOVELISTS AND WRITERS (cont.)

Lively, Penelope (Margaret) (née **Low**) (1933–   )
British, born Cairo, Egypt; *The Road to Lichfield* (1977), *Moon Tiger* (1987) Booker Prize, *City of the Mind* (1991).

Lodge, David (1935–   )
English novelist, born London; *The British Museum is Falling Down* (1965), *Changing Places* (1975), *Small World* (1984).

London, Jack (John) Griffith (1876–1916)
American novelist, born San Francisco; *Call of the Wild* (1903), *White Fang* (1907), *Martin Eden* (1909).

Lowry, (Clarence) Malcolm (1909–57)
English novelist, born Cheshire; *Under The Volcano* (1947).

Lurie, Alison (1926–   )
American novelist, born Chicago, Illinois; *Love and Friendship* (1962), *The War Between the Tates* (1974), *The Truth about Lorin Jones* (1988).

McEwan, Ian (Russell) (1948–   )
English novelist, short-story writer, playwright, born Aldershot, Hampshire; *First Love, Last Rites* (1975), *The Cement Garden* (1978), *The Child in Time* (1987), *The Innocent* (1990), *Black Dogs* (1992).

MacKenzie, Sir (Edward Montague) Compton (1883–1972)
English novelist, born West Hartlepool; *Whisky Galore* (1942).

MacLean, Alistair (1922–87)
Scottish novelist, born Glasgow; *The Guns of Navarone* (1957), *Where Eagles Dare* (1967).

Mailer, Norman (Kingsley) (1923–   )
American novelist, born Long Beach, New Jersey; *The Naked and the Dead* (1949), *Barbary Shore* (1951), *An American Dream* (1965), *The Executioner's Song* (1979).

Mann, Thomas (1875–1955)
German novelist, born Lubeck; *Death in Venice* (1912), *The Magic Mountain* (1924).

Mansfield, Katherine (Katherine Mansfield Beauchamp) (1888–1923)
New Zealand short-story writer, born Wellington; *Prelude* (1918), *Bliss, and other stories* (1920), *The Garden Party, and other stories* (1922).

Marsh, Ngaio (1899–1982)
New Zealand novelist, born Christchurch; *Death in a White Tie* (1958), *A Grave Mistake* (1978).

Maugham, (William) Somerset (1874–1965)
English novelist, born Paris; *Of Human Bondage* (1915), *The Moon and Sixpence* (1919), *The Razor's Edge* (1945).

Maupassant, Guy de (1850–93)
French short-story writer, novelist, born Miromesnil; *Claire de Lune* (1884), *Bel Ami* (1885).

Mauriac, François (1885–1970)
French novelist, born Bordeaux; *Le Baiser au Lépreux* (1922); Nobel Prize for Literature 1952.

Melville, Herman (1819–1909)
American novelist, poet, born New York; *Moby Dick* (1851).

Meredith, George (1828–1909)
English novelist, poet, born Portsmouth; *The Egoist* (1879), *Diana of the Crossways* (1885).

Michener, James A(lbert) (1907–   )
American novelist, short-story writer; *Tales of the South Pacific* (1947), *Hawaii* (1959), *Chesapeake* (1978).

Miller, Henry Valentine (1891–1980)
  American novelist, born New York; *Tropic of Cancer* (1934), *Tropic of Capricorn* (1938), *The Rosy Crucifixion Trilogy* (1949–60).
Mitchell, Margaret (1900–49)
  American novelist, born Atlanta, Georgia; *Gone with the Wind* (1936).
Morrison, Toni (1931–   )
  American novelist, born Ohio; *The Bluest Eye* (1970), *Song of Solomon* (1977), *Tar Baby* (1981) *Beloved* (1987) , *Jazz* (1992); Nobel Prize for Literature 1993.
Mortimer, John (Clifford) (1923–   )
  English novelist, short-story writer, playwright, born London; *A Cat Among the Pigeons* (1964), *Rumpole of the Bailey* (1978), *Paradise Postponed* (1985).
Murdoch, Iris (1919–   )
  Irish novelist, born Dublin; *The Bell* (1958), *The Sea, The Sea* (1978) Booker Prize, *The Philosopher's Pupil* (1983).

Nabokov, Vladimir Vladimirovich (1899–1977)
  Russian/US novelist, poet, born St Petersburg; *Lolita* (1955), *Look at the Harlequins!* (1974).
Naipaul, V(idiadhar) S(urajprasad) (1932–   )
  Trinidadian novelist, born Trinidad; *A House for Mr Biswas* (1961), *In a Free State* (1971) Booker Prize, *A Bend in the River* (1979).

Okri, Ben (1959–   )
  Nigerian novelist, born Minna; *The Famished Road* (1991) Booker Prize, *Songs of Enchantment* (1993).
Orwell, George (Eric Arthur Blair) (1903–50)
  English novelist, born Bengal; *Down and Out in Paris and London* (1933), *The Road to Wigan Pier* (1937), *Animal Farm* (1945), *Nineteen Eighty-Four* (1949).

Pasternak, Boris (Leonidovich) (1890–1960)
  Russian novelist, born Moscow; *Doctor Zhivago* (1957); Nobel Prize for Literature 1958.
Paton, Allan (Stewart) (1903–88)
  South African novelist, short-story writer, born Pietermaritzburg, Natal; *Cry, the Beloved Country* (1948).
Poe, Edgar Allan (1809–49)
  American short-story writer, poet, born Boston; *Tales of the Grotesque and Arabesque* (eg 'The Fall of the House of Usher') (1840), *The Pit and the Pendulum* (1843).
Porter, Katherine Anne (Maria Veronica Callista Russell) (1890–1980)
  American novelist, short-story writer, born Indian Creek, Texas; *Pale Horse, Pale Rider* (1939), *Ship of Fools* (1962).
Powell, Anthony (Dymoke) (1905–   )
  English novelist, born London; *A Dance to the Music of Time* (1951–75), *The Fisher King* (1986).
Priestley, J(ohn) B(oynton) (1894–1984)
  English novelist, playwright, born Bradford; *The Good Companions* (1929), *Angel Pavement* (1930).
Proust, Marcel (1871–1922)
  French novelist, born Paris; *Remembrance of Things Past* (1913–27).

Queen, Ellery (Patrick Dannay (1905–82) **and his cousin Manfred B Lee** (1905–71))
  American novelists and short-story writers, both born Brooklyn, New York; *The French Powder Mystery* (1930), *The Tragedy of X* (1940), *The Glass Village* (1954).

NOVELISTS AND WRITERS (cont.)

Remarque, Erich Maria (1898–1970)
German novelist, born Osnabrück; *All Quiet on the Western Front* (1929), *The Road Back* (1931), *The Black Obelisk* (1957).

Rendell, Ruth (1930–)
English novelist, born London; *A Judgement in Stone* (1977), *The Killing Doll* (1980), *Heartstones* (1987); as Barbara Vine *The House of Stairs* (1989).

Richardson, Samuel (1689–1761)
English novelist, born near Derby; *Pamela* (1740), *Clarissa* (1747–8), *Sir Charles Grandison* (1753–4).

Roth, Philip Milton (1933–)
American novelist, short-story writer, born Newark, New Jersey; *Portnoy's Complaint* (1969), *The Great American Novel* (1973), *My Life as a Man* (1974) *The Ghost Writer* (1979), *The Counterlife* (1987), *Operation Shylock* (1993).

Rushdie, Salman (1947–)
British novelist, short-story writer, born Bombay; *Midnight's Children* (1981) Booker Prize, *Shame* (1983), *The Satanic Verses* (1988), *Haroun and the Sea of Stories* (1990), *Imaginary Homelands* (1991).

Sade, Donatien Alphonse François, Comte de, (known as **Marquis**) (1740–1814)
French novelist, born Paris; *Les 120 Journées de Sodome* (1784), *Justine* (1791), *La Philosophie dans le boudoir* (1793), *Juliette* (1798), *Les Crimes de l'amour* (1800).

Saki (Hector Hugh Munro) (1870–1916)
British novelist, short-story writer, born Akyab, Burma; *The Chronicles of Clovis* (1912), *The Unbearable Bassington* (1912).

Salinger, J(erome) D(avid) (1919–)
American novelist, born New York; *The Catcher in the Rye* (1951), *Franny and Zooey* (1961).

Sand, George (Amandine Aurore Lucille Dupin) (1804–76)
French novelist, born Paris; *Lélia* (1833), *La Petite Fadette* (1849).

Sartre, Jean-Paul (1905–80)
French novelist, playwright, born Paris; *Nausea* (1949), *The Roads to Freedom* (1945–7); Nobel Prize for Literature 1964.

Sayers, Dorothy L (1893–1957)
English novelist, short-story writer, born Oxford; *Lord Peter Views the Body* (1928), *Gaudy Night* (1935).

Scott, Sir Walter (1771–1832)
Scottish novelist, poet, born Edinburgh; *Waverley* (1814), *The Heart of Midlothian* (1818), *The Bride of Lammermoor* (1819), *Ivanhoe* (1820).

Sharpe, Tom (Thomas Ridley) (1928–)
British novelist, born London; *Riotous Assembly* (1971), *Porterhouse Blue* (1974), *Blott on the Landscape* (1975), *Wilt* (1976).

Shelley, Mary (Wollstonecraft) (1797–1851)
English novelist, born London; *Frankenstein* (1818), *The Last Man* (1826), *Perkin Warbeck* (1830).

Sholokhov, Mikhail Alexandrovich (1905–84)
Russian novelist, born near Veshenskaya; *And Quiet Flows the Don* (1928–40), *The Upturned Soil* (1940); Nobel Prize for Literature 1965.

Shute, Nevil (Nevil Shute Norway) (1899–1960)
English/Australian novelist, born Ealing; *The Pied Piper* (1942), *A Town Like Alice* (1950), *On the Beach* (1957).

Sillitoe, Alan (1928–)
English novelist, poet, short-story writer, born Nottingham; *Saturday Night and Sunday Morning* (1958), *The Loneliness of the Long Distance Runner* (1959).

Simenon, Georges (1903–89)
Belgian-born French writer, born Liège; almost 100 novels featuring Jules Maigret, 400 other novels.

Singer, Isaac Bashevis (1904–91)
American novelist, playwright, born Radzymin, Poland; *The Family Moskat* (1950), *The Satan in Goray* (1955); Nobel Prize for Literature 1978.

Smollett, Tobias George (1721–71)
Scottish novelist, born Dalquharn, Dunbartonshire; *Roderick Random* (1748), *The Adventures of Peregrine Pickle* (1751), *The Expedition of Humphry Clinker* (1771).

Snow, C(harles) P(ercy) (1905–80)
English novelist, born Leicester; *Strangers and Brothers* (1940–70).

Solzhenitsyn, Aleksandr Isayevich (1918–)
Russian novelist, born Kislovodsk, Caucasus; *One Day in the Life of Ivan Denisovich* (1962), *Cancer Ward* (1968), *The First Circle* (1969); Nobel Prize for Literature 1970.

Spark, Muriel (1918–)
Scottish novelist, short-story writer, poet, born Edinburgh; *The Ballad of Peckham Rye* (1960), *The Prime of Miss Jean Brodie* (1962), *The Girls of Slender Means* (1963).

Steinbeck, John Ernest (1902–68)
American novelist born Salinas, California; *Of Mice and Men* (1937), *The Grapes of Wrath* (1939), *Cannery Row* (1945), *East of Eden* (1952); Nobel Prize for Literature 1962.

Stendhal (Henri Marie Beyle) (1788–1842)
French novelist, born Grenoble; *Le Rouge et le noir* (1830), *La Chartreuse de Parme* (1839).

Sterne, Lawrence (1713–68)
Irish novelist, born Clonmel, Tipperary; *Tristram Shandy* (1759–67), *A Sentimental Journey* (1768).

Stevenson, Robert Louis (Balfour) (1850–94)
Scottish novelist, short-story writer, poet, born Edinburgh; *Travels with a Donkey* (1879), *Treasure Island* (1883), *Kidnapped* (1886), *The Strange Case of Dr Jekyll and Mr Hyde* (1886), *Weir of Hermiston* (1896).

Stewart, Mary (1916–)
English novelist born Sunderland; *This Rough Magic* (1964), *The Last Enchantment* (1979).

Stoker, Bram (Abraham) (1847–1912)
Irish novelist, short-story writer, born Dublin; *Dracula* (1897).

Stowe, Harriet (Elizabeth) Beecher (1811–96)
American novelist, born Litchfield, Connecticut; *Uncle Tom's Cabin* (1852).

Styron, William (Clark) (1925–)
American novelist, born Newport News, Virginia; *Lie Down in Darkness* (1951), *The Confessions of Nat Turner* (1967), *Sophie's Choice* (1979).

Swift, Jonathan (1667–1754)
Irish novelist, poet, born Dublin; *A Tale of a Tub* (1704), *Gulliver's Travels* (1726).

Thackeray, William Makepeace (1811–63)
English novelist, born Calcutta; *Vanity Fair* (1847–8), *Pendennis* (1848–50).

Theroux, Paul (Edward) (1941–)
American novelist, short-story writer, born Medford, Massachusetts; *The Mosquito Coast* (1981), *Doctor Slaughter* (1984), *My Secret History* (1989).

Tolkien, J(ohn) R(onald) R(euel) (1892–1973)
English novelist, born Bloemfontein, South Africa; *The Hobbit* (1937), *The Lord of the Rings* (1954–5).

NOVELISTS AND WRITERS (cont.)

Tolstoy, Count Leo Nikolayevich (1828–1910)
  Russian novelist, born Yasnaya Polyana, Central Russia; *War and Peace* (1863–9), *Anna Karenina* (1873–7), *Resurrection* (1899).
Trollope, Anthony (1815–82)
  English novelist, born London; *Barchester Towers* (1857), *Can You Forgive Her?* (1864), *The Way We Live Now* (1875).
Turgenev, Ivan Sergeevich (1818–83)
  Russian novelist, born province of Orel; *Sportsman's Sketches* (1952), *Fathers and Children* (1862).
Twain, Mark (Samuel Langhorne Clemens) (1835–1910)
  American novelist, born Florida, Missouri; *The Celebrated Jumping Frog of Calaveras County* (1865), *The Adventures of Tom Sawyer* (1876), *The Prince and the Pauper* (1882), *The Adventures of Huckleberry Finn* (1884), *A Connecticut Yankee in King Arthur's Court* (1889).

Updike, John (Hoyer) (1932–   )
  American novelist, short-story writer, born Shillington, Pennsylvania; *Rabbit, Run* (1960), *Pigeon Feathers and other stories* (1962).

Van der Post, Sir Laurens (Jan) (1906–96)
  South African novelist, playwright, born Philippolis; *Flamingo Feather* (1955), *Journey into Russia* (1964), *A Far-Off Place* (1974).
Vargas Llosa, Mario (1936–   )
  Peruvian novelist; *The Time of the Hero* (1963), *Aunt Julia and the Scriptwriter* (1977), *The War at the End of the World* (1982), *The Green House* (1986).
Verne, Jules (1828–1905)
  French novelist, born Nantes; *Voyage to the Centre of the Earth* (1864), *Twenty Thousand Leagues under the Sea* (1870).
Voltaire, François-Marie Arouet de (1694–1778)
  French novelist, poet, born Paris; *Zadig* (1747), *Candide* (1759).
Vonnegut, Kurt (1922–   )
  American novelist, short-story writer, born Indianapolis, Indiana; *Cat's Cradle* (1963), *Slaughterhouse-Five* (1969).

Wain, John (Barrington) (1925–94)
  English novelist, poet, short-story writer, playwright, born Stoke-on-Trent, Staffordshire; *Hurry on Down* (1953), *The Young Visitors* (1965), *Where the Rivers Meet* (1988).
Walker, Alice (1944–   )
  American novelist, short-story writer, born Eatonville, Georgia; *The Third Life of Grange Copeland* (1970), *In Love and Trouble* (1973), *The Color Purple* (1983).
Walpole, Horace (1717–97)
  English novelist, poet, born London; *Letter from Xotto to his friend Lien Chi at Pekin* (1757), *Anecdotes of Painting in England* (1761–71), *The Castle of Otranto* (1764), *The Mysterious Mother* (1768), *Historic Doubts on the Life and Reign of King Richard the Third* (1768).
Waugh, Evelyn (Arthur St John) (1903–66)
  English novelist, born Hampstead; *Decline and Fall* (1928), *A Handful of Dust* (1934), *Brideshead Revisited* (1945).
Weldon, Fay (1933–   )
  English novelist, born Alvechurch, Worcestershire; *Down Among the Women* (1971), *Female Friends* (1975), *Life and Loves of a She-Devil* (1983).

Wells, H(erbert) G(eorge) (1866–1946)
English novelist, born Bromley, Kent; *The Time Machine* (1895), *The War of the Worlds* (1898), *The History of Mr Polly* (1910).

Welty, Eudora (1909–   )
American novelist, short-story writer, born Jackson, Mississippi; *A Curtain of Green* (1941), *The Golden Apples* (1949), *The Ponder Heart* (1954), *The Optimist's Daughter* (1972).

Wesley, Mary (née **Farmar**) (1912–   )
British novelist, born Englefield Green, Berkshire; *The Camomile Lawn* (1984), *A Sensible Life* (1990).

Wharton, Edith (Newbold) (1862–1937)
American novelist, short-story writer, born New York; *The House of Mirth* (1905), *Ethan Frome* (1911), *The Age of Innocence* (1920).

White, Patrick Victor Martindale (1912–90)
Australian novelist, playwright, short-story writer, born London; *Voss* (1957), *The Vivisector* (1970), *A Fringe of Leaves* (1976); Nobel Prize for Literature 1973.

Wilde, Oscar (1854–1900)
Irish novelist, short-story writer, playwright, poet, born Dublin; *The Happy Prince and Other Tales* (1888), *The Picture of Dorian Gray* (1890), *The Importance of Being Earnest* (play) (1895).

Wilder, Thornton Niven (1897–1976)
American novelist, playwright, born Madison, Wisconsin; *The Bridge of San Luis Rey* (1927), *The Woman of Andros* (1930), *Heaven's My Destination* (1935).

Wodehouse, Sir P(elham) G(renville) (1881–1975)
English novelist, short-story writer, born Guildford; *The Inimitable Jeeves* (1923), *Carry on, Jeeves* (1925).

Wolfe, Thomas Clayton (1900–38)
American novelist, born Asheville, North Carolina; *Look Homeward, Angel* (1929), *Of time and the River* (1935), *From Death to Morning* (1935).

Wolfe, Tom (Thomas Kennerley) (1931–   )
American novelist, born Richmond, Virginia; *The Electric Kool-Aid Acid Test* (1968), *The Right Stuff* (1979), *The Bonfire of the Vanities* (1988).

Woolf, (Adeline) Virginia (1882–1941)
English novelist, born London; *Mrs Dalloway* (1925), *To The Lighthouse* (1927), *Orlando* (1928), *A Room of One's Own* (1929), *The Waves* (1931).

Wouk, Herman (1915–   )
American novelist, playwright, born New York City; *The Caine Mutiny* (1951), *The Winds of War* (1971), *War and Remembrance* (1978).

Yourcenar, Marguerite (Marguerite de Crayencour) (1903–87)
French novelist, poet, born Brussels; *Memoirs of Hadrian* (1941).

Zola, Émile (1840–1902)
French novelist, born Paris; *Thérèse Raquin* (1867), *Les Rougon-Macquart* (1871–93), *Germinal* (1885).

POETS

Selected volumes of poetry are listed.

Abse, Dannie (Daniel) (1923–)
  Welsh, born Cardiff; *After Every Green Thing* (1948), *Tenants of the House* (1957).
Adcock, (Kareen) Fleur (1934–)
  New Zealander, born Papakura; *The Eye of the Hurricane* (1964), *The Incident Book* (1986).
Aiken, Conrad (Potter) (1889–1973)
  American, born Georgia; *Earth Triumphant* (1914), *Preludes for Memnon* (1931).
Akhmatova, Anna (pseudonym of **Anna Andreeyevna Gorenko**) (1889–1966)
  Russian, born Odessa; *Evening* (1912), *Poem without a Hero* (1940–62), *Requiem* (1963).
Angelou, Maya (pseudonym of **Marguerite Annie Johnson**) (1928–)
  American, born St Louis, Missouri; *And Still I Rise* (1978), *I Shall Not Be Moved* (1990), *Wouldn't Take Nothing For My Journey Now* (1994).
Apollinaire, Guillaume (1880–1918)
  French, born Rome; *Alcools* (1913), *Calligrammes* (1918).
Ariosto, Ludovico (1474–1535)
  Italian, born Reggio; *Furioso* (1532).
Auden, W(ystan) H(ugh) (1907–73)
  British, naturalized American citizen, born York; *Another Time* (1940), *The Sea and the Mirror* (1944), *The Age of Anxiety* (1947).

Baudelaire, Charles (Pierre) (1821–67)
  French, born Paris; *Les Fleurs du mal* (1857).
Beer, Patricia (1924–)
  English, born Exmouth, Devon; *The Loss of the Magyar* (1959), *The Lie of the Land* (1983).
Belloc, (Joseph) Hilaire (Pierre) (1870–1953)
  British, born St Cloud, France; *Cautionary Tales* (1907), *Sonnets and Verse* (1923).
Berryman, John (1914–72)
  American, born McAlester, Oklahoma; *Homage to Mistress Bradsheet* (1966), *Dream Songs* (1969).
Betjeman, John (1906–84)
  English, born Highgate; *Mount Zion* (1931), *New Bats in Old Belfries* (1945), *A Nip in the Air* (1972).
Bishop, Elizabeth (1911–79)
  American, born Worcester, Massachusetts; *North and South* (1946), *Geography III* (1978).
Blake, William (1757–1827)
  English, born London; *The Marriage of Heaven and Hell* (1793), *The Vision of the Daughter of Albion* (1793), *Songs of Innocence and Experience* (1794), *Vala, or The Four Zoas* (1800), *Milton* (1810).
Blunden, Edmund (Charles) (1896–1974)
  English, born Yalding, Kent; *The Waggoner and Other Poems* (1920), *Undertones of War* (1928).
Brooke, Rupert (Chawner) (1887–1915)
  English, born Rugby; *Poems* (1911); *1914 and Other Poems* (1915), *New Numbers* (1915).
Brooks, Gwendolyn (1917–)
  American, born Topeka, Kansas; *A Street in Bronzeville* (1945), *Annie Allen* (1949), *In The Mecca* (1968).
Browning, Elizabeth, née **Barrett** (1806–61)
  English, born Coxhoe Hall, near Durham; *Sonnets from the Portuguese* (1850), *Aurora Leigh* (1855).

Browning, Robert (1812–89)
English, born Camberwell; *Bells and Pomegranates, Dramatic Lyrics, Men and Women* (1855), *The Ring and the Book* (1868–9).
Burns, Robert (1759–96)
Scottish, born Alloway, Ayr; *Poems Chiefly in the Scottish Dialect* (1786), *Tam O'Shanter* (1790).
Byron, George Gordon (1788–1824)
English, born London; *Hours of Idleness* (1807), *Childe Harolde* (1817), *Don Juan* (1819–24).

Catullus, Gaius Valerius (c.84–c.54 BC)
Roman, born Verona; lyric poet, over one hundred poems survive.
Causley, Charles (1917–   )
English, born Lanceton, Cornwall; *Union St* (1957), *Johnny Alleluia* (1961), *Underneath the Water* (1968).
Chaucer, Geoffrey (c.1345–1400)
English, born London; *Book of the Duchess* (1370), *Troilus and Cressida* (c.1385), *The Canterbury Tales* (1387–1400).
Clampitt, Amy (1920–   )
American, born Iowa; *The Kingfisher* (1983), *Archaic Figure* (1987).
Clare, John (1793–1864)
English, born Helpstone, Northamptonshire.
Coleridge, Samuel Taylor (1772–1834)
English, born Otterly St Mary, Devonshire; *Poems on Various Subjects* (1796), 'Kubla Khan' (1797), 'The Rime of the Ancient Mariner' (1798), *Christabel and Other Poems* (1816), *Sybylline Leaves* (1817).
Cowper, William (1731–1800)
English, born Great Berkhampstead, Hertfordshire; *The Task* (1785).
Crabbe, George (1754–1832)
English, born Aldeburgh, Suffolk; *The Village* (1783).
cummings, e(dward) e(stlin) (1894–1962)
American, born Cambridge, Massachusetts; *Tulips and Chimneys* (1923), *XLI Poems* (1925), *is 5* (1926).

Dante, Alighieri (1265–1321)
Italian, born Florence; *Vita nuova* (1294), *Divine Comedy* (1321).
Day Lewis, Cecil (1904–72)
Irish, born Ballintogher, Sligo; *Overtures to Death* (1938), *The Aeneid of Virgil* (1952).
de la Mare, Walter (1873–1956)
English, born Charleston, Kent; *The Listeners* (1912), *The Burning Glass and Other Poems* (1945).
Dickinson, Emily (Elizabeth) (1830–86)
American, born Amherst, Massachusetts; only 7 poems published in her lifetime; posthumous publications, eg *Poems* (1890).
Donne, John (?1572–1631)
English, born London; *Satires & Elegies* (1590s), *Holy Sonnets* (1610–11), *Songs and Sonnets* (most verse published posthumously).
Doolittle, Hilda (known as **H D**) (1886–1961)
American, born Bethlehem, Pennsylvania; *Sea Garden* (1916), *The Walls Do Not Fall* (1944), *Helen in Egypt* (1961).
Dryden, John (1631–1700)
English, born Adwinckle All Saints, Northamptonshire; 'Astrea Redux' (1660), 'Absalom and Achitophel' (1681), 'MacFlecknoe' (1684).

POETS (cont.)

Dunbar, William (c.1460–c.1520)
  Scottish, birthplace probably E Lothian; *'The Thrissill and the Rois' (1503)*, *'Lament for the Makaris'* (c.1507).
Dunn, Douglas (Eaglesham) (1942–)
  Scottish, born Inchinnan; *Love or Nothing* (1974), *Elegies* (1985), *Dante's Drum-kit* (1993).
Dutton, Geoffrey (Piers Henry) (1922–)
  Australian, born Anlaby; *Antipedes in Shoes* (1955), *Poems, Soft and Loud* (1968).

Eliot, T(homas) S(tearns) (1888–1965)
  American (British citizen 1927), born St Louis, Missouri; *Prufrock and Other Observations* (1917), *The Waste Land* (1922), *Ash Wednesday* (1930), *Four Quartets* (1944).
Éluard, Paul (pseudonym of **Eugène Grindal**) (1895–1952)
  French, born Saint-Denis; *La Vie immédiate* (1934), *Poésie et vérité* (1942).
Emerson, Ralph Waldo (1803–82)
  American, born Boston; poems published posthumously in *Complete Works* (1903–4).
Empson, Sir William (1906–84)
  English, born Yokefleet, E Yorkshire; *Poems* (1935), *The Gathering Storm* (1940).

Fitzgerald, Edward (1809–83)
  English, born near Woodbridge, Suffolk; translator of *The Rubaiyat of Omar Khayyam* (1859).
Fitzgerald, Robert (David) (1902–87)
  Australian, born Hunters Hill, New South Wales; *To Meet the Sun* (1929), *The Wind at Your Door* (1959), *Product* (1974).
Frost, Robert (Lee) (1874–1963)
  American, born San Francisco; *North of Boston* (1914), *Mountain Interval* (1916), *New Hampshire* (1923), *In the Clearing* (1962).

Ginsberg, Allen (1926–97)
  American, born Newark, New Jersey; *Howl and Other Poems* (1956), *Empty Mirror* (1961), *The Fall of America* (1973).
Graves, Robert (van Ranke) (1895–1985)
  English, born London; *Fairies and Fusiliers* (1917).
Gunn, Thom(son William) (1929–)
  English, born Gravesend, Kent; *The Sense of Movement* (1957), *Touch* (1967), *Jack Straw's Castle* (1976).

Heaney, Seamus (Justin) (1939–)
  Irish, born Castledawson, County Derry; *Death of a Naturalist* (1966), *Door into the Dark* (1969), *Field Work* (1979), *Seeing Things* (1991).
Henri, Adrian (Maurice) (1932–)
  English, born Birkenhead; *Tonight at Noon* (1968), *City* (1969), *From the Loveless Motel* (1980).
Henryson, Robert (c.1425–1506)
  Scottish, birthplace unknown; *Testament of Cresseid*, *Morall Fables of Esope the Phrygian*.
Herbert, George (1593–1633)
  English, born Montgomery; *The Temple* (1633).
Herrick, Robert (1591–1674)
  English, born London; *Hesperides* (1648).
Hill, Geoffrey (William) (1932–)
  English, born Bromsgrove, Worcestershire; *King Log* (1968), *Mercian Hymns* (1971).

Hodgson, Ralph (Edwin) (1871–1962)
  English, born Yorkshire; *Poems* (1917), *The Skylark and Other Poems* (1958).
Homer (10th–8th-c BC) Greek, birthplace and existence disputed; he is credited with the writing or
  writing down of *The Iliad* and *The Odyssey*.
Hopkins, Gerard Manley (1844–89)
  English, born Stratford, London; *'The Wreck of the Deutschland'* (1876), posthumously published
  Poems (1918).
Horace, Quintus Horatius Flaccus (65–8 BC)
  Roman, born Venusia, Apulia; *Epodes* (30 BC), *Odes* (23–13 BC).
Housman, A(lfred) E(dward) (1859–1936)
  English, born Flockbury, Worcestershire; *A Shropshire Lad* (1896), *Last Poems* (1922).
Hughes, Ted (1930–   )
  English, born Mytholmroyd, Yorkshire; *The Hawk in the Rain* (1957), *Lupereal* (1960), *Wodwo*
  (1967), *Crow* (1970), *Care Birds* (1975), *Season Songs* (1976), *Gaudete* (1977), *Moortown* (1979),
  Wolfwatching (1989).

Jennings, Elizabeth (Joan) (1926–   )
  English, born Boston, Lincolnshire; *Poems* (1953), *The Animals' Arrival* (1969), *The Mind Has
  Mountains* (1966).
Johnson, Samuel (1709–84)
  English, born Lichfield, Staffordshire; *The Vanity of Human Wishes* (1749).

Kavanagh, Patrick (1905–67)
  Irish, born Inniskeen; *Ploughman and Other Poems* (1936), *The Great Hunger* (1942).
Keats, John (1795–1821)
  English, born London; *Endymion* (1818), *Lamia and Other Poems* (1820).
Keyes, Sidney (Arthur Kilworth) (1922–43)
  English, born Dartford, Kent; *The Iron Laurel* (1942), *The Cruel Solstice* (1943).

La Fontaine, Jean de (1621–95)
  French, born Château-Thierry, Champagne; *Contes et nouvelles en vers* (1665), *Fables choisies
  mises en vers* (1668).
Langland, or Langley, William (c.1332–c.1400)
  English, birthplace uncertain, possibly Ledbury, Herefordshire; *Piers Plowman* (1362–99).
Larkin, Philip (Arthur) (1922–85)
  English, born Coventry; *The North Ship* (1945), *The Whitsun Weddings* (1964), *High Windows* (1974).
Longfellow, Henry (Wadsworth) (1807–82)
  American, born Portland, Maine; *Voices of the Night* (1839), *Ballads and Other Poems* (1842),
  Hiawatha (1855), *'Divina Comedia'* (1872).
Lowell, Amy (Laurence) (1874–1925)
  American, born Brookline, Massachusetts; *A Dome of Many-Colored Glass* (1912), *Legends* (1921).
Lowell, Robert (Traill Spence, Jr) (1917–77)
  American, born Boston, Massachusetts; *Lord Weary's Castle* (1946), *Life Studies* (1959),
  Prometheus Bound (1967).

Macaulay, Thomas (Babington) (1800–59)
  English, born Rothey Temple, Leicestershire; *The Lays of Ancient Home* (1842).
MacCaig, Norman (Alexander) (1910–96)
  Scottish, born Edinburgh; *Far Cry* (1943), *Riding Lights* (1955), *A Round of Applause* (1962),
  A Man in My Position (1969), *Voice-Over* (1988).

POETS (cont.)

MacDiarmid, Hugh (pseudonym of **Christopher Murray Grieve**) (1892–1978)
  Scottish, born Langholm, Dumfriesshire; *A Drunk Man Looks at the Thistle* (1926).
McGough, Roger (1937–)
  English, educated Liverpool; *Waving at Trains* (1982), *The Mersey Sound: Penguin Modern Poets 10* (with Adrian Henri and Brian Patten) (1967), *An Imaginary Menagerie* (1988).
MacLean, Sorley (Somhairle Macgill-Eain) (1911–96)
  Scottish, born Isle of Raasay; *Reothairt is Contraigh* (Spring Tide and Neap Tide) (1977).
MacNeice, (Frederick) Louis (1907–63)
  Irish, born Belfast; *Blind Fireworks* (1929), *Solstices* (1961).
Mallarmé, Stéphane (1842–98)
  French, born Paris; *L'Après-midi d'un faune* (1876), *Poésies* (1899).
Marvell, Andrew (1621–78)
  English, born Winestead, near Hull; *Miscellaneous Poems by Andrew Marvell, Esq.* (1681).
Masefield, John (Edward) (1878–1967)
  English, born Ledbury, Herefordshire; *Salt-Water Ballads* (1902).
Millay, Edna St Vincent (1892–1950)
  American, born Rockland, Maine; *A Few Figs from Thistles* (1920), *The Ballad of Harp-Weaver* (1922).
Milton, John (1608–74)
  English, born London; *Lycidas* (1637), *Paradise Lost* (1667, 74), *Samson Agonistes* (1667).
Moore, Marianne (Craig) (1887–1972)
  American, born Kirkwood, Missouri; *The Pangolin and Other Verse* (1936).
Muir, Edwin (1887–1959)
  Scottish, born Deerness, Orkney; *First Poems* (1925), *Chorus of the Newly Dead* (1926), *Variations on a Time Theme* (1934), *The Labyrinth* (1949), *New Poems* (1949–51).

Nash, (Frederick) Ogden (1902–71)
  American, born New York; *Free Wheeling* (1931).

O'Hara, Frank (Francis Russell) (1926–66)
  American, born Baltimore, Maryland; *A City Winter and Other Poems* (1952), *Lunch Poems* (1964).
Ovid (Publius Ovidius Naso) (43 BC–c.17 AD)
  Roman, born Sulmo; *Amores* (c.16 BC), *Metamorphoses, Ars Amatoria*.
Owen, Wildred (Edward Salter) (1893–1918)
  English, born Oswestry, Shropshire; most poems published posthumously, 1920 by Siegfried Sassoon.

Paz, Octavio (1914–)
  Mexican, born Mexico City; *Liberty on Parole, Salamander, Collected Poems* (1988); Nobel Prize for Literature 1990.
Petrarch, (Francesco Petrarca) (1304–74)
  Italian, born Arezzo; *Canzoniere*.
Plath, Sylvia (1932–63)
  American, born Boston, Massachusetts; *The Colossus and Other Poems* (1960), *Ariel* (1965), *Crossing the Water* (1971), *Winter Trees* (1972).
Porter, Peter (Neville Frederick) (1929–)
  Australian, born Brisbane; *Poems, Ancient and Modern* (1964), *English Subtitles* (1981).

Pound, Ezra (Weston Loomir) (1885–1972)
American, born Haile, Idaho; *The Cantos* (1917, 48, 59).
Pushkin, Alexander (Sergevich) (1799–1837)
Russian, born Moscow; *Eugene Onegin* (1828), *Ruslam and Lyudmilla* (1820).

Raine, Kathleen (Jessie) (1908–)
English, born London; *Stone and Flower* (1943).
Rich, Adrienne (Cecile) (1929–)
American, born Baltimore, Maryland; *The Diamond Cutters and Other Poems* (1955), *Snapshots of a Daughter-in-Law* (1963).
Riding, Laura, née Reichenfeld (1901–91)
American, born New York; *The Close Chaplet* (1926).
Rilke, Rainer Maria (1875–1926)
Austrian, born Prague; *Die Sonnettean Orpheus* (1923).
Rimbaud, (Jean Nicholas) Arthur (1854–91)
French, born Charleville, Ardennes; *Les Illuminations* (1886).
Rochester, John Wilmot, Earl of (1647–80)
English, born Ditchley, Oxfordshire; *A Satyre against Mankind* (1675).
Roethke, Theodore (1908–63)
American, born Saginaw, Michigan; *Open House* (1941), *The Lost Son and Other Poems* (1948).
Rosenberg, Isaac (1890–1918)
English, born Bristol; *Night and Day* (1912), *Youth* (1915), *Poems* (1922).

Saint-John Perse (pseudonym of **Marie René Auguste Alexis Saint-Léger Léger**) (1887–1975)
French, born St Léger des Feuilles; *Anabase* (1924), *Exil* (1942), *Chroniques* (1960); Nobel Prize for Literature 1960.
Sassoon, Siegfried (Lovain) (1886–1967)
English, born Kent; *Counter-Attack and Other Poems* (1917), *The Road to Ruin* (1933).
Schwartz, Delmore (1913–66)
American, born New York; *In Dreams Begin Responsibilities* (1938), *Vaudeville for a Princess and Other Poems* (1950).
Shelley, Percy Bysshe (1792–1822)
English, born Field Place, Horsham, Sussex; *'Love's Philosophy'*, *'Alastor'* (1816), *'The Revolt of Islam'* (1818), *'Julian and Maddalo'* (1818), *'The Triumph of Life'* (1922).
Sidney, Sir Philip (1554–86)
English, born Penshurst, Kent; *Arcadia* (1580), *Astrophel and Stella* (1591).
Sitwell, Dame Edith (Louisa) (1887–1964)
English, born Scarborough; *Façade* (1922), *Colonel Fantock* (1926).
Smart, Christopher (1722–71)
English, born Shipborne, Kent; *Jubilate Agno* (first published 1939).
Smith, Stevie (pseudonym of **Florence Margaret Smith**) (1902–71)
English, born Hull; *Not Waving but Drowning: Poems* (1957).
Spender, Sir Stephen (Harold) (1909–95)
English, born London; *Twenty Poems* (1933), *Poems from Spain* (1939).
Spenser, Edmund (1552–99)
English, born London; *The Shepheardes Calender* (1570), *The Faerie Queene* (1590, 96).
Stevens, Wallace (1879–1955)
American, born Reading, Pennsylvania; *Harmonium* (1923), *Transport to Summer* (1947).

POETS (cont.)

Tennyson, Alfred, 1st Baron Tennyson (1809–92)
English, born Somersby Rectory, Lincolnshire; *Poems* (1832) (eg 'The Lotos-Eaters' and 'The Lady of Shalott'), *The Princess* (1847), *In Memoriam* (1850), *Idylls of the King* (1859), *Maud* (1885).

Thomas, Dylan (Marlais) (1914–53)
Welsh, born Swansea; *Twenty-five Poems* (1936), *Deaths and Entrances* (1946), *In Country Sleep and Other Poems* (1952).

Thomas, (Philip) Edward (1878–1917)
English, born London; *Six poems* (1916), *Last Poems* (1918).

Thomas, R(onald) S(tuart) (1913–   )
Welsh, born Cardiff; *The Stones of the Field* (1946), *Song at the Year's Turning* (1955).

Thomson, James (1700–48)
Scottish, born Ednam, Roxburghshire; *The Seasons* (1730), *The Castle of Indolence* (1748).

Verlaine, Paul (1844–96)
French, born Metz; *Fêtes galantes* (1869), *Sagesse* (1881).

Virgil, Publius Vergilius Maro (70–19 BC)
Roman, born near Mantua; *Eclogues* (37 BC), *Georgics* (29 BC), *The Aeneid* (19 BC).

Webb, Francis Charles (1925–73)
Australian, born Adelaide; *A Drum for Ben Boyd* (1948), *The Ghost of the Cock* (1964).

Whitman, Walt (1819–92)
American, born West Hills, Long Island, New York; *Leaves of Grass* (1855–89).

Wordsworth, William (1770–1850)
English, born Cockermouth; *Lyrical Ballads* (with S T Coleridge, 1798), *The Prelude* (1799, 1805, 1850), *The Excursion* (1814).

Wright, Judith (1915–   )
Australian, born Armidale, New South Wales; *The Moving Image* (1946), *The Two Fires* (1955), *Birds* (1962).

Wyatt, Sir Thomas (1503–42)
English, born Allington Castle, Kent; poems first published in *Tottel's Miscellany* (1557).

Yeats, W(illiam) B(utler) (1865–1939)
Irish, born Sandymount, County Dublin; *The Wanderings of Oisin and Other Poems* (1889), *The Wind Among the Reeds* (1894), *The Wild Swans at Coole* (1917), *Michael Robartes and the Dancer* (1921), *The Winding Stair and Other Poems* (1933); Nobel Prize for Literature 1923.

PLAYWRIGHTS

Selected plays are listed.

Aeschylus (c.525–c.456 BC) Athenian; *The Oresteia trilogy (Agamemnon, Choephoroe, Eumenides)* (458 BC), *Prometheus Bound, Seven Against Thebes*.

Albee, Edward Franklin (1928–   )
American, born Washington DC; *The American Dream* (1961), *Who's Afraid of Virginia Woolf?* (1962).

Amos, Robert (1920–   )
Australian, born Austria; *When the Gravediggers Come* (1961).

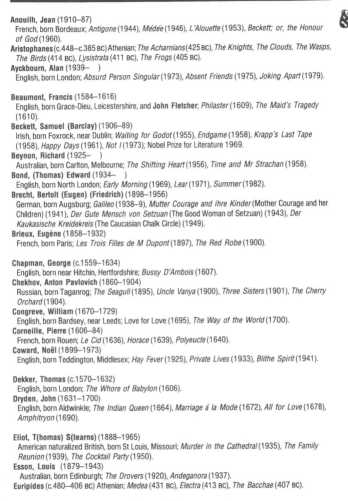

Anouilh, Jean (1910–87)
French, born Bordeaux; *Antigone* (1944), *Médée* (1946), *L'Alouette* (1953), *Beckett; or, the Honour of God* (1960).
Aristophanes (c.448–c.385 BC) Athenian; *The Acharnians* (425 BC), *The Knights*, *The Clouds*, *The Wasps*, *The Birds* (414 BC), *Lysistrata* (411 BC), *The Frogs* (405 BC).
Ayckbourn, Alan (1939–   )
English, born London; *Absurd Person Singular* (1973), *Absent Friends* (1975), *Joking Apart* (1979).

Beaumont, Francis (1584–1616)
English, born Grace-Dieu, Leicestershire, and **John Fletcher**; *Philaster* (1609), *The Maid's Tragedy* (1610).
Beckett, Samuel (Barclay) (1906–89)
Irish, born Foxrock, near Dublin; *Waiting for Godot* (1955), *Endgame* (1958), *Krapp's Last Tape* (1958), *Happy Days* (1961), *Not I* (1973); Nobel Prize for Literature 1969.
Beynon, Richard (1925–   )
Australian, born Carlton, Melbourne; *The Shifting Heart* (1956), *Time and Mr Strachan* (1958).
Bond, (Thomas) Edward (1934–   )
English, born North London; *Early Morning* (1969), *Lear* (1971), *Summer* (1982).
Brecht, Bertolt (Eugen) (Friedrich) (1898–1956)
German, born Augsburg; *Galileo* (1938–9), *Mutter Courage and ihre Kinder* (Mother Courage and her Children) (1941), *Der Gute Mensch von Setzuan* (The Good Woman of Setzuan) (1943), *Der Kaukasische Kreidekreis* (The Caucasian Chalk Circle) (1949).
Brieux, Eugène (1858–1932)
French, born Paris; *Les Trois Filles de M Dupont* (1897), *The Red Robe* (1900).

Chapman, George (c.1559–1634)
English, born near Hitchin, Hertfordshire; *Bussy D'Ambois* (1607).
Chekhov, Anton Pavlovich (1860–1904)
Russian, born Taganrog; *The Seagull* (1895), *Uncle Vanya* (1900), *Three Sisters* (1901), *The Cherry Orchard* (1904).
Congreve, William (1670–1729)
English, born Bardsey, near Leeds; *Love for Love* (1695), *The Way of the World* (1700).
Corneille, Pierre (1606–84)
French, born Rouen; *Le Cid* (1636), *Horace* (1639), *Polyeucte* (1640).
Coward, Noël (1899–1973)
English, born Teddington, Middlesex; *Hay Fever* (1925), *Private Lives* (1933), *Blithe Spirit* (1941).

Dekker, Thomas (c.1570–1632)
English, born London; *The Whore of Babylon* (1606).
Dryden, John (1631–1700)
English, born Aldwinkle; *The Indian Queen* (1664), *Marriage à la Mode* (1672), *All for Love* (1678), *Amphitryon* (1690).

Eliot, T(homas) S(tearns) (1888–1965)
American naturalized British, born St Louis, Missouri; *Murder in the Cathedral* (1935), *The Family Reunion* (1939), *The Cocktail Party* (1950).
Esson, Louis (1879–1943)
Australian, born Edinburgh; *The Drovers* (1920), *Andeganora* (1937).
Euripides (c.480–406 BC) Athenian; *Medea* (431 BC), *Electra* (413 BC), *The Bacchae* (407 BC).

PLAYWRIGHTS (cont.)

Fletcher, John (1579–1625)
English, born Rye, Sussex; *The Faithful Shepherdess* (1610), *A Wife for a Month* (1624).
Fo, Dario (1926–   )
Italian, born Lombardy; *Accidental Death of an Anarchist* (1970), *Can't Pay! Won't Pay!* (1978).
Ford, John (1586–c.1640) English, born Devonshire; *'Tis Pity She's a Whore* (1633), *Perkin Warbeck* (1634).

Galsworthy, John (1867–1933)
English, born Coombe, Surrey; *Strife* (1909), *Justice* (1910); Nobel Prize for Literature 1932.
Genet, Jean (1910–86)
French, born Paris; *The Maids* (1948), *The Balcony* (1956).
Giraudoux, (Hippolyte) Jean (1882–1944)
French, born Bellac; *Judith* (1931), *Ondine* (1939).
Goethe, Johann Wolfgang von (1749–1832)
German, born Frankfurt am Main; *Faust* (1808, 1832).
Gogol, Nikolai (Vasilievich) (1809–52)
Russian, born Ukraine; *The Inspector General* (1836).
Goldsmith, Oliver (1730–74)
Irish, born Pallas, County Longford; *She Stoops to Conquer* (1773).
Gray, Oriel (1921–   )
Australian, born Sydney; *The Torrents* (1955), *Burst of Summer* (1960).
Greene, Robert (1558–92)
English, born Norwich; *Orlando Furioso* (1594), *James the Fourth* (1598).

Hauptmann, Gerhart (1862–1946)
German, born Obersalzbrunn, Silesia; *Before Sunrise* (1889), *The Weavers* (1892); Nobel Prize for Literature 1912.
Hayes, Alfred (1911–85)
American, born England; *The Girl on the Via Flaminia* (1954).
Hebbel Friedrich (1813–63)
German, born Wesselburen, Dithmarschen; *Judith* (1841), *Maria Magdalena* (1844).
Hewett, Dorothy Coade (1923–   )
Australian, born Wickepin, West Australia; *The Chapel Perilous* (1972), *This Old Man Comes Rolling Home* (1976).
Heywood, Thomas (c.1574–1641)
English, born Lincolnshire; *A Woman Killed with Kindness* (1603), *The Fair Maid of the West* (1631), *The English Traveller* (1633).
Hibberd, Jack (1940–   )
Australian, born Warracknabeal, Victoria; *Dimboola* (1969), *White with Wire Wheels* (1970), *A Stretch of the Imagination* (1973).
Howard, Sidney (Coe) (1891–1939)
American, born Oakland, California; *They Knew What They Wanted* (1924), *The Silver Cord* (1926).

Ibsen, Henrik (1828–1906)
Norwegian, born Skien; *Peer Gynt* (1867), *A Doll's House* (1879), *The Pillars of Society* (1880), *The Wild Duck* (1884), *Hedda Gabler* (1890), *The Master Builder* (1892).

Inge, William (1913–73)
American, born Kansas; *Picnic* (1953), *Where's Daddy?* (1966).

Ionesco, Eugène (1912–94)
French, born Romania; *The Bald Prima Donna* (1948), *The Picture* (1958), *Le Rhinocéros* (1960).

Jonson, Ben(jamin) (c.1572–1637)
English, born Westminster; *Every man in his Humour* (1598), *Sejanus* (1603), *Volpone* (1606),
The Alchemist (1610), *Bartholomew Fair* (1614).

Kaiser, Georg (1878–1945)
German, born Magdeburg; *The Burghers of Calais* (1914), *Gas* (1920).

Kyd, Thomas (1558–94)
English, born London; *The Spanish Tragedy* (1587).

Lawler, Ray(mond Evenor) (1922–)
Australian, born Footscrag; *The Summer of the Seventeenth Doll* (1955), *The Man Who Shot the
Albatross* (1970).

Lorca, Federico Garcia (1898–1936)
Spanish, born Fuente Vaqueros; *Blood Wedding* (1933), *The House of Bernarda Alba* (1945).

Maeterlinck, Count Maurice (1862–1949)
Belgian, born Gand; *La Princesse Maleine* (1889), *Pelleas et Melisande* (1892), *The Blue Bird*
(1909).

Mamet, David Alan (1947–)
American, born Chicago; *Sexual Perversity in Chicago* (1974), *Duck Variations* (1974), *American
Buffalo* (1975), *Edmond* (1982).

Marlowe, Christopher (1564–93)
English, born Canterbury; *Tamburlaine the Great* (in two parts, 1587), *Dr Faustus* (1588), *The Jew
of Malta* (c.1589), *Edward II* (1592).

Marston, John (1576–1634)
English, born Wardington, Oxfordshire; *Antonio's Revenge* (1602), *The Malcontent* (1604).

Miller, Arthur (1915–)
American, born New York; *All My Sons* (1947), *Death of a Salesman* (1949), *The Crucible* (1952),
A View from the Bridge (1955), *The Misfits* (1961), *After the Fall* (1964).

Molière (pseudonym of **Jean-Baptiste Poquelin**) (1622–73)
French, born Paris; *Le Bourgeois Gentilhomme* (The Bourgeois Gentleman) (1660), *Tartuffe*
(1664), *Le Misanthrope* (The Misanthropist) (1666), *Le Malade Imaginaire* (The Hypochondriac)
(1673).

Oakley, Barry (1931–)
Australian, born Melbourne; *The Feet of Daniel Mannix* (1975), *Bedfellows* (1975).

O'Casey, Sean (originally **John Casey**) (1880–1964)
Irish, born Dublin; *Juno and the Paycock* (1924), *The Plough and the Stars* (1926).

O'Neill, Eugene (1888–1953)
American, born New York; *Beyond the Horizon* (1920), *Desire under the Elms* (1924), *Mourning
Becomes Electra* (1931), *Long Day's Journey into Night* (1041), *The Iceman Cometh* (1940); Nobel
Prize for Literature 1936.

Orton, Joe (John Kingsley) (1933–67)
English, born Leicester; *Entertaining Mr Sloane* (1964), *Loot* (1965), *What the Butler Saw* (1969).

PLAYWRIGHTS (cont.)

Osborne, John (James) (1929–94)
Welsh, born Fulham, London; *Look Back in Anger* (1956), *The Entertainer* (1957), *Inadmissible Evidence* (1964).
Otway, Thomas (1652–85)
English, born Milland, Sussex; *Don Carlos* (1676), *The Orphan* (1680), *Venice Preserv'd* (1682).

Patrick, John (1905–95)
American, born Louisville, Kentucky; *The Teahouse of the August Moon* (1953).
Pinter, Harold (1930–)
English, born East London; *The Birthday Party* (1958), *The Caretaker* (1960), *The Homecoming* (1965).
Pirandello, Luigi (1867–1936)
Italian, born near Agrigento, Sicily; *Six Characters in Search of an Author* (1921), *Henry IV* (1922); Nobel Prize for Literature 1934.
Plautus, Titus Maccius (c.254–184 BC) Roman; *Menachmi, Miles Gloriosus*.
Porter, Hal (1911–84)
Australian, born Melbourne; *The Tower* (1963), *The Professor* (1966), *Eden House* (1969).
Potter, Dennis (Christopher George) (1935–94)
English, born Forest of Dean. *Vote, Vote, Vote for Nigel Barton* (1965), *Brimstone and Treacle* (1978), *Pennies from Heaven* (1978), *The Singing Detective* (1986), *Sufficient Carbohydrate* (1984), *Lipstick on Your Collar* (1993).

Racine, Jean (1639–99)
French, born near Soissons; *Andromaque* (1667), *Phèdre* (1677), *Bajazet* (1672), *Esther* (1689).
Romeril, John (1945–)
Australian, born Melbourne; *Chicago, Chicago* (1970), *I Don't Know Who to Feel Sorry For* (1973).

Sackville, Thomas (1553–1608)
English, born Buckhurst, Sussex; *Gorboduc* (1592).
Sartre, Jean-Paul (1905–80)
French, born Paris; *The Flies* (1943), *Huis Clos* (1945), *The Condemned of Altona* (1961).
Schiller, Johann Christoph Friedrich von (1759–1805)
German, born Marbach; *The Robbers* (1781), *Wallenstein* (1799), *Maria Stuart* (1800).
Seneca, Lucius Annaeus (c.4 BC–AD 65)
Roman, born Corduba; *Hercules, Medea, Thyestes*.
Seymour, Alan (1927–)
Australian, born Perth; *The One Day of the Year* (1962), *Swamp Creatures* (1958), *Danny Johnson* (1960).
Shakespeare, William *see* PLAYS OF SHAKESPEARE
Shaffer, Peter (Levin) (1926–)
English, born Liverpool; *The Royal Hunt of the Sun* (1964), *Equus* (1973), *Amadeus* (1979).
Shaw, George Bernard (1856–1950)
Irish, born Dublin; *Arms and the Man* (1894), *Man and Superman* (1903), *Pygmalion* (1913), *Saint Joan* (1924); Nobel Prize for Literature 1925.
Shepard, Sam (Samuel Shepard Rogers) (1943–)
American, born Illinois; *La Turista* (1967), *The Tooth of Crime* (1972), *Buried Child* (1978), *True West* (1979), *Fool for Love* (1983).

Sheridan, Richard Brinsley (1751–1816)
Irish, born Dublin; *The Rivals* (1775), *The School for Scandal* (1777), *The Critic* (1779).
Sherwood, Robert (Emmet) (1896–1955)
American, born New York; *Idiot's Delight* (1936), *Abe Lincoln in Illinois* (1938), *There Shall Be No Night* (1940).
Sophocles (496–406 BC) Athenian, born Colonus; *Antigone, Oedipus Rex, Oedipus at Colonus.*
Soyinka, Wole (Akinwande Olnwole Soyinka) (1934–   )
Nigerian, born Abeokata, West Nigeria; *The Swamp Dwellers* (1958), *The Bacchae of Euripides* (1973).
Stoppard, Tom (Thomas Straussler) (1937–   )
English, born Czechoslovakia; *Rosencrantz and Guildenstern are Dead* (1966), *The Real Inspector Hound* (1968), *Travesties* (1974).
Strindberg, (Johan) August (1849–1912)
Swedish, born Stockholm; *Miss Julie* (1888), *Master Olof* (1877), *The Dance of Death* (1901).
Synge, (Edmund) J(ohn) M(illington) (1871–1909)
Irish, born near Dublin; *The Well of Saints* (1905), *The Playboy of the Western World* (1907).

Webster, John (c.1578–c.1632)
English, born London; *The White Devil* (1612), *The Duchess of Malfi* (1614).
Wilde, Oscar (Fingal O'Flahertie Wills) (1854–1906)
Irish, born Dublin; *Lady Windermere's Fan* (1892), *The Importance of Being Earnest* (1895), *Salomé* (1896).
Wilder, Thornton (Niven) (1897–1975)
American, born Wisconsin; *Our Town* (1938), *The Merchant of Yonkers* (1938), *The Skin of Our Teeth* (1942), *The Matchmaker* (1954, later a musical *Hello, Dolly!*, 1964).
Williams, Tennessee (originally Thomas Lanier Williams) (1911–83)
American, born Mississippi; *The Glass Menagerie* (1944), *A Streetcar Named Desire* (1947), *Cat on a Hot Tin Roof* (1955), *Sweet Bird of Youth* (1959).
Williamson, David Keith (1942–   )
Australian, born Melbourne; *The Removalists* (1971), *Don's Party* (1971).
Wycherly, William (1641–1715)
English, born Clive, near Shrewsbury; *The Gentleman Dancing-Master* (1672), *The Country Wife* (1675), *The Plain-Dealer* (1676).

PLAYS OF SHAKESPEARE

William Shakespeare (1564–1616), English playwright and poet, born Stratford-upon-Avon.

Title	Date	Category
The Two Gentlemen of Verona	1590–1	comedy
Henry VI Part One	1592	history
Henry VI Part Two	1592	history
Henry VI Part Three	1592	history
Titus Andronicus	1592	tragedy
Richard III	1592–3	history
The Taming of the Shrew	1593	comedy
The Comedy of Errors	1594	comedy

PLAYS OF SHAKESPEARE (cont.)

Title	Date	Category
Love's Labour Lost	1594–5	comedy
Richard II	1595	history
Romeo and Juliet	1595	tragedy
A Midsummer Night's Dream	1595	comedy
King John	1596	history
The Merchant of Venice	1596–7	comedy
Henry IV Part One	1596–7	history
The Merry Wives of Windsor	1597–8	comedy
Henry IV Part Two	1597–8	history
Much Ado About Nothing	1598	dark comedy
Henry V	1598–9	history
Julius Caesar	1599	Roman
As You Like It	1599–1600	comedy
Hamlet, Prince of Denmark	1600–1	tragedy
Twelfth Night, or What You Will	1601	comedy
Troilus and Cressida	1602	tragedy
Measure for Measure	1603	dark comedy
Othello	1603–4	tragedy
All's Well That Ends Well	1604–5	dark comedy
Timon of Athens	1605	romantic drama
The Tragedy of King Lear	1605–6	tragedy
Macbeth	1606	tragedy
Antony and Cleopatra	1606	tragedy
Pericles	1607	romance
Coriolanus	1608	Roman
The Winter's Tale	1609	romance
Cymbeline	1610	comedy
The Tempest	1611	comedy
Henry VIII	1613	history

POETS LAUREATE

1617 Ben Jonson[1]
1638 Sir William Davenant[1]
1668 John Dryden
1689 Thomas Shadwell
1692 Nahum Tate
1715 Nicholas Rowe
1718 Laurence Eusden

1730 Colley Cibber
1757 William Whitehead
1785 Thomas Warton
1790 Henry Pye
1813 Robert Southey
1843 William Wordsworth
1850 Alfred, Lord Tennyson

1896 Alfred Austin
1913 Robert Bridges
1930 John Masefield
1968 Cecil Day Lewis
1972 Sir John Betjeman
1984 Ted Hughes

[1] The post was not officially established until 1668.

LITERARY PRIZES

Booker Prize (UK)

1970 Bernice Rubens *The Elected Member*

1971 V S Naipaul *In a Free State*

1972 John Berger *G*

1973 J G Farrell *The Siege of Krishnapur*

1974 Nadine Gordimer *The Conservationist*; Stanley Middleton *Holiday*

1975 Ruth Prawer Jhabvala *Heat and Dust*

1976 David Storey *Saville*

1977 Paul Scott *Staying On*

1978 Irish Murdoch *The Sea, The Sea*

1979 Penelope Fitzgerald *Offshore*

1980 William Golding *Rites of Passage*

1981 Salman Rushdie *Midnight's Children*

1982 Thomas Keneally *Schindler's Ark*

1983 J M Coetzee *Life and Times of Michael K*

1984 Anita Brookner *Hotel du Lac*

1985 Keri Hulme *The Bone People*

1986 Kingsley Amis *The Old Devils*

1987 Penelope Lively *Moon Tiger*

1988 Peter Carey *Oscar and Lucinda*

1989 Kazuo Ishiguro *The Remains of the Day*

1990 A S Byatt *Possession*

1991 Ben Okri *The Famished Road*

1992 Barry Unsworth *Sacred Hunger*; Michael Ondaatje *The English Patient*

1993 Roddy Doyle *Paddy Clarke Ha Ha Ha*

1994 James Kelman *How late it was, how late*

1995 Pat Barker *The Ghost Road*

1996 Graham Swift *Last Orders*

Pulitzer Prize in Letters: Fiction (USA)

1970 Jean Stafford *Collected Stories*

1972 Wallace Stegner *Angle of Repose*

1973 Eudora Welty *The Optimist's Daughter*

1975 Michael Shaara *The Killer Angels*

1976 Saul Bellow *Humboldt's Gift*

1978 James Alan McPherson *Elbow Room*

1979 John Cheever *The Stories of John Cheever*

1980 Norman Mailer *The Executioner's Song*

1981 John Kennedy Toole *A Confederacy of Dunces*

1982 John Updike *Rabbit is Rich*

1983 Alice Walker *The Color Purple*

1984 William Kennedy *Ironweed*

1985 Alison Lurie *Foreign Affairs*

1986 Larry McMurtry *Lonesome Dove*

1987 Peter Taylor *A Summons to Memphis*

1988 Toni Morrison *Beloved*

1989 Anne Tyler *Breathing Lessons*

1990 Oscar Hijuelos *The Mambo Kings Play Songs of Love*

1991 John Updike *Rabbit at Rest*

1992 Jane Smiley *A Thousand Acres*

1993 Robert Olen Butler *A Good Scent from a Strange Mountain*

1994 E Annie Proulx *The Shipping News*

1995 Carol Shields *The Stone Diaries*

1996 Richard Ford *Independence Day*

FILM ACTORS

Selected films and television productions are listed.
Original and full names of actors are given in parentheses.

Allen, Woody (Allen Stewart Konigsberg) (1935–   )
American, born Brooklyn, New York; *What's New Pussycat?* (1965), *Casino Royale* (1967), *Bananas* (1971), *Play it Again Sam* (1972), *Sleeper* (1973), *Annie Hall* (1977), *Manhattan* (1979), *Stardust Memories* (1980), *Hannah and Her Sisters* (1986), *New York Stories* (1989), *Crimes and Misdemeanors* (1989), *Scenes from the Mall* (1990), *Shadows and Fog* (1992), *Husbands and Wives* (1992), *Manhattan Murder Mystery* (1994).

Andrews, Julie, (Julia Elizabeth Wells) (1935–   )
British born Walton-on-Thames, Surrey; *Mary Poppins* (1964), *The Sound of Music* (1965), *Star!* (1968), *Victor/Victoria* (1982), *Duet for One* (1986).

Astaire, Fred (Frederick Austerlitz) (1899–1987)
American, born Omaha, Nebraska; *Flying Down to Rio* (1933), *Top Hat* (1935), *Swing Time* (1936), *Easter Parade* (1948), *The Bandwagon* (1953), *Funny Face* (1957), *Finian's Rainbow* (1968), *Towering Inferno* (1974).

Bacall, Lauren (Betty Joan Perske) (1924–   )
American, born New York City; *To Have and Have Not* (1944), *The Big Sleep* (1946), *Key Largo* (1948), *How to Marry a Millionaire* (1953), *Murder on the Orient Express* (1974), *The Shootist* (1976), *The Fan* (1981), *The Portrait* (TV 1993), *Pret-A-Porter (1994)*.

Bardot, Brigitte (Camille Javal) (1934–   )
French, born Paris; *And God Created Woman* (1956), *La Verite* (1960), *La Vie Privée* (1961), *Le Mepris* (1963), *Viva Maria* (1965).

Beatty, Warren (Henry Warren Beaty) (1937–   )
American, born Richmond, Virginia; *Splendour in the Grass* (1961), *The Roman Spring of Mrs Stone* (1961), *All Fall Down* (1962), *Bonnie and Clyde* (1967), *The Parallax View* (1974), *Shampoo* (1975), *Heaven Can Wait* (1978), *Reds* (1981), *Ishtar* (1987), *Dick Tracy* (1990), *Bugsy* (1991), *Love Affair* (1994).

Bergman, Ingrid (1915–82)
Swedish, born Stockholm; *Intermezzo* (1939), *Casablanca* (1942), *For Whom the Bell Tolls* (1943), *Gaslight* (1944), *Notorious* (1946), *Stromboli* (1949), *Anastasia* (1956), *Cactus Flower* (1969), *Murder on the Orient Express* (1974), *Autumn Sonata* (1978), *Golda* (TV 1981).

Bogarde, Dirk (Derek Niven Van Den Bogaerde) (1921–   )
Dutch/British, born Hampstead; *The Blue Lamp* (1949), *Hunted* (1952), *Doctor in the House* (1954), *Victim* (1961), *The Servant* (1963), *Darling* (1965), *Accident* (1967), *The Damned* (1969), *Death in Venice* (1971), *Providence* (1977), *These Foolish Things* (1990).

Bogart, Humphrey (De Forest) (1899–1957)
American, born New York City; *Broadway's Like That* (1930), *The Petrified Forest* (1936), *High Sierra* (1941), *The Maltese Falcon* (1941), *Casablanca* (1942), *To Have and Have Not* (1944), *The Big Sleep* (1946), *The Treasure of the Sierra Madre* (1947), *The African Queen* (1951), *The Barefoot Contessa* (1954), *The Caine Mutiny* (1954).

Branagh, Kenneth (1960–   )
British, born Belfast; also stage; *High Season* (1987), *A Month in the Country* (1988), *Hennry V*

(1989), *Dead Again* (1991), *Peter's Friends* (1992), *Much Ado about Nothing* (1993), *Frankenstein* (1994), *In the Bleak Mid Winter* (1995).

Brando, Marlon (1924–)
American, born Omaha, Nebraska; *A Streetcar Named Desire* (1951), *Viva Zapata* (1952), *Julius Caesar* (1953), *The Wild One* (1953), *On the Waterfront* (1954), *Guys and Dolls* (1955), *The Young Lions* (1958), *One-Eyed Jacks* (1961), *Mutiny on the Bounty* (1962), *The Chase* (1966), *The Godfather* (1972), *Last Tango in Paris* (1972), *Apocalypse Now* (1979), *A Dry White Season* (1988), *The Freshman* (1990), *Don Juan De Marco and the Centerfold* (1995).

Bridges, Jeff (1949–)
American, born Los Angeles; *The Last Picture Show* (1971), *Fat City* (1972), *Thunderbolt and Lightfoot* (1974), *Stay Hungry* (1976), *Heaven's Gate* (1980), *Cutter's Way* (1981), *Tron* (1982), *Starman* (1984), *Jagged Edge* (1985), *Tucker: The Man and His Dream* (1987), *The Fabulous Baker Boys* (1989), *Texasville* (1990), *The Fisher King* (1991), *Fearless* (1993).

Bronson, Charles (Charles Buchinski) (1920–)
American, born Ehrenfield, Pennsylvania; *Pat and Mike* (1952), *The Magnificent Seven* (1960), *The Dirty Dozen* (1967), *Death Wish* (1974), *Hard Times* (1975), *The Indian Runner* (1991).

Burton, Richard (Richard Jenkins) (1925–84)
British, born Pontrhydfen, S Wales: *My Cousin Rachel* (1952), *Alexander the Great* (1956), *Look Back in Anger* (1959), *Cleopatra* (1962), *The Night of the Iguana* (1964), *The Spy Who Came in from the Cold* (1965), *Who's Afraid of Virginia Woolf?* (1966), *The Taming of the Shrew* (1967), *Where Eagles Dare* (1969), *Equus* (1977), *1984* (1984).

Cagney, James (Francis Jr) (1899–1986)
American, born New York City; *Public Enemy* (1931), *Lady Killer* (1933), *A Midsummer Night's Dream* (1935), *The Roaring Twenties* (1939), *Yankee Doodle Dandy* (1942), *White Heat* (1949), *Love Me or Leave Me* (1955), *Mister Roberts* (1955), *One, Two, or Three* (1961), *Ragtime* (1981).

Caine, Michael (Maurice Micklewhite) (1933–)
British, born London; *Zulu* (1963), *The Ipcress File* (1965), *Alfie* (1966), *The Italian Job* (1969), *Sleuth* (1972), *The Man Who Would Be King* (1975), *California Suite* (1978), *Dressed to Kill* (1980), *Educating Rita* (1983), *Hannah and Her Sisters* (1986), *The Muppet Christmas Carol* (1992).

Chaplin, Sir Charles (Spencer) (1889–1977)
British, born London; *The Champion* (1915), *The Tramp* (1915), *Easy Street* (1917), *A Dog's Life* (1918), *Shoulder Arms* (1918), *The Kid* (1920), *The Idle Class* (1921), *The Gold Rush* (1924), *City Lights* (1931), *Modern Times* (1936), *The Great Dictator* (1940), *Limelight* (1952), *A King in New York* (1957).

Cher (Cher Bono, formerly Cherilyn Sarkisian) (1946–)
American, born El Centro, California; *Silkwood* (1983), *Mask* (1985), *Moonstruck* (1987), *Suspect* (1987), *The Witches of Eastwick* (1987), *Mermaids* (1990).

Clift, (Edward) Montgomery (1920–66)
American, born Omaha, Nebraska; *Red River* (1946), *The Search* (1948), *A Place in the Sun* (1951), *From Here to Eternity* (1953), *Suddenly Last Summer* (1959), *Freud* (1962).

Close, Glenn (1947–)
American, born Greenwich, Connecticut; *The World According to Garp* (1982), *The Big Chill* (1983), *The Natural* (1984), *Something About Amelia* (TV 1984), *Jagged Edge* (1985), *Fatal Attraction* (1987), *Dangerous Liaisons* (1988), *Reversal of Fortune* (1990), *Hamlet* (1990), *Meeting Venus* (1991), *The Paper* (1994).

FILM ACTORS (cont.)

Connery, Sean (Thomas Connery) (1930–)
British, born Edinburgh; *Dr No* (1963), *Marnie* (1964), *From Russia With Love* (1964), *Goldfinger* (1965), *The Hill* (1965), *The Molly Maguires* (1969), *The Anderson Tapes* (1971), *Diamonds are Forever* (1971), *The Offence* (1972), *Murder on the Orient Express* (1974), *The Man Who Would Be King* (1975), *Never Say Never Again* (1983), *The Name of the Rose* (1986), *The Untouchables* (1987), *Indiana Jones and the Last Crusade* (1989), *Family Business* (1989), *The Hunt for Red October* (1990), *The Russia House* (1990), *Rising Sun* (1992), *First Night* (1995).

Cooper, Gary (Frank J Cooper) (1901–61)
American, born Helena, Montana; *The Virginian* (1929), *A Farewell to Arms* (1932), *The Lives of a Bengal Lancer* (1935), *Mr Deeds goes to Town* (1936), *Beau Geste* (1939), *Sergeant York* (1941), *The Pride of the Yankees* (1942), *For Whom the Bell Tolls* (1943), *High Noon* (1952), *Friendly Persuasion* (1956).

Costner, Kevin (1955–)
American, born Los Angeles; *Silverado* (1985), *The Untouchables* (1987), *No Way Out* (1987), *Bull Durham* (1988), *Field of Dreams* (1989), *Dances with Wolves* (1990), *Robin Hood, Prince of Thieves* (1991), *JFK* (1991), *The Bodyguard* (1992), *A Perfect World* (1993), *Wyatt Earp* (1994), *The War* (1994), Waterworld (1995).

Crawford, Joan (Lucille Le Sueur) (1904–77)
American, born San Antonio, Texas; *Our Dancing Daughters* (1928), *Grand Hotel* (1932), *The Women* (1939), *Mildred Pierce* (1945), *Possessed* (1947), *Sudden Fear* (1952), *Johnny Guitar* (1954), *Whatever Happened to Baby Jane?* (1962), *Trog* (1970).

Crosby, Bing (Harry Lillis Crosby) (1904–77)
American, born Tacoma, Washington; *King of Jazz* (1930), *Mississippi* (1935), *Anything Goes* (1936), *Road to Singapore* (1940), *Road to Zanzibar* (1941), *Holiday Inn* (1942), *Road to Morrocco* (1942), *Going My Way* (1944), *The Bells of St Mary's* (1945), *Blue Skies* (1946), *A Connecticut Yankee in King Arthur's Court* (1949), *White Christmas* (1954), *The Country Girl* (1954), *High Society* (1956), *Road to Hong Kong* (1962).

Cruise, Tom (Tom Cruise Mapother IV) (1962–)
American, born Syracuse, New York; *Taps* (1981), *The Outsiders* (1983), *Legend* (1984), *Risky Business* (1983), *Top Gun* (1986), *The Color of Money* (1986), *Rain Man* (1988), *Born on the 4th of July* (1989), *A Few Good Men* (1992), *The Firm* (1993), *Interview with the Vampire* (1994), *Mission Impossible* (1995).

Curtis, Tony (Bernard Schwarz) (1925–)
American, born New York City; *The Prince who was a Thief* (1950), *Sweet smell of Success* (1957), *The Defiant Ones* (1958), *Some Like it Hot* (1959), *Spartacus* (1960), *The Boston Strangler* (1968), *The Persuaders* (TV 1971–2), *Insignificance* (1958).

Dafoe, Willem (1955–)
American, born Appleton, Wisconsin; *Heaven's Gate* (1980), *Platoon* (1986), *The Last Temptation of Christ* (1988), *Mississippi Burning* (1988), *Triumph of the Spirit* (1989), *Born on the 4th of July* (1989), *Wild At Heart* (1990), *Cry Baby* (1990), *Flight of The Intruder* (1990), *Light Sleeper* (1992), *Body of Evidence* (1992), *Tom and Viv* (1994), *Clear and Present Danger* (1994).

Davis, Bette (Ruth Elizabeth Davis) (1908–89)
American, born Lowell, Massachusetts; *Bad Sister* (1931), *Of Human Bondage* (1934), *Dangerous* (1935), *Jezebel* (1938), *Dark Victory* (1939), *The Letter* (1940), *The Little Foxes* (1941),

Now Voyager (1942), *All About Eve* (1950), *The Star* (1952), *Whatever Happened to Baby Jane?* (1962), *The Great Lie* (1941), *Strangers* (TV 1979), *The Whales of August* (1987).

Day, Doris (Doris von Kappelhoff) (1924–   )
American, born Cincinnati, Ohio; *Romance on the High Seas* (1948), *Storm Warning* (1950), *Calamity Jane* (1953), *Young at Heart* (1954), *Love Me or Leave Me* (1955), *The Pajama Game* (1957), *Pillow Talk* (1959), *That Touch of Mink* (1962), *With Six You Get Egg Roll* (1968), *The Doris Day Show* (TV 1968–73).

Day-Lewis, Daniel (1958–   )
Irish, born London; *Sunday, Bloody Sunday* (1971), *Gandhi* (1982), *My Beautiful Laundrette* (1985), *Room with a View* (1985), *The Unbearable Lightness of Being* (1988), *My Left Foot* (1989), *The Last of the Mohicans* (1992), *Age of Innocence* (1993), *In the Name of the Father* (1993).

Dean, James (Byron) (1931–55)
American, born Fairmount, Indiana; *East of Eden* (1955), *Rebel without a Cause* (1955), *Giant* (1956).

De Havilland, Olivia (1916–   )
British, born Tokyo, Japan; *Midsummer Night's Dream* (1935), *The Adventures of Robin Hood* (1938), *Gone with the Wind* (1939), *The Dark Mirror* (1946), *To Each his Own* (1946), *The Heiress* (1949).

Deneuve, Catherine (Catherine Dorleac) (1943–   )
French, born Paris; *Les Parapluies de Cherbourg* (1964), *Repulsion* (1965), *Belle de Jour* (1967), *Tristana* (1970), *The Last Metro* (1980), *The Hunger* (1983), *Indochine* (1991).

De Niro, Robert (1943–   )
American, born New York City; *Bang the Drum Slowly* (1973), *Mean Streets* (1973), *The Godfather, Part II* (1974), *1900* (1976), *Taxi Driver* (1976), *The Deer Hunter* (1978), *Raging Bull* (1980), *King of Comedy* (1982), *The Untouchables* (1987), *Midnight Run* (1988), *GoodFellas* (1990), *Awakenings* (1990), *Backdraft* (1991), *Cape Fear* (1991), *This Boy's Life* (1993), *A Bronx Tale* (1993), *Frankenstein* (1994), *Casino* (1995).

Depardieu, Gérard (1948–   )
French, born Châteauroux; *1900* (1976), *Get Out Your Handkerchiefs* (1977), *Loulou* (1980), *The Last Metro* (1980), *The Return of Martin Guerre* (1981), *Danton* (1982), *The Moon in the Gutter* (1983), *Police* (1985), *Jean de Florette* (1986), *Under the Sun of Satan* (1987), *Cyrano de Bergerac* (1990), *Green Card* (1990), *Tous les Matins du Monde* (1991), *1492: Conquest of Paradise* (1992), *Le Colonel Chabert* (1994).

Depp, Johnny (1963–   )
American, born Owensboro, Kentucky; *A Nightmare on Elm Street* (1984), *Platoon* (1986), *Cry Baby* (1990), *Edward Scissorhands* (1990), *Benny and Joon* (1993), *What's Eating Gilbert Grape?* (1993), *Ed Wood* (1994), *Don Juan Marco and the Centerfold* (1995).

De Vito, Danny (1944–   )
American, born Neptune, New Jersey; *One Flew Over the Cuckoo's Nest* (1975), *Taxi* (TV 1978–82), *Terms of Endearment* (1983), *Romancing the Stone* (1984), *Ruthless People* (1986), *Tin Men* (1987), *Throw Momma from the Train* (1987), *War of the Roses* (1989), *Batman Returns* (1992), *Renaissance Man* (1994), *Junior* (1994), *Get Shorty* (1995).

Dietrich, Marlene (Maria Magdalena von Losch) (1901–92)
German/American, born Berlin; *The Blue Angel* (1930), *Morocco* (1930), *Blonde Venus* (1932), *Shanghai Express* (1932), *The Scarlett Empress* (1934), *The Devil is a Woman* (1935), *Desire* (1936), *Destry Rides Again* (1939), *A Foreign Affair* (1948), *Rancho Notorious* (1952), *Judgement at Nuremberg* (1961).

FILM ACTORS (cont.)

Donat, Robert (1905–58)
British, born Withington; *The Count of Monte Cristo* (1934), *The Thirty-Nine Steps* (1935), *The Ghost Goes West* (1936), *The Citadel* (1938), *Goodbye Mr Chips* (1939), *The Winslow Boy* (1948), *The Inn of the Sixth Happiness* (1958).

Douglas, Kirk (Issur Danielovitch Demsky) (1916–)
American, born Amsterdam, New York; *The Strange Love of Martha Ivers* (1946), *Champion* (1949), *Detective Story (1950)*, *Ace in the Hole* (1951), *The Bad and The Beautiful* (1952), *Lust for Life* (1956), *Paths of Glory* (1957), *The Vikings* (1958), *Spartacus* (1960), *Lonely are the Brave* (1962), *Posse* (1975), *Amos* (TV 1985).

Douglas, Michael (1944–)
American, born New Brunswick, New Jersey; *The Streets of San Francisco* (TV 1972–5), *Coma* (1978), *The China Syndrome* (1979), *Romancing the Stone* (1984), *Fatal Attraction* (1987), *Wall Street* (1987), *The War of the Roses* (1989), *Basic Instinct* (1992), *Falling Down* (1993), *Disclosure* (1994).

Dreyfuss, Richard (1947–)
American, born Brooklyn, New York; *American Graffiti* (1973), *The Apprenticeship of Duddy Kravitz* (1974), *Jaws* (1975), *Close Encounters of the Third Kind* (1977), *The Goodbye Girl* (1977), *Whose Life is it Anyway?* (1981), *Down and Out in Beverly Hills* (1986), *Stakeout* (1987), *Tin Men* (1987), *Always* (1989), *What About Bob?* (1991).

Dunaway, (Dorothy) Faye (1941–)
American, born Bascom, Florida; *Bonnie and Clyde* (1967), *The Thomas Crown Affair* (1968), *Little Big Man* (1970), *Chinatown* (1974), *The Towering Inferno* (1974), *Network* (1976), *The Eyes of Laura Mars* (1978), *Mommie Dearest* (1981), *Barfly* (1987), *Cold Sassy Tree* (TV 1989), *Don Juan De Marco and the Centerfold* (1995).

Durbin, Deanna (Edna Mae Durbin) (1921–)
Canadian, born Winnipeg, Manitoba; *Three Smart Girls* (1936), *One Hundred Men and a Girl* (1937), *Mad About Music* (1938), *That Certain Age* (1938), *Three Smart Girls Grow Up* (1939), *It Started With Eve* (1941), *Christmas Holiday* (1944), *Lady on a Train* (1945).

Eastwood, Clint (1930–)
American, born San Francisco, California; *Rawhide* (TV 1958–65), *A Fistful of Dollars* (1964), *The Good, The Bad, and the Ugly* (1966), *Coogan's Bluff* (1968), *Where Eagles Dare* (1969), *Play Misty for Me* (1971), *Dirty Harry* (1971), *The Outlaw Josey Wales* (1976), *Every Which Way But Loose* (1978), *Escape from Alcatraz* (1979), *Bronco Billy* (1980), *Tightrope* (1984), *Pale Rider* (1985), *White Hunter Black Heart* (1990), *Unforgiven* (1992), *In the Line of Fire* (1993), *The Bridges of Madison County* (1995).

Fairbanks, Douglas Sr (Douglas Elton Ullman) (1883–1939)
American, born Denver, Colorado; *The Mark of Zorro* (1920), *The Three Musketeers* (1921), *Robin Hood* (1922), *The Thief of Baghdad* (1924), *The Black Pirate* (1926).

Field, Sally (1946–)
American, born Pasadena, California; *Gidget* (TV 1965), *The Flying Nun* (TV 1967–9), *Sybil* (TV 1976), *Stay Hungry* (1976), *Smokey and the Bandit* (1977), *Norma Rae* (1979), *Absence of Malice* (1981), *Places in the Heart* (1984), *Punchline* (1988), *Steel Magnolias* (1990), *Mrs Doubtfire* (1993), *Forrest Gump* (1994).

Flynn, Errol (1909–59)
Australian/American, born Hobart, Tasmania; *In the Wake of the Bounty* (1933), *Captain Blood*

(1935), *The Charge of the Light Brigade* (1936), *The Adventures of Robin Hood* (1938), *The Sea Hawk* (1940), *The Sun Also Rises* (1957).

Fonda, Henry (James) (1905–82)
American, born Grand Island, Nebraska; *Young Mr Lincoln* (1939), *The Grapes of Wrath* (1940), *The Lady Eve* (1941), *The Oxbow Incident* (1943), *My Darling Clementine* (1946), *Twelve Angry Men* (1957), *Once Upon a Time in the West* (1968), *On Golden Pond* (1981).

Fonda, Jane (Seymour) (1937–)
American, born New York City; *Walk on the Wild Side* (1962), *Barbarella* (1968), *They Shoot Horses Don't They?* (1969), *Klute* (1971), *Julia* (1977), *Coming Home* (1978), *The Electric Horseman* (1979), *The China Syndrome* (1979), *Nine to Five* (1980), *On Golden Pond* (1981), *The Dollmaker* (TV 1983), *The Morning After* (1986), *Old Gringo* (1989), *Stanley and Iris* (1989).

Ford, Harrison (1942–)
American, born Chicago; *Dead Heat on a Merry-Go-Round* (1966), *American Graffiti* (1974), *Star Wars* (1977), *Apocalypse Now* (1979), *The Empire Strikes Back* (1980), *Raiders of the Lost Ark* (1981), *Blade Runner* (1982), *Return of the Jedi* (1983), *Indiana Jones and the Temple of Doom* (1984), *Witness* (1985), *The Mosquito Coast* (1986), *Frantic* (1988), *Working Girl* (1988), *Indiana Jones and the Last Crusade* (1989), *Presumed Innocent* (1990), *The Fugitive* (1993), *Clear and Present Danger* (1994), *Sabrina* (1995).

Foster, Jodie (Ariane Munker) (1962–)
American, born Bronx, New York; *Alice Doesn't Live Here Anymore* (1974), *Bugsy Malone* (1976), *Taxi Driver* (1976), *The Accused* (1988), *Silence of the Lambs* (1991), *Little Man Tate* (1991), *Sommersby* (1993), *Maverick* (1994), *Nell* (1994).

Fox, Michael J (1961–)
Canadian, born Edmonton, Alberta; *Family Ties* (TV 1983–88), *Back to the Future* (1985), *The Secret of My Success* (1987), *Casualties of War* (1989), *Back to the Future II* (1989), *Back to the Future III* (1990), *'Doc' Hollywood* (1991), *Don't Drink the Water* (TV 1994).

Gable, (William) Clark (1901–60)
American, born Cadiz, Ohio; *Red Dust* (1932), *It Happened One Night* (1934), *Mutiny on the Bounty* (1935), *San Francisco* (1936), *Gone with the Wind* (1939), *The Hucksters* (1947), *Mogambo* (1953), *The Misfits* (1961).

Garbo, Greta (Greta Lovisa Gustafsson) (1905–90)
Swedish/American, born Stockholm; *Flesh and the Devil* (1927), *Anna Christie* (1930), *Grand Hotel* (1932), *Queen Christina* (1933), *Anna Karenina* (1935), *Camille* (1936), *Ninotchka* (1939).

Gardner, Ava (Lucy Johnson) (1922–90)
American, born Smithfield, North Carolina; *The Killers* (1946), *The Hucksters* (1947), *Show Boat* (1951), *Pandora and the Flying Dutchman* (1951), *The Snows of Kilimanjaro* (1952), *Mogambo* (1953), *The Barefoot Contessa* (1954), *The Sun Also Rises* (1957), *The Night of the Iguana* (1964).

Garland, Judy (Frances Gumm) (1922–69)
American, born Grand Rapids, Minnesota; *The Wizard of Oz* (1939), *Babes in Arms* (1939), *For Me and My Gal* (1942), *Meet Me in St Louis* (1944), *The Clock* (1945), *Easter Parade* (1948), *Summer Stock* (1950), *A Star is Born* (1954), *Judgement at Nuremberg* (1961).

Gere, Richard (1949–)
American, born Philadelphia, Pennsylvania; *Looking For Mr Goodbar* (1977), *Days of Heaven* (1978), *American Gigolo* (1980), *An Officer and a Gentleman* (1982), *The Cotton Club* (1984), *Internal Affairs* (1989), *Pretty Woman* (1990), *Sommersby* (1993), *And the Band Played On* (TV 1993), *First Knight* (1995).

FILM ACTORS (cont.)

Gibson, Mel (1956–   )

American/Australian, born Peekshill, New York; *Tim* (1979), *Mad Max* (1979), *Gallipoli* (1980), *Mad Max 2: The Road Warrior* (1982), *The Year of Living Dangerously* (1982), *The Bounty* (1984), *Mad Max Beyond Thunderdrome* (1985), *Lethal Weapon* (1987), *Lethal Weapon 2* (1989), *Hamlet* (1990), *Lethal Weapon 3* (1992), *Forever Young* (1992), *Man without a Face* (1993), *Maverick* (1994), *Braveheart* (1995).

Gish, Lillian (Diana) (Lillian de Guiche) (1893–1993)

American, born Springfield, Ohio; *An Unseen Enemy* (1912), *Birth of a Nation* (1915), *Intolerance* (1916), *Broken Blossoms* (1919), *Way Down East* (1920), *Duel in the Sun* (1946), *Night of the Hunter* (1955), *The Whales of August* (1987).

Goldberg, Whoopi (Caryn Johnson) (1949–   )

American, born Manhattan, New York; *The Color Purple* (1985), *Burglar* (1985), *Jumping Jack Flash* (1986), *Clara's Heart* (1988), *The Telephone* (1988), *Ghost* (1990), *Soapdish* (1991), *Sister Act* (1992), *Change of Heart* (1992), *Serafina!* (1992), *The Player* (1992).

Granger, Stewart (James Lablanche Stewart) (1913–93)

British–American, born London; *The Man in Grey* (1943), *Waterloo Road* (1944), *Love Story* (1944), *Caesar and Cleopatra* (1945), *Captain Boycott* (1947), *King Solomon's Mines* (1950), *Scaramouch* (1952), *The Prisoner of Zenda* (1952), *Beau Brummell* (1954), *The Wild Geese* (1977).

Grant, Cary (Archibald Alexander Leach) (1904–86)

British, born Bristol; *Blonde Venus* (1932), *She Done Him Wrong* (1933), *The Awful Truth* (1937), *Bringing Up Baby* (1938), *Gunga Din* (1939), *The Philadelphia Story* (1940), *His Girl Friday* (1940), *Arsenic and Old Lace* (1944), *Notorious* (1946), *To Catch a Thief* (1953), *North by Northwest* (1959), *Charade* (1963).

Grant, Hugh (1960–   )

British, born London; *Maurice* (1987), *Bitter Moon* (1992), *Sirens* (1993), *Four Weddings and a Funeral* (1994), *An Awfully Big Adventure* (1995), *Nine Months* (1995).

Griffith, Melanie (1957–   )

American, born New York City; *Night Moves* (1985), *Body Double* (1984), *Working Girl* (1988), *Nobody's Fool* (1994).

Guinness, Sir Alec (1914–   )

British, born London; also stage; *Oliver Twist* (1948), *Kind Hearts and Coronets* (1949), *The Lavender Hill Mob* (1951), *The Man in the White Suit* (1951), *The Ladykillers* (1955), *The Bridge on the River Kwai* (1957), *Tunes of Glory* (1960), *Lawrence of Arabia* (1962), *Doctor Zhivago* (1966), *Star Wars* (1977), *Tinker Tailor Soldier Spy* (TV 1979), *Smiley's People* (TV 1981), *Return of the Jedi* (1983), *A Passage to India* (1984), *Little Dorrit* (1987).

Hackman, Gene (1931–   )

American, born San Bernardino, California; *Bonnie and Clyde* (1967), *I Never Sang for my Father* (1970), *French Connection* (1971), *The Poseidon Adventure* (1972), *Scarecrow* (1973), *The Conversation* (1974), *French Connection II* (1975), *Night Moves* (1975), *Superman* (1978), *Eureka* (1983), *No Way Out* (1987), *Mississippi Burning* (1989), *Unforgiven* (1992), *The Firm* (1993), *The Quick and the Dead* (1995), *Crimson Tide* (1995).

Hanks, Tom (1957–   )

American, born Oakland, California; *He Knows You're Alone* (1981), *Splash!* (1984), *Big* (1988), *Punchline* (1988), *A League of Their Own* (1992), *Sleepless in Seattle* (1993), *Philadelphia* (1993), *Forrest Gump* (1994), *Apollo 13* (1995).

Hardy, Oliver (Norvell Hardy Junior) (1892–1957)
American, born near Atlanta, Georgia; many Laurel and Hardy films including *Putting Pants on Philip* (1927), *The Battle of the Century* (1927), *Two Tars* (1928), *The Perfect Day* (1929), *Laughing Gravy* (1931), *The Music Box* (1932), *Babes in Toyland* (1934), *Bonnie Scotland* (1935), *Way Out West* (1937), *The Flying Deuces* (1939), *Atoll K* (1950).

Hawn, Goldie (Jeanne) (1945–)
American, born Washington D.C.; *Laugh In* (TV 1968–73), *Cactus Flower* (1969), *There's a Girl in My Soup* (1970), *Butterflies are Free* (1971), *Sugarland Express* (1974), *Shampoo* (1975), *Foul Play* (1978), *Seems Like Old Times* (1980), *Private Benjamin* (1980), *Best Friends* (1982), *Swing Shift* (1984), *Bird on a Wire* (1990), *CrissCross* (1991), *Deceived* (1991), *Housesitter* (1992), *Death Becomes Her* (1992).

Hayward, Susan (Edythe Marrenner) (1917–75)
American, born Brooklyn, New York; *Smash-Up: The Story of a Woman* (1947), *With a Song In My Heart* (1952), *I'll Cry Tomorrow* (1955), *I Want to Live!* (1958), *Where Love Has Gone* (1964), *Valley of the Dolls* (1967), *The Revengers* (1972).

Hayworth, Rita (Margarita Carmen Cansino) (1918–87)
American, born New York City; *Charlie Chan in Egypt* (1935), *Only Angels Have Wings* (1939), *The Strawberry Blonde* (1940), *Blood and Sand* (1941), *You'll Never Get Rich* (1941), *You were Never Lovlier* (1942), *Cover Girl* (1944), *Gilda* (1946), *The Lady from Shanghai* (1948), *Separate Tables* (1958), *The Wrath of God* (1972).

Hepburn, Audrey (Audrey Hepburn-Ruston) (1929–93)
British/Dutch, born Brussels, Belgium; *Roman Holiday* (1953), *War and Peace* (1956), *Funny Face* (1957), *The Nun's Story* (1959), *Breakfast at Tiffany's* (1961), *My Fair Lady* (1964), *How to Steal a Million* (1966), *Wait Until Dark* (1967), *Robin and Marian* (1976), *Always* (1989).

Hepburn, Katharine (1907–)
American, born Hartford, Connecticut; *A Bill of Divorcement* (1932), *Morning Glory* (1933), *Stage Door* (1937), *Bringing Up Baby* (1938), *The Philadelphia Story* (1940), *Woman of the Year* (1942), *Adam's Rib* (1949), *The African Queen* (1951), *Long Day's Journey into Night* (1962), *Guess Who's Coming to Dinner?* (1967), *The Lion in Winter* (1968), *A Delicate Balance* (1973), *Love Among the Ruins* (TV 1975) *On Golden Pond* (1981), *Love Affair* (1994).

Heston, Charlton (John Charlton Carter) (1922–)
American, born Evanston, Illinois; *The Greatest Show on Earth* (1952), *The Ten Commandments* (1956), *Touch of Evil* (1958), *Ben Hur* (1959), *El Cid* (1961), *Major Dundee* (1965), *The War Lord* (1965), *Khartoum* (1966), *Planet of the Apes* (1968), *Will Penny* (1968), *Soylent Green* (1973), *Treasure Island* (TV 1990).

Hoffman, Dustin (1937–)
American, born Los Angeles; *The Graduate* (1967), *Midnight Cowboy* (1969), *Little Big Man* (1970), *Papillon* (1973), *Lenny* (1974), *All the President's Men* (1976), *Kramer Vs Kramer* (1979), *Tootsie* (1982), *Death of a Salesman* (TV 1984), *Rain Man* (1988), *Dick Tracy* (1990), *Billy Bathgate* (1991), *Hook* (1991), *Hero* (1992), *Outbreak* (1995).

Holden, William (William Franklin Beedle Jr) (1918–82)
American, born O'Fallon, Illinois; *Golden Boy* (1939), *Sunset Boulevard* (1950), *Born Yesterday* (1950), *Stalag 17* (1953), *Love is a Many-Spendored Thing* (1955), *Picnic* (1955), *The Bridge on the River Kwai* (1957), *The Wild Bunch* (1969), *The Towering Inferno* (1974), *Network* (1976), *S.O.B.* (1981).

Hope, Bob (Leslie Townes Hope) (1903–)
British/American, born Eltham; *Thanks for the Memory* (1938), *The Cat and the Canary* (1939), *Road to Singapore* (1940), *The Ghost Breakers* (1940), *Road to Zanzibar* (1941), *My Favorite Blonde* (1942), *Road to Morocco* (1942), *The Paleface* (1948), *Fancy Pants* (1950), *The Facts of Life* (1960), *Road to Hong Kong* (1961), *How to Commit Marriage* (1969).

FILM ACTORS (cont.)

Hopkins, Anthony (1941–   )
British, born Port Talbot, Wales; *The Lion in Winter* (1968), *War and Peace* (TV 1972), *The Elephant Man* (1980), *The Bunker* (TV 1981), *The Bounty* (1984), *Silence of the Lambs* (1991), *Dracula* (1992), *Howard's End* (1992), *The Remains of the Day* (1993), *Shadowlands* (1993), *The Road to Wellville* (1994), *Legends of the Fall* (1994).

Hopper, Dennis (1936–   )
American, born Dodge City, Kansas; *Rebel Without a Cause* (1955), *Giant* (1956), *Cool Hand Luke* (1967), *Easy Rider* (1969), *Apocalypse Now* (1979), *Blue Velvet* (1986), *River's Edge* (1986), *Blood Red* (1990), *Catchfire* (1990), *Paris Trout* (1991), *The Indian Runner* (1991), *Money Men* (1992), *True Romance* (1993), *Speed* (1994), *Waterworld* (1995)..

Hoskins, Bob (Robert William) (1942–   )
British, born Bury St Edmunds, Suffolk; *Pennies from Heaven* (TV 1978), *The Long Good Friday* (1980), *Pink Floyd: The Wall* (1982), *The Honorary Consul* (1983), *The Cotton Club* (1984), *Brazil* (1985), *Sweet Liberty* (1985), *Mona Lisa* (1986), *A Prayer for the Dying* (1987), *Who Framed Roger Rabbit* (1988), *Heart Condition* (1990), *Mermaids* (1990), *Shattered* (1991), *Hook* (1991), *The Favour, The Watch And The Very Big Fish* (1991), *The Inner Circle* (1992), *Rainbow* (1995).

Hudson, Rock (Roy Scherer Jr) (1925–85)
American, born Winnetka, Illinois; *Magnificent Obsession* (1954), *Giant* (1956), *Written on the Wind* (1956), *The Tarnished Angel* (1957), *Pillow Talk* (1959), *Send Me No Flowers* (1964), *Seconds* (1966), *Darling Lili* (1969), *McMillan and Wife* (TV 1971–5), *McMillan* (TV 1976), *Embryo* (1976), *The Martian Chronicles* (TV 1980), *Dynasty* (TV 1985).

Hunter, Holly (1958–   )
American, born Conyers, Georgia; *Raising Arozona* (1987), *Broadcast News* (1987), *Roe Vs Wade* (TV 1989), *Once Around* (1990), *The Piano* (1993), *The Firm* (1993), *The Positively True Adventures of the Alleged Texas Cheerleader-Murdering Mom* (TV 1993).

Hurt, William (1950–   )
American, born Washington DC; *Altered States* (1980), *Body Heat* (1981), *The Big Chill* (1983), *Kiss of the Spider Woman* (1985), *Children of a Lesser God* (1986), *Broadcast News* (1987), *The Accidental Tourist* (1989), *The Doctor* (1991), *Second Best* (1994), *Smoke* (1995).

Huston, Anjelica (1952–   )
Irish/American, born Ireland; *The Last Tycoon* (1976), *Frances* (1982), *This is Spinal Tap* (1983), *Prizzi's Honor* (1985), *The Dead* (1987), *Gardens of Stone* (1987), *A Handful of Dust* (1988), *Mr North* (1988), *The Witches* (1990), *The Grifters* (1990), *The Addams Family* (1991), *Addams Family Values* (1993), *Manhattan Murder Mystery* (1994), *The Crossing Guard* (1995).

Jackson, Glenda (1936–   )
British, born Liverpool; also stage; *Women in Love* (1969), *Sunday, Bloody Sunday* (1971), *Elizabeth R* (TV 1971), *A Touch of Class* (1972), *Hedda* (1975), *Stevie* (1978), *The Patricia Neal Story* (TV 1981), *Turtle Diary* (1985), *Business as Usual* (1987).

Keaton, Buster (Joseph Francis Keaton) (1895–1966)
American, born Pickway; *Our Hospitality* (1923), *The Navigator* (1924), *The General* (1927), *Sunset Boulevard* (1950), *Limelight* (1952) *A Funny Thing Happened on the Way to the Forum* (1966).

Keaton, Diane (Diane Hall) (1946–   )
American, born Los Angeles, California; *The Godfather* (1972), *(part II*— 1974), *Sleeper* (1973), *Annie Hall* (1977), *Manhattan* (1979), *Reds* (1981), *Shoot the Moon* (1982), *Mrs Soffel* (1984), *Baby Boom* (1987), *The Good Mother* (1988), *The Godfather Part III* (1990), *Manhattan Murder Mystery* (1994).

Keitel, Harvey (1947–)
American, born Brooklyn, New York; *Mean Streets* (1973), *Taxi Driver* (1976), *The Duellists* (1977), *Bad Timing* (1980), *The Last Temptation of Christ* (1988), *Bugsy* (1991), *Thelma and Louise* (1991), *Reservoir Dogs* (1992), *The Bad Lieutenant (1992)*, *The Piano* (1993), *Pulp Fiction* (1994), *Smoke* (1995), *Clockers* (1995).

Kelly, Gene (Eugene Curran Kelly) (1912–96)
American, born Pittsburgh, Pennsylvania; *For Me and My Girl* (1942), *Cover Girl* (1944), *Anchors Aweigh* (1945), *Ziegfeld Follies* (1946), *The Pirate* (1948), *The Three Musketeers* (1948), *Take Me Out to the Ball Game* (1949), *On the Town* (1949), *Summer Stock* (1950), *An American in Paris* (1951), *Singin' in the Rain* (1952), *Brigadoon* (1954), *Invitation to Dance* (1956), *Les Girls* (1957), *Marjorie Morningstar* (1958), *Inherit the Wind* (1960), *Sins* (TV 1987).

Kelly, Grace (Patricia) (1928–82)
American, born Philadelphia, Pennsylvania; *High Noon* (1952), *Mogambo* (1953), *Dial M for Murder* (1954), *Rear Window* (1954), *The Country Girl* (1954), *To Catch a Thief* (1955), *High Society* (1956).

Kennedy, George (1925–)
American, born New York City; *Charade* (1963), *The Flight of the Phoenix* (1967), *The Dirty Dozen* (1967), *Cool Hand Luke* (1967), *Sarge* (TV 1971), *Thunderbolt and Lightfoot* (1974), *Earthquake* (1974), *The Blue Knight* (TV 1975–6), *The Eiger Sanction* (1977), *Death on the Nile* (1979), *Bolero* (1984), *Delta Force* (1985), *Creepshow 2* (1987), *Dallas* (TV 1988–91).

Kerr, Deborah (Deborah Jane Kerr-Trimmer) (1921–)
British, born Helensburgh, Scotland; *Major Barbara* (1940), *Love on the Dole* (1941), *The Life and Death of Colonel Blimp* (1943), *Perfect Strangers* (1945), *I See a Dark Stranger* (1945), *Black Narcissus* (1947), *From Here to Eternity* (1953), *The King and I* (1956), *Tea and Sympathy* (1956), *An Affair to Remember* (1957), *Separate Tables* (1958), *The Sundowners* (1960), *The Innocents* (1961), *The Night of the Iguana* (1964), *Casino Royale* (1967), *Prudence and the Pill* (1968), *The Assam Garden* (1985).

Ladd, Alan (1913–64)
American, born Hot Springs, Arkansas; *This Gun for Hire* (1942), *The Glass Key* (1942), *The Blue Dahlia* (1946), *The Great Gatsby* (1949), *Shane* (1953), *The Carpetbaggers* (1964).

Lancaster, Burt (Stephen Burton) (1913–94)
American, born New York City; *The Killers* (1946), *Brute Force* (1947), *The Flame and the Arrow* (1950), *Come Back Little Sheba* (1952), *From Here to Eternity* (1953), *Vera Cruz* (1954), *Gunfight at the OK Corral* (1957), *Elmer Gantry* (1960), *Birdman of Alcatraz* (1962), *The Professionals* (1966), *The Swimmer* (1967), *1900* (1976), *Atlantic City* (1980), *Local Hero* (1983), *Rocket Gibraltar* (1988), *Field of Dreams* (1989).

Lange, Jessica (1949–)
American, born Cloquet, Minnesota; *King Kong* (1976), *All That Jazz* (1979), *The Postman Always Rings Twice* (1981), *Tootsie* (1982), *Frances* (1982), *Country* (1984), *Sweet Dreams* (1985), *Crimes of the Heart* (1986), *Far North* (1988), *Music Box* (1989), *Men Don't Leave* (1990), *Blue Sky* (1991), *Cape Fear* (1991), *Night and The City* (1992), *Leaving Isiah* (1995), *Rob Roy* (1995).

Laughton, Charles (1899–1962)
British, born Scarborough; *The Sign of the Cross* (1932), *The Private Life of Henry VIII* (1932), *The Barretts of Wimpole Street* (1934), *Ruggles of Red Gap* (1935), *Mutiny on the Bounty* (1935), *Les Misérables* (1935), *Rembrandt* (1936), *The Hunchback of Notre Dame* (1939), *Hobsons Choice* (1954), *Witness for the Prosecution* (1957), *Advise and Consent* (1962).

Laurel, Stan (Arthur Stanley Jefferson) (1890–1965)
British/American, born Ulverston, Lancashire; *Nuts in May* (1917), *Monsieur Don't Care* (1925); for films with Hardy *see* **Hardy, Oliver**

FILM ACTORS (cont.)

Leigh, Vivien (Vivien Hartley) (1913–67)
British, born Darjeeling, India; *Dark Journey* (1937), *A Yank at Oxford* (1938), *Gone with the Wind* (1939), *Lady Hamilton* (1941), *Caesar and Cleopatra* (1945), *Anna Karenina* (1948), *A Streetcar Named Desire* (1951), *The Roman Spring of Mrs Stone* (1961), *Ship of Fools* (1965).

Lemmon, Jack (John Uhler Lemmon III) (1925–)
American, born Boston, Massachusetts; *Mister Roberts* (1955), *Some Like It Hot* (1959), *The Apartment* (1960), *Days of Wine and Roses* (1962), *The Odd Couple* (1968), *Save the Tiger* (1973), *The China Syndrome* (1979), *Missing* (1982), *Glengarry Glen Ross* (1992), *Short Cuts* (1993).

Lewis, Jerry (Joseph Levitch) (1926–)
American, born Newark, New Jersey; *My Friend Irma* (1949), *The Nutty Professor* (1963), *King of Comedy* (1983), *Funny Bones* (1995).

Lloyd, Harold (Clayton) (1893–1971)
American, born Burchard, Nebraska; *High and Dizzy* (1920), *Grandma's Boy* (1922), *Safety Last* (1923), *Why Worry?* (1923), *The Freshman* (1925), *The Kid Brother* (1927), *Feet First* (1930), *Movie Crazy* (1932).

Loren, Sophia (Sofia Scicolone) (1934–)
Italian, born Rome; *Woman of the River* (1955), *Boy on a Dolphin* (1957), *The Key* (1958), *El Cid* (1961), *Two Women* (1961), *The Millionairess* (1961), *Marriage Italian Style* (1964), *Cinderella Italian Style* (1967), *A Special Day* (1977), *Pret-A-Porter* (1994).

MacLaine, Shirley (Shirley Beaty) (1934–)
American, born Richmond, Virginia; *The Trouble with Harry* (1955), *Some Came Running* (1958), *The Apartment* (1959), *Sweet Charity* (1968), *The Turning Point* (1977), *Terms of Endearment* (1983), *Postcards from the Edge* (1990), *Guarding Tess* (1992).

McQueen, Steve (Terence Steven McQueen) (1930–80)
American, born Slater, Missouri; *Wanted Dead or Alive* (TV 1958), *The Blob* (1958), *The Magnificent Seven* (1960), *The Great Escape* (1963), *Love with the Proper Stranger* (1963), *The Cincinnatti Kid* (1965), *Bullitt* (1968), *Le Mans* (1971), *Getaway* (1972), *Papillon* (1973), *Towering Inferno* (1974), *An Enemy of the People* (1977), *Tom Horn* (1980), *Hunter* (1980).

Martin, Steve (1945–)
American, born Waco, Texas; *The Jerk* (1979), *Pennies from Heaven* (1981), *The Man With Two Brains* (1983), *All of Me* (1984), *Planes, Trains and Automobiles* (1987), *Roxanne* (1987), *Parenthood* (1989), *Father of the Bride* (1991), *Grand Canyon* (1991), *A Simple Twist of Faith* (1994), *Sgt Bilko* (1995).

Marx Brothers, The: Chico (Leonard Marx) (1886–1961); **Harpo** (Adolph Marx) (1888–1964); **Groucho** (Julius Henry Marx) (1890–1977); **Zeppo** (Herbert Marx) (1901–79)
all American, born New York City; (joint) *The Cocoanuts* (1929), *Monkey Business* (1931), *Horse Feathers* (1932), *Duck Soup* (1933), *A Night at the Opera* (1935), *A Day at the Races* (1937), *A Night in Casablanca* (1946).

Mason, James (1909–84)
British, born Huddersfield; *I Met a Murderer* (1939), *The Man in Grey* (1943), *Fanny by Gaslight* (1944), *The Seventh Veil* (1945), *The Wicked Lady* (1946), *Odd Man Out* (1946), *Pandora and the Flying Dutchman* (1951), *The Desert Fox* (1951), *Five Fingers* (1952), *The Prisoner of Zenda* (1952), *Julius Caesar* (1953), *20 000 Leagues Under the Sea* (1954), *A Star is Born* (1954), *Journey to the Center of the Earth* (1959), *Lolita* (1962), *The Pumpkin Eater* (1964), *Georgy Girl* (1966), *The Blue Max* (1966), *The Deadly Affair* (1967), *Heaven Can Wait* (1978), *Murder by Decree* (1979), *The Verdict* (1982), *The Shooting Party* (1984).

Mastroianni, Marcello (1924–96)
Italian, born Fontana Liri, near Frosinone; *White Nights* (1957), *La Dolce Vita* (1959), *8½* (1963), *Yesterday, Today and Tomorrow* (1963), *Marriage Italian Style* (1964), *A Special Day* (1977), *Ginger and Fred* (1986), *Dark Eyes* (1987), *Everybody's Fine* (1990), *Pret-A-Porter* (1994).

Midler, Bette (1945–)
American, born Honolulu, Hawaii; *The Rose* (1979), *Down and Out in Beverly Hills* (1986), *Ruthless People* (1986), *Outrageous Fortune* (1987), *Beaches* (1988), *Big Business* (1988), *Stella* (1990), *Scenes from The Mall* (1991), *For the Boys* (1991), *Hocus Pocus* (1993), *Gypsy* (1993).

Minnelli, Liza (1946–)
American, born Los Angeles; *Charlie Bubbles*, *The Sterile Cuckoo* (1969), *Tell Me That You Love Me Junie Moon* (1970), *Cabaret* (1972), *New York New York* (1977), *Arthur* (1981), *Arthur 2: On the Rocks* (1988), *Rent-a-Cop* (1988), *Stepping Out* (1991).

Mitchum, Robert (1917–)
American, born Bridgeport, Connecticut; *The Story of G.I. Joe* (1945), *Pursued* (1947), *Crossfire* (1947), *Out of the Past* (1947), *The Big Steal* (1949), *Night of the Hunter* (1955), *Home from the Hill* (1960), *The Sundowners* (1960), *Cape Fear* (1962), *Ryan's Daughter* (1970), *Farewell My Lovely* (1975), *The Winds of War* (TV 1983), *War and Remembrance* (TV 1987), *Cape Fear* (1991).

Monroe, Marilyn (Norma Jean Mortenson or Baker) (1926–62)
American, born Los Angeles; *How to Marry a Millionaire* (1953), *Gentlemen Prefer Blondes* (1953), *The Seven Year Itch* (1955), *Bus Stop* (1956), *Some Like It Hot* (1959), *The Misfits* (1960).

Montand, Yves (Ivo Levi) (1921–91)
French, born Monsumagno, Italy; *The Wages of Fear* (1953), *Let's Make Love* (1960), *Jean de Florette* (1986), *Manon des Sources* (1986), *IP5* (1992).

Moore, Demi (Demi Guines) (1962–)
American, born Roswell, New Mexico; *St Elmo's Fire* (1986), *About Last Night* (1987), *The Seventh Sign (1988)*, *We're No Angels* (1990), *Ghost* (1990), *The Butcher's Wife* (1991), *A Few Good Men* (1992), *Indecent Proposal* (1993), *Disclosure* (1994), *The Scarlet Letter* (1995), *The Gaslight Addition* (1995).

Moreau, Jeanne (1928–)
French, born Paris; *Les Amants* (1958), *Ascenseur Pour L'Echafaud* (1957), *Jules et Jim* (1961), *Eva* (1962), *The Trial* (1963), *Journal D'une Femme de Chambre* (1964), *Viva Maria* (1965), *Nikita* (1990), *La Vielle Qui Marchait Dans La Mer* (1991).

Murphy, Eddie (1961–)
American, born Brooklyn, New York; *48 Hours* (1982), *Trading Places* (1983), *Beverly Hills Cop* (1985), *The Golden Child* (1986), *Beverly Hills Cop II* (1987), *Coming to America* (1988), *Harlem Nights* (1989), *Another 48 Hours* (1990), *Boomerang* (1992), *Distinguished Gentleman* (1992), *Beverly Hills Cop III* (1994), *The Nutty Professor* (1995).

Neeson, Liam (1952–)
British, born Ballymena, Northern Ireland; *Excalibur* (1981), *The Bounty* (1984), *Lamb* (1985), *The Mission* (1986), *Suspect* (1987), *The Big Man* (1990), *Dark Man* (1990), *Husbands and Wives* (1992), *Schindler's List* (1993), *Nell* (1994), *Rob Roy* (1995).

Newman, Paul (1925–)
American, born Cleveland, Ohio; *Somebody Up There Likes Me* (1956), *The Long Hot Summer* (1958), *The Hustler* (1961), *Hud* (1963), *The Prize* (1963), *Torn Curtain* (1966), *Cool Hand Luke* (1967), *Butch Cassidy and the Sundance Kid* (1969), *Judge Roy Bean* (1972), *The Sting* (1973), *Absence of Malice* (1981), *The Verdict* (1982), *The Color of Money* (1986), *Blaze* (1990), *Mr & Mrs Bridge* (1990), *The Hudsucker Proxy* (1994), *Nobody's Fool* (1994).

FILM ACTORS (cont.)

Nicholson, Jack (1937–   )
American, born Neptune, New Jersey; *The Little Shop of Horrors* (1960), *Easy Rider* (1969), *Five Easy Pieces* (1970), *Carnal Knowledge* (1971), *The Last Detail* (1973), *Chinatown* (1974), *One Flew Over the Cuckoo's Nest* (1975), *Tommy* (1975), *The Shining* (1980), *The Postman Always Rings Twice* (1981), *Reds* (1981), *Terms of Endearment* (1983), *Prizzi's Honour* (1985), *Broadcast News* (1987), *Ironweed* (1987), *The Witches of Eastwick* (1987), *Batman* (1989), *Two Jakes* (1990), *The Death of Napoleon* (1991), *Man Trouble* (1992), *A Few Good Men* (1992), *Hoffa* (1992), *Wolf* (1994), *The Crossing Guard* (1995).

Niven, David (James David Graham Niven) (1910–83)
British, born London; *Thank You Jeeves* (1936), *The Prisoner of Zenda* (1937), *Wuthering Heights* (1939), *Bachelor Mother* (1939), *Raffles* (1940), *The Way Ahead* (1944), *A Matter of Life and Death* (1946), *Carrington V.C.* (1955), *Around the World in Eighty Days* (1956), *Separate Tables* (1958), *The Guns of Navarone* (1961), *The Pink Panther* (1964), *Casino Royale* (1967), *Candleshoe* (1977), *Death on the Nile* (1978), *Escape to Athena* (1979), *Trail of the Pink Panther* (1982), *Curse of the Pink Panther* (1982).

Nolte, Nick (1940–   )
American, born Omaha, Nebraska; *Rich Man Poor Man* (TV 1976), *Cannery Row* (1982), *48 Hours* (1982), *Down and Out in Beverly Hills* (1986), *Weeds* (1987), *New York Stories* (1989), *Three Fugitives* (1989), *Another 48 Hours* (1990), *Cape Fear* (1991), *Prince of Tides* (1991), *The Player* (1992), *Lorenzo's Oil* (1992), *Blue Chips* (1993), *I'll Do Anything* (1994), *I Love Trouble* (1994), *Jefferson in Paris* (1995).

Olivier, Sir Laurence (Kerr) (1907–89)
British, born Dorking; also stage; *The Divorce of Lady X* (1938), *Wuthering Heights* (1939), *Rebecca* (1940), *Pride and Prejudice* (1940), *Henry V* (1944), *Hamlet* (1948), *Richard III* (1956), *The Prince and the Showgirl* (1958), *The Devil's Disciple* (1959), *The Entertainer* (1960), *Sleuth* (1972), *Marathon Man* (1976), *A Bridge Too Far* (1977), *Brideshead Revisited* (TV 1981), *A Voyage Round My Father* (TV 1982).

O'Toole, Peter (Seamus) (1932–   )
Irish, born Kerry, Connemara; *Lawrence of Arabia* (1962), *How to Steal a Million* (1966), *The Lion in Winter* (1968), *Goodbye Mr Chips* (1969), *The Ruling Class* (1972), *The Stunt Man* (1980), *My Favourite Year* (1982), *The Last Emperor* (1987), *King Ralph* (1991).

Pacino, Al (Alfredo Pacino) (1940–   )
American, born New York City; *The Godfather* (1972), (*part II* — 1974, *part III* — 1991), *Dog Day Afternoon* (1975), *Scarface* (1983), *Sea of Love* (1989), *Dick Tracy* (1990), *Frankie and Johnny* (1991), *Glengarry Glen Ross* (1992), *Scent Of A Woman* (1992), *Carlito's Way* (1993), *City Hall* (1995).

Peck, Gregory (Eldred) (1916–   )
American, born La Jolla, California; *The Keys to the Kingdom* (1944), *Spellbound* (1945), *Duel in the Sun* (1946), *Gentleman's Agreement* (1947), *The Macomber Affair* (1947), *The Paradine Case* (1947), *Twelve O'Clock High* (1949), *The Gunfighter* (1950), *Captain Horatio Hornblower* (1951), *The Million Pound Note* (1954), *The Purple Plain* (1955), *The Man in the Grey Flannel Suit* (1956), *The Big Country* (1958), *The Guns of Navarone* (1961), *Cape Fear* (1962), *To Kill a Mockingbird* (1962), *The Omen* (1976), *Old Gringo* (1989), *Other People's Money* (1991), *Cape Fear* (1991).

Penn, Sean (1960–   )
American, born Burbank, California; *Taps* (1981), *Fast Times at Ridgemont High* (1982), *Racing with

the Moon (1984), *The Falcon and the Snowman* (1985), *At Close Range* (1986), *Shanghai Surprise* (1986), *Colors* (1988), *Judgement in Berlin* (1988), *Casualties of War* (1989), *We're No Angels* (1989), *State of Grace* (1990), *Carlito's Way* (1993).

Pfeiffer, Michelle (1957–)
American, born Santa Ana, California; *Grease 2* (1982), *Scarface* (1983), *Sweet Liberty* (1985), *The Witches of Eastwick* (1987), *Married to the Mob* (1989), *The Fabulous Baker Boys* (1989), *Batman Returns* (1992), *Age of Innocence* (1993), *My Posse don't do Homework* (1995).

Phoenix, River (1970–93)
American, born Madras, Oregon; *Explorers* (1985), *Mosquito Coast* (1986), *Running on Empty* (1988), *Indiana Jones and the Last Crusade* (1989), *Dogfight* (1991), *My Own Private Idaho* (1991), *The Thing Called Love* (1993).

Pickford, Mary (Gladys Mary Smith) (1893–1979)
Canadian, born Toronto, Ontario; *The Violin Maker of Cremona* (1909), *Rebecca of Sunnybrook Farm* (1917), *Poor Little Rich Girl* (1917), *Pollyanna* (1919), *Little Lord Fauntleroy* (1921), *Tess of the Storm Country* (1922), *The Taming of the Shrew* (1929), *Coquette* (1929), *Secrets* (1933).

Poitier, Sidney (1924–)
American, born Miami, Florida; *No Way Out* (1950), *Cry, the Beloved Country* (1952), *The Blackboard Jungle* (1955), *The Defiant Ones* (1958), *Porgy and Bess* (1959), *Lilies of the Field* (1963), *To Sir with Love* (1967), *In the Heat of the Night* (1967), *Guess Who's Coming to Dinner* (1967), *Little Nikita* (1988), *Shoot to Kill* (1988), *Separate But Equal* (TV 1991), *Sneakers* (1992).

Redford, (Charles) Robert (1937–)
American, born Santa Monica, California; *Barefoot in the Park* (1967), *Butch Cassidy and the Sundance Kid* (1969), *The Candidate* (1972), *The Great Gatsby* (1974), *The Sting* (1973), *The Way We Were* (1973), *All the President's Men* (1976), *The Electric Horseman* (1979), *The Natural* (1984), *Out of Africa* (1985), *Legal Eagles* (1986), *Havana* (1990), *Sneakers* (1992), *Indecent Proposal* (1993), *Up Close and Personal* (1995).

Redgrave, Vanessa (1937–)
British, born London; also stage; *Morgan!* (1965), *Blow-Up* (1966), *Camelot* (1967), *Mary, Queen of Scots* (1971), *Julia* (1977), *Playing for Time* (TV 1980), *The Bostonians* (1984), *Wetherby* (1985), *Three Sovereigns for Sarah* (TV 1985), *Prick Up Your Ears* (1987), *Consuming Passions* (1988), *The Ballad of The Sad Café* (1991), *What Ever Happened to Baby Jane?* (1991), *Howard's End* (1992), *Little Odessa* (1994).

Reeves, Keanu (1965–)
American; *River's Edge* (1986), *Prince of Pennsylvania* (1988), *The Night Before* (1988), *Dangerous Liaisons* (1988), *Permanent Record* (1988), *Bill and Ted's Excellent Adventure* (1989), *Parenthood* (1989), *I Love You to Death* (1990), *Bill and Ted's Bogus Journey* (1991), *My Own Private Idaho* (1991), *Dracula* (1992), *Much Ado About Nothing* (1993), *Little Buddha* (1993), *Speed* (1994), *A Walk in the Clouds, Feeling Minnesota* (1995).

Roberts, Julia (1967–)
American, born Smyrna, Georgia; *Mystic Pizza* (1988), *Steel Magnolias* (1989), *Flatliners* (1990), *Pretty Woman* (1990), *Sleeping with the Enemy* (1991), *Dying Young* (1991), *Hook* (1991), *The Player* (1992), *The Pelican Brief* (1993), *I Love Trouble* (1994), *Pret-A-Porter* (1994), *Mary Reilly* (1995).

Ryder, Winona (1971–)
American, born Winona, Michigan; *Beetlejuice* (1988), *1969* (1988), *Great Balls of Fire* (1989), *Heathers* (1989), *Edward Scissorhands* (1990), *Mermaids* (1990), *Night on Earth* (1992), *Dracula* (1992), *Age of Innocence* (1993), *Reality Bites* (1994), *Little Women* (1994), *The Making of an American Quilt* (1995).

FILM ACTORS (cont.)

Sarandon, Susan (Susan Abigail Tomalin) (1946–   )
American, born New York City; *The Front Page* (1974), *Dragonfly* (1977), *Atlantic City* (1981), *Tempest* (1982), *The Hunger* (1983), *The Witches of Eastwick* (1987), *Bull Durham* (1988), *A Dry White Season* (1989), *White Palace* (1991), *Thelma and Louise* (1991), *Light Sleeper* (1991), *Lorenzo's Oil* (1992), *The Client* (1994), *Little Women* (1994).

Schwarzenegger, Arnold (1947–   )
American, born Graz, Austria; *Stay Hungry* (1976), *Pumping Iron* (1977), *Conan the Barbarian* (1982), *Conan the Destroyer* (1984), *The Terminator* (1984), *Red Sonja* (1985), *Commando* (1985), *Raw Deal* (1986), *Predator* (1987), *The Running Man* (1987), *Red Heat* (1989), *Total Recall* (1990), *Kindergarten Cop* (1990), *T2 — Terminator 2: Judgment Day* (1991), *The Last Action Hero* (1993), *True Lies* (1994), *Junior* (1994).

Sellers, Peter (1925–80)
British, born Southsea; *The Ladykillers* (1955) *I'm Alright Jack* (1959), *Only Two Can Play* (1962), *Lolita* (1962), *Dr Strangelove* (1964), *The Pink Panther* (1964), *The Optimists of Nine Elms* (1973), *Being There* (1979).

Signoret, Simone (Simon-Henriette Charlotte Kaminker) (1921–85)
French, born Wiesbaden, Germany; *La Ronde* (1950), *Casque d'Or* (1952), *Les Diaboliques* (1955), *Room at the Top* (1959), *Ship of Fools* (1965), *Le Chat* (1971), *Madame Rosa* (1977).

Sinatra, Frank (Francis Albert Sinatra) (1915–   )
American, born Hoboken, New Jersey; *Anchors Aweigh* (1945), *On the Town* (1949), *From Here to Eternity* (1953), *The Man With the Golden Gun* (1955), *Pal Joey* (1957), *The Manchurian Candidate* (1962), *The Detective* (1968).

Stallone, Sylvester (1946–   )
American, born New York City; *The Lords of Flatbush* (1973), *Rocky* (1976), (*part II*— 1979, *III*— 1982, *IV*— 1985, *V*— 1990), *Paradise Alley* (1978), *Victory* (1981), *Nighthawks* (1981), *First Blood* (1981), *Rambo* (1985), *Over the Top* (1987), *Rambo III* (1988), *Lock Up* (1989), *Tango and Cash* (1990), *Oscar* (1991), *Stop, Or My Mom Will Shoot* (1992), *Cliffhanger* (1993), *Demolition Man* (1993), *The Specialist* (1994), *Judge Dredd* (1995).

Stanwyck, Barbara (Ruby Stevens) (1907–90)
American, born Brooklyn, New York; *Broadway Nights* (1927), *Miracle Woman* (1931), *Night Nurse* (1931), *The Bitter Tea of General Yen* (1933), *Baby Face* (1933), *Annie Oakley* (1935), *Stella Dallas* (1937), *Union Pacific* (1939), *The Lady Eve* (1941), *Meet John Doe* (1941), *Ball of Fire* (1941), *Double Indemnity* (1944), *The Strange Love of Martha Ivers* (1946), *Sorry Wrong Number* (1948), *The Furies* (1950), *Executive Suite* (1954), *Walk on the Wild Side* (1962), *The Big Valley* (TV 1965–9), *The Thorn Birds* (TV 1983).

Stewart, James (Maitland) (1908–   )
American, born Indiana, Pennsylvania; *Seventh Heaven* (1937), *You Can't Take It With You* (1938), *Mr Smith Goes to Washington* (1939), *Destry Rides Again* (1939), *The Shop around the Corner* (1940), *The Philadelphia Story* (1940), *It's a Wonderful Life* (1946), *Harvey* (1950), *Broken Arrow* (1950), *The Glenn Miller Story* (1953), *Rear Window* (1954), *The Man from Laramie* (1955), *Vertigo* (1958), *Anatomy of a Murder* (1959), *Mr Hobbs Takes a Vacation* (1962), *Shenandoah* (1965), *The Shootist* (1976), *North and South II* (TV 1986).

Streep, Meryl (Mary Louise Streep) (1949–   )
American, born Summit, New Jersey: *Julia* (1977), *The Deer Hunter* (1978), *Kramer Vs Kramer* (1979), *Manhattan* (1979), *The French Lieutenant's Woman* (1981), *Sophie's Choice* (1982), *Still of the Night* (1982), *Silkwood* (1983), *Plenty* (1985), *Out of Africa* (1986), *Ironweed* (1987), *A Cry in the Dark* (1988), *She-Devil* (1989), *Postcards from the Edge* (1990), *Death Becomes Her* (1992),

The River Wild (1994), *The Bridges of Madison County* (1995).
Streisand, Barbra (Joan) (1942–)
American, born Brooklyn, New York; *Funny Girl* (1968), *Hello Dolly* (1969), *On a Clear Day You Can See Forever* (1970), *Whats Up, Doc?* (1972), *The Way We Were* (1973), *A Star is Born* (1976), *Yentl* (1983), *Nuts* (1987), *Prince of Tides* (1991).

Taylor, Elizabeth (Rosemond) (1932–)
British, born London; *National Velvet* (1944), *Little Women* (1949), *The Father of the Bride* (1950), *A Place in the Sun* (1951), *Giant* (1956), *Raintree Country* (1957), *Cat on a Hot Tin Roof* (1958), *Butterfield 8* (1960), *Cleopatra* (1962), *Who's Afraid of Virginia Woolf?* (1966), *Reflections in a Golden Eye* (1967), *The Taming of the Shrew* (1967), *A Little Night Music* (1977), *The Mirror Crack'd* (1981), *Malice in Wonderland* (TV 1985), *Poker Alice* (TV 1986), *Young Toscanini* (1988), *Sweet Bird of Youth* (TV 1989), *The Flintstones* (1994).
Temple, Shirley (1928–)
American, born Santa Monica, California; *Little Miss Marker* (1934), *Curly Top* (1935), *Dimples* (1936), *Heidi* (1937), *The Little Princess* (1939).
Thompson, Emma (1959–)
British, born Cambridge; *The Tall Guy* (1989), *Henry V* (1989), *Dead Again* (1991), *Impromptu* (1991), *Howard's End* (1992), *Peter's Friends* (1992), *Much Ado About Nothing* (1993), *The Remains of the Day* (1993), *In the Name of the Father* (1993), *Junior* (1994), *Carrington* (1995).
Tracy, Spencer (1900–67)
American, born Milwaukee, Wisconsin; *Twenty Thousand Years in Sing Sing* (1932), *The Power and the Glory* (1933), *A Man's Castle* (1933), *Fury* (1936), *San Francisco* (1936), *Libeled Lady* (1936), *Captains Courageous* (1937), *Boy's Town* (1938), *Stanley and Livingstone* (1939), *Northwest Passage* (1939), *Edison the Man* (1940), *Dr Jekyll and Mr Hyde* (1941), *Woman of the Year* (1942), *The Seventh Cross* (1944), *State of the Union* (1948), *Adam's Rib* (1949), *Father of the Bride* (1950), *Bad Day at Black Rock* (1955), *The Last Hurrah* (1958), *Inherit the Wind* (1960), *Judgment at Nuremberg* (1961), *It's a Mad, Mad, Mad, Mad World* (1963), *Guess Who's Coming to Dinner* (1967).
Travolta, John (1954–)
American, born Englewood, New Jersey; *Welcome Back Kotter* (TV 1975–8), *Carrie* (1976), *Saturday Night Fever* (1977), *Grease* (1978), *Blow Out* (1981), *Staying Alive* (1983), *Perfect* (1985), *Look Who's Talking* (1989), *Pulp Fiction* (1994), *White Man's Burden (1995), Get Shorty* (1995).
Turner, Kathleen (1954–)
American, born Springfield, Missouri; *The Doctors* (TV 1977–8), *Body Heat* (1981), *The Man With Two Brains* (1983), *Romancing the Stone* (1984), *Crimes of Passion* (1984), *The Jewel of the Nile* (1985), *Prizzi's Honour* (1985), *Peggy Sue Got Married* (1986), *War of the Roses* (1989), *V. I. Warshawski* (1991), *Serial Mom* (1994), *Moonlight and Valentino* (1995).

Ullmann, Liv (1939–)
Norwegian, born Tokyo, Japan; *Persona* (1966), *The Emigrants* (1972), *Face to Face* (1975), *Autumn Sonata* (1978), *Dangerous Moves* (1983), *Gaby — The True Story* (1987), *La Amiga* (1988), *The Rose Garden* (1989), *Mindwalk* (1990), *The Ox* (1991).

Valentino, Rudolph (Rodolpho Alphonso Guglielmi di Valentina d'Antonguolla) (1895–1926)
Italian/US, born Castellaneta; *The Four Horsemen of the Apocalypse* (1921), *The Sheikh* (1921), *Blood and Sand* (1922), *The Young Rajah* (1922), *Monsieur Beaucaire* (1924), *The Eagle* (1925), *The Son of the Sheikh* (1926).

FILM ACTORS (cont.)

Van Damme, Jean-Claude (1961–)
Belgian, born Brussels; *No Retreat No Surrender* (1985), *Kickboxer* (1989), *Universal Soldier* (1992), *Nowhere to Run* (1993), *Timecop* (1994), *Streetfighter* (1994).

Washington, Denzel (1954–)
American, born Mt. Vernon, New York; *St Elsewhere* (1982–9), *Cry Freedom* (1987), *Queen and Country* (1988), *Glory* (1989), *Mo' Better Blues* (1990), *Mississippi Masala* (1991), *Ricochet* (1991), *Malcolm X* (1992), *Philadelphia* (1993), *Much Ado About Nothing* (1993), *Devil in a Blue Dress* (1995), *Crimson Tide* (1995).

Wayne, John (Marion Michael Morrison) (1907–79)
American, born Winterset, Iowa; *The Big Trail* (1930), *Stagecoach* (1939), *The Long Voyage Home* (1940), *Red River* (1948), *She Wore a Yellow Ribbon* (1949), *Sands of Iwo Jima* (1949), *The Quiet Man* (1952), *The High and the Mighty* (1954), *The Searchers* (1956), *Rio Bravo* (1959), *The Alamo* (1960), *True Grit* (1969), *The Shootist* (1976).

West, Mae (1892–1980)
American, born Brooklyn, New York; *She Done Him Wrong* (1933), *I'm No Angel* (1933), *My Little Chickadee* (1940) *Myra Breckenridge* (1970).

Williams, Robin (1952–)
American, born Chicago; *Mork and Mindy* (TV 1978–82), *Popeye* (1980), *The World According to Garp* (1982), *Good Morning Vietnam* (1987), *Dead Poets' Society* (1989), *Cadillac Man* (1990), *Awakenings* (1990), *Dead Again* (1991), *The Fisher King* (1991), *Hook* (1991), *Toys* (1992), *Aladdin* (1992), *Mrs Doubtfire* (1993), *Being Human* (1994), *Jumanji* (1995).

Willis, Bruce (1955–)
American, born Penns Grove, New Jersey; *Moonlighting* (TV 1985–9), *Blind Date* (1987), *Die Hard* (1988), *Sunset* (1988), *In Country* (1989), *Die Hard 2: Die Harder* (1990), *Bonfire of the Vanities* (1991), *Hudson Hawk* (1991), *Billy Bathgate* (1991), *The Last Boy Scout* (1991), *Death Becomes Her* (1992), *Striking Distance (1993)*, *Pulp Fiction* (1994), *Nobody's Fool* (1994), *Die Hard With a Vengeance* (1995).

Winger, Debra (1955–)
American, born Columbus, Ohio; *Urban Cowboy* (1980), *Cannery Row* (1981), *An Officer and a Gentleman* (1982), *Terms of Endearment* (1983), *Legal Eagles* (1985), *Black Widow* (1987), *Made in Heaven* (1987), *Betrayed* (1988), *The Sheltering Sky* (1990), *Wilder Napalm* (1992), *A Dangerous Woman* (1993), *Shadowlands* (1993), *Forget Paris* (1995).

Wood, Natalie (Natasha Gurdin) (1938–81)
American, born San Francisco, California; *Miracle on 34th Street* (1947), *The Ghost and Mrs. Muir* (1947), *Rebel Without a Cause* (1955), *The Searchers* (1956), *Marjorie Morningstar* (1958), *All The Fine Young Cannibals* (1959), *Splendour in the Grass* (1961), *Westside Story* (1961), *Love with the Proper Stranger* (1964), *The Great Race* (1965), *This Property is Condemned* (1966), *Bob and Carol and Ted and Alice* (1969), *From Here to Eternity* (TV 1979), *Meteor* (1979), *Brainstorm* (1983).

Woodward, Joanne (1930–)
American, born Thomasville, Georgia; *Three Faces of Eve* (1957), *No Down Payment* (1957), *The Long Hot Summer* (1958), *The Stripper* (1963), *A Big Hand for the Little Lady* (1966), *Rachel, Rachel* (1968), *Summer Wishes, Winter Dreams* (1973), *The Glass Menagerie* (1987), *Mr and Mrs Bridge* (1990), *Philadelphia* (1993), *Breathing Lessons* (TV 1994).

DIRECTORS

Aldrich, Robert (1918–83)
American, born Cranston, Rhode Island; *Kiss Me Deadly* (1955), *Attack!* (1956), *What Ever Happened to Baby Jane?* (1962), *The Dirty Dozen* (1967), *Ulzana's Raid* (1972).

Allen, Woody (Allen Stewart Konigsberg) (1935–)
American, born Brooklyn, New York; *Take the Money and Run Sleeper* (1973), *Love and Death* (1975), *Annie Hall* (1977), *Interiors* (1978), *Manhattan* (1979), *Broadway Danny Rose* (1984), *The Purple Rose of Cairo* (1985), *Hannah and Her Sisters* (1986), *Crimes and Misdemeanors* (1989), *Husbands and Wives* (1992), *Bullets Over Broadway* (1994).

Almódovar, Pedro (1951–)
Spanish, born Calzada de Calatrava; *Dark Habits* (1983), *Matador* (1986), *Law of Desire* (1987), *Women on the Verge of a Nervous Breakdown* (1988), *Kika* (1993).

Altman, Robert (1925–)
American, born Kansas City, Missouri; *The James Dean Story* (1957), *M*A*S*H* (1970), *McCabe and Mrs Miller* (1971), *The Long Goodbye* (1973), *Nashville* (1975), *Popeye* (1980), *Come Back to the Five & Dime Jimmy Dean, Jimmy Dean* (1982), *The Player* (1992), *Short Cuts* (1993).

Antonioni, Michelangelo (1912–)
Italian, born in Ferrara; *L'Avventura* (1959), *La Notte* (1960), *L'Eclisse* (1962), *Blow-Up* (1966), *The Passenger* (1975).

Attenborough, Richard Samuel Attenborough, Baron (1923–)
British, born Cambridge; *Oh! What a Lovely War* (1968), *Gandhi* (1982), *A Chorus Line* (1985), *Cry Freedom* (1987), *Shadowlands* (1993).

Bergman, (Ernst) Ingmar (1918–)
Swedish, born Uppsala; *Sawdust and Tinsel* (1953), *The Face* (1955), *Smiles of a Summer Night* (1955), *The Seventh Seal* (1957), *Wild Strawberries* (1957), *The Silence* (1963), *Persona* (1966), *Cries and Whispers* (1972), *Fanny and Alexander* (1982).

Bertolucci, Bernardo (1940–)
Italian, born Parma; *The Spider's Stratagem* (1969), *The Conformist* (1970), *Last Tango in Paris* (1972), *The Last Emperor* (1987).

Besson, Luc (1959–)
French, born Paris; *The Last Battle* (1983), *Subway* (1985), *The Big Blue* (1988), *Nikita* (1990), *Leon* (1994).

Bogdanovich, Peter (1939–)
American, born Kingston, New York; *Targets* (1967), *The Last Picture Show* (1971), *Paper Moon* (1973), *Saint Jack* (1979), *Mask* (1985), *The Thing Called Love (1993)*.

Boorman, John (1933–)
English, born Epsom, Surrey; *Point Blank* (1967), *Deliverance* (1972), *Excalibur* (1981), *The Emerald Forest* (1984), *Hope and Glory* (1987), *Beyond Rangoon* (1995).

Bresson, Robert (1907–)
French, born Bromont-Lamothe; Les Dames Do Bois De Boulogne (1946), *Journal D'Un Cure de Campagne* (1950), *Pickpocket* (1959), *Au Hasard Balthazar* (1966), *L'Argent* (1983).

Brooks, Mel (Melvin Kaminski) (1926–)
American, born Brooklyn, New York; *The Producers* (1966), *Blazing Saddles* (1974), *Young Frankenstein* (1974), *To Be Or Not To Be* (1983), *Robin Hood: Men in Tights* (1993).

DIRECTORS (cont.)

Buñuel, Luis (1900–83)
Spanish, born Calanda; *Un Chien Andalou* (with Salvador Dali) (1928), *L'Age d'Or* (1930), *Los Olvidados* (1950), *Viridiana* (1961), *Belle de Jour* (1967), *The Discreet Charm of the Bourgeoisie* (1972), *That Obscure Object of Desire* (1977).

Burton, Tim (1958–   )
American, born Burbank, California; *Peewee's Big Adventure* (1985), *Beetlejuice* (1988), *Batman* (1989), *Edward Scissorhands* (1990), *Batman Returns* (1992), *Ed Wood* (1994).

Capra, Frank (1897–91)
Italian/American, born Bisacquino, Sicily; *The Strong Man* (1926), *Platinum Blonde* (1932), *It Happened One Night* (1934), *Mr Deeds Goes to Town* (1936), *Lost Horizon* (1937), *Mr Smith Goes to Washington* (1939), *Arsenic and Old Lace* (1944), *It's a Wonderful Life* (1946).

Carpenter, John (1948–   )
American, born Carthage, New York; *Dark Star* (1974), *Assault on Precinct 13 (1976)*, *Halloween* (1978), *The Fog* (1979), *Escape from New York* (1981), *The Thing* (1982), *Christine* (1983), *Starman* (1984), *Big Trouble in Little China* (1986), *Prince of Darkness* (1987).

Carné, Marcel (1909–96)
French, born Batignolles, Paris; *Quai Des Brumes* (1938), *Le Jour Se Leve* (1939), *Les Enfants Du Paradise* (1944).

Cassavetes, John (1929–89)
American, born New York City; *Shadows* (1959), *Faces* (1968), *Husbands* (1970), *A Woman Under the Influence* (1974), *Gloria* (1980).

Clair, René (originally **René Lucien Chomette**) (1898–1981)
French, born Paris; *An Italian Straw Hat* (1927), *Sous Les Toits de Paris* (1929), *Le Million* (1931), *A Nous la Liberté* (1931), *The Ghost goes West* (1935), *Les Belles de Nuit* (1952).

Cocteau, Jean (1889–1963)
French, born Maisons-Lafitte; *Le Sang d'un poète* (1930), *La Belle et La Bête* (1946), *Orphée* (1950), *Le Testament d'Orphée* (1959).

Coppola, Francis Ford (1939–   )
American, born Detroit, Michigan; *The Godfather* (1972), (*Part II* — 1974, *Part III* — 1991), *The Conversation* (1974), *Apocalypse Now* (1979), *The Cotton Club* (1984), *Tucker: The Man and His Dream* (1988), *Dracula* (1992).

Corman, Roger (1926–   )
American, born Detroit, Michigan; *The Fall of the House of Usher* (1960), *Little Shop of Horrors* (1960), *The Intruder* (1961), *The Masque of the Red Death* (1964), *The St Valentine's Day Massacre* (1967), *Frankenstein Unbound* (1990).

Cronenberg, David (1943–   )
Canadian, born Toronto; *Shivers* (1974), *Scanners* (1979), *Videodrome* (1982), *The Dead Zone* (1983), *The Fly* (1986), *Dead Ringers* (1988), *Naked Lunch* (1991), *M. Butterfly* (1993).

Curtiz, Michael (**Mihály Kertész**) (1888–1962)
American/Hungarian, born Budapest, Hungary; *Noah's Ark* (1929), *The Mystery of the Wax Museum* (1933), *Captain Blood* (1935), *The Adventures of Robin Hood* (1938), *Angels with Dirty Faces* (1938), *The Sea Hawk* (1940), *Yankee Doodle Dandy* (1942), *Casablanca* (1942), *Mildred Pierce* (1945), *White Christmas* (1954), *King Creole* (1958), *The Comancheros* (1962).

Davies, Terence (1945–   )
British, born Liverpool; *Distant Voices, Still Lives* (1988), *The Long Day Closes* (1992), *The Neon Bible* (1995).

de Mille, Cecil B(lount) (1881–1959)
American, born Ashfield, Massachusetts; *The Squaw Man* (1914), *Male and Female* (1919), *The Ten Commandments* (1923 & 1956), *The King of Kings* (1927), *The Sign of the Cross* (1932), *Union Pacific* (1939), *The Greatest Show on Earth* (1952).

Demme, Jonathan (1944–   )
American, born Baldwin, New York; *Caged Heat* (1974), *Citizen's Band* (1977), *Melvin and Howard* (1980), *Stop Making Sense* (1984), *Something Wild* (1986), *The Silence of the Lambs* (1991), *Philadelphia* (1993).

de Palma, Brian (1940–   )
American, born Newark, New Jersey; *Greetings* (1968), *Phantom of the Paradise* (1974), *Carrie* (1976), *Dressed to Kill* (1980), *Blow Out* (1981), *Scarface* (1983), *The Untouchables* (1987), *Bonfire of the Vanities* (1990), *Carlito's Way* (1993), *Mission Impossible* (1995).

Donner, Richard (1939–   )
American, born New York City; *X-15* (1961), *The Omen* (1976), *Superman* (1978), *Lethal Weapon* (1987), *Maverick* (1994).

Dreyer, Carl (1889–1968)
Danish, born Copenhagen; *La Passion de Jeanne D'Arc* (1928), *Vampyr* (1932), *Day of Wrath* (1943), *Ordet* (1955), *Gertrud* (1964).

Eastwood, Clint (1930–   )
American, born San Francisco; *Play Misty for Me* (1971), *The Outlaw Josey Wales* (1976), *Pale Rider* (1985), *Birdy* (1988), *Unforgiven* (1992), *The Bridges of Madison County* (1995).

Edwards, Blake (William Blake McEdwards) (1922–   )
American, born Tulsa, Oklahoma; *Operation Petticoat (1959)*, *Breakfast at Tiffany's* (1961), *Days of Wine and Roses* (1962), *The Pink Panther* (1964), *The Great Race* (1965), *10* (1979), *Victor/Victoria* (1982).

Eisenstein, Sergei Mikhailovich (1898–1948)
Soviet, born Riga, Latvia; *The Battleship Potemkin* (1925), *Ten Days that Shook the World* (1928), *Alexander Nevsky* (1938), *Ivan the Terrible* (1942–46).

Fassbinder, Rainer Werner (1946–82)
German, born Bad Wörishofen; *Love is colder than Death* (1969), *Fear eats the Soul* (1974), *The Marriage of Maria Braun* (1978), *Lola* (1981), *Querelle* (1982).

Fellini, Federico (1920–93)
Italian, born Rimini; *I Vitelloni* (1953), *La Strada* (1954), *La Dolce Vita* (1960), *Otto E Mezzo* (1963), *Satyricon* (1969), *Amarcord* (1973), *Ginger and Fred* (1986).

Fleming, Victor (1883–1949)
American, born Pasadena, California; *The Virginian* (1929), *Red Dust* (1932), *The Wizard of Oz* (1939), *Gone with the Wind* (1939), *A Guy Named Joe* (1943).

Ford, John (Sean Aloysius O'Feeney) (1894–1973)
American, born Cape Elizabeth, Maine; *The Tornado* (1917), *The Iron Horse* (1924), *Arrowsmith* (1931), *The Informer* (1935), *Stagecoach* (1939), *Young Mr Lincoln* (1939), *The Grapes of Wrath* (1940), *My Darling Clementine* (1946), *The Quiet Man* (1952), *The Searchers* (1956), *The Man Who Shot Liberty Valance* (1962).

Forman, Miloš (1932–   )
Czechoslovakian, born Kaslov; *The Fireman's Ball* (1967), *Taking-Off* (1971), *One Flew over the Cuckoo's Nest* (1975), *Amadeus* (1984).

Forsyth, Bill (William David) (1946–   )
British, born Whiteinch, Glasgow; *That Sinking Feeling* (1979), *Gregory's Girl* (1980), *Local Hero* (1983), *Housekeeping* (1987), *Being Human* (1994).

DIRECTORS (cont.)

Frankenheimer, John (1930–)
American, born Malba, New York; *The Manchurian Candidate* (1962), *Birdman of Alcatraz* (1962), *Seven Days in May* (1963), *Seconds* (1966), *Black Sunday (1976)*.

Frears, Stephen (1941–)
British, born Leicester; *Gumshoe* (1971), *The Hit* (1984), *My Beautiful Laundrette* (1985), *Prick Up Your Ears* (1987), *Dangerous Liaisons (1988)*, *The Grifters* (1990), *The Snapper* (1993), *Mary Reilly* (1995).

Fuller, Samuel Michael (1911–)
American, born Worcester, Massachusetts; *I Shot Jesse James (1948)*, *Pickup on South Street* (1953), *Underworld USA* (1960), *Shock Corridor* (1963), *The Big Red One* (1980).

Gilliam, Terry (1940–)
American, born Minneapolis, Minnesota; *Jabberwocky* (1977), *Time Bandits* (1980), *Brazil* (1985), *The Adventures of Baron Munchausen* (1988), *The Fisher King* (1991).

Godard, Jean-Luc (1930–)
French, born Paris; *A Bout de Souffle* (1959), *Alphaville* (1965), *Weekend* (1967), *Sauve Qui Peut La Vie* (1980), *Hail Mary* (1985), *Nouvelle Vague* (1990).

Greenaway, Peter (1942–)
British, born London; *The Falls* (1980), *The Draughtman's Contract* (1982), *Drowning by Numbers* (1988), *The Cook, The Thief, His Wife and Her Lover* (1989), *Prospero's Books* (1991), *The Baby of Macon* (1993).

Griffith, D(avid) W(ark) (1875–1948)
American, born Oldham County Farm, near Centerfield, Kentucky; *The Birth of a Nation* (1915), *Intolerance* (1916), *Broken Blossoms* (1919), *Way Down East* (1920), *Orphans of the Storm* (1922), *Abraham Lincoln* (1930).

Hawks, Howard Winchester (1896–1977)
American, born Goshen, Indiana; *The Road to Glory* (1926), *The Dawn Patrol* (1930), *Scarface* (1932), *Bringing Up Baby* (1938), *His Girl Friday* (1940), *The Big Sleep* (1946), *Red River* (1948), *Rio Bravo* (1959), *El Dorado* (1967).

Hitchcock, Sir Alfred Joseph (1899–1980)
British, born Leytonstone, London; *The Lodger* (1926), *Blackmail* (1929), *Murder* (1930), *The Thirty-Nine Steps* (1935), *The Lady Vanishes* (1938), *Rebecca* (1940), *Shadow of a Doubt* (1943), *Notorious* (1946), *Strangers on a Train* (1951), *Rear Window* (1954), *Vertigo* (1958), *North by Northwest* (1959), *Psycho* (1960), *The Birds* (1963), *Frenzy* (1972).

Huston, John Marcellus (1906–87)
American, born Nevada, Missouri; *The Maltese Falcon* (1941), *Key Largo* (1948), *The Treasure of Sierra Madre* (1948), *The Asphalt Jungle* (1950), *The African Queen* (1951), *Moulin Rouge* (1952), *The Night of the Iguana* (1964), *Fat City* (1972), *The Man Who Would Be King* (1975), *Wise Blood* (1979), *Prizzi's Honour* (1985), *The Dead* (1987).

Ivory, James Francis (1928–)
American, born Berkeley, California; *Shakespeare Wallah* (1965), *Roseland* (1977), *Heat and Dust* (1982), *The Bostonians* (1984), *Room with a View* (1985), *Maurice* (1987), *Howard's End* (1992), *The Remains of the Day* (1993), *Jefferson in Paris* (1995).

Jarman, (Michael) Derek (1942–94)
British, born Northwood, Middlesex; *Sebastiane* (1976), *Jubilee* (1977), *The Tempest* (1979), *Caravaggio* (1985), *The Last of England* (1987), *Edward II* (1991), *Wittgenstein* (1993).

Jarmsuch, Jim (1953–)
American, born Akron, Ohio; *Stranger than Paradise* (1984), *Down By Law* (1986), *Mystery Train* (1989), *Night on Earth* (1992), *Dead Man* (1995).

Jordan, Neil (1950–)
Irish, born Sligo; *Angel* (1982), *The Company of Wolves* (1984), *Mona Lisa* (1986), *The Crying Game* (1992), *Interview with the Vampire* (1994).

Kasdan, Lawrence (1949–)
American, born Miami Beach, Florida; *Body Heat* (1981), *The Big Chill* (1983), *Silverado* (1985), *The Accidental Tourist* (1989), *Grand Canyon* (1991), *Wyatt Earp* (1994).

Kazan, Elia (Elia Kazanjoglou) (1909–)
American, born Istanbul, Turkey; *Gentleman's Agreement (1947)*, *Panic in the Streets* (1950), *A Streetcar Named Desire* (1951), *On the Waterfront* (1954), *East of Eden* (1955), *America, America* (1963), *The Last Tycoon* (1976).

Kieslowski, Krzysztof (1941–96)
Polish, born Warsaw; *From the City of Lodz* (1969), *Camera Bluff* (1979), *A Short Film about Killing* (1988), *The Double Life of Veronique* (1991), *Three Colours: Blue, White and Red* (1993–94).

Kubrick, Stanley (1928–)
American, born New York; *Killer's Kiss* (1955), *The Killing* (1956), *Paths of Glory* (1957), *Spartacus* (1960), *Lolita* (1962), *Dr Strangelove* (1964), *2001: A Space Odyssey* (1968), *A Clockwork Orange* (1971), *Barry Lyndon* (1975), *The Shining* (1980), *Full Metal Jacket* (1987).

Kurosawa, Akira (1910–)
Japanese, born Tokyo; *Rashomon* (1950), *Seven Samurai* (1954), *Throne of Blood* (1957), *Yojimbo* (1961), *Dersu Uzala* (1975), *Kagemusha* (1980), *Ran* (1985).

Lang, Fritz (1890–1976)
German, born Vienna; *Destiny* (1921), *Dr Mabuse the Gambler* (1922), *Metropolis* (1926), *M* (1931), *Fury* (1936), *You Only Live Once* (1937), *The Woman in the Window* (1944), *The Big Heat* (1953), *Beyond a Reasonable Doubt* (1956).

Lean, Sir David (1908–91)
English, born Croydon; *In Which We Serve* (1942), *Brief Encounter* (1945), *Great Expectations* (1946), *The Bridge on the River Kwai* (1957), *Lawrence of Arabia* (1962), *Doctor Zhivago* (1965), *Ryan's Daughter* (1970), *A Passage to India* (1984).

Lee, Spike (Shelton Jackson) (1957–)
American, born Atlanta, Georgia; *She's Gotta Have It* (1986), *Do the Right Thing* (1989), *Malcolm X* (1992), *Clockers* (1995).

Leone, Sergio (1929–89)
Italian, born Rome; *A Fistful of Dollars* (1964), *Once Upon A Time In The West* (1968), *Once Upon A Time In America* (1983).

Levinson, Barry (1942–)
American, born Baltimore, Maryland; *Diner* (1982), *Good Morning Vietnam* (1987), *Rain Man* (1988), *Avalon* (1990), *Disclosure* (1994).

Loach, Kenneth (1937–)
British, born Nuneaton; *Cathy Come Home* (TV 1986), *Looks and Smiles* (1981), *Hidden Agenda* (1990), *Riff Raff* (1991), *Raining Stones* (1993), *Ladybird Ladybird* (1994), *Land and Freedom* (1995).

Losey, Joseph (1909–84)
American, born La Crosse, Wisconsin; *The Boy with the Green Hair* (1948), *The Servant* (1963), *Accident* (1967), *The Go-Between* (1971), *Don Giovanni* (1979).

DIRECTORS (cont.)

Lubitsch, Ernst (1892–1947)
German/American, born Berlin; *The Marriage Circle* (1924), *The Love Parade* (1929), *Trouble in Paradise* (1932), *The Merry Widow* (1934), *Ninotchka* (1939), *To Be Or Not To Be* (1942), *Heaven Can Wait* (1943).

Lumet, Sidney (1924–)
American, born Philadelphia; *Twelve Angry Men* (1957), *The Pawnbroker* (1965), *The Hill* (1965), *Murder on the Orient Express* (1974), *Dog Day Afternoon* (1975), *Network* (1976), *The Verdict* (1982), *Q & A* (1982).

Lynch, David K (1946–)
American, born Missoula, Montana; *Eraserhead* (1976), *The Elephant Man* (1980), *Dune* (1984), *Blue Velvet* (1986), *Wild at Heart* (1990), *Twin Peaks: Fire Walk with me* (1992).

Mankiewicz, Joseph Leo (1909–93)
American, born Wilkes-Barre, Pennsylvania; *A Letter to Three Wives* (1949), *All About Eve* (1950), *The Barefoot Contessa* (1954), *Guys and Dolls* (1955), *Cleopatra* (1963), *Sleuth* (1972).

Minnelli, Vincente (1913–86)
American, born Chicago; *Meet me in St Louis* (1944), *The Pirate* (1948), *An American in Paris* (1951), *The Bandwagon* (1953), *Lust for Life* (1956), *Gigi* (1958).

Nichols, Mike (Michael Igor Peschkowsky) (1931–)
American, born Berlin; *Who's Afraid of Virginia Woolf?* (1966), *The Graduate* (1967), *Catch-22* (1970), *Carnal Knowledge* (1971), *Silkwood* (1983), *Working Girl* (1988), *Wolf* (1994).

Olivier, Lord Laurence Kerr (1907–89)
English, born Dorking, Surrey; *Henry V* (1944), *Hamlet* (1948), *Richard III* (1956).

Parker, Alan (1944–)
British, born London; *Bugsy Malone* (1976), *Midnight Express* (1978), *Fame* (1980), *Birdy* (1985), *Mississippi Burning* (1988), *The Commitments* (1991).

Pasolini, Pier Paolo (1922–75)
Italian, born Bologna; *Accatone* (1961), *The Gospel According to St Matthew* (1964), *Teorema* (1968), *Salo* (1975).

Peckinpah, (David) Sam(uel) (1925–84)
American, born Fresno, California; *Ride the High Country* (1962), *The Wild Bunch* (1969), *Straw Dogs* (1971).

Polanski, Roman (1933–)
Polish, born Paris; *Knife in the Water* (1962), *Repulsion* (1965), *Rosemary's Baby* (1968), *Macbeth* (1971), *Chinatown* (1974), *Tess* (1979), *Pirates* (1986), *Death and the Maiden* (1994).

Pollack, Sydney (1934–)
American, born Lafayette, Indiana; *They Shoot Horses Don't They?* (1969), *The Way We Were* (1973), *Tootsie* (1982), *Out of Africa* (1985), *The Firm* (1993).

Powell, Michael Latham (1905–90)
British, born Bekesbourne, near Canterbury; with **Emeric Pressburger** (1902–88)
Hungarian/British, born Miskolc, Hungary; *The Life and Death of Colonel Blimp* (1943), *I Know Where I'm Going* (1945), *A Matter of Life and Death* (1946), *Black Narcissus* (1947), *The Red Shoes* (1948), *Peeping Tom* (1959).

Preminger, Otto (1905–86)
  Austrian/American, born Vienna; *Laura* (1944), *The Man With the Golden Arm* (1955), *Anatomy of a Murder* (1959), *Exodus* (1960), *Advise and Consent* (1962), *Such God Friends* (1971).

Ray, Satyajit (1921–92)
  Indian, born Calcutta; *Pather Panchali* (1955), *Apur Sansar* (1959), *Charulata* (1964), *Distant Thunder* (1973), *The Chess Players* (1977), *Home and the World* (1984).

Redford, (Charles) Robert (1937–   )
  American, born Santa Monica, California; *Ordinary People* (1980), *The Milagro Beanfield War* (1987), *A River Runs Through It* (1992), *Quiz Show* (1994).

Reed, Sir Carol (1906–76)
  British, born London; *Bank Holiday* (1938), *Night Train to Munich* (1940), *Odd Man Out* (1946), *The Third Man* (1949), *Trapeze* (1956), *Oliver!* (1968).

Renoir, Jean (1894–1979)
  French/American, born Paris; *Bodu Saved from Drowning* (1932), *La Grande Illusion* (1937), *La Règle du Jeu* (1939), *The Southerner* (1945), *The River* (1951), *Le Petit Theatre de Jean Renoir* (1969).

Roeg, Nicolas Jack (1928–   )
  British, born London; *Performance* (1970), *Walkabout* (1971), *Don't Look Now* (1973), *The Man Who Fell to Earth* (1976), *Bad Timing* (1980), *Eureka* (1983), *Heart of Darkness* (1994).

Rossellini, Roberto (1906–77)
  Italian, born Rome; *Rome, Open City* (1945), *Paisan* (1946), *Stromboli* (1950), *Voyage to Italy* (1953), *The Rise of Louis XIV* (1965).

Russell, Ken (Henry Kenneth Alfred Russell) (1927–   )
  British, born Southampton; *Women in Love* (1969), *The Music Lovers* (1970), *The Devils* (1971), *Tommy* (1975), *Crimes of Passion* (1984).

Schlesinger, John Richard (1926–   )
  British, born London; *A Kind of Loving* (1962), *Billy Liar* (1963), *Darling* (1965), *Far from the Madding Crowd* (1967), *Midnight Cowboy* (1969), *Sunday, Bloody Sunday* (1971), *Marathon Man* (1976), *An Englishman Abroad* (TV 1982), *The Innocent* (1993).

Scorsese, Martin (1942–   )
  American, born Queens, New York; *Mean Streets* (1973), *Alice Doesn't Live Here Any More* (1974), *Taxi Driver* (1976), *Raging Bull* (1980), *King of Comedy* (1983), *The Mission* (1986), *The Color of Money* (1986), *The Last Temptation of Christ* (1988), *GoodFellas* (1990), *Cape Fear* (1991), *Age of Innocence* (1992), *Casino* (1995).

Scott, Ridley (1937–   )
  British, born South Shields; *The Duellists* (1977), *Alien* (1979), *Blade Runner* (1982), *Thelma & Louise* (1991).

Siegel, Don (1912–91)
  American, born Chicago; *Riot in Cell Block 11* (1954), *Invasion of the Bodysnatchers* (1956), *Madigan* (1968), *The Beguiled* (1970), *Dirty Harry* (1971), *The Shootist* (1976), *Escape from Alcatraz* (1979).

Spielberg, Steven (1946–   )
  American, born Cincinnati, Ohio; *Duel* (TV 1971), *Jaws* (1975), *1941* (1979), *Close Encounters of the Third Kind* (1977), *Raiders of the Lost Ark* (1981), *ET* (1982), *Indiana Jones and the Temple of Doom* (1984), *The Color Purple* (1985), *Indiana Jones and the Last Crusade* (1989), *Hook* (1992), *Jurassic Park* (1993), *Schindler's List* (1993).

DIRECTORS (cont.)

Stone, Oliver (1946–   )
American, born New York City; *Seizure* (1974), *Salvador* (1986), *Platoon* (1987), *Wall Street* (1987), *Born on the 4th of July* (1989), *The Doors* (1991), *JFK* (1991), *Natural Born Killers* (1994).
Sturges, Preston (Ernest P Biden) (1898–1959)
American, born Chicago, Illinois; *The Great McGinty* (1940), *The Lady Eve* (1941), *Sullivan's Travels* (1941), *The Palm Beach Story* (1942), *The Miracle of Morgan's Creek* (1944).

Tarantino, Quentin (1963–   )
American, born Knoxville, Tennessee; *Reservoir Dogs* (1992), *Pulp Fiction* (1994), *Four Rooms* (1995) (co-director).
Truffaut, François (1932–84)
French, born Paris; *Les Quatre Cents Coups* (1959), *Jules et Jim* (1961), *L'Enfant Sauvage* (1969), *Day for Night* (1973), *The Last Metro* (1980).

Visconti, Count Luchino (Don Luchino Visconti Di Modrone) (1906–76)
Italian, born Milan; *Ossessione* (1942), *Rocco and his Brothers* (1961), *The Leopard* (1963), *The Damned* (1969), *Death in Venice* (1971).

Weir, Peter Lindsay (1944–   )
Australian, born Sydney; *The Cars that Ate Paris* (1974), *Picnic at Hanging Rock* (1975), *Gallipoli* (1981), *The Year of Living Dangerously* (1982), *Witness* (1985), *Dead Poet's Society* (1989), *Fearless* (1993).
Welles, (George) Orson (1915–85)
American, born Kenosha, Wisconsin; *Citizen Kane* (1941), *The Magnificent Ambersons* (1942), *The Lady from Shanghai (1948)*, *Macbeth* (1948), *Othello* (1952), *Touch of Evil* (1958), *The Trial* (1962), *Chimes at Midnight* (1966), *The Other Side of the Wind* (1972–75).
Wenders, Wim (Wilhelm) (1945–   )
German, born Dusseldorf; *The Goalkeeper's Fear of the Penalty* (1971), *Kings of the Road* (1976), *The American Friend* (1977), *Paris Texas* (1984), *Wings of Desire* (1987), *Far Away So Close* (1993).
Wilder, Billy (Samuel) (1906–   )
Austrian/American, born Sucha, Austria; *Double Indemnity* (1944), *The Lost Weekend* (1945), *Sunset Boulevard* (1950), *The Seven Year Itch (1955)*, *Some Like It Hot* (1959), *The Apartment* (1960), *Avanti!* (1972), *The Front Page* (1974), *Buddy Buddy* (1981).
Wise, Robert (1914–   )
American, born Winchester, Indiana; *The Set-Up* (1949), *The Day the Earth Stood Still* (1951), *I Want to Live (1958)*, *West Side Story* (1961), *The Sound of Music* (1965), *Star Trek The Motion Picture* (1979).
Wyler, William (1902–81)
American, born Mulhausen, Alsace-Lorraine; *These Three* (1936), *Dodsworth* (1936), *Jezebel* (1938), *Wuthering Heights* (1939), *The Letter* (1940), *The Little Foxes* (1941), *Mrs Miniver* (1942), *The Best Years of Our Lives* (1946), *Roman Holiday* (1953), *Ben-Hur* (1959), *Funny Girl* (1968).

Zeffirelli, Franco (Gianfranco Corsi) (1923–   )
Italian, born Florence; *The Taming of the Shrew* (1967), *Romeo and Juliet* (1968), *Jesus of Nazareth* (TV 1977), *La Traviata* (1982), *Hamlet* (1990), *Jane Eyre* (TV 1995).
Zemeckis, Robert (1951–   )
American, born Chicago; *Romancing The Stone* (1984), *Back to the Future* (1985), *Who Framed Roger Rabbit?* (1988), *Back to the Future II* (1989), *Back to the Future III* (1990), *Forrest Gump* (1994).

Zinnemann, Fred (1907–97)
Austrian/American, born Vienna, Austria; *The Search* (1948), *High Noon* (1952), *From Here to Eternity* (1953), *The Nun's Story* (1959), *A Man for All Seasons* (1966), *Day of the Jackal* (1973), *Julia* (1977), *Five Days One Summer* (1982).

MOTION PICTURE ACADEMY AWARDS

	Best film	Best actor	Best actress
1970	*Patton* (Franklin J Schaffner)	George C Scott *Patton*	Glenda Jackson *Women in Love*
1971	*The French Connection* (William Friedkin)	Gene Hackman *The French Connection*	Jane Fonda *Klute*
1972	*The Godfather* (Francis Ford Coppola)	Marlon Brando *The Godfather*	Liza Minnelli *Cabaret*
1973	*The Sting* (George Roy Hill)	Jack Lemmon *Save the Tiger*	Glenda Jackson *A Touch of Class*
1974	*The Godfather Part II* (Francis Ford Coppola)	Art Carney *Harry and Tonto*	Ellen Burstyn *Alice Doesn't Live Here Anymore*
1975	*One Flew Over the Cuckoo's Nest* (Milos Forman)	Jack Nicholson *One Flew Over the Cuckoo's Nest*	Louise Fletcher *One Flew Over the Cuckoo's Nest*
1976	*Rocky* (John G Avildsen)	Peter Finch *Network*	Faye Dunaway *Network*
1977	*Annie Hall* (Woody Allen)	Richard Dreyfuss *The Goodbye Girl*	Diane Keaton *Annie Hall*
1978	*The Deer Hunter* (Michael Cimino)	Jon Voight *Coming Home*	Jane Fonda *Coming Home*
1979	*Kramer vs Kramer* (Robert Beaton)	Dustin Hoffman *Kramer vs Kramer*	Sally Field *Norma Rae*
1980	*Ordinary People* (Robert Redford)	Robert de Niro *Raging Bull*	Sissy Spacek *Coal Miner's Daughter*
1981	*Chariots of Fire* (Hugh Hudson)	Henry Fonda *On Golden Pond*	Katharine Hepburn *On Golden Pond*
1982	*Gandhi* (Richard Attenborough)	Ben Kingsley *Gandhi*	Meryl Streep *Sophie's Choice*
1983	*Terms of Endearment* (James L Brooks)	Robert Duval *Tender Mercies*	Shirley MacLaine *Terms of Endearment*
1984	*Amadeus* (Milos Forman)	F Murray Abraham *Amadeus*	Sally Field *Places in the Heart*
1985	*Out of Africa* (Sydney Pollack)	William Hurt *Kiss of the Spider Woman*	Geraldine Page *The Trip to Bountiful*
1986	*Platoon* (Oliver Stone)	Paul Newman *The Color of Money*	Marlee Matlin *Children of a Lesser God*
1987	*The Last Emperor* (Bernardo Bertolucci)	Michael Douglas *Wall Street*	Cher *Moonstruck*

MOTION PICTURE ACADEMY AWARDS (cont.)

	Best film	Best actor	Best actress
1988	*Rain Man* (Barry Levinson)	Dustin Hoffman *Rain Man*	Jody Foster *The Accused*
1989	*Driving Miss Daisy* (Bruce Beresford)	Daniel Day-Lewis *My Left Foot*	Jessica Tandy *Driving Miss Daisy*
1990	*Dances with Wolves* (Kevin Costner)	Jeremy Irons *Reversal of Fortune*	Kathy Bates *Misery*
1991	*The Silence of the Lambs* (Jonathan Demme)	Anthony Hopkins *The Silence of the Lambs*	Jody Foster *The Silence of the Lambs*
1992	*Unforgiven* (Clint Eeastwood)	Al Pacino *Scent of a Woman*	Emma Thompson *Howards End*
1993	*Schindler's List* (Steven Spielberg)	Tom Hanks *Philadelphia*	Holly Hunter *The Piano*
1994	*Forrest Gump* (Robert Zemeckis)	Tom Hanks *Forrest Gump*	Jessica Lange *Blue Sky*
1995	*Braveheart* (Mel Gibson)	Nicolas Cage *Leaving Las Vegas*	Susan Sarandon *Dead Man Walking*
1996	*The English Patient* (Anthony Minghella)	Geoffrey Rush *Shine*	Frances McDormand *Fargo*

COMPOSERS

Albéniz, Isaac (1860–1909)
Spanish, born Camprodón, Catalonia; works include operas and works for piano based on Spanish folk music (eg *Iberia*).

Bach, Johann Sebastian (1685–1750)
German, born Eisenach; prolific composer, works include over 190 cantatas and oratorios, concertos, chamber music, keyboard music, and orchestral works (eg *Toccata and Fugue in D minor*, *The Well-tempered Clavier*, *Six Brandenburg Concertos*, *St Matthew Passion*, *Mass in B minor*, *Goldberg Variations*, *The Musical Offering*, *The Art of Fugue*).

Bartók, Béla (1881–1945)
Hungarian, born Nagyszentmiklós (now Sînnicolau Mare, Romania); six string quartets, *Sonata for 2 pianos and percussion*, concertos (for piano, violin, viola and notably the *Concerto for Orchestra*), opera, (*Duke Bluebeard's Castle*), two ballets (*The Wooden Prince*, *The Miraculous Mandarin*), songs, choruses, folksong arrangements.

Beethoven, Ludwig van (1770–1827)
German, born Bonn; works include 33 piano sonatas (eg the 'Pathetique', 'Moonlight', *Waldstein*, *Appassionata*), nine symphonies (eg *Eroica*, 'Pastoral', *Choral* Symphony (no.9)), string quartets, concertos, *Lebewohl* and the opera *Fidelio*.

Berg, Alban (1885–1935)
Austrian, born Vienna; works include songs (*Four Songs*), operas (*Wozzeck*, *Lulu*, unfinished), a violin concerto and a string quartet (*Lyric Suite*).

Berio, Luciano (1925–)
Italian, born Oneglia; works include compositions using tapes and electronic music (eg *Mutazioni*, *Omaggio a James Joyce*), works for solo instruments (*Sequenzas*), stage works (eg *Laborintus II*, *Opera*) and symphonies (*Synfonia*).

Berlioz, (Louis) Hector (1803–69)
   French, born Côte-St-André, near Grenoble; works include the overture *Le carnival romain*, the cantata (*La Damnation de Faust*), symphonies (eg *Symphonie Fantastique, Romeo et Juliette*) and operas (eq *Béatrice et Bénédict, Les Toyens*).

Bernstein, Leonard (1918–90)
   American, born Lawrence, Massachusetts; works include ballets (*Jeremiah, The Age of Anxiety, Kaddish*), symphonies (eg *Fancy Free, The Dybbuk*), and musicals, (eg *Candide, West Side Story, On The Town, Songfest, Halil*).

Bizet, Georges (1838–75)
   French, born Paris; works include opera (eg *Carmen, Les Pêcheurs de Perles, La Jolie Fille de Perth*) incidental music to Daudet's play *L'Arlésienne* and a symphony.

Boulez, Pierre (1925–)
   French, born Montbrison; works include three piano sonatas and works for piano and flute (eg *Sonatine*).

Brahms, Johannes (1833–97)
   German, born Hamburg; works include songs, four symphonies, two piano concertos, choral work (eg *German Requiem*), orchestral work (eg *Variations on a Theme of Haydn*), programme work (eg *Tragic overture*), also the *Academic Festival Overture* and *Hungarian Dances*.

Bruckner, Anton (1824–96)
   Austrian, born Ansfelden; works include nine symphonies, a string quartet, choral-orchestral Masses and other church music (eg *Te Deum*).

Cage, John (1912–92)
   American, born Los Angeles; works include unorthodox modern compositions, eg *Sonatas and Interludes for the prepared piano*.

Carter, Elliott Cook Jr (1908–)
   American, born New York City; works include quartets, symphonies, concertos, songs and chamber music.

Chabrier, Emmanuel (1841–94)
   French, born Ambert; works include operas (*Gwendoline, Le Roi malgré lui, Briséis*) and an orchestral rhapsody (*España*).

Chausson, Ernest (1855–99)
   French, born Paris; works include songs and orchestral works (eg *Poème*).

Chopin, Frédéric François (1810–49)
   Polish, born Zelazowa Wola, near Warsaw; wrote almost exclusively for piano — nocturnes, polonaises, mazurkas, preludes, concertos, and a funeral march.

Copland, Aaron (1900–90)
   American, born Brooklyn, New York; ballets (eg *Billy The Kid, Appalachian Spring*), film scores (eg *Our Town, The Hucis*), symphonies (eg *Symphonie Ode, Connotations, Clarinet Concerto*).

Corelli, Arcangelo (1653–1713)
   Italian, born Fusignano, near Bologna; works include 12 concertos (eg *Concerto for Christmas Night*), and solo and trio sonatas for violin.

Couperin, François (1668–1733)
   French, born Paris; works include chamber music, four books containing 240 harpsichord pieces, motets and other church music.

Debussy, Claude Achille (1862–1918)
   French, born St Germalnc-en-Laye, near Paris; songs (eg the cantata *L'Enfant prodigue*), opera (*Pelléas et Mélisande*), orchestral works (eg *Prélude à l'après-midi d'un faune, La Mer*), chamber and piano music (eg *Feux d'artifice, La Cathédrale engloutie*).

COMPOSERS (cont.)

Delius, Frederick (1862–1934)
English (of German Scandinavian descent), born Bradford; works include songs (eg *A Song of Summer, Idyll, Songs of Farewell*), concertos, operas (eg *Koanga, A Village Romeo and Juliette*), chamber music and orchestral variations (eg *Appalachia, Sea Drift, A Mass of Life*).

Dukas, Paul (1865–1935)
French, born Paris; works include a symphonic poem (*L'Apprenti sorcier*) and opera (*Ariane et Barbe-Bleue*).

Dutilleux, Henri (1916–   )
French, born Angers; works include a piano sonata, two symphonies, a violin concerto, a string quartet (*Ainsi la nuit*), compositions for two pianos and other orchestral works.

Dvořák, Antonin (1841–1904)
Czech, born near Prague; works include songs, concertos, choral (eg *Hymnus*) and chamber music, symphonies (notably 'From the New World'), operas (eg *Rusalka* (The Water Nymph), *Armida, Slavonic Dances*).

Elgar, Sir Edward (William) (1857–1934)
English, born Broadheath, near Worcester; works include chamber music, two symphonies, oratorios (eg *The Dream of Gerontius, The Apostles, The Kingdom*), and the orchestral work *Enigma Variations*.

Falla, Manuel de (1876–1946)
Spanish, born Cadiz; works include opera (eg *La Vida Breve, Master Peter's Puppet Show*, ballet (eg *The Three-Cornered Hat, Love the Magician*) and orchestral suites (eg *Nights in the Gardens of Spain*).

Fauré, Gabriel Urbain (1845–1924)
French, born Pamiers; works include songs (eg *Après un rêve*), chamber music, choral music (eg the *Requiem*), operas and orchestral music (eg *Marques et bergamasques*).

Franck, César Auguste (1822–90)
naturalized French, born Liège, Belgium; works include tone-poems, (eg *Les Béatitudes*), sonatas for violin and piano, symphony in D minor and *Variations symphoniques* for piano and orchestra.

Gershwin, George (1898–1937)
American, born Brooklyn, New York; Broadway musicals (eg *Lady Be Good, Of Thee I Sing*), symphonies, songs (notably 'I Got Rhythm', 'The Man I Love'), operas (eg *Porgy and Bess*), and concert works (eg *Rhapsody in Blue, Concerto in F, An American in Paris*).

Grainger, Percy Aldridge (1882–1961)
Australian, born Melbourne; works include songs, piano and chamber music (eg *Molly on the Shore, Mock Morris, Shepherds Hey*).

Grieg, Edvard Hagerup (1843–1907)
Norwegian, born Bergen; works include songs, a piano concerto, orchestral suites, violin sonatas, choral music and incidental music for *Peer Gynt* and *Sigurd Jorsalfar*.

Handel, George Friederic (1685–1759)
naturalized English, born Halle, Saxony; prolific output including over 27 operas (eg *Almira, Rinaldo*), 20 oratorios (eg *The Messiah, Saul, Israel in Egypt, Samson, Jephthah*), orchestral suites (eg the *Water Music* and *Music for the Royal Fireworks*), organ concertos and chamber music.

Haydn, (Franz) Joseph (1732–1809)
Austrian, born Rohrau, Lower Austria; prolific output including 104 symphonies (eg the 'Salomon' or 'London' Symphonies), string quartets and oratorios (notably *The Creation, The Seasons*).

Holst, Gustav Theodore (originally **von Holst**) (1874–1934)
English of Swedish origin, born Cheltenham; works include choral and ballet music, operas (eg *The Perfect Fool, At the Boar's Head*), orchestral suites (eg *The Planets, St Paul's Suite for Strings*), choral music (eg *The Hymn of Jesus, Ode to Death*), and *Concerto for Two Violins*.

Honegger, Arthur (1892–1955)
French, born Le Havre; works include five symphonies and dramatic oratorios (*King David, Joan of Arc at the Stake*).

Ireland, John Nicholson (1879–1962)
English, born Bowden, Cheshire; works include sonatas (eg Violin Sonata in A), piano music, songs (eg 'Sea Fever'), the rhapsody *Mai-dun* and orchestral works (eg *The Forgotten Rite, These Things Shall Be*).

Ives, Charles (1874–1954)
American, born Danbury, Connecticut; works include five symphonies, chamber music (eg *Concord Sonata*) and many songs.

Janáček, Leoš (1854–1928)
Czech, born Hukvaldy, Moravia; works include chamber, orchestral and choral music (eg the song cycle *The Diary of One Who Has Vanished*), operas (eg *Janufa, The Cunning Little Vixen, The Excursions of Mr Brouček, From the House of the Dead*), two string quartets and a mass.

Lalo, (Victor Antoine) Édouard (1823–92)
French, born Lille. Works include compositions for violin (eg *Symphonie espagnole*), opera (eg *Le Roi d'Ys*) and ballet (*Namouna*).

Ligeti, Györgi Sándor (1923–   )
Hungarian, born Dicsöszentmárton; works include orchestral compositions (eg *Apparitions, Lontano, Double Concerto*), choral works (eg *Requiem*) and music for harpsichord, organ and wind and string ensembles.

Liszt, Franz (1811–1886)
Hungarian, born Raiding; 400 original compositions including symphonic poems, piano music and masses (eg *The Legend of St Elizabeth, Christus*).

Mahler, Gustav (1860–1911)
Austrian, born Kalist, Bohemia; works include ten symphonies, songs, the cantata *Das klagende Lied*, and the song-symphony *Das lied von der Erde* (The Song of the Earth).

Mendelssohn, (Jacob Ludwig) Felix (1809–47)
German, born Hamburg; prolific output, including concerto overtures (eg *Fingal's Cave*, Midsummer Night's Dream, *Hebrides, Scottish Symphony*), symphonies (Symphony in C minor), quartets (B minor Quartet), operas (eg *Camacho's Wedding*), and oratorios (eg *Elijah*).

Messiaen, Olivier Eugène Prosper Charles (1908–92)
French, born Avignon; works include compositions for piano (*Vingt regards sur l'enfant Jésus, Catalogue d'oiseaux*), the symphony *Turangalila*, an oratorio (*La Transfiguration de Notre Seigneur Jésus-Christ*) and an opera (*St François d'Assisi*).

Milhaud, Darius (1892–1974)
French, born Aix-en-Provence; works include several operas, incidental music for plays, ballets (eg the jazz ballet *La Création du monde*), symphonies and orchestral, choral and chamber works.

Monteverdi, Claudio (Giovanni Antonio) (1567–1643)
Italian, born Cremona; works include masses (eg *Mass* and *Vespers* of the Virgin), cantatas and operas (eg *Orfeo, Il Ritorno d'Ulisse, L'Incoronazione di Poppea* (The Coronation of Poppea)).

COMPOSERS (cont.)

Mozart, (Johann Chrysostom) Wolfgang Amadeus (1756–91)
Austrian, born Salzburg; 600 compositions including symphonies (eg 'Jupiter', *Linz, Prague*), concertos, string quartets, sonatas, operas (eg *Marriage of Figaro, Don Giovanni, Cosi fan tutte*) and the Singspiels *The Abduction from the Seraglio, Die Zauberflöte*.

Mussorgsky, Modeste (1839–81)
Russian, born Karevo, government of Pskov; works include operas (eg *Boris Godunov*), song cycles and instrumental works (eg *Pictures from an Exhibition, Night on the Bare Mountain*).

Nielsen, Carl August (1865–1931)
Danish, born Furen; works include operas (eg *Saul and David, Masquerade*), symphonies (eg 'The Four Temperaments'), string quartets, choral and piano music.

Palestrina, Giovanni Pierluigi da (c.1525–1594)
Italian, born Palestrina, near Rome; works include chamber music and the organ work *Commotion*, masses, choral music (eg *Song of Songs*), madrigals.

Prokofiev, Sergei (1891–1953)
Russian, born Sontsovka in the Ukraine; works include 11 operas (eg *The Gambler, The Love for Three Oranges, The Fiery Angels, Semyon Kotko, Betrothal in a Monastery, War and Peace, The Story of a Real Man*), ballets (eg *Romeo and Juliet, Cinderella*), concertos, sonatas, cantatas (eg *We are Seven, Hail to Stalin*), film scores (eg *Alexander Nevsky*), and the 'children's piece' *Peter and the Wolf*.

Puccini, Giacomo (Antonio Domenico Michele Secondo Maria) (1858–1924)
Italian, born Lucca; 12 operas (eg *Manon Lescaut, La Bohème, Tosca, Madama Butterfly, Turandot*).

Purcell, Henry (1659–95)
English, born London; works include songs (eg 'Nymphs and Shepherds', 'Arise, ye Subterrean Winds'), sonatas, string fantasies, church music and opera (eg *Dido and Aeneas*).

Rachmaninov, Sergei Vasilyevich (1873–1943)
Russian, born Nizhi-Novgorod; works include operas, three symphonies, four piano concertos (eg *Prelude in C Sharp Minor*), the tone-poem *The Isle of the Dead*, and *Rhapsody on a Theme of Paganini* for piano and orchestra.

Rameau, Jean Philippe (1683–1764)
French, born Dijon; works include over 30 ballets and operas (eg *Hippolyte et Aricie, Castor et Pollux*) and harpsichord pieces.

Ravel, Maurice (1875–1937)
French, born Ciboure, in the Basque country; works include piano compositions (eg *Sonatina, Miroirs, Ma Mère L'Oye, Gaspard de la nuit*), string quartets, operas (eg *L'Heure espagnol, L'Enfant et les sortilèges*), ballets (eg *Daphnis and Chloë*), the 'choreographic poem' *La Valse* and the miniature ballet *Boléro*.

Rimsky-Korsakov, Nikolai Andreievich (1844–1908)
Russian, born Tikhvin, Novgorod; works include orchestral music (eg the symphonic suite *Sheherazade, Capriccio Espagnol, Easter Festival*) and 15 operas (eg *Sadko, The Snow Maiden, The Tsar Sultan, The Invisible City of Kitesh, The Goldern Cockerel*).

Rossini, Gioacchino Antonio (1792–1868)
Italian, born Pesaro; works include many operas (eg *Il Barbiere de Seviglia, Otella, Guillaume Tell*) and a number of vocal and piano pieces.

Roussel, Albert (1869–1937)
French, born Tourcoing; works include four symphonies, numerous choral works (eg *Évocations*), ballets (eg *Bacchus and Ariane, Le Festin de l'araignée*) and an opera (*Padmâvati*).

Saint-Saëns, (Charles) Camille (1835–1921)

French, born Paris; works include four symphonic poems (eg *Danse macabre*), piano (*Le Rouet d'Omphale, Phaëton, La Jeunesse d'Hercule*), violin and cello concertos, symphonies, the opera *Samson et Dalila*, church music (eg *Messe solennelle*), and *Carnival des animaux* for two pianos and orchestra.

Satie, Erik Alfred Leslie (1866–1925)

French, born Honfleur; works include ballets (eg *Parade*), lyric dramas and whimsical pieces.

Scarlatti, (Guiseppe) Domenico (1685–1757)

Italian, born Naples; works include over 600 harpsichord sonatas.

Schönberg, Arnold (1874–1951)

naturalized American, born Vienna; works include chamber music (eg *Chamber Symphony*), concertos (eg *Piano Concerto*), and symphonic poems (eg *Pelleas und Melisande*), the choral-orchestral *Gurrelieder*, string quartets, the oratorio *Die Jacobsiter*, and opera (*Von Heute auf Morgen, Moses and Aaron*).

Schubert, Franz Peter (1797–1828)

Austrian, born Vienna; prolific output, works include symphonies, piano sonatas, string quartets and songs (eg *Gretchen am Spinnrade, Erlkönig, Die schöne Müllerin, Winterreise, Who is Sylvia?, Hark, Hark the Lark, Schwanengesang* ('Swan-song').

Schumann, Robert Alexander (1810–56)

German, born Zwickau, Saxony; works include piano music (eg *Fantasiestücke*), songs (eg The Fool's Song in *Twelfth Night*, the Chamisso songs *Frauenliebe und Leben* or 'Woman's Love and Life'), chamber music, and four symphonies (eg the *Rhenish*).

Scriabin, Alexander (1872–1915)

Russian, born Moscow; works include a piano concerto, three symphonies, two tone poems (eg *Poem of Ecstasy*), 10 sonatas, studies and preludes.

Shostakovich, Dmitri (1906–75)

Russian, born St Petersburg; works include 15 symphonies, operas (eg *The Nose, A Lady Macbeth of Mtensk*), concertos, string quartets and film music.

Sibelius, Jean (1865–1957)

Finnish, born Tavastehus; works include symphonic poems (eg *Swan of Tuonela, En Saga*), songs, a violin concerto, and seven symphonies.

Stockhausen, Karlheinz (1928–   )

German, born Mödrath, near Cologne; works include orchestral (eg *Gruppen*), choral and instrumental compositions.

Strauss, Johann (the Younger) (1825–99)

Austrian, born Vienna; works include over 400 waltzes (eg *The Blue Danube, Wine, Women, and Song, Perpetuum Mobile, Artist's Life, Tales from the Vienna Woods, Voices from Spring, The Emperor*), and operettas (eg *Die Fledermaus, A Night in Venice*).

Strauss, Richard (1864–1949)

German, born Munich; works include symphonic poems (eg *Don Juan, Till Eulenspiegel, Also Sprach Zarathustra, Tod und Verklärung* ('Death and Transfiguration'), *Don Quixote, Ein Heldenleben*) and operas (eg *Der Rosenkavalier, Ariadne auf Naxos, Capriccio*).

Stravinsky, Igor (1882–1971)

Russian, born Oranienbaum, near St Petersburg (naturalized French, then American); works include operas (eg *The Rake's Progress*), oratorios (eg *Oedipus Rex, Symphony of Psalms*), concertos, ballets (eg *The Firebird, The Rite of Spring, Petrushka, Pulcinella, Apollo Musogetes, The Card Game, Orpheus, Agon*), and a musical play *Elegy for J.F.K.* for voice and clarinets.

Tchaikovsky, Piotr Ilyich (1840–93)

Russian, born Kamsko-Votinsk; works include ten operas (eg *Eugene Onegin, The Queen of Spades*),

COMPOSERS (cont.)

a violin concerto, six symphonies, two piano concertos, three ballets (*The Nutcracker, Swan Lake, The Sleeping Beauty*) and tone-poems (eg *Romeo and Juliet, Italian Capriccio*).

Telemann, George Philipp (1681–1767)
German, born Magdeburg; prolific composer, works include 600 overtures, 40 operas, 200 concertos, sonatas, suites, and overtures (eg *Der Tag de Gerichts, Die Tageszeiten*).

Tippett, Sir Michael Kemp (1905–   )
English, born London; works include operas (eg *The Midsummer Marriage, King Priam, The Knot Garden, The Ice Break*), concertos, symphonies, cantatas and oratorios (eg *A Child of our Time, The Vision of St Augustine*).

Varèse, Edgar (1883–1965)
American, born Paris; works are almost entirely orchestral (eg *Metal, Ionization, Hyperprism*).

Vaughan Williams, Ralph (1872–1958)
English, born Down Ampney, Gloucestershire; works include songs, symphonies (eg *London Symphony, Pastoral Symphony*), choral-orchestral works (eg *Sea Symphony, Magnificat*), operas (eg *Hugh the Drover, The Pilgrim's Progress*), a ballet *Job*, and film music (eg for Scott of the Antarctic).

Verdi, Giuseppe (1813–1901)
Italian, born le Roncole, near Busseto; church music (eg *Requiem*), operas (eg *Oberto, Nabucco, Rigoletto, Il Trovatore, La Traviata, Un Ballo in Maschera, La Forza del Destino, Aïda, Otello, Falstaff*).

Vivaldi, Antonio (1678–1741)
Italian, born Venice; prolific output, works include over 400 concertos (eg *L'Estro Armonico, The Four Seasons*), 40 operas and an oratorio, *Juditha triumphans*.

Wagner, (Wilhelm) Richard (1813–83)
German, born Leipzig; operas include *Lohengrin, Rienzi*, the *Ring* cycle (*Das Rheingold, Die Walk re, Siegfried, Götterdämmerung*), *Die Meistersinger, Tristan und Isolde, Parsifal*.

Walton, Sir William Turner (1902–83)
English, born Oldham; works include concertos, operas (*Troilus and Cressida, The Bear*), a cantata (*Belshazzar's Feast*), ballet music for *The Wise Virgins*, a song-cycle (*Anon in Love*) and film music.

Weber, Carl Maria von (1786–1826)
German, born Eutin, near Lübeck; works include operas (eg *Oberon, Euryanthe, Silvana*), concertos, symphonies, sonatas, scenas, cantatas (eg *Kampf und Sieg*) and songs.

Webern, Anton von (1883–1945)
Austrian, born Vienna; works include a symphony, three cantatas, *Four Pieces for Violin and Pianoforte, Five Pieces for Orchestra*, a concerto for nine instruments and songs.

Xenakis, Iannis (1922–   )
Greek, born Romania; works include compositions for piano and orchestra (eg *Erikhthon*), *Shaar* for strings, *Tetras* for string quartet and solo pieces (eg *Nomos Alpha* for cello, *Herma* for piano), *Pithoprakta* for 50 instruments.

ARTISTS

Selected paintings are listed.

Altdorfer, Albrecht (c.1480–1538)
German, born Regensburg; *Danube Landscape* (1520), *Alexander's Victory* (1529).

Andrea del Sarto (Andrea d'Agnolo di Francesco) (1486–1530)
Italian, born Florence; *Miracles of S Filippo Benizzi* (1509–10), *Madonna del Saeco* (1525).
Angelico, Fra (Guido di Pietro) (c.1400–55)
Italian, born Vicchio, Tuscany; *Coronation of the Virgin* (1430–5), *San Marco altarpiece* (c.1440).
Auerbach, Frank (1931–)
German/British, born Berlin; *Mornington Crescent* (1967).

Bacon, Francis (1909–92)
British, born Dublin; *Three Figures at the Base of a Crucifixion* (1945), *Two figures with a Monkey* (1973), *Triptych Inspired by the Oresteia of Aeschylus* (1981).
Beardsley, Aubrey (Vincent) (1872–98)
British, born Brighton; illustrations to Malory's *Morte d'Arthur* (1893), Wilde's *Salome* (1894).
Bell, Vanessa (1879–1961)
British, born Kensington, London; *Still Life on Corner of a Mantlepiece* (1914).
Bellini, Gentile (c.1429–1507)
Italian, born Venice; *Procession of the Relic of the True Cross* (1496), *Miracle at Ponte di Lorenzo* (1500).
Blackadder, Elizabeth (1931–)
Scottish, born Falkirk; *Interior with Self-Portrait* (1972), *White Anemones* (1983), *Texas Flame* (1986).
Blake, William (1757–1827)
British, born London; illustrations for his own *Songs of Innocence and Experience* (1794), *Newton* (1795), illustrations for the *Book of Job* (1826).
Böcklin, Arnold (1827–1901)
Swiss, born Basel; *Pan in the Reeds* (1857), *The Island of the Dead* (1880).
Bomberg, David (1890–1957)
British, born Birmingham; *In the Hold* (1913–14), *The Mud Bath* (1913–14).
Bonnard, Pierre (1867–1947)
French, born Paris; *Young Woman in Lamplight* (1900), *Dining Room in the Country* (1913), *Seascape of the Mediterranean* (1941).
Bosch, Hieronymus (Jerome von Aken) (c.1460–1516)
Dutch, born 's-Hertogenbosch, Brabant; *The Temptation of St Anthony*, *The Garden of Earthly Delights* (work undated).
Botticelli, Sandro (Alessandro di Mariano Filipepi) (1444–1510)
Italian, born Florence; *Primavera* (c.1478), *The Birth of Venus* (c.1485), *Mystic Nativity* (1500).
Braque, Georges (1882–1963)
French, born Argenteuil-sur-Seine; *Still Life with Violin* (1910), *The Portuguese* (1911), *Blue Wash-Basin* (1942).
Brueghel, Pieter (the Elder) (c.1525–69)
Dutch, born Bruegel, near Breda; *Road to Calvary* (1564), *Massacre of the Innocents* (c.1566), *The Blind Leading the Blind* (1568), *The Peasant Wedding* (1568), *The Peasant Dance* (1568).
Burne-Jones, Sir Edward (Coley) (1833–98)
British, born Birmingham; *The Beguiling of Merlin* (1874), *The Arming of Perseus* (1877), *King Cophetea and the Beggar Maid* (1880–4).
Burra, Edward (1905–76)
British, born London; *Dancing Skeletons* (1934), *Soldiers* (1942), *Scene in Harlem (Simply Heavenly)* (1952).

Canaletto (Giovanni Antonio Canal) (1697–1768)
Italian, born Venice; *Stone Mason's Yard* (c.1730).

ARTISTS (cont.)

Caravaggio, Michelangelo (Merisi da) (1573–1610)
Italian, born Caravaggio, near Burgamo; *The Supper at Emmaus* (c.1598–1600), *Martyrdom of St Matthew* (1599–1600), *The Death of the Virgin* (1605–6).

Cézanne, Paul (1839–1906)
French, born Aix-en-Provence; *The Black Marble Clock* (c.1869–70), *Maison du Pendu* (c.1873), *Bathing Women* (1900–5), *Le Jardinier* (1906).

Chagall, Marc (1887–1985)
Russian/French, born Vitebsk; *The Musician* (1912–13), *Bouquet of Flying Lovers* (1947).

Chirico, Giorgio de (1888–1978)
Italian, born Volos, Greece; *Portrait of Guillame Apollinaire* (1914), *The Jewish Angel* (1916), *The Return of Ulysses* (1968).

Cimabue (Cenni de Pepo) (c.1240–c.1302) Italian, born Florence; *Crucifix* (date unknown), *Saint John the Evangelist* (1302).

Claude Lorrain(e) (le Lorrain) (Claude Gêllée) (1600–82)
French, born near Nancy; *The Mill* (1631), *The Embarkation of St Ursula* (1641), *Ascanius Shooting the Stag of Silvia* (1682).

Constable, John (1776–1837)
English, born East Bergholt, Suffolk; *A Country Lane (c.1810)*, *The White Horse* (1819), *The Hay Wain* (1821), *Stonehenge* (1835).

Corot, (Jean Baptiste Camille) (1796–1875)
French, born Paris; *Bridge at Narni* (1827), *Souvenir de Marcoussis* (1869), *Woman Reading in a Landscape* (1869).

Correggio (Antonio Allegri) (c.1494–1534)
Italian, born Correggio; *The Agony in the Garden* (c.1528).

Courbet (Jean Désiré) Gustave (1819–77)
French, born Ornans; *The After-Dinner at Ornans* (1848–9), *The Bathers* (1853), *The Painter's Studio* (1855), *The Stormy Sea* (1869).

Cranach, Lucas (the Elder) (1472–1553)
German, born Kronach, near Bamberg; *The Crucifixion* (1503), *The Fountain of Youth* (1550).

Dali, Salvador (Felipe Jacinto) (1904–89)
Spanish, born Figueras, Gerona; *The Persistence of Memory* (1931), *The Transformation of Narcissus* (1934), *Christ of St John of the Cross* (1951).

David, Jacques Louis (1748–1825)
French, born Paris; *Death of Socrates* (1788), *The Death of Marat* (1793), *The Rape of the Sabines* (1799), *Madame Récamier* (1800).

Degas, (Hilaire Germain) Edgar (1834–1917)
French, born Paris; *Cotton-brokers Office* (1873), *L'Absinthe* (1875–6), *Little Fourteen-year-old Dancer* (sculpture) (1881), *Dancer at the Bar* (c.1900).

Delacroix, (Ferdinand Victor) Eugène (1798–1863)
French, born St-Maurice-Charenton; *Dante and Vergil in Hell* (1822), *Liberty Guiding the People* (1831), *Jacob and the Angel* (1853–61).

Delvaux, Paul (1897–1994)
Belgian, born Antheit, near Huys; *Vénus endormie* (1932), *Phases of the Moon* (1939), *In Praise of Melancholy* (1951).

Doré, (Louis Auguste) Gustave (1832–1883)
French, born Strasbourg; Illustrations to Dante's *Inferno* (1861), Milton's *Paradise Lost* (1866).

Duccio di Buoninsegna (c.1260–c.1320)
Italian; *Maestà* (Siena Cathedral alterpiece) (1308–11).
Duchamp, Marcel (1887–1968)
French/American, born Blainville, Normandy; *Nude descending a Staircase* (1912), *The Bride Stripped Bare by her Bachelors Even* (1915–23).
Dufy, Raoul (1877–1953)
French, born Le Havre; *Posters at Trouville* (1906), illustrations to Guillame Appollinaire's *Bestiary* (1911), *Riders in the Wood* (1931).

Eardley, Joan (1921–63)
British, born Warnham, Sussex; *Winter Sea IV* (1958), *Two Children* (1962).
Ernst, Max (1891–1976)
German/American/French, born Brühl, near Cologne, Germany; *Europe after the Rain* (1940–2), *The Elephant Célèbes* (1921), *Moonmad* (1944) (sculpture), *The King Playing with the Queen* (1959) (sculpture).
Eyck, Jan van (c.1389–1441)
Dutch, born Maaseyck, near Maastricht; *The Adoration of the Holy Lamb* (Ghent altarpiece) (1432), *Man in a Red Turban* (1433), *Arnolfni Marriage Portrait* (1434), *Madonna by the Fountain* (1439).

Fini, Léonor (1908–96)
Italian/Argentine, born Bueonos Aires; *The End of the World* (1944).
Freud, Lucian (1922–   )
German/British, born Berlin; *Woman with a Daffodil* (1945), *Interior in Paddington* (1951), *Hotel Room* (1953–4).
Friedrich, Caspar David (1774–1840)
German, born Pomerania; *The Cross in the Mountains* (1807–8).
Fuseli, Henri (Johann Heinrich Füssli) (1741–1825)
Swiss/English, born Zurich; *The Nightmare* (1781), *Appearance of the Ghost* (1796).

Gainsborough, Thomas (1727–88)
English, born Sudbury, Suffolk; *Peasant Girl Gathering Sticks* (1782), *The Watering Place* (1777).
Gauguin, (Eugène Henri) Paul (1848–1903)
French, born Paris; *The Vision after the Sermon* (1888), *Still Life with Three Puppies* (1888), *The White Horse* (1898), *Women of Tahiti* (1891), *Tahitian Landscape* (1891), *Where Do We Come From? What Are We? Where Are We Going?* (1897–8), *Golden Bodies* (1901).
Géricault, (Jean Louis André) Theodore (1791–1824)
French, born Rouen; *Officer of Light Horse* (c.1812), *Raft of the Medusa* (1819).
Ghirlandaio, Domenico (Domenico di Tommaso Bigordi) (1449–1494)
Italian, born Florence; *Virgin of Mercy* (1472), *St Jerome* (1480), *Nativity* (1485).
Giorgione (da Castelfranco), or Giorgio Barbarelli (c.1478–1511)
Italian, born Castelfranco; *The Tempest* (c.1508), *Three Philosophers* (c.1508), *Portrait of a Man* (1510).
Giotto (di Bondone) (c.1266–1337)
Italian, born near Florence; frescoes in *Arena Chapel*, Padua (1304–12), *Ognissanti Madonna* (1311–12).
Goes, Hugo van der (c.1440–82)
Dutch, born probably Ghent; *Portinari Alterpiece* (1475), *Ghent Altarpiece* (1495).
Goya (y Lucientes), Francisco (José) de (1746–1828)
Spanish, born Fuendetotos; *Family of Charles IV* (1799), *Los Desastres de la Guerra* (1810–14), *Black Paintings* (1820s).

ARTISTS (cont.)

Greco, El (Domenikos Theotokopoulos) (1541–1614)
Greek, born Candia, Crete; *Lady in Fur Wrap* (c.1577–8), *El Espolio* (The Disrobing of Christ) (1577–9), *The Saviour of the World* (1600), *Portrait of Brother Hortensio Felix Paravicino* (1609), *Toledo Landscape* (c.1610).

Grünewald, Matthias (Mathis Nithardt or **Gothardt)** (c.1480–1528)
German, born probably Würzburg; *Isenheim Altarpiece* (1515).

Hilliard, Nicholas (c.1547–1619)
English, born Exeter; miniature of *Queen Elizabeth I* (1572), *Henry Wriothesley* (1594).

Hockney, David (1937–   )
British, born Bradford, Yorkshire; *We Two Boys Together Clinging* (1961), *The Rake's Progress* (1963), *A Bigger Splash* (1967), *Invented Man Revealing a Still Life* (1975), *Dancer* (1980).

Hogarth, William (1697–1764)
English, born Smithfield, London; *Before and After* (1731), *A Rake's Progress* (1733–5).

Hokusai, Katsushika (1760–1849)
Japanese, born Tokyo; *Tametomo and the Demon* (1811), *Mangwa* (1814–19), *Hundred Views of Mount Fuji* (1835).

Holbein, Hans, 'the younger' (1497–1543)
German, born Augsburg; *Bonifacius Amerbach* (1519), *Solothurn Madonna* (1522), *Anne of Cleves* (1539).

Hundertwasser, Fritz (Friedrich Stowasser) (1928–   )
Austrian, born Vienna; *Many Transparent Heads* (1949–50), *The End of Greece* (1963), *The Court of Sulaiman* (1967).

Hunt, (William) Holman (1827–1910)
English, born London; *Our English Coasts* (1852), *Claudio and Isabella* (1853), *The Light of the World* (1854), *Isabella and the Pot of Basil* (1867).

Ingres, Jean Auguste Dominique (1780–1867)
French, born Montauban; *Gilbert* (1805), *La Sources* (1807–59), *Bather* (1808), *Turkish Bath* (1863).

John, Augustus (Edwin) (1878–1961)
British, born Tenby; *The Smiling Woman* (1908), *Portrait of a Lady in Black* (1917).

John, Gwen (1876–1939)
British, born Haverfordwest, Pembrokeshire; *Girl with bare shoulders* (1909–10).

Kandinsky, Vasily or Wasily (1866–1944)
Russian/French, born Moscow; *Kossacks* (1910–11), *Swinging* (1925), *Two Green Points* (1935), *Sky Blue* (1940).

Kirchner, Ernst Ludwig (1880–1938)
German, born Aschaffenburg; *Recumbent Blue Nude with Straw Hat* (1908–9), *The Drinker* (1915), *Die Amselfluh* (1923).

Kitaj, R(onald) B(rooks) (1932–   )
American, born Cleveland, Ohio; *The Orientalists*, *The Ohio Gang* (1964), *If not, not* (1975–6).

Klee, Paul (1879–1940)
Swiss, born Münchenbuchsee, near Berne; *Der Vollmond* (1919), *Rosegarden* (1920), *A tiny tale of a tiny dwarf* (1925), *Fire in the Evening* (1929), *Twittering Machine*.

Klimt, Gustav (1862–1918)
Austrian, born Baumgarten, near Vienna; *Music* (1895), *The Kiss* (1907–8), *Judith II* (Salome) (1909).
Kokoschka, Oskar (1886–1980)
Austrian/British, born Pöchlarn; *The Dreaming Boys* (1908).

Landseer, Sir Edwin (Henry) (1803–73)
English, born London; *The Old Shepherd's Chief Mourner* (1837), *The Monarch of the Glen* (1850).
La Tour, Georges (Dumesnil) de (1593–1652)
French, born Vic-sur-Seille, Lorraine; *St Jerome Reading* (1620s), *The Denial of St Peter* (1650).
Léger, Fernand (1881–1955)
French, born Argentan; *Contrast of Forms* (1913), *Black Profile* (1928), *The Great Parade* (1954).
Lely, Sir Peter (Pietar van der Faes) (1618–80)
Dutch/British, born Soest, Westphalia; *The Windsor Beauties* (1668), *Admirals* series (1666–7).
Leonardo da Vinci (1452–1519)
Italian, born Vinci; *The Last Supper* (1495–7), *Madonna and Child with St Anne* (begun 1503), *Mona Lisa* (1500–6), *The Virgin of the Rocks* (c.1508).
Lichtenstein, Roy (1923–   )
American, born New York City; *Whaam!* (1963), *As I Opened Fire* (1964).
Lippi, Fra Filippo, called Lippo (c.1406–69)
Italian, born Florence; *Tarquinia Madonna* (1437), *Barbadori Altarpiece* (begun 1437).
Lochner, Stefan (c.1400–1451)
German, born Meersburg am Bodense; *The Adoration of the Magi* (c.1448), triptych in Cologne Cathedral.

Macke, August (1887–1914)
German, born Meschede; *Greeting* (1912), *The Zoo* (1912), *Girls Under Trees* (1914).
Magritte, René (François Ghislain) (1898–1967)
Belgian, born Lessines, Hainault; *The Menaced Assassin* (1926), *Loving Perspective* (1935), *Presence of Mind* (1960).
Manet, Édouard (1932–83)
French, born Paris; *Déjeuner sur l'herbe* (1863), *Olympia* (1865), *A Bar at the Folies-Bergère* (1882).
Mantegna, Andrea (1431–1506)
Italian, born Vicenza; *Madonna of Victory* (altarpiece), *San Zeno Altarpiece* (1457–9), *Triumphs of Caesar* (c.1486–94).
Martin, John (1789–1854)
English, born Haydon Bridge; *Joshua Commanding the Sun to Stand Still* (1816), *The Last Judgement* (1851–4).
Martini, Simone (c.1284–1344)
Italian, born Siena; *S Caterina Polyptych* (1319), *Annunciation* (1333).
Masaccio (Tomaso di Ser Mone) (1401–28)
Italian, born Castel San Giovanni di Val d'Arno; *polyptych* for the *Carmelite Church* in Pisa (1426), frescoes in *Sta Maria del Carmine*, Florence, (1424–7).
Masson, André (1896–1987)
French, born Balgny, Oise; *Massacres* (1933), *The Labyrinth* (1939).
Matisse, Henri (Emile Benoît) (1869–1954)
French, born Le Cateau-Cambrésis; *La Desserte* (1908), *Notre Dame* (1914), *The Large Red Studio* (1948), *L'Escargot* (1953).

ARTISTS (cont.)

Michelangelo (Michelangelo di Lodovico Buonarroti Simoni) (1475–1564)
Italian, born Caprese, Tuscany; *The Pietà* (1497) (sculpture), *David* (1501–4) (sculpture), *Madonna* (c.1502), ceiling of the *Sistine Chapel*, Rome (1508–12), *The Last Judgement* (begun 1537).

Millais, Sir John Everett (1829–96)
English, born Southampton; *Ophelia* (1851–2), *The Bridesmaid* (1851), *Tennyson* (1881), *Bubbles* (1886).

Millet, Jean François (1814–75)
French, born Grouchy; *Sower* (1850), *The Gleaners* (1857).

Mondrian, Piet (Pieter Cornelis Mondriaan) (1872–1944)
Dutch, born Amersfoort; *Still Life with Gingerpot II* (1911), *Composition with red, black, blue, yellow, and grey* (1920), *Broadway Boogie-Woogie* (1942–3).

Monet, Claude (1840–1926)
French, born Paris; *Impression: Sunrise* (1872), *Haystacks* (1890–1), *Rouen Cathedral* (1892–5), *Water-lilies* (1899 onwards).

Moreau, Gustave (1826–98)
French, born Paris; *Oedipus and the Sphinx* (1864), *Apparition* (1876), *Jupiter and Semele* (1889–95).

Morisot, Berthe (1841–95)
French, born Bourges; *The Harbour at Cherbourg* (1874), *In the Dining Room* (1886).

Morris, William (1834–96)
British, born Walthamstow; *Queen Guinevere* (1858).

Motherwell, Robert (1915–91)
American, born Aberdeen, Washington; *Gauloises* (1967), *Opens* (1968–72).

Munch, Edvard (1863–1944)
Norwegian, born Löten; *The Scream* (1895), *Mother and Daughter* (c.1897), *Self-Portrait between the clock and the bed* (1940–2).

Nash, Paul (1899–1946)
British, born London; *We Are Making a New World* (1918), *Menin Road* (1919).

Newman, Barnett (1905–70)
American, born New York; *The Moment* (1946), *Onement I* (1948), *Vir Heroicus Sublimis* (1950–1).

Nicholson, Ben (1894–1982)
British, born Denham, London; *White Relief* (1935), *November 11, 1947* (1947).

Nicholson, Winifred (1893–1981)
British, born Oxford; *Honeysuckle and Sweet Peas* (1950), *The Copper and Capari* (1967), *The Gate to The Isles* (1980).

Nolde, Emil (1867–1956)
German, born Nolde; *The Missionary* (1912), *Candle Dancers* (1912).

Oliver, Isaac (c.1560–1617)
French/English, born Rouen; *Self-Portrait* (c.1590), *Henry, Prince of Wales* (c.1612).

Palmer, Samuel (1805–81)
English, born London; *Repose of the Holy Family* (1824), *The Magic Apple Tree* (1830), *Opening the Fold* (1880).

Parmigiano, or Pamiganino (Girolamo Francesco Maria Mazzola) (1503–40)
Italian, born Parma; frescoes in *S Giovanni Evangelista*, Parma (c.1522), *Self-Portrait in a convex mirror* (1524), *Vision of St Jerome* (1526–7), *Madonna Altarpiece*, Bologna (c.1528–30), *The Madonna of the Long Neck* (c.1535).

Pasmore, Victor (1908–)
  British, born Chelsham, Surrey; *The Evening Star* (1945–7), *Black Symphony — the Pistol Shot* (1977).
Peploe, S(amuel) J(ohn) (1871–1935)
  Scottish, born Edinburgh; one of the 'Scottish colourists'; *Boats of Royan* (1910).
Perugino (Pietro di Cristoforo Vannucci) (c.1450–1523)
  Italian, born Città della Pieve, Umbria; *Christ giving the Keys to Peter* (fresco in the Sistine Chapel) (c.1483).
Picabia, Francis (1879–1953)
  French, born Paris; *I See Again in Memory my Dear Undine* (1913), *The Kiss* (1924).
Picasso, Pablo (Ruiz y) (1881–1973)
  Spanish, born Málaga; *Mother and Child* (1921), *Three Dances* (1925), *Guernica* (1937), *The Charnel House* (1945), *The Artist and his Model* (1968).
Piero della Francesca (c.1420–92)
  Italian, born Borgo san Sepolcro; *Madonna of the Misericordia* (1445–8), *Resurrection* (c.1450).
Piper, John (1903–92)
  English, born Epsom; *Windor Castle* watercolours (1941–2), *Council Chamber, House of Commons* (1941); also stage designs and illustrated publications.
Pissarro, Camille (1830–1903)
  French, born St Thomas, Danish W Indies; *Landscape at Chaponval* (1880), *The Boieldieu Bridge at Rouen* (1896), *Boulevard Montmartre* (1897).
Pollock, (Paul) Jackson (1912–56)
  American, born Cody, Wyoming; *No 14* (1948), *Guardians of the Secret* (1943).
Poussin, Nicolas (1594–1665)
  French, born Les Andelys, Normandy; *The Adoration of the Golden Calf* (1624), *Inspiration of the Poet* (c.1628), *Seven Sacraments* (1644–8), *Self-Portrait* (1650).

Raeburn, Sir Henry (1756–1823)
  Scottish, born Edinburgh; *Rev Robert Walker Skating* (1784), *Isabella McLeod, Mrs James Gregory* (c.1798).
Ramsay, Allan (1713–84)
  Scottish, born Edinburgh; *The Artist's Wife* (1754–5).
Raphael (Raffaello Sanzio) (1483–1520)
  Italian, born Urbino; *Assumption of the Virgin* (1504), *Madonna of the Meadow* (1505–6), *Transfiguration* (1518–20).
Redon, Odilon (1840–1916)
  French, born Bordeaux; *Woman with outstretched arms* (c.1910–14).
Redpath, Anne (1895–1965)
  Scottish, born Galashiels; *Pinks* (1947).
Rembrandt (Harmenszoon van Rijn) (1606–69)
  Dutch, born Leiden; *Anatomy Lesson of Dr Tulp* (1632), *Blinding of Samson* (1636), *The Night Watch* (1642), *The Conspiracy of Claudius* (1661–2).
Renoir, Pierre Auguste (1841–1919)
  French, born Limoges; *Woman in Blue* (1874), *Woman Reading* (1876), *The Bathers* (1887).
Reynolds, Sir Joshua (1723–92)
  English, born Plympton Earls, near Plymouth; *Portrait of Miss Bowles with her dog* (1775), *Master Henry Hoare* (1788).
Riley, Bridget (Louise) (1931–)
  British, born London; *Pink Landscapes* (1959–60), *Zig-Zag* (1961), *Fall* (1963), *Apprehend* (1970).

ARTISTS (cont.)

Rosa, Salvator (1615–73)
Italian, born Arenella, near Naples; *Self-Portrait with a Skull* (1656), *Humana Fragilitas* (c.1657).

Rosetti, Dante Gabriel (1828–82)
British, born London; *Beat Beatrix* (1849–50), *Ecce Ancilla Domini!* (1850), *Astarte Syriaca* (1877).

Rothko, Mark (1903–70)
Latvian/American, born Dvinsk; *The Omen of the Eagle* (1942), *Red on Maroon* (1959).

Rousseau, Henri, known as **Le Douanier** (1844–1910)
French, born Laval; *Monsieur et Madame Stevens* (1884), *Sleeping Gipsy* (1897), *Portrait of Joseph Brunner* (1909).

Rubens, Sir Peter Paul (1577–1640)
Flemish, born Siegen, Westphalia; *Marchesa Brigida Spinola-Doria* (1606), *Hélène Fourment with two of her Children* (c.1637).

Sargent, John Singer (1856–1925)
American, born Florence; *Madame X* (1884), *Lady Agnew* (1893), *Gassel* (1918).

Schiele, Egon (1890–1918)
Austrian, born Tulln; *Autumn Tree* (1909), *Pregnant Woman and Death* (1911), *Edith Seated* (1917–18).

Seurat, Georges (Pierre) (1859–91)
French, born Paris; *Bathers at Asnières* (1884), *Sunday on the Island of La Grande Jatte* (1885–6), *Le Cirque* (1891).

Sickert, Walter (Richard) (1860–1942)
British, born Munich; *La Hollandaise* (1905–6), *Ennui* (c.1914).

Sisley, Alfred (1839–99)
French, born Paris; *Avenue of Chestnut Trees near La Celle Saint-Cloud* (1868), *Mosley Weir, Hampton Court* (1874).

Spencer, Sir Stanley (1891–1959)
British, born Cookham-on-Thames, Berkshire; *The Resurrection* (1927), *The Leg of Mutton Nude* (1937).

Steen, Jan (1627–79)
Dutch, born Leiden; *A Woman at her Toilet* (1663), *The World upside Down* (1663).

Stubbs, George (1724–1806)
English, born Liverpool; *James Stanley* (1755), *Anatomy of the Horse* (1766), *Hambletonian, Rubbing Town* (1799).

Sutherland, Graham (Vivian) (1903–80)
British, born London; *Entrance to a Lane* (1939), *Crucifixion* (1946), *A Bestiary and some Correspondences* (1968).

Tanguy, Yves (1900–55)
French/American, born Paris; *He did what he wanted* (1927), *The Invisibles* (1951).

Tintoretto, (Jacopo Robusti) (1518–94)
Italian, born probably Venice; *The Miracle of the Slave* (1548), *St George and the Dragon* (c.1558), *The Golden Calf* (c.1560).

Titian, (Tiziano Vecellio) (c.1488–1576)
Italian, born Pieve di Cadore; *The Assumption of the Virgin* (1516–18), *Bacchus and Ariadne* (1522–3), *Pesaro Madonna* (1519–26), *Crowning with Thorns* (c.1570).

Toulouse-Lautrec, Henri (Marie Raymond de) (1864–1901)
  French, born Albi; *The Jockey* (1899), *At the Moulin Rouge* (1895), *The Modiste* (1900).
Turner, Joseph Mallord William (1775–1851)
  English, born London; *Frosty Morning* (1813), *The Shipwreck* (1805), *Crossing the Brook* (1815),
  The Fighting Téméraire (1839), *Rain, Steam and Speed* (1844).

Uccello, Paolo (Paolo di Dono) (c.1396–1475)
  Italian, born Pratovecchio; *The Flood* (c.1445), *The Rout of San Romano* (1454–7).
Utamaro, Kitagawa (1753–1806)
  Japanese, born Edo (modern Tokyo); *Ohisa* (c.1788), *The Twelve Hours of the Green Houses*
  (c.1795).

Van Dyck, Sir Anthony (1599–1641)
  Flemish, born Antwerp; *Marchesa Elena Grimaldi* (c.1625), *The Deposition* (1634–5), *Le Roi à la
  chasse* (c.1638).
Van Gogh, Vincent (Willem) (1853–90)
  Dutch, born Groot-Zundert, near Breda; *The Potato Eaters* (1885), *Self-Portrait with Bandaged Ear*
  (1888), *The Harvest* (1888), *The Sunflowers* (1888), *Starry Night* (1889), *Cornfields with Flight of
  Birds* (1890).
Velázquez, Diego (Rodríguez de Silva) (1599–1660)
  Spanish, born Seville; *The Immaculate Conception* (c.1618), *The Waterseller of Seville* (c.1620),
  The Surrender of Breda (1634–5), *Pope Innocent X* (1650), *Las Meninas* (c.1656).
Vermeer, Jan (1632–75)
  Dutch, born Delft; *The Astronomer* (1668), *Christ in the House of Mary and Martha* (date unknown),
  A Lady with a Gentleman at the Virginals (c.1665), *The Lacemaker* (date unknown).
Veronese, Paolo (Paolo Caliari) (1528–88)
  Italian, born Verona; *The Feast in the House of Levi* (1573), *Marriage at Cana* (1573), *Triumph of
  Venice* (c.1585).
Verrocchio, Andrea del (Andrea di Cioni) (c.1435–c.1488) Italian, born Florence; *Baptism of Christ*
  (c.1470), *David* (c.1475) (sculpture).

Warhol, Andy (Andrew Warhola) (1828–87)
  American, born McKeesport, Pennsylvania; *Marilyn* (1962), *Electric Chair* (1963).
Watteau, (Jean) Antoine (1684–1721)
  French, born Valenciennes; *The Pilgrimage to the Island of Cythera* (1717), *L'Enseigne de Gersaint*
  (1721).
Whistler, James (Abbott) McNeill (1834–1903)
  American, born Lowell, Massachusetts; *The Artist's Mother* (1871), *Nocturne in blue and silver: Old
  Battersea Bridge* (1872–5), *Falling Rocket* (1875).
Wilkie, Sir David (1785–1841)
  Scottish, born Cults, Fife; *The Village Politicians* (1806), *Chelsea Pensioners Reading the Waterloo
  Despatch* (1822).
Wood, Grant (1891–1942)
  American, born Iowa; *American Gothic* (1930), *Spring Turning* (1936).
Wright, Joseph ('of Derby') (1734–97)
  English, born Derby; *Experiment with an Air Pump* (1766), *The Alchemist in Search of the
  Philosopher's Stone Discovers Phosphorous* (1795).
Wyeth, Andrew (Newell) (1917–)
  American, born Chadds Ford, Pennsylvania; *Christina's World* (1948).

SCULPTORS

Selected works are listed.

Arp, Hans (Jean) (1887–1966)
French, born Strasbourg; *Eggboard* (1922), *Kore* (1958).

Barlach, Ernst (1870–1938)
German, born Wedel; *Moeller-Jarke Tomb* (1901), *Have Pity!* (1919).

Bernini, Gianlorenzo (1598–1680)
Italian, born Naples; *Neptune and Triton* (1620), *David* (1623), *Ecstasy of St Theresa* (1640s), *Fountain of the Four Rivers* (1648–51).

Bologna, Giovanni da (Jean de Boulogne) (1529–1608)
French, born Douai; *Mercury* (1564–5), *Rape of the Sabines* (1579–83).

Brancusi, Constantin (1876–1957)
Romanian/French, born Hobitza, Gorj; *The Kiss* (1909), *Torso of a Young Man* (1922).

Calder, Alexander (1898–1976)
American, born Philadelphia, Pennsylvania; *Stabiles and Mobiles* (1932), *A Universe* (1934).

Caro, Sir Anthony (1924–)
English, born London; *Sailing Tonight* (1971–74), *Veduggio Sound* (1973), *Ledge Piece* (1978).

Cellini, Benvenuto (1500–71)
Italian, born Florence; salt cellar of *Neptune and Ceres* (1543), *Cosimo de 'Medici* (1545–7), *Perseus with the Head of Medusa* (1564).

Donatello (Donato di Niccolo di Betti di Bardi) (c.1386–1466)
Italian, born Florence; *St Mark* (1411–12), *St George Killing the Dragon* (c.1417), *Feast of Herod* (1423–37), *David, Judith and Holofernes*, Piazza della Signoria, Florence.

Epstein, Sir Jacob (1880–1959)
American/British, born New York; *Rima* (1925), *Genesis* (1930), *Ecce Homo* (1934–5), *Christ in Majesty* (Llandaff Cathedral), *St Michael and the Devil* (on the façade of Coventry Cathedral) (1958–9), *Adam* (1939).

Frink, Dame Elizabeth (1930–93)
British, born Thurlow, Suffolk; *Horse Lying Down* (1975), *Running Man* (1985), *Seated Man* (1986).

Gaudier-Brzeska, Henri (1891–1915)
French, born St Jean de Braye, near Orléans; *Red stone dancer* (1913).

Ghiberti, Lorenzo (di Cione di Ser Buonaccorso) (c.1378–1455)
Italian, born in or near Florence; *St John the Baptist* (1412–15), *St Matthew* (1419–22), *The Gates of Paradise* (1425–52).

Giacometti, Alberto (1901–66)
Swiss, born Bogonova, near Stampa; *Head* (c.1928), *Woman with her Throat Cut* (1932).

Goldsworthy, Andy (1956–)
British, born Cheshire; *Hazel Stick Throws* (1980), *Slate Cone* (1988), *The Wall* (1988–9).

González, Julio (1876–1942)
Spanish, born Barcelona; *Angel* (1933), *Woman Combing her Hair* (1936), *Cactus People* (1930–40).

Hepworth, Dame (Jocelyn) Barbara (1903–75)
British, born Wakefield, Yorkshire; *Figure of a Woman* (1929–30), *Large and Small Forms* (1945), *Single Form* (1963).

Leonardo Da Vinci (1452–1519)
Italian, born Vinci, between Pisa and Florence; *St John the Baptist.*

Michelangelo (Michelangelo di Lodovico Buonarotti) (1475–1564)
Italian, born Caprese, Tuscany; *Cupid* (1495), *Bacchus* (1496), *Pieta* (1497), *David* (c.1500).
Moore, Henry (Spencer) (1898–1986)
British, born Castleford, Yorkshire; *Recumbent figure* (1938), *Fallen Warrior* (1956–7).

Paolozzi, Eduardo Luigi (1924–)
Scottish, born Leith, Edinburgh; *Krokodeel* (c.1956–7), *Japanese War God* (1958), *Medea* (1964), *Piscator* (1981), *Manuscript of Monte Cassino*, Edinburgh (1991).
Pheidias (c.490–c.417 BC)
Greek, born Athens; *Athena Promachos* (460–450 BC), marble sculptures of the *Parthenon* (447–432 BC).
Pisano, Andrea (c.1270–1349)
Italian, born Pontedera; bronze doors of the *Baptistry* of Florence (1330–6).
Pisano, Giovanni (c.1248–c.1320)
Italian, born Pisa; *Fontana Magiore*, Perugia (1278), *Duomo pulpit*, Pisa (1302–10).
Pisano, Nicola (c.1225–c.1284)
Italian, birthplace unknown; *Baptistry* at Pisa (1260).
Praxiteles (5th-c BC)
Greek, born probably Athens; *Hermes Carrying the Boy Dionysus* (date unknown).

Robbia, Luca della (Luca di Simone di Marco) (c.1400–1482)
Italian, born Florence; *Cantoria* (1432–7).
Rodin, (François) Auguste (René) (1840–1917)
French, born Paris; *The Age of Bronze* (1875–6), *The Gates of Hell* (1880–1917), *The Burghers of Calais* (1884), *The Thinker* (1904).

Schwitters, Kurt (1887–1948)
German, born Hanover; *Merzbau* (1920–43).

Tinguely, Jean (1925–91)
Swiss, born Fribourg; *Baluba No 3* (1959), *Métamécanique No 9* (1959), *Homage to New York* (1960), *EOSX* (1967).

ARCHITECTS

Aalto, Alvar (1898–1976)
Finnish, born Kuortane; *Convalescent Home*, Paimio, near Turku (1929–30), *Town Hall*, Saynatsab (1950–2), *Finlandia Concert Hall*, Helsinki (1971).
Adam, Robert (1728–92)
Scottish, born Kirkcaldy; *Adelphi*, London (1769–71, demolished 1936), *General Register House* (begun 1774), *Charlotte Square* (1791), *Edinburgh University* (1789–94) — all Edinburgh; *Culzean Castle*, Ayrshire (1772–92).

ARCHITECTS (cont.)

Adam, William (1689–1748)
  Scottish, born Maryburgh; *Hopetoun House*, near Edinburgh (1721).
Alberti, Leone Battista (1404–72)
  Italian, born Genoa; facade of the *Palazzo Recellai*, Florence (1460), *San Andrea*, Mantua (1470).
Anthemias of Tralles (dates unknown)
  Greek, born Tralles, Lydia; *Hagia Sophia*, Constantinople (now Istanbul) (532–7).
Apollodorus of Damascus (dates unknown)
  Greek, born Syria; *Trajan's Forum*, Rome, *The Baths of Trajan*, Rome.
Arnolfo di Cambio (1232–1302)
  Italian, born Colledi Valdelsa, Tuscany; *Florence Cathedral* (1299–1310).
Asplund, Erik Gunnar (1885–1940)
  Swedish, born Stockholm; *Stockholm City Library* (1924–7), *Law Courts*, Gothenburg (1934–7).

Baker, Sir Herbert (1862–1946)
  English, born Kent; *Groote Schuur*, near Cape Town (1892–1902), *Union Government Buildings*, Pretoria (1907).
Barry, Sir Charles (1795–1860)
  English, born London; *Royal Institution of the Arts*, Manchester (1824), *Houses of Parliament*, London (opened 1852).
Behrens, Peter (1868–1940)
  German, born Hamburg; *Turbine Assembly Works*, Berlin (1909), *German Embassy*, St Petersburg (1912).
Berlage, Hendrick Petrus (1856–1934)
  Dutch, born Amsterdam; *Amsterdam Bourse* (1903), *Holland House*, London (1914), *Gemeente Museum*, the Hague (1934).
Bernini, Gian Lorenzo (1598–1680)
  Italian, born Naples; *St Peter's Baldacchino*, Rome (1625).
Borromini, Francesco (1599–1667)
  Italian, born Bissone, on Lake Lugano; *S Carlo alle Quattro Fontane* (1637–41), *S Ivo* (1642–61), both Rome.
Boullée, Étienne-Louis (1728–99)
  French, born Paris; *Hôtel de Brunoy*, Paris (1772), *Monument to Isaac Newton* (never built) (1794).
Bramante, Donato (Donato di Pascuccion d'Antonio) (1444–1514)
  Italian, born near Urbino; *San Maria presso S Satiro*, Milan (begun 1482), *Tempietto of S Pietro*, Rome (1502).
Breuer, Marcel Lajos (1902–81)
  Hungarian–American, born Pécs; *UNESCO Building*, Paris (1953–8).
Brosse, Salomon de (1565–1626)
  French, born Verneuil-sur-Oise; *Luxembourg Palace*, Paris (1615–20), *Louis XIII's Hunting Lodge*, Versailles (1624–6).
Brunelleschi, Filippo (1377–1446)
  Italian, born Florence; *San Lorenzo*, Florence (begun 1418), *dome* of *Florence Cathedral* (begun 1420), *Ospedale degli Innocenti*, Florence (1419).
Bryce, David (1803–76)
  Scottish, born Edinburgh; *Fettes College* (1863–9), *Royal Infirmary* (begun 1870) — both Edinburgh.
Burnham, David Hudson (1846–1912)
  American, born Henderson, New York; *Reliance Building*, Chicago (1890–5), *Monadnock Building*, Chicago (1890–1), *Selfridge Building*, London (1908).

Burton, Decimus (1800–81)
English, born London; *Regents Park Colosseum* (1823), *Arch at Hyde Park Corner* (1825) — both London.
Butterfield, William (1814–1900)
English, born London; *Keble College*, Oxford (1866–86), *St Augustine's College*, Canterbury (1844–73), *All Saints'*, Margaret Street, London (1849–59).

Campen, Jacob van (1595–1657)
Dutch, born Haarlem; *Maurithuis*, The Hague (1633), *Amsterdam Theatre* (1637), *Amsterdam Town Hall* (1647–55).
Candela, Felix (1910–)
Spanish–Mexican, born Madrid; *Sports Palace* for Olympic Games, Mexico City (1968).
Chambers, Sir William (1726–96)
Scottish, born Stockholm; *Somerset House* (1776), pagoda in *Kew Gardens* (1757) — both London.
Chermayeff, Serge (1900–96)
American, born the Caucasus; *De La Warr Pavilion*, Bexhill-on-Sea (1933–5).
Churriguera, Don José (1650–1725)
Spanish, born Salamanca; *Salamanca Cathedral* (1692–4).
Coates, Wells Wintemute (1895–1958)
English, born Tokyo; *BBC Studios* (1932), *EKCO Laboratories* (1936), *Cinema*, Festival of Great Britain Exhibition (1951).
Cockerell, Charles Robert (1788–1863)
English, born London; *Taylorian Institute*, Oxford (1841–5), *Fitzwilliam Museum*, Cambridge (1837–40).
Cortona, Pietro Berrettini da (1596–1669)
Italian, born Cortona; *Villa Sacchetti*, Castel Fusano (1626–7), *San Firenze*, Florence (1645).

Dance, George the elder (1700–68)
English, born London; *Mansion House*, London (1739).
Dance, George the younger (1741–1825)
English, born London; rebuilt *Newgate Prison* (1770–83).
Delorme, Philibert (c.1510–70)
French, born Lyons; *Tuileries* (1565–70), *Châteaux of Anet*, Meudon (1547–55).
Doesburg, Theo van (originally **Christian Emil Marie Kupper**) (1883–1931)
Dutch, born Utrecht; *L'Art Nouveau Shop*, Paris (1896), *Keller und Reiner Art Gallery*, Berlin (1898).
Doshi, Balkrishna Vithaldas (1927–)
Indian, born Poona; *City Hall*, Toronto (1958), *Indian Institute of Management*, Ahmedabad (1951–7).
Dudok, Willem Marinus (1884–1974)
Dutch, born Amsterdam; *Hilversum Town Hall* (1928–30), *Bijenkorf Department Store*, Rotterdam (1929).

Engel, Johann Carl Ludwig (1778–1840)
Finnish, born Berlin; layout of Helsinki (1818–26).
Erickson, Arthur Charles (1924–)
Canadian, born Vancouver; *Simon Fraser University Buildings*, British Columbia (1963), *Lethbridge University*, Alberta (1971).
Fischer von Erlach, Johann Bernard (1656–1723)
Austrian, born Graz; *Kariskirche*, Vienna (1716), *Hofbibliotek*, Vienna (1723), *Kollegienkirche*, Salzburg (1707).

ARCHITECTS (cont.)

Foster, Sir Norman (1935–   )
English, born Manchester; *Willis Faber Dumas Building*, Ipswich (1975), *Sainsbury Centre*, University of East Anglia (1978), *Hong Kong and Shanghai Bank*, Hong Kong (1979–85).

Francesco di Giorgio (1439–1501/2) Italian, born Siena; *Church of San Bernardino all'Osservanza*, Siena (1474–84), *Palazzo Ducale*, Gubbio (1476–82).

Gabriel, Ange-Jacques (1698–1782)
French, born Paris; *Pavillon de Pompadour*, Fontainebleu (begun 1749), Paris; layout of *Place de la Concorde*, Paris (1753), *Petit Trianon*, Versailles (1761–8).

Garnier, Tony (Antoine) (1869–1948)
French, born Lyons; *Grange Blanche Hospital*, Lyons (1911–27), *Stadium*, Lyons (1913–18), *Hôtel de Ville*, Boulogne-Bilancourt (1931–3).

Gaudí, Antonio y Cornet (1852–1926)
Spanish, born Reus, Tarragona; *Casa Vicens* (1878–80), *Sagrada Familia* (1884 onwards), *Casa Battló* (1904–17), *Casa Milá* (1905–9) — all Barcelona.

Geddes, Sir Patrick (1854–1932)
Scottish, born Perth; *Ramsay Gardens*, Edinburgh (1892), *Edinburgh Zoo* (1913), *Scots College*, Montpelier, France (1924).

Gibbs, James (1682–1754)
Scottish, born Aberdeen; *St-Martin-in-the-Fields*, London (1722–6), *King's College Fellows' Building*, Cambridge (1724–49).

Gilbert, Cass (1859–1934)
American, born Zanesville, Ohio; *Woolworth Building*, New York City (1913).

Gilly, Friedrich (1772–1800)
German, born Berlin; *Funerary Precinct and Temple* to Frederick II, the Great of Prussia (1796), *Prussian National Theatre*, Berlin (1798).

Giotto de Bondone (c.1266–1337)
Italian, born Vespignano, near Florence; *Campanile*, Florence Cathedral (from 1334).

Giulio Romano (properly Giulio Pippi de' Giannuzzi) (c.1492–1546)
Italian, born Rome; *Oakazzi dek Te'*, Mantua (1524), church of *S Petronio* façade, Bologna (1546).

Greenway, Francis Howard (1777–1837)
British/Australian, born Bristol; *Macquarie Lighthouse*, Sydney Harbour (1818), *St James' Church*, Sydney (1824).

Gropius, Walter (1883–1969)
German/American, born Berlin; *Fagus Shoe Factory*, Alfeld (1911), *The Bauhaus*, Dessau (1925) — both Germany; *Harvard University Graduate Centre* (1950), USA.

Guarini, Guarino, (originally Camillo) (1624–83)
Italian, born Modena; *San Lorenzo* church, Turin (1688–80), *Capella della SS Sindone* church, Turin (1668), *Palazzo Carignano*, Racconigi (1679).

Hamilton, Thomas (1784–1858)
Scottish, born Glasgow; *Royal High School* (1825–9), *Royal College of Physicians Hall* (1844–5), *George IV Bridge* (1827–34) — all Edinburgh.

Haussmann, Georges Eugène (1809–91)
French, born Paris; layout of *Bois de Boulogne, Bois de Vincennes*, Paris (1853–1870).

Hawksmoor, Nicholas (1661–1736)
English, born Nottinghamshire; *St Mary Woolnoth* church (1716–24), *St George's*, Bloomsbury (1716–30) — both London.

Hildebrandt, Johann Lukas von (1668–1745)
Austrian, born Genoa; *Lower and Upper Belvedere*, Vienna, (1714–15, 1720–3).

Hoffmann, Josef (1870–1956)
Austrian architect, born Pirnitz; *Purkersdorf Sanatorium* (1903–5), *Stociet House*, Brussels (1905–11).

Holland, Henry (1746–1806)
English, born London; *Carlton House*, London (1783–96), *Brighton Pavilion* (1787).

Howard, Sir Ebenezer (1850–1928)
English, born London; *Letchworth Garden City* (1903).

Ikinos and **Callicrates** (dates and place of birth unknown)
Greek; *The Parthenon*, Athens (447/6–438 BC).

Jacobsen, Arne (1902–71)
Danish, born Copenhagen; *Town Hall of Aarhus* (with Erik Moller, 1938–42), *Town Hall of Rodovre* (1955–6), *SAS Tower*, Copenhagen (1960) — all Denmark; new *St Catherine's College*, Oxford (1959).

Jefferson, Thomas (1743–1826)
American, born Shadwell, Virginia; *'Monticello'*, Albermale County (1769), *Virginia State Capitol* (1796).

Johnson Philip Cortelyou (1906–   )
American, born Cleveland, Ohio; *Glass House*, New Canaan, Connecticut (1949–50), *Seagram Building*, New York City (1945), *Amon Carter Museum of Western Art*, Texas (1961), *New York State Theater*, Lincoln Center (1964).

Jones, Inigo (1573–1652)
English, born London; *The Queen's House*, Greenwich (1616–18, 1629–35), *Banqueting House*, Whitehall, London (1619–22).

Kahn, Louis Isadore (1901–74)
American architect, born Osel (now Saaremaa, Estonia); *Richards Medical Research Building*, Pennsylvania (1957–61), *City Tower Municipal Building*, Philadelphia (1952–7).

Kent, William (1685–1748)
English, born Bridlington; *Holkham Hall* (begun 1734).

Labrouste, (Pierre François) Henri (1801–75)
French, born Paris; *Bibliothèque Sainte Geneviève* (1838–50), *Bibliothèque Nationale* reading room (1860–7) — both Paris.

Lasdun, Sir Denys Louis (1914–   )
English, born London; *Royal College of Musicians* (1958–64), *National Theatre* (1965–76) — both London.

Le Corbusier, (Charles-Edouard Jeanneret) (1887–1966)
French, born La Chaux-de-Fonds, Switzerland; *Salvation Army Hostel*, Paris (begun 1929), *Chapel of Ronchamp*, near Belfort (1950–4), *Museum of Modern Art*, Tokyo (1957).

Ledoux, Claude Nicolas (1736–1806)
French, born Dormans, Champagne; *Château*, Louveciennes (1771–3), *Theatre*, Besançon (1771–3).

Leonardo da Vinci (1452–1519)
Italian, born Vinci; *Mariolo de Guiscardi House*, Milan (1497), *La Veruca Fortress*, near Pisa (1504), *Villa Melzi*, Vaprio, Milan (1513).

ARCHITECTS (cont.)

Lescot, Pierre (c.1510–78)
French, born Paris; rebuilt one wing of the *Louvre*, Paris (1546), screen of *St Germain l'Auxerrois* (1541–4).

Lethaby, William Richard (1857–1931)
English, born Barnstaple; *Avon Tyrell*, Christchurch, Hampshire (1891–2), *Eagle Insurance Buildings*, Birmingham (1899–1900).

Le Vau, or Levau, Louis (1612–70)
French, born Paris; *Hôtel Lambert*, Paris (1640–4), part of *Palace of Versailles* (from 1661), *Collège des Quatre Nations*, Paris (1661).

Loos, Adolf (1870–1933)
Austrian, born Bruno, Moravia; *Steiner House*, Vienna (1910).

Lorimer, Sir Robert Stodart (1864–1929)
Scottish, born Edinburgh; *Thistle Chapel, St Giles*, Edinburgh (1909–11), *Scottish National War Memorial*, Edinburgh Castle (1923–8).

Lutyens, Sir Edwin Landseer (1869–1944)
English, born London; *Cenotaph*, Whitehall, London (1919–20), *Liverpool Roman Catholic Cathedral* (1929–c.1941), *Viceroy's House*, New Delhi (1921–5).

Mackintosh, Charles Rennie (1868–1928)
Scottish, born Glasgow; *Glasgow School of Art* (1897–9), *Hill House*, Helensburgh (1902–3).

Mackmurdo, Arthur Heygate (1851–1942)
English, born London; *Gordon Institute for Boys*, St Helens (1890).

Maderna, or Maderno, Carlo (1556–1629)
Italian, born Capalago; façade of *St Peter's* (1606–12), *S Susanna* (1597–1603), *Palazzo Barberini* (1628–38) — all Rome.

Mansard, or Mansart, François (1598–1666)
French, born Paris; north wing of *Châteaux de Blois* (1635), *Sainte-Marie de la Visitation*, Paris (1632).

Mansard, or Mansart, Jules Hardouin (1645–1708)
French, born Paris; *Grand Trianon, Palace of Versailles* (1678–89).

Mendelsohn, Eric (1887–1953)
German, born Allenstein; *De La Warr Pavilion*, Bexhill, UK (1934–5), *Anglo-Palestine Bank* Jerusalem (1938), Israel.

Michelozzo di Bartolommeo (1396–1472)
Italian, born Florence; *Villa Medici*, Fiesole (1458–61), *San Marco*, Florence (begun 1437).

Mies van der Rohe, Ludwig (1886–1969)
German–American, born Aachen; *Seagram Building*, New York City (1956–8), *Public Library*, Washington (1967).

Nash, John (1752–1835)
English, born London; layout of *Regent's Park* and *Regent Street*, London (1811 onwards), *Brighton Pavilion* (1815).

Nervi, Pier Luigi (1891–1979)
Italian, born Sondrio; *Berta Stadium*, Florence (1930–2), *Olympic Stadia*, Rome (1960), *San Francisco Cathedral* (1970).

Neumann, (Johann) Balthasar (1687–1753)
German, born Eger; *Würzburg Palace* (1730–43), *Schloss Bruchsal* (1738–53).

Niemeyer, Oscar (1907–)
Brazilian, born Rio de Janeiro; *Church of St Francis of Assisi*, Pampúlha, Belo Horizonte, Brazil (1942–4), *Niemeyer House*, Rio de Janeiro (1953).

Oud, Jacobus Johann Pieter (1890–1963)
Dutch, born Purmerend; *Alida Hartog-Ond House*, Purmerend (1906), *Café de Unie*, Rotterdam (1924), *Convention Centre*, The Hague (1957–63).

Palladio, Andrea (1508–80)
Italian, born Padua; *Godi-Porto* (villa at Lonedo) (1540), *La Malcontenta* (villa near Padua) (1560), *San Giorgio Maggiore*, Venice (begun 1566).

Paxton, Sir Joseph (1801–65)
English, born Milton-Bryant, near Woburn; building for *Great Exhibition* of 1851, later re-erected as the *Crystal Palace*, Sydenham (1852–4).

Pei, Ieoh Meng (1917–)
Chinese–American, born Canton; *Mile High Center*, Denver (1954–9), *John Hancock Tower*, Boston (1973), *Glass Pyramids*, the Louvre, Paris (1983–9).

Perret, Auguste (1874–1954)
French, born Brussels; *Théâtre des Champs Élysées*, Paris (1911–13), *Musée des travaux publics*, Paris (1936).

Piranesi, Giambattista (1720–78)
Italian, born Venice; *Santa Maria Arentina*, Rome (1764–6).

Pisano, Nicola (c.1225–c.1284) Italian, born Tuscany; *Pisa Baptistry* (1260), façade renovation of *Pisa Cathedral* (1260–70).

Playfair, William Henry (1789–1857)
Scottish, born London; *National Gallery of Scotland* (1850–7), *Royal Scottish Academy* (1832–5), *Surgeon's Hall* (1829–32) — all Edinburgh.

Poelzig, Hans (1869–1936)
German, born Berlin; *Exhibition Hall*, Posen (1910–11), *Salzburg Festival Theatre* (1920–2).

Pugin, August Welby Northmore (1812–52)
English, born London; decorations and sculpture for the *Houses of Parliament*, London (1836–7), *Birmingham Cathedral* (1839–41).

Rietveld, Gerrit Thomas (1888–1964)
Dutch, born Utrecht; *Schröder House*, Utrecht (1924), *Van Gogh Museum*, Amsterdam (1963–4).

Rogers, Richard Rogers, Baron (1933–)
English, born Florence; *Pompidou Centre*, Paris (1971–9), *Lloyds*, London (1979–85).

Saarinen, (Gottlieb) Eliel (1873–1950)
Finnish–American, born Rantasalmi; *Cranbrook Academy of Art*, Michigan (1934–40).

Saarinen, Eero (1910–61)
Finnish–American, born Kirkknonummi; *Jefferson Memorial Arch*, St Louis (1948–64), *American Embassy*, London (1955–60).

Sanmichele, Michele (c.1484–1559)
Italian, born Verona; *Capella Pelegrini*, Verona (1527–57), *Palazzo Grimani*, Venice (1551–9).

Sansovino, Jacopo (1486–1570)
Italian, born Florence; *Library* and *Mint*, Venice.

Schinkel, Karl Friederich (1781–1841)
German, born Neurippen, Brandenburg; *Old Museum*, Berlin (1823–30), *War Memorial on the Kreuzberg* (1818).

ARCHITECTS (cont.)

Scott, Sir George Gilbert (1811–78)
English, born Gawcott, Buckinghamshire; *Albert Memorial*, London (1862–3), *St Pancras station and hotel*, London (1865), *Glasgow University* (1865).

Serlio, Sebastiano (1475–1554)
Italian, born Bologna; *Grand Ferrare*, Fontainebleau (1541–8), *Château*, Ancy-le-Franc, Tonnerre (from 1546).

Shaw, (Richard) Norman (1831–1912)
English, born Edinburgh; *Old Swan House*, Chelsea (1876), *New Scotland Yard*, London (1888).

Smirke, Sir Robert (1781–1867)
English, born London; *Covent Garden Theatre*, London (1809), *British Museum*, London (1823–47).

Smythson, Robert (c.1535–1614)
English, place of birth unknown; *Wollaton Hall*, Nottingham (1580–8), *Hardwick Hall*, Derbyshire (1591–7).

Soane, Sir John (1753–1837)
English, born near Reading; altered interior of *Bank of England* (1788–1833), *Dulwich College Art Gallery* (1811–14).

Sottsass, Ettore Jnr (1917–   )
Italian, born Innsbruck; *Apartment Building*, Turin (1934), *Galleria del Cavalliro*, Venice (1956).

Soufflot, Jacques Germain (1713–80)
French, born Irancy; *Hôtel Dieu*, Lyons (1741), *St Geneviève* (Panthéon), Paris (begun 1757).

Spence, Sir Basil Urwin (1907–76)
Scottish, born India; pavilions for *Festival of Britain*, Heavy Industries Exhibition, London (1951), *New Coventry Cathedral* (1951).

Stirling, Sir James (1926–92)
Scottish; *Department of Engineering*, Leicester University (1959–63)
(with James Gowan), *History Faculty*, Cambridge (1965–8), *Florey Building*, Queen's College, Oxford (1966), *Neue Staatsgalerie*, Stuttgart (1980–4).

Street, George Edmund (1824–81)
English, born Woodford, Essex; *London Law Courts* (1870–81).

Stuart, James (1713–88)
English, born London; rebuilt interior, *Chapel of Greenwich Hospital* (1779).

Sullivan, Louis Henry (1856–1924)
American, born Boston; *Wainwright Building*, St Louis (1890), *Carson, Pirie and Scott Store*, Chicago (1899–1904).

Tange, Kenzo (1913–   )
Japanese, born Tokyo; *Hiroshima Peace Centre* (1949–55), *Shizoka Press and Broadcasting Centre*, Tokyo (1966–7).

Utzon, Jørn (1918–   )
Danish, born Copenhagen; *Sydney Opera House* (1956–68), *Kuwait House of Parliament* (begun 1972).

Vanbrugh, Sir John (1664–1726)
English, born London; *Castle Howard* (1699–1726), *Blenheim Palace* (1705–20).

Vignola, Giacomo Barozzi da (1507–73)
Italian, born Vignola; *Villa di Papa Giulio* (1550–5), church of the *Il Gesu*, Rome (1586–73).

Viollet-le-Duc, Eugène Emmanuel (1814–79)
  French, born Paris; restored cathedral of *Notre Dame*, Paris (1845–64), *Château de Pierrefonds* (1858–70).
Voysey, Charles Francis Annesley (1857–1941)
  English, born London; *Grove Town Houses*, Kensington (1891–2), *Sanderson's Wallpaper Factory*, Chiswick (1902).

Wagner, Otto (1841–1918)
  Austrian, born Penzing, near Vienna; stations for *Vienna Stadtbahn* (1894–7), *Post Office Savings Bank*, Vienna (1904–6).
Waterhouse, Alfred (1830–1905)
  English, born Liverpool; *Manchester Town Hall* (1867–77), *Natural History Museum*, South Kensington, London (1873–81).
Webb, Sir Aston (1849–1930)
  English, born London; eastern façade of *Buckingham Palace* (1912), *Admiralty Arch* (1903–10), *Imperial College of Science* (1906) — all London.
Webb, Philip (1831–1915)
  English, born Oxford; *Red House*, Bexley (1859), *Clouds*, Wiltshire (1881–6), *Standen*, East Grinstead (1891).
Wood, John, the elder (1704–54)
  North and South Parades, Bath (1728), *Queen Square*, Bath (1735), *Prior Park*, (1735–48), *Royal Mineral Water Hospital*, Bath (1738), *Circus*, Bath (completed 1764 by his son, John Wood, the younger), *Royal Crescent*, Bath (1767–75, built by 'the younger' based on 'the elder's' design).
Wren, Sir Christopher (1632–1723)
  English, born East Knoyle, Wiltshire; *Pembroke College Chapel*, Cambridge (1663–5), *The Sheldonian Theatre*, Oxford (1664), *Royal Greenwich Observatory* (1675–6), *St Paul's*, London (1675–1710), *Greenwich Hospital* (1696).
Wright, Frank Lloyd (1869–1959)
  American, born Richland Center, Wisconsin; *Larkin Building*, Buffalo (1904), *Robie House*, Chicago (1908), *Johnson Wax Factory*, Racine, Wisconsin (1936–9), *Guggenheim Museum*, New York (begun 1942).
Wyatt, James (1746–1813)
  English, born Staffordshire; *London Pantheon* (1772), *Gothic Revival Country House*, Fonthill Abbey, Wiltshire (1796–1813).

NOBEL PRIZES 1970–96

Year	Peace	Literature	Economic Science
1970	Norman E Borlaug	Alexandr Solzhenitsyn	Paul A Samuelson
1971	Willy Brandt	Pablo Neruda	Simon Kuznets
1972	*none*	Heinrich Böll	John R Hicks Kenneth J Arrow
1973	Henry A Kissinger Le Duc Tho (*declined*)	Patrick White	Wassily Leontief
1974	Sean MacBride Sato Eisaku	Eyvind Johnson Harry Martinson	Gunnar Myrdal Friedrich A von Hayek
1975	Andrei D Sakharov	Eugenio Montale	Leonid V Kantorovich Tjalling C Koopmans
1976	Mairead Corrigan Betty Williams	Saul Bellow	Milton Friedman
1977	Amnesty International	Vicente Aleixandre	James E Meade Bertil Ohlin
1978	Menachem Begin Anwar al-Sadat	Isaac B Singer	Herbert A Simon
1979	Mother Teresa	Odysseus Elytis	Arthur Lewis Theodore W Schultz
1980	Adolfo Pérez Esquivel	Czeslaw Milosz	Lawrence R Klein
1981	Office of the UN High Commissioner for Refugees	Elisas Canetti	James Tobin
1982	Alfonso García Robles Alva Myrdal	Gabriel García Márquez	George J Stigler
1983	Lech Walesa	William Golding	Gerard Debreu
1984	Desmond Tutu	Jaroslav Seifert	Richard Stone
1985	International Physicians for the Prevention of Nuclear War	Claude Simon	Franco Modigliani

Year	Peace	Literature	Economic Science
1986	Elie Wiesel	Wole Soyinka	James M Buchanan
1987	Oscar Arias Sánchez	Joseph Brodsky	Robert M Solow
1988	UK Peacekeeping Forces	Naguib Mahfouz	Maurice Allais
1989	Tenzin Ciyatso (Dalai Lama)	Camilo José Cela	Trygve Haavelmo
1990	Mikhail Gorbachev	Octavio Paz	Harry M Markovitz Merton Miller William Sharpe
1991	Aung San Suu Kyi	Nadine Gordimer	Ronald Coase
1992	Rigoberta Menchú	Derek Walcott	Gary S Becker
1993	Nelson Mandela F W de Klerk	Toni Morrison	Robert Fugel Douglas North
1994	Yasser Arafat Shimon Peres Yitzhak Rabin	Kenzaburo Oe	John Nash John Harsanyi Reinhard Selten
1995	Joseph Rotblat Pugwash Conferences on Science and World Affairs	Seamus Heaney	Robert E Lucas
1996	Carlos Filipe Ximenes Belo José Ramos-Horta	Wislawa Szymborska	James Mirrlees William Vickrey

SPORTS AND GAMES

OLYMPIC GAMES

First Modern Olympic Games took place in 1896, founded by Frenchman Baron de Coubertin; held every four years; women first competed in 1900; first separate Winter Games celebration in 1924.

VENUES

Olympic games were also held in 1906 to commemorate the 10th anniversary of the birth of the Modern Games. The 1956 equestrian events were held at Stockholm, Sweden, due to quarantine laws in Australia.

Summer Games

1896	Athens, Greece	1932	Los Angeles, USA	1972	Munich, West Germany
1900	Paris, France	1936	Berlin, Germany	1976	Montreal, Canada
1904	St Louis, USA	1948	London, UK	1980	Moscow, USSR
1908	London, UK	1952	Helsinki, Finland	1984	Los Angeles, USA
1912	Stockholm, Sweden	1956	Melbourne, Australia	1988	Seoul, South Korea
1920	Antwerp, Belgium	1960	Rome, Italy	1992	Barcelona, Spain
1924	Paris, France	1964	Tokyo, Japan	1996	Atlanta, USA
1928	Amsterdam, Holland	1968	Mexico City, Mexico	2000	Sydney, Australia

Winter Games

1924	Chamonix, France	1952	Oslo, Norway	1976	Innsbruck, Austria
1928	St Moritz, Switzerland	1956	Cortina, Italy	1980	Lake Placid, New York, USA
1932	Lake Placid, New York, USA	1960	Squaw Valley, California, USA	1984	Sarajevo, Yugoslavia
1936	Garmisch-Partenkirchen, Germany	1964	Innsbruck, Austria	1988	Calgary, Canada
		1968	Grenoble, France	1992	Albertville, France
1948	St Moritz, Switzerland	1972	Sapporo, Japan	1994	Lillehammer, Norway
				1998	Nugano, Japan

LEADING MEDAL WINNERS

Summer Games	Gold	Silver	Bronze	Total		Winter Games	Gold	Silver	Bronze	Total
1 USA	783	594	512	1 889		1 Russia[1]	99	71	71	241
2 Unified Team[1]	440	361	328	1 129		2 Norway	73	77	64	214
3 West Germany[2]	190	228	235	653		3 USA	53	51	41	145
4 Great Britain	178	225	218	621		4 Austria	36	48	44	128
5 France	161	173	192	526		5 Finland	36	45	42	123

Summer Games	Gold	Silver	Bronze	Total		Winter Games	Gold	Silver	Bronze	Total
6 Sweden	132	146	173	451		6 East Germany	39	36	35	110
7 Italy	153	126	132	411		7 West Germany[3]	45	43	37	125
8 East Germany	153	129	127	409		8 Sweden	39	26	34	99
9 Hungary	135	124	143	402		9 Switzerland	27	29	29	85
10 Finland	98	77	112	287		10 Canada	19	24	23	66

[1] Includes medals won as USSR
[2] Includes medals won as Germany 1896–1964 and 1992.
[3] Includes medals won as Germany 1896–1964, 1992 and 1994.

COMMONWEALTH GAMES

First held as the British Empire Games in 1930; take place every four years and between Olympic celebrations; became the British Empire and Commonwealth Games in 1954; current title adopted in 1970.

VENUES

1930 Hamilton, Canada	1962 Perth, Australia	1982 Brisbane, Australia
1934 London, England	1966 Kingston, Jamaica	1986 Edinburgh, Scotland
1938 Sydney, Australia	1970 Edinburgh, Scotland	1990 Auckland, New Zealand
1950 Auckland, New Zealand	1974 Christchurch, New	1994 Victoria, Canada
1954 Vancouver, Canada	Zealand	1998 Kuala Lumpur, Malaysia
1958 Cardiff, Wales	1978 Edmonton, Canada	

LEADING MEDAL WINNERS

Nation	Gold	Silver	Bronze	Total
1 Australia	484	426	425	1 335
2 England	451	413	411	1 275
3 Canada	327	343	345	1 015
4 New Zealand	99	137	181	417
5 Scotland	62	77	120	259
6 South Africa	62	48	52	162
7 Wales	37	47	66	150
8 India	33	47	38	118
9 Kenya	42	28	41	111
10 Northern Ireland	20	22	37	79

RECENT CHAMPIONS

For 1992 Summer Olympic events the designation (UT) is given for members of the Unified Team (Armenia, Azerbaijan, Byelorussia, Georgia, Kazakhstan, Kirghizia, Moldavia, Tadzhikistan, Ukraine and Uzbekistan).

AMERICAN FOOTBALL

Superbowl
First held in 1967; takes place each January; an end-of-season meeting between the champions of the two major US leagues, the National Football Conference (NFC) and the American Football Conference (AFC).

Recent winners

1984	Los Angeles Raiders (AFC)
1985	San Francisco 49ers (NFC)
1986	Chicago Bears (NFC)
1987	New York Giants (NFC)
1988	Washington Redskins (NFC)
1989	San Francisco 49ers (NFC)
1990	San Francisco 49ers (NFC)
1991	New York Giants (NFC)
1992	Washington Redskins (NFC)
1993	Dallas Cowboys (NFC)
1994	Dallas Cowboys (NFC)
1995	San Francisco 49ers (NFC)

ASSOCIATION FOOTBALL

FIFA World Cup
Association Football's premier event; first contested for the Jules Rimet Trophy in 1930; Brazil won it outright after winning for the third time in 1970; since then teams have competed for the FIFA (*Féderation Internationale de Football Association*) World Cup; held every four years.

Post-war winners

1950	Uruguay
1954	West Germany

Post-war winners

1958	Brazil
1962	Brazil
1966	England
1970	Brazil
1974	West Germany
1978	Argentina
1982	Italy
1986	Argentina
1990	West Germany
1994	Brazil

European Championship
Held every four years since 1960; qualifying group matches held over the two years preceding the final.

Winners

1960	USSR
1964	Spain
1968	Italy
1972	West Germany
1976	Czechoslovakia
1980	West Germany
1984	France
1988	Holland
1992	Denmark

South American Championship
First held in 1916, for South American national sides; discontinued in 1967, but revived eight years later; now played every two years.

Recent winners

1956	Uruguay
1957	Argentina
1959[1]	Argentina
1959[1]	Uruguay
1963	Bolivia
1967	Uruguay
1975	Peru

Recent winners

1979	Paraguay
1983	Uruguay
1987	Uruguay
1989	Brazil
1991	Argentina
1993	Argentina

[1] There were two tournaments in 1959.

European Champions Cup
The leading club competition in Europe; open to the League champions of countries affiliated to UEFA (Union of European Football Associations); commonly known as the 'European Cup'; inaugurated in the 1955–6 season; played annually.

Recent winners

1984	Liverpool (England)
1985	Juventus (Italy)
1986	Steaua Bucharest (Romania)
1987	FC Porto (Portugal)
1988	PSV Eindhoven (Holland)
1989	AC Milan (Italy)
1990	AC Milan (Italy)
1991	Red Star Belgrade (Yugoslavia)
1992	Barcelona (Spain)
1993	Marseille (France)
1994	AC Milan (Italy)

Football Association Challenge Cup
The world's oldest club knockout competition (the 'FA cup'), held annually; first contested in the 1871–2 season; first final at the Kennington Oval on 16 March 1872; first winners were The Wanderers.

Recent winners

1984	Everton
1985	Manchester United
1986	Liverpool
1987	Coventry City
1988	Wimbledon
1989	Liverpool
1990	Manchester United
1991	Tottenham Hotspur
1992	Liverpool
1993	Arsenal
1994	Manchester United

Football League
The oldest league in the world; founded in 1888; consists of four divisions; the current complement of 92 teams achieved in 1950.

Recent winners

1983–4	Liverpool
1984–5	Everton
1985–6	Liverpool
1986–7	Everton
1987–8	Liverpool
1988–9	Arsenal
1989–90	Liverpool
1990–1	Arsenal
1991–2	Leeds United
1992–3	Manchester United
1993–4	Manchester United

ATHLETICS

World Championships
First held in Helsinki, Finland in 1983, then in Rome, Italy in 1987; take place every four years.

Event	Winners (Men)
1983	
100 m	Carl Lewis (USA)
200 m	Calvin Smith (USA)
400 m	Bert Cameron (Jamaica)
800 m	Willi Wülbeck (East Germany)
1 500 m	Steve Cram (UK)
5 000 m	Eamonn Coghlan (Ireland)
10 000 m	Alberto Cova (Italy)
Marathon	Rob de Castella (Austria)
3 000 m steeplechase	Patriz Ilg (West Germany)
110 m hurdles	Greg Foster (USA)
400 m hurdles	Ed Moses (USA)
20 km walk	Ernesto Canto (Mexico)
50 km walk	Ronald Weigel (East Germany)
4 x 100 m relay	USA
4 x 400 m relay	USSR
High jump	Gennadiy Avdeyenko (USSR)
Long jump	Carl Lewis (USA)

ATHLETICS (cont.)

Event	Winners (Men)	Event	Winners (Men)
Triple jump	Zdzislaw Hoffma (Poland)	800 m	Billy Konchellah (Kenya)
Pole vault	Sergey Bubka (USSR)	1 500 m	Noureddine Morceli
Shot	Edward Sarul (Poland)		(Algeria)
Discus	Imrich Bugar	5 000 m	Yobes Ondieki (Kenya)
	(Czechoslovakia)	10 000 m	Moses Tanui (Kenya)
Hammer	Sergey Litvinov (USSR)	Marathon	Hiromi Taniguchi (Japan)
Javelin	Detlef Michel (East	3 000 m steeplechase	Moses Kiptanui (Kenya)
	Germany)	110 m hurdles	Greg Foster (Zambia)
Decathlon	Daley Thompson (UK)	400 m hurdles	Samuel Matete (Zambia)
		20 km walk	Maurizio Damilano
1987			(Italy)
100 m	Ben Johnson (Canada)	50 km walk	Alexandr Potashov
200 m	Calvin Smith (USA)		(USSR)
400 m	Thomas Schoenlebe (East		
	Germany)	4 x 100 m relay	USA
800 m	Billy Konchellah (Kenya)	4 x 400 m relay	UK
1 500 m	Abdi Bile (Somalia)	High jump	Charles Austin (USA)
5 000 m	Said Aouita (Morocco)	Long jump	Mike Powell (USA)
10 000 m	Paul Kipkoech (Kenya)	Triple jump	Kenny Harrison (USA)
Marathon	Douglas Waikihuru	Pole vault	Sergey Bubka (USSR)
3 000 m steeplechase	Francesco Panetta (Italy)	Shot	Werner Gunthor
110 m hurdles	Greg Foster (USA)		(Switzerland)
400 m hurdles	Ed Moses (USA)	Discus	Lars Riedel (Germany)
25 km walk	Maurizio Damilano (Italy)	Hammer	Yuriy Sedykh (USSR)
50 km walk	Hartwig Gauder (East	Javelin	Kimmo Kinnunen
	Germany)		(Finland)
4 x 100 m relay	USA	Decathlon	Dan O'Brien (USA)
4 x 400 m relay	USA		
High jump	Patrik Sjoeberg (Sweden)	Event	Winners (Women)
Long jump	Carl Lewis (USA)		
Triple jump	Khristo Markov (Bulgaria)	**1983**	
Pole vault	Sergey Bubka (USSR)	100 m	Marlies Göhr (East
Shot	Werner Gunthoer		Germany)
	(Switzerland)	200 m	Marita Koch (East
Discus	Jurgen Schult (East		Germany)
	Germany)	400 m	Jarmila Kratochvilova
Hammer	Sergey Litvinov (USSR)		(Czechoslovakia)
Javelin	Seppo Raty (Finland)	800 m	Jarmila Kratochvilova
Decathlon	Torsten Voss (East		(Czechoslovakia)
	Germany)	1 500 m	Mary Decker (USA)
		3 000 m	Mary Decker (USA)
1991		Marathon	Greta Waitz (Norway)
100 m	Carl Lewis (USA)	100 m hurdles	Bettina Jahn (East
200 m	Michael Johnson (USA)		Germany)
400 m	Antonio Pettigrew (USA)	400 m hurdles	Ekaterina Fesenko
			(USSR)

Event	Winners (Women)	Event	Winners (Women)
4 x 100 m relay	East Germany	200 m	Katrin Krabbe (Germany)
4 x 400 m relay	East Germany	400 m	Marle-Jose Perec (France)
High jump	Tamara Bykova (USSR)		
Long jump	Heike Daute (East Germany)	800 m	Lilia Nurutdinova (USSR)
Shot	Helene Fibingerova (Czechoslovakia)	1 500 m	Hassiba Boulmerka (Algeria)
Discus	Martina Opitz (East Germany)	3 000 m	Tatyana Dorovskikh (USSR)
Javelin	Tilna Lillak (Finland)	10 000 m	Liz McColgan (UK)
Heptathlon	Tamona Neubert (East Germany)	Marathon	Wanda Panfil (Poland)
		100 m hurdles	Lyudmila Narozhilenko (USSR)
1987		400 m hurdles	Tatyana Ledovskaya (USSR)
100 m	Silke Gladisch (East Germany)		
200 m	Silke Gladisch (East Germany)	10 km walk	Alina Ivanova (USSR)
		4 x 100 m relay	Jamaica
400 m	Olga Bryzgina (USSR)	4 x 400 m relay	USSR
800 m	Sigrun Wodars (East Germany)	High jump	Heike Henkel (Germany)
1 500 m	Tatyana Samolenko (USSR)	Long jump	Jackie Joyner-Kersee (USA)
3 000 m	Tatyana Samolenko (USSR)	Shot	Huang Zhihong (China)
Marathon	Rosa Mota (Portugal)	Discus	Tsvetanka Khristova (Bulgaria)
100 m hurdles	Ginka Zagorcheva (Bulgaria)	Javelin	Xu Demei (China)
400 m hurdles	Sabine Busche (East Germany)	Heptathlon	Sabine Braun (Germany)
10 km walk	Irinia Strakhova (USSR)		
4 x 100 m relay	USA		
4 x 400 m relay	East Germany		
High jump	Stefka Kostadinova (Bulgaria)		
Long jump	Jackie Joyner-Kersee (USA)		
Shot	Natalya Lisovskaya (USSR)		
Discus	Martina Hellman (*née* Opitz) (East Germany)		
Javelin	Fatima Whitbread (UK)		
Heptathlon	Jackie Joyner-Kersee (USA)		
1991			
100 m	Katrin Krabbe (Germany)		

AUSTRALIAN RULES FOOTBALL

Victoria Football League
The top prize is the Australian Football League Trophy (Victoria Football League 1897–1989); inaugural winners in 1897 were Essendon.

1984	Essendon
1985	Essendon
1986	Hawthorn
1987	Carlton
1988	Hawthorn
1989	Hawthorn
1990	Collingwood
1991	Hawthorn
1992	West Coast Eagles
1993	Essendon
1994	West Coast Eagles

BASEBALL

World Series
First held in 1903; takes place each October, the best of seven matches; professional Baseball's leading event, the end-of-season meeting between the winners of the two Major Baseball leagues in the USA, the National League (NL) and American League (AL).

Recent winners

1984	Detroit Tigers (AL)
1985	Kansas City Royals (AL)
1986	New York Mets (NL)
1987	Minnesota Twins (AL)
1988	Los Angeles Dodgers (NL)
1989	Oakland Athletics (AL)
1990	Cincinatti Reds (NL)
1991	Minnesota Twins (AL)
1992	Toronto Blue Jays (AL)
1993	Toronto Blue Jays (AL)
1994	*cancelled*

World Amateur Championship
Instituted in 1938; since 1974 held every two years.

Recent winners

1972	Cuba
1973	Cuba & USA (*shared*)
1974	USA
1976	Cuba
1978	Cuba
1980	Cuba
1982	South Korea
1984	Cuba
1986	Cuba
1988	Cuba
1990	Cuba
1992	Cuba

BASKETBALL

World Championship
First held 1950 for men, 1953 for women; takes place every four years.

Winners (Men)

1950	Argentina
1954	USA
1959	Brazil
1963	Brazil
1967	USSR
1970	Yugoslavia
1974	USSR
1978	Yugoslavia
1982	USSR
1986	USA
1990	Yugoslavia
1994	USA

Winners (Women)

1953	USA
1957	USA
1959	USSR
1964	USSR
1967	USSR
1971	USSR
1975	USSR
1979	USA
1983	USSR
1987	USA
1991	USA

National Basketball Association Championship
First held in 1947; the major competition in professional basketball in the USA, end-of-season NBA Play-off involving the champion teams from the Eastern (EC) Conference and Western Conference (WC).

Recent winners

1984	Boston Celtics (EC)
1985	Los Angeles Lakers (WC)
1986	Boston Celtics (EC)

Recent winners

1987	Los Angeles Lakers (WC)
1988	Los Angeles Lakers (WC)
1989	Detroit Pistons (EC)
1990	Detroit Pistons (EC)
1991	Chicago Bulls (EC)
1992	Chicago Bulls (EC)
1993	Chicago Bulls (EC)
1994	New York Knicks (EC)

BOXING

World Heavyweight Champions
The first world heavyweight champion under Queensbury Rules with gloves was James J Corbett in 1892.

Recent champions	Recognizing Body
1984 Larry Holmes (USA)	IBF
1984 Tim Witherspoon (USA)	WBC
1984 Pinklon Thomas (USA)	WBC
1984 Greg Page (USA)	WBA
1985 Michael Spinks (USA)	IBF
1985 Tony Tubbs (USA)	WBA
1986 Tim Witherspoon (USA)	WBA
1986 Trevor Berbick (Canada)	WBC
1986 Mike Tyson (USA)	WBC
1986 James Smith (USA)	WBA
1987 Tony Tucker (USA)	IBF
1987 Mike Tyson (USA)	WBA/WBC
1987 Mike Tyson (USA)	UND
1989 Francesco Damiani (Italy)	WBO
1989 Mike Tyson (USA)	WBA/WBC/IBF
1990 James (Buster) Douglas (USA)	WBA/WBC/IBF
1990 Evander Holyfield (USA)	WBA/WBC/ IBF
1991 Ray Mercer (USA)	WBO
1992 Riddick Bowe	WBA/WBC/IBF
1992 Lennox Lewis	WBC
1992 Michael Moorer	WBO
1992 Tommy Morrison	WBO
1993 Michael Bentt	WBO
1994 Oliver McCall	WBC
1994 Herbie Hyde	WBO
1994 Michael Moorer	WBA/WBC/IBF

Recent champions	Recognizing Body
1994 Oliver McCall	WBC
1994 George Foreman	WBA/WBC/IBF

UND = Undisputed Champion
WBC = World Boxing Council
WBA = World Boxing Association
IBF = International Boxing Federation
WBO = World Boxing Organization

CHESS

World Champions
World Champions have been recognized since 1886. The first international tournament was held in London in 1851, and won by Adolf Anderssen (Germany), first women's champion recognized in 1927.

Post-war champions (Men)

1948–57	Mikhail Botvinnik (USSR)
1957–8	Vassiliy Smyslov (USSR)
1958–60	Mikhail Botvinnik (USSR)
1960–1	Mikhail Tal (USSR)
1961–3	Mikhail Botvinnik (USSR)
1963–9	Tigran Petrosian (USSR)
1969–72	Boris Spassky (USSR)
1972–5	Bobby Fischer (USA)
1975–85	Anatoliy Karpov (USSR)
1985–93	Gary Kasparov (USSR)[1]
1993–	Anatoly Karpov (Russia)
1993–	Gary Kasparov (Russia) (PCA)

[1] Kasparov split from the International Chess Federation (FIDE) and formed the Professional Chess Association (PCA) in 1993.

Champions (Women)

1927–44	Vera Menchik-Stevenson (UK)
1950–3	Lyudmila Rudenko (USSR)
1953–6	Elizaveta Bykova (USSR)
1956–8	Olga Rubtsova (USSR)
1958–62	Elizaveta Bykova (USSR)
1962–78	Nona Gaprindashvili (USSR)
1978–91	Maya Chiburdanidze (USSR)
1991–	Xie Jun (China)

CRICKET

World Cup
First played in England in 1975; held every four years; the 1987 competition was the first to be played outside England, in India and Pakistan.

Winners

1975	West Indies
1979	West Indies
1983	India
1987	Australia
1992	Pakistan

County Championship
The oldest cricket competition in the world; first won by Sussex in 1827; not officially recognized until 1890, when a proper points system was introduced.

Recent winners

1984	Essex
1985	Middlesex
1986	Essex
1987	Nottinghamshire
1988	Worcestershire
1989	Worcestershire
1990	Middlesex
1991	Essex
1992	Essex
1993	Middlesex
1994	Warwickshire

AXA Equity and Law League
First held in 1969; known as the John Player League until 1987 and as the Refuge Assurance League until 1991.

Recent winners

1984	Essex
1985	Essex
1986	Hampshire
1987	Worcestershire
1988	Worcestershire
1989	Lancashire
1990	Derbyshire

Recent winners

1991	Nottinghamshire
1992	Middlesex
1993	Glamorgan
1994	Warwickshire

Natwest Bank Trophy
First held in 1963; known as the Gillette Cup until 1981.

Recent winners

1984	Middlesex
1985	Essex
1986	Sussex
1987	Nottinghamshire
1988	Middlesex
1989	Warwickshire
1990	Lancashire
1991	Hampshire
1992	Northhamptonshire
1993	Warwickshire
1994	Worcestershire

Benson and Hedges Cup
First held in 1972.

Recent winners

1984	Lancashire
1985	Leicestershire
1986	Middlesex
1987	Yorkshire
1988	Hampshire
1989	Nottinghamshire
1990	Lancashire
1991	Worcestershire
1992	Hampshire
1993	Derbyshire
1994	Warwickshire

Sheffield Shield
Australia's leading domestic competition; contested inter-state since 1891–2.

Recent winners

1984	Western Australia
1985	New South Wales

Recent winners

1986	New South Wales
1987	Western Australia
1988	Western Australia
1989	Western Australia
1990	New South Wales
1991	Victoria
1992	Western Australia
1993	New South Wales
1994	New South Wales

CYCLING

Tour de France
World's premier cycling event; first held in 1903.

Recent winners

1984	Laurent Fignon (France)
1985	Bernard Hinault (France)
1986	Greg Le Mond (USA)
1987	Stephen Roche (Ireland)
1988	Pedro Delgado (Spain)
1989	Greg Le Mond (USA)
1990	Greg Le Mond (USA)
1991	Miguel Indurain (Spain)
1992	Miguel Indurain (Spain)
1993	Miguel Indurain (Spain)
1994	Miguel Indurain (Spain)

World Road Race Championships
Men's race first held in 1927; first women's race in 1958; takes place annually.

Recent winners (Professional Men)

1984	Claude Criquielion (Belgium)
1985	Joop Zoetemelk (Holland)
1986	Moreno Argentin (Italy)
1987	Stephen Roche (Ireland)
1988	Maurizio Fondriest (Italy)
1989	Greg Le Mond (USA)
1990	Rudy Dhaenens (Belgium)
1991	Gianni Bugno (Italy)
1992	Gianni Bugno (Italy)
1993	Gianni Bugno (Italy)
1994	Luc Leblanc (France)

Recent winners (Women)

1984	*not held*
1985	Jeannie Longo (France)
1986	Jeannie Longo (France)
1987	Jeannie Longo (France)
1988	Jeannie Longo (France)
1989	Jeannie Longo (France)
1990	Catherine Marsal (France)
1991	Leontien van Moorsel (The Netherlands)
1992	Kathryn Watt (Australia)
1993	Leontien van Moorsel (The Netherlands)
1994	Monica Valvik (Norway)

GOLF

British Open
First held at Prestwick in 1860, and won by Willie Park; takes place annually; regarded as the world's leading golf tournament.

Recent winners

1984	Severiano Ballesteros (Spain)
1985	Sandy Lyle (Great Britain)
1986	Greg Norman (Australia)
1987	Nick Faldo (Great Britain)
1988	Severiano Ballesteros (Spain)
1989	Mark Calcavecchia (USA)
1990	Nick Faldo (Great Britain)
1991	Ian Baker-Finch (Australia)
1992	Nick Faldo (Great Britain)
1993	Greg Norman (Australia)
1994	Nick Price (Zimbabwe)

United States Open
First Held at Newport, Rhode Island in 1895, and won by Horace Rawlins; takes place annually.

Recent winners

1984	Fuzzy Zoeller (USA)
1985	Andy North (USA)
1986	Ray Floyd (USA)
1987	Scott Simpson (USA)
1988	Curtis Strange (USA)
1989	Curtis Strange (USA)
1990	Hale Irwin (USA)

GOLF (cont.)

Recent winners

1991	Payne Stewart (USA)
1992	Tom Kite (USA)
1993	Lee Janzen (USA)
1994	Ernie Els (South Africa)

US Masters
First held in 1934; takes place at the Augusta National course in Georgia every April.

Recent winners

1984	Ben Crenshaw (USA)
1985	Bernhard Langer (West Germany)
1986	Jack Nicklaus (USA)
1987	Larry Mize (USA)
1988	Sandy Lyle (Great Britain)
1989	Nick Faldo (Great Britain)
1990	Nick Faldo (Great Britain)
1991	Ian Woosnam (Great Britain)
1992	Fred Couples (USA)
1993	Bernhard Langer (Germany)
1994	José María Olazábal (Spain)

United States PGA Championship
The last of the season's four 'Majors'; first held in 1916, and a match-play event until 1958; takes place annually.

Recent winners

1984	Lee Trevino (USA)
1985	Hubert Green (USA)
1986	Bob Tway (USA)
1987	Larry Nelson (USA)
1988	Jeff Sluman (USA)
1989	Payne Stewart (USA)
1990	Wayne Grady (Australia)
1991	John Daly (USA)
1992	Nick Price (Zimbabwe)
1993	Paul Azinger (USA)
1994	Nick Price (Zimbabwe)

Ryder Cup
The leading international team tournament; first held at Worcester, Massachusetts in 1927; takes place every two years between teams from the USA and Europe (Great Britain 1927–71; Great Britain and Ireland 1973–7).

Recent winners

1973	USA	19–13
1975	USA	21–11
1977	USA	12½–7½
1979	USA	17–11
1981	USA	18½–9½
1983	USA	14½–13½
1985	Europe	16½–11½
1987	Europe	15–13
1989	Drawn	14–14
1991	USA	14½–13½
1993	USA	15–13

GYMNASTICS

World Championships
First held in 1903; took place every four years, 1922–78; since 1979, every two years.

Recent winners

Individual (Men)

1962	Yuriy Titov (USSR)
1966	Mikhail Voronin (USSR)
1970	Eizo Kenmotsu (Japan)
1974	Shigeru Kasamatsu (Japan)
1978	Nikolai Adrianov (USSR)
1979	Aleksandr Ditiatin (USSR)
1981	Yuri Korolev (USSR)
1983	Dmitri Belozerchev (USSR)
1985	Yuri Korolev (USSR)
1987	Dmitri Belozerchev (USSR)
1989	Igor Korobichensky (USSR)
1991	Vitaly Scherbo (USSR)
1993	Vitaly Scherbo (Russia)

Recent winners

Team (Men)

1962	Japan
1966	Japan

Recent winners

1970	Japan
1974	Japan
1978	Japan
1979	USSR
1981	USSR
1983	China
1985	USSR
1987	USSR
1989	USSR
1991	USSR
1993	Belorussia

Recent winners

Individual (Women)

1962	Larissa Latynina (USSR)
1966	Vera Caslavska (Czechoslovakia)
1970	Ludmila Tourischeva (USSR)
1974	Ludmila Tourischeva (USSR)
1978	Yelena Mukhina (USSR)
1979	Nelli Kim (USSR)
1981	Olga Bicherova (USSR)
1983	Natalia Yurchenko (USSR)
1985	Yelena Shoushounova (USSR) and Oksana Omeliantchuk (USSR)
1987	Aurelia Dobre (Romania)
1989	Svetlana Boginskaya
1991	Kirn Zmeskal (USA)
1993	Shannon Miller (USA)

Recent winners

Team (Women)

1962	USSR
1966	Czechoslovakia
1970	USSR
1974	USSR
1978	USSR
1979	Romania
1981	USSR
1983	USSR
1985	USSR
1987	Romania
1989	USSR
1991	USSR
1993	USA

HORSE RACING

The Derby
The 'Blue Riband' of the Turf; run at Epsom over 1½ miles; first run in 1780.

Recent winners	Horse (Jockey)
1984	Secreto (Christy Roche)
1985	Slip Anchor (Steve Cauthen)
1986	Shahrastani (Walter Swinburn)
1987	Reference Point (Steve Cauthen)
1988	Kahyasi (Ray Cochrane)
1989	Nashwan (Willie Carson)
1990	Quest For Fame (Pat Eddery)
1991	Generous (Alan Munro)
1992	Dr Devious (John Reid)
1993	Commander In Chief (Michael Kinane)
1994	Erhaab (Willie Carson)

The Oaks
Raced at Epsom over 1½ miles; for fillies only; first run in 1779.

Recent winners	Horse (Jockey)
1984	Circus Plume (Lester Piggott)
1985	Oh So Sharp (Steve Cauthen)
1986	Midway Lady (Ray Cochrane)
1987	Unite (Walter Swinburn)
1988	Diminuendo (Steve Cauthen)
1989	Aliysa (Walter Swinburn)
1990	Salsabil (Willie Carson)
1991	Jet Ski Lady (Christy Roche)
1992	User Friendly (George Duffield)
1993	Intrepidity (Michael Roberts)
1994	Balanchine (Lanfranco Dettori)

One Thousand Guineas
Run over 1 mile at Newmarket; for fillies only; first run in 1814.

Recent winners	Horse (Jockey)
1984	Pebbles (Philip Robinson)
1985	Oh So Sharp (Steve Cauthen)

HORSE RACING (cont.)

Recent winners	Horse (Jockey)
1986	Midway Lady (Ray Cochrane)
1987	Miesque (Freddy Head)
1988	Ravinella (Gary Moore)
1989	Musical Bliss (Walter Swinburn)
1990	Salsabil (Willie Carson)
1991	Shadayid (Willie Carson)
1992	Hatoof (Walter Swinburn)
1993	Sayyedati (Walter Swinburn)
1994	Las Meninas (John Reid)

Two Thousand Guineas
Run at Newmarket over 1 mile; first run in 1809.

Recent winners	Horse (Jockey)
1984	El Gran Senor (Pat Eddery)
1985	Shadeed (Lester Piggott)
1986	Dancing Brave (Greville Starkey)
1987	Don't Forget Me (Willie Carson)
1988	Doyoun (Walter Swinburn)
1989	Nashwan (Willie Carson)
1990	Tirol (Michael Kinane)
1991	Mystiko (Michael Roberts)
1992	Rodrigo De Triano (Lester Piggott)
1993	Zafonic (Pat Eddery)
1994	Mister Baileys (Jason Weaver)

St Leger
The oldest of the five English classics; first run in 1776; raced at Doncaster annually over 1 mile 6 furlongs 127 yards.

Recent winners	Horse (Jockey)
1984	Commanche Run (Lester Piggott)
1985	Oh So Sharp (Steve Cauthen)
1986	Moon Madness (Pat Eddery)
1987	Reference Point (Steve Cauthen)
1988	Minster Son (Willie Carson)
1989	Michelozzo (Steve Cauthen)
1990	Snurge (Richard Quinn)
1991	Toulon (Pat Eddery)

Recent winners	Horse (Jockey)
1992	User Friendly (George Duffield)
1993	Bob's Return (Philip Robinson)
1994	Moonax (Pat Eddery)

Grand National
Steeplechasing's most famous race; first run at Maghull in 1836; at Aintree since 1839; war-time races at Gatwick 1916–18.

Recent winners	Horse (Jockey)
1984	Hallo Dandy (Neale Doughty)
1985	Last Suspect (Hywel Davies)
1986	West Tip (Richard Dunwoody)
1987	Maori Venture (Steve Knight)
1988	Rhyme 'N' Reason (Brendan Powell)
1989	Little Polveir (Jimmy Frost)
1990	Mr Frisk (Marcus Armytage)
1991	Seagram (Nigel Hawke)
1992	Party Politics (Carl Llewellyn)
1993	*declared void*
1994	Miinnehoma (Richard Dunwoody)

Prix de l'Arc de Triomphe
The leading end of season race in Europe; raced over 2 400 metres at Longchamp; first run in 1920.

Recent winners	Horse (Jockey)
1984	Sagace (Yves Saint-Martin)
1985	Rainbow Quest (Pat Eddery)
1986	Dancing Brave (Pat Eddery)
1987	Trempolino (Pat Eddery)
1988	Tony Bin (John Reid)
1989	Caroll House (Michael Kinane)
1990	Suamarez (Gerard Mosse)
1991	Suave Dancer (Cash Asmussen)
1992	Subotica (Thierry Jarnet)
1993	Urban Sea (E. Saint-Martin)
1994	Carnegie (Thierry Jarnet)

ICE HOCKEY

World Championship
First held in 1930; takes place annually (except 1980); up to 1968 Olympic champions also regarded as world champions.

Recent winners

1984	USSR
1985	Czechoslovakia
1986	USSR
1987	Sweden
1988	USSR
1989	USSR
1990	USSR
1991	Sweden
1992	Unified Team
1993	Russia
1994	Canada

Stanley Cup
The most sought-after trophy at club level; the end-of-season meeting between the winners of the two conferences in the National Hockey League in the USA and Canada.

Recent winners

1984	Edmonton Oilers
1985	Edmonton Oilers
1986	Montreal Canadiens
1987	Edmonton Oilers
1988	Edmonton Oilers
1989	Calgary Flames
1990	Edmonton Oilers
1991	Pittsburgh Penguins
1992	Pittsburgh Penguins
1993	Montreal Canadiens
1994	New York Rangers

ICE SKATING

World Championships
First men's championships in 1896; first women's event in 1906; pairs first contested in 1908; Ice Dance officially recognized in 1952.

Recent winners (Men)

1984	Scott Hamilton (USA)
1985	Alexander Fadeyev (USSR)
1986	Brian Boitano (USA)
1987	Brian Orser (Canada)
1988	Brian Boitano (USA)
1989	Kurt Browning (Canada)
1990	Kurt Browning (Canada)
1991	Kurt Browning (Canada)
1992	Viktor Petrenko (CIS)
1993	Kurt Browning (Canada)
1994	Elvis Stojko (Canada)

Recent winners (Women)

1984	Katarina Witt (East Germany)
1985	Katarina Witt (East Germany)
1986	Debbie Thomas (USA)
1987	Katarina Witt (East Germany)
1988	Katarina Witt (East Germany)
1989	Midori Ito (Japan)
1990	Jill Trenary (USA)
1991	Kristi Yamaguchi (USA)
1992	Kristi Yamaguchi (USA)
1993	Oksana Baiul (Ukraine)
1994	Yuka Sato (Japan)

Recent winners (Pairs)

1984	Paul Martini/Barbara Underhill (Canada)
1985	Oleg Vasilev/Yelena Valova (USSR)
1986	Sergey Grinkov/Yekaterina Gordeeva (USSR)
1987	Sergey Grinkov/Yekaterina Gordeeva (USSR)
1988	Oleg Vasilev/Yelena Valova (USSR)
1989	Sergey Grinkov/Yekaterina Gordeeva (USSR)
1990	Sergey Grinkov/Yekaterina Gordeeva (USSR)
1991	Arthur Dmtriev/Natalya Mishkutienok (USSR)
1992	Arthur Dmtriev/Natalya Mishkutienok (USSR)
1993	Lloyd Eisler/Isabelle Brasseur (Canada)
1994	Vadim Naumov/Evgenia Shiskova (Russia)

ICE SKATING (cont.)

Recent winners (Ice Dance)

1984	Christopher Dean/Jayne Torvill (Great Britain)
1985	Andrey Bukin/Natalya Bestemianova (USSR)
1986	Andrey Bukin/Natalya Bestemianova (USSR)
1987	Andrey Bukin/Natalya Bestemianova (USSR)
1988	Andrey Bukin/Natalya Bestemianova (USSR)
1989	Sergey Ponomarenko/Marina Klimova (USSR)
1990	Sergey Ponomarenko/Marina Klimova (USSR)
1991	Alexandra Zhulin/Maia Usova (USSR)
1992	Sergey Ponomarenko/Marina Klimova (CIS)
1993	Alexander Zhulin/Maia Usova (Russia)
1994	Evgeny Platov/Oksana Gritschuk (Russia)

MOTOR RACING

World Championship

A Formula One drivers' world championship instituted in 1950; constructor's championship instituted in 1958.

Recent winners

1984	Niki Lauda (Austria)	*McLaren*
1985	Alain Prost (France)	*McLaren*
1986	Alain Prost (France)	*Williams*
1987	Nelson Piquet (Brazil)	*Williams*
1988	Ayrton Senna (Brazil)	*McLaren*
1989	Alain Prost (France)	*McLaren*
1990	Ayrton Senna (Brazil)	*McLaren*
1991	Ayrton Senna (Brazil)	*McLaren*
1992	Nigel Mansell (England)	*Williams*
1993	Alain Prost (French)	*Williams*
1994	Michael Schumacher (German)	*Benetton*

Le Mans 24-Hour Race

The greatest of all endurance races; first held in 1923.

Recent winners

1984	Klaus Ludwig (West Germany)
	Henri Pescarolo (France)
1985	Klaus Ludwig (West Germany)
	'John Winter'[1] (West Germany)
	Paolo Barilla (Italy)
1986	Hans Stück (West Germany)
	Derek Bell (Great Britain)
	Al Holbert (USA)
1987	Hans Stück (West Germany)
	Derek Bell (Great Britain)
	Al Holbert (USA)
1988	Jan Lammers (Holland)
	Johnny Dumfries (Great Britain)
	Andy Wallace (Great Britain)
1989	Jochen Mass (West Germany)
	Manuel Reuter (West Germany)
	Stanley Dickens (Sweden)
1990	John Nielsen (Denmark)
	Price Cobb (USA)
	Martin Brundle (Great Britain)
1991	Volker Weidler (Germany)
	Johnny Herbert (Great Britain)
	Bertrand Gachot (Belgium)
1992	Derek Warwick (Great Britain)
	Mark Blundell (Great Britain)
	Yannick Dalmas (France)
1993	Christophe Bouchut (France)
	Eric Helary (France
	Geoff Brabham (Australia)
1994	Hurley Haywood (USA)
	Yannic Dalmas (France)
	Mauro Baldi (Italy)

[1] pseudonym

Indianapolis 500

First held in 1911; raced over the Indianapolis Raceway as part of the Memorial Day celebrations at the end of May each year.

Recent winners

1984	Rick Mears (USA)
1985	Danny Sullivan (USA)
1986	Bobby Rahal (USA)
1987	Al Unser (USA)

Recent winners

1988	Rick Mears (USA)
1989	Emerson Fittipaldi (Brazil)
1990	Arie Luyendyk (Holland)
1991	Rick Mears (USA)
1992	Al Unser (USA)
1993	Emerson Fittipaldi (Brazil)
1994	Al Unser jun. (USA)

Monte Carlo Rally
The world's leading rally; first held in 1911.

Recent winners

1984	Walter Röhrl (West Germany)
	Christian Geistdörfer (West Germany)
1985	Ari Vatanen (Finland)
	Terry Harryman (Great Britain)
1986	Henri Toivonen (Finland)
	Sergio Cresto (Italy)
1987	Miki Biasion (Italy)
	Tiziano Siviero (Italy)
1988	Bruno Saby (France)
	Jean-François Fauchille (France)
1989	Miki Biasion (Italy)
	Tiziano Siviero (Italy)
1990	Didier Auriol (France)
	Bernard Occelli (France)
1991	Carlos Sainz (Spain)
	Luis Moya (Spain)
1992	Didier Auriol (France)
	Bernard Occelli (France)
1993	Didier Auriol (France)
	Bernard Occelli (France)
1994	Francois Delecour (France)

ROWING

World Championships
First held for men in 1962 and for women in 1974; Olympic champions assume the role of world champion in Olympic years; principal events are the single sculls.

Recent winners Single Sculls (Men)

1984	Pertti Karppinen (Finland)
1985	Pertti Karppinen (Finland)

Recent winners Single Sculls (Men)

1986	Peter-Michael Kolbe (West Germany)
1987	Thomas Lange (East Germany)
1988	Thomas Lange (East Germany)
1989	Thomas Lange (East Germany)
1990	Yuri Janson (USSR)
1991	Thomas Lange (Germany)
1992	Thomas Lange (Germany)
1993	Derek Porter (Canada)
1994	Andre Wilms (Germany)

Recent winners Single Sculls (Women)

1984	Valeria Racila (Romania)
1985	Cornelia Linse (East Germany)
1986	Jutta Hampe (East Germany)
1987	Magdelena Georgieva (Bulgaria)
1988	Jutta Behrendt (East Germany)
1989	Elisabeta Lipa (Romania)
1990	Brigit Peter (East Germany)
1991	Silke Laumann (Canada)
1992	Elisabeta Lipa (Romania)
1993	Jana Thieme (Germany)
1994	Trine Hansen (Denmark)

The Boat Race
An annual contest between the crews from the Oxford and Cambridge University rowing clubs; first contested in 1829; the current course is from Putney to Mortlake.

Recent winners

1984	Oxford
1985	Oxford
1986	Cambridge
1987	Oxford
1988	Oxford
1989	Oxford
1990	Oxford
1991	Oxford
1992	Oxford
1993	Cambridge
1994	Cambridge

ROWING (cont.)

Diamond Sculls
Highlight of Henley Royal Regatta held every July; first contested in 1884.

Recent winners

1984	Chris Baillieu (Great Britain)
1985	Steve Redgrave (Great Britain)
1986	Bjarne Eltang (Denmark)
1987	Peter-Michael Kolbe (West Germany)
1988	Hamish McGlashan (Australia)
1989	Vaclav Chlupa (Czechoslovakia)
1990	Erik Verdonk (New Zealand)
1991	Wim van Belleghem (Belgium)
1992	Rorie Henderson (Great Britain)
1993	Thomas Lange (Germany)
1994	Xeno Muller (Switzerland)

RUGBY LEAGUE

Challenge Cup Final
First contested in 1897 and won by Batley; first final at Wembley Stadium in 1929.

Recent winners

1984	Widnes
1985	Wigan
1986	Castleford
1987	Halifax
1988	Wigan
1989	Wigan
1990	Wigan
1991	Wigan
1992	Wigan
1993	Wigan
1994	Wigan

Premiership Trophy
End-of-season knockout competition involving the top eight teams in the first division; first contested at the end of the 1974–5 season.

Recent winners

1984	Hull Kingston Rovers
1985	St Helens

Recent winners

1986	Warrington
1987	Wigan
1988	Widnes
1989	Widnes
1990	Widnes
1991	Hull
1992	Wigan
1993	St Helens
1994	Wigan

Regal Trophy
A knockout competition, first held in 1971–2. Formerly known as the John Player Special Trophy, it adopted its current style in 1989–90.

Recent winners

1984	Hull Kingston Rovers
1985	Wigan
1986	Wigan
1987	St Helens
1988	Wigan
1989	Wigan
1990	Warrington
1991	Widnes
1992	Widnes
1993	Wigan
1994	Castleford

RUGBY UNION

World Cup
The first Rugby Union World Cup was staged in 1987; New Zealand were crowned the first champions after beating France in the final. Australia won the second World Cup in 1991, defeating England in the final.

International Championship
A round robin competition involving England, Ireland, Scotland, Wales and France; first contested in 1884.

Recent winners

1984	Scotland
1985	Ireland

Recent winners

1986	France and Scotland
1987	France
1988	France and Wales
1989	France
1990	Scotland
1991	England
1992	England
1993	France
1994	Wales

County Championship
First held in 1889.

Recent winners

1984	Gloucestershire
1985	Middlesex
1986	Warwickshire
1987	Yorkshire
1988	Lancashire
1989	Durham
1990	Lancashire
1991	Cornwall
1992	Lancashire
1993	Lancashire
1994	Yorkshire

Pilkington Cup
An annual knockout competition for English Club sides; first held in the 1971–2 season. Known as the John Player Special Cup until 1988.

Recent winners

1984	Bath
1985	Bath
1986	Bath
1987	Bath
1988	Harlequins
1989	Bath
1990	Bath
1991	Harlequins
1992	Bath
1993	Bath
1994	Leicester

Schweppes Welsh Cup
The knockout tournament for Welsh clubs; first held in 1971–2.

Recent winners

1984	Cardiff
1985	Llanelli
1986	Cardiff
1987	Cardiff
1988	Llanelli
1989	Neath
1990	Neath
1991	Llanelli
1992	Llanelli
1993	Llanelli
1994	Cardiff

SKIING

World Cup
A season-long competition first organized in 1967; champions are declared in downhill, slalom, giant slalom and super-giant slalom, as well as the overall champion; points are obtained for performances in each category.

Recent overall winners (Men)

1984	Pirmin Zurbriggen (Switzerland)
1985	Marc Girardelli (Luxembourg)
1986	Marc Girardelli (Luxembourg)
1987	Pirmin Zurbriggen (Switzerland)
1988	Pirmin Zurbriggen (Switzerland)
1989	Marc Girardelli (Luxembourg)
1990	Pirmin Zurbriggen (Switzerland)
1991	Marc Girardelli (Luxembourg)
1992	Paul Accola (Switzerland)
1993	Marc Girardelli (Luxembourg)
1994	Kjetil-Andre Aamodt (Norway)

Recent overall winners (Women)

1984	Frika Hess (Switzerland)
1985	Michela Figini (Switzerland)
1986	Maria Walliser (Switzerland)
1987	Maria Walliser (Switzerland)
1988	Michela Figini (Switzerland)

SKIING (cont.)

Recent overall winners (Women)

1989	Vreni Schneider (Switzerland)
1990	Petra Kronberger (Austria)
1991	Petra Kronberger (Austria)
1992	Petra Kronberger (Austria)
1993	Anita Wachter (Austria)
1994	Vreni Schneider (Swit)

SNOOKER

World Professional Championship
Instituted in the 1926–7 season; a knockout competition open to professional players who are members of the World Professional Billiards and Snooker Association; played at the Crucible Theatre, Sheffield.

Recent winners

1984	Steve Davis (England)
1985	Dennis Taylor (England)
1986	Joe Johnson (England)
1987	Steve Davis (England)
1988	Steve Davis (England)
1989	Steve Davis (England)
1990	Stephen Hendry (Scotland)
1991	John Parrott (England)
1992	Stephen Hendry (Scotland)
1993	Stephen Hendry (Scotland)
1994	Stephen Hendry (Scotland)

World Amateur Championship
First held in 1963; originally took place every two years, but annual since 1984.

Recent winners

1984	O. B. Agrawal (India)
1985	Paul Mifsud (Malta)
1986	Paul Mifsud (Malta)
1987	Darren, Morgan (Wales)
1988	James Wattana (Thailand)
1989	Ken Doherty (Republic of Ireland)
1990	Stephen O'Connor (Republic of Ireland)
1991	Noppodol Noppajorn (Thailand)

Recent winners

1992	Neil Mosley (England)
1993	Tai Pichit (Thailand)
1994	Mohammed Yusuf (Pakistan)

SOFTBALL

World Championships
First held for women in 1965 and for men the following year; now held every four years.

Winners (Men)

1966	USA
1968	USA
1972	Canada
1976	Canada, New Zealand & USA (*shared*)
1980	USA
1984	New Zealand
1988	USA
1992	Canada

Winners (Women)

1965	Australia
1970	Japan
1974	USA
1978	USA
1982	New Zealand
1986	USA
1990	USA

SQUASH

World Open Championship
First held in 1976; takes place annually for men, every two years for women.

Winners (Men)

1984	Jahangir Khan (Pakistan)
1985	Jahangir Khan (Pakistan)
1986	Ross Norman (New Zealand)

Winners (Men)

1987	Jansher Khan (Pakistan)
1988	Jahangir Khan (Pakistan)
1989	Jansher Khan (Pakistan)
1990	Jansher Khan (Pakistan)
1991	Rodney Martin (Australia)
1992	Jansher Khan (Pakistan)
1993	Jansher Khan (Pakistan)
1994	Jansher Khan (Pakistan)

Winners (Women)

1976	Heather McKay (Australia)
1979	Heather McKay (Australia)
1981	Rhonda Thorne (Australia)
1983	Vicky Cardwell (Australia)
1985	Sue Devoy (New Zealand)
1987	Sue Devoy (New Zealand)
1989	Martine Le Moignan (Great Britain)
1990	Sue Devoy (New Zealand)
1991	Susan Devoy (New Zealand)
1992	Susan Devoy (New Zealand)
1993	Michelle Martin (Australia)
1994	Michelle Martin (Australia)

SURFING

World Professional Championship
A season-long series of Grand Prix events; first held in 1970.

Recent winners (Men)

1984	Tom Carroll (Australia)
1985	Tom Carroll (Australia)
1986	Tommy Curren (USA)
1987	Damien Hardman (Australia)
1988	Barton Lynch (Australia)
1989	Martin Potter (Great Britain)
1990	Heifara Tahutini (Tahiti)
1991	Damien Hardman (Australia)
1992	Kelly Slater (USA)
1993	Derek Ho (USA)
1994	Kelly Slater (USA)

Recent winners (Women)

1984	Kim Mearig (USA)
1985	Frieda Zamba (USA)
1986	Frieda Zamba (USA)
1987	Wendy Botha (South Africa)
1988	Frieda Zamba (USA)
1989	Wendy Botha (South Africa)
1990	Kathy Newman (Australia)
1991	Wendy Botha (South Africa)
1992	Wendy Botha (South Africa)
1993	Pauline Menczer (Australia
1994	Lisa Andersen (USA)

SWIMMING AND DIVING

World Championships
First held in 1973 and again in 1975; since 1978 take place every four years; 1990 championships postponed until 1991.

1994 World Champions (Men)

50 metres freestyle	Alexander Popov (Russia)
100 metres freestyle	Alexander Popov (Russia)
200 metres freestyle	Anti Casvio (Finland)
400 metres freestyle	Kieren Perkins (Australia)
1 500 metres freestyle	Kieren Perkins (Australia)
100 metres backstroke	Martin Lopez Zubero (Spain)
200 metres backstroke	Vladimir Selkov (Russia)
100 metres breaststroke	Norbert Rosza (Hungary)
200 metres breaststroke	Norbert Rosza (Hungary)
100 metres butterfly	Rafal Szukala (Poland)
200 metres butterfly	Dennis Pankratov (Russia)
200 metres individual medley	Jani Sievinen (Finland)
400 metres individual medley	Tom Dolan (USA)

SWIMMING AND DIVING (cont.)

1994 World Champions (Men)

4 x 100 metres freestyle medley	USA
4 x 200 metres freestyle medley	Sweden
4 x 100 metres medley relay	USA
Springboard diving (1 m)	Evan Stewart (Zimbabwe)
Highboard diving (10m)	Dmitri Sautin (Russia)

1994 World Champions (Women)

50 metres freestyle	Le Jingyi (China)
100 metres freestyle	Le Jingyi (China)
200 metres freestyle	Franziska van Almsick (Germany)
400 metres freestyle	Yang Ai Hua (China)
800 metres freestyle	Janet Evans (USA)
100 metres backstroke	He Chihong (China)
200 metres backstroke	He Chihong (China)
100 metres breaststroke	Samantha Riley (Australia)
200 metres breaststroke	Samantha Riley (Australia)
100 metres butterfly	Liu Limin (China)
200 metres butterfly	Liu Limin (China)
200 metres individual medley	Lu Bin (China)
400 metres individual medley	Dai Guohong (China)
4 x 100 metres freestyle relay	China
4 x 200 metres freestyle relay	China
4 x 100 metres medley relay	China
Springboard diving (1m)	Lixia Chen (China)
Highboard diving (10m)	Mingxia Fu (China)

Synchronized swimming

Solo	Becky Dyroen Lance (USA)
Duet	Lancer and Sudduth (USA)
Team	USA

TABLE TENNIS

World Championships
First held in 1926 and every two years since 1957.

Recent winners

Swaythling Cup (Men's Team)
1983	China
1985	China
1987	China
1989	Sweden
1991	Sweden
1993	Sweden

Recent winners

Corbillon Cup (Women's Team)
1983	China
1985	China
1987	China
1989	China
1991	United Korea
1993	China

Recent winners

Men's Singles
1983	Guo Yuehua (China)
1985	Jiang Jialiang (China)
1987	Jiang Jialiang (China)
1989	Jan-Ove Waldner (Sweden)
1991	Jorgen Persson (Sweden)
1993	Jean-Philippe Gatien (France)

Recent winners

Women's singles
1983	Cao Yanhua (China)
1985	Cao Yanhua (China)
1987	He Zhili (China)
1989	Qiao Hong (China)
1991	Deng Yaping (China)
1993	Hyun Jung-hwa (South Korea)

Recent winners

Men's Doubles

1983 Dragutin Surbek/Zoran Kalinic
        (Yugoslavia)
1985 Mikael Applegren/Ulf Carlsson (Sweden)
1987 Chen Longcan/Wei Quinguang (China)
1989 Jaerg Rosskopf/Stefen Fetzner (West
        Germany)
1991 Peter Karlsson/Tomas von Scheele
        (Sweden)
1993 Wang Tao/Lu Lin (China)

Recent winners

Women's Doubles

1983 Shen Jianping/Dai Lili (China)
1985 Dai Lili/Geng Lijuan (China)
1987 Yang Young-Ja/Hyun Jung-Hwa
        (Korea)
1989 Quio Hong/Deng Yaping (China)
1991 Chen Zhie/Liu Wei (China)
1993 Liu Wei/Qiao Hong (China)

Recent winners

Mixed Doubles

1983 Guo Yuehua/Ni Xialian (China)
1985 Cai Zhenua/Cao Yanhua (China)
1987 Hui Jun/Geng Lijuan (China)
1989 Yoo Nam-Kyu/Hyun Jung-Hwa (South
        Korea)
1991 Wang Tao/Liu Wei (China)
1993 Wang Tao/Liu Wei (China)

TENNIS (LAWN)

Wimbledon Championships
The All-England Championships at Wimbledon are
Lawn Tennis's most prestigious championships;
first held in 1877.

Recent winners

Men's Singles

1984 John McEnroe (USA)
1985 Boris Becker (West Germany)
1986 Boris Becker (West Germany)

Recent winners

1987 Pat Cash (Australia)
1988 Stefan Edberg (Sweden)
1989 Boris Becker (West Germany)
1990 Stefan Edberg (Sweden)
1991 Michael Stich (Germany)
1992 André Agassi (USA)
1993 Pete Sampras (USA)
1994 Pete Sampras (USA)

Recent winners

Women's Singles

1984 Martina Navratilova (USA)
1985 Martina Navratilova (USA)
1986 Martina Navratilova (USA)
1987 Martina Navratilova (USA)
1988 Steffi Graf (West Germany)
1989 Steffi Graf (West Germany)
1990 Martina Navratilova (USA)
1991 Steffi Graf (Germany)
1992 Steffi Graf (Germany)
1993 Steffi Graf (Germany)
1994 Conchita Martinez (Spain)

Recent winners

Men's Doubles

1984 Peter Fleming/John McEnroe (USA)
1985 Heinz Gunthardt (Switzerland)/Balazs
        Taroczy (Hungary)
1986 Joakim Nystrom/Mats Wilander
        (Sweden)
1987 Ken Flach/Robert Seguso (USA)
1988 Ken Flach/Robert Seguso (USA)
1989 John Fitzgerald (Australia)/Anders Jarryd
        (Sweden)
1990 Rick Leach/Jim Pugh (USA)
1991 John Fitzgerald (Australia)/Anders Jarryd
        (Sweden)
1992 John McEnroe (USA)/Michael Stich
        (Germany)
1993 Todd Woodbridge/Mark Woodforde
        (Australia)
1994 Todd Woodbridge/Mark Woodforde
        (Australia)

TENNIS (LAWN) (cont.)

Recent winners

Women's Doubles
1984   Martina Navratilova/Pam Shriver (USA)
1985   Kathy Jordan/Elizabeth Smylie (Aus)
1986   Martina Navratilova/Pam Shriver (USA)
1987   Claudia Kohde-Kilsch (West Germany)/
        Helena Sukova (Czechoslovakia)
1988   Steffi Graf (West Germany)/Gabriela
        Sabatini (Argentina)
1989   Jana Novotna/Helena Sukova
        (Czechoslovakia)
1990   Jana Novotna/Helena Sukova
        (Czechoslovakia)
1991   Natalya Zvereva/Larisa Savchenko
        (USSR)
1992   Gigi Fernandez (USA)/Natalya Zvereva (CIS)
1993   Gigi Fernandez (USA) and Natalya
        Zvereva (Belarus)
1994   Gigi Fernandez (USA) and Natalya
        Zvereva (Belarus)

Recent winners

Mixed Doubles
1984   Wendy Turnbull (Australia)/John Lloyd
        (Great Britain)
1985   Martina Navratilova (USA)/Paul McNamee
        (Australia)
1986   Kathy Jordan/Ken Flach (USA)
1987   Jo Durie/Jeremy Bates (Great Britain)
1988   Sherwood Stewart/Zina Garrison (USA)
1989   Jim Pugh (USA)/Jan Novotna
        (Czechoslovakia)
1990   Rick Leach/Zina Garrison (USA)
1991   John Fitzgerald/Elizabeth Smylie
        (Australia)
1992   Cyril Suk (Czechoslovakia)/Larisa
        Savchenko-Neiland (Latvia)
1993   Mark Woodforde (Australia)/Martina
        Navratilova (USA)
1994   Todd Woodbridge (Australia)/Helena
        Sukova (Czech Republic)

United States Open
First held in 1891 as the United States Championship;
became the United States Open in 1968.
Recent winners

Men's Singles
1979   John McEnroe (USA)
1980   John McEnroe (USA)
1981   John McEnroe (USA)
1982   Jimmy Connors (USA)
1983   Jimmy Connors (USA)
1984   John McEnroe (USA)
1985   Ivan Lendl (Czechoslovakia)
1986   Ivan Lendl (Czechoslovakia)
1987   Ivan Lendl (Czechoslovakia)
1988   Mats Wilander (Sweden)
1989   Boris Becker (West Germany)
1990   Pete Sampras (USA)
1991   Stefan Edberg (Sweden)
1992   Stefan Edberg (Sweden)
1993   Pete Sampras (USA)
1994   Andre Agassi (USA)

Recent winners

Women's Singles
1979   Tracy Austin (USA)
1980   Chris Evert-Lloyd (USA)
1981   Tracy Austin (USA)
1982   Chris Evert-Lloyd (USA)
1983   Martina Navratilova (USA)
1984   Martina Navratilova (USA)
1985   Hana Mandlikova (Czechoslovakia)
1986   Martina Navratilova (USA)
1987   Martina Navratilova (USA)
1988   Steffi Graf (West Germany)
1989   Steffi Graf (West Germany)
1990   Gabriela Sabatini (Argentina)
1991   Monica Seles (Yugoslavia)
1992   Monica Seles (Yugoslavia)
1993   Steffi Graf (Germany)
1994   Arantxa Sánchez Vicario (Spain)

Davis Cup

International team competition organized on a knockout basis; first held in 1900; contested on a challenge basis until 1972.

Recent winners

1984	Sweden
1985	Sweden
1986	Australia
1987	Sweden
1988	West Germany
1989	West Germany
1990	USA
1991	France
1992	USA
1993	Germany
1994	Sweden

WEIGHTLIFTING

World Championships

First held in 1898; 11 weight divisions; the most prestigious is the 108 kg-plus category (formerly known as Super Heavyweight); Olympic champions are automatically world champions in Olympic years.

Recent champions (108+ kg)

1984	Dean Lukin (Australia)
1985	Antonio Krastev (Bulgaria)
1986	Antonio Krastev (Bulgaria)
1987	Aleksander Kurlovich (USSR)
1988	Aleksander Kurlovich (USSR)
1989	Stefan Botev (Bulgaria)
1990	Stefan Botev (Bulgaria)
1991	Aleksander Kurlovich (USSR)
1992	Aleksander Kurlovich (UT)
1993	Ronnie Weller (Germany)
1994	Aleksandr Kurlovich (Belorussia)

WRESTLING

World Championships

Graeco-Roman world championships first held in 1921; first freestyle championships in 1951; each style contests 10 weight divisions, the heaviest being the 130 kg (formerly over 100 kg) category; Olympic champions become world champions in Olympic years.

Recent winners (Super-heavyweight/over 100 kg)

Freestyle

1984	Bruce Baumgartner (USA)
1985	David Gobedichviliy (USSR)
1986	Bruce Baumgartner (USA)
1987	Khadartsv Aslam (USSR)
1988	David Gobedzhishvilli (USSR)
1989	Ali Reiza Soleimani (Iran)
1990	David Gobedzhishvilli (USSR)
1991	Andreas Schroder (Germany)
1992	Bruce Baumgartner (USA)
1993	Mikael Ljunberg (Sweden)
1994	Mahmut Demir (Turkey)

Graeco-Roman

1984	Jeffrey Blatnick (USA)
1985	Igor Rostozotskiy (USSR)
1986	Thomas Johansson (Sweden)
1987	Igor Rostozotskiy (USSR)
1988	Alexsander Karoline (USSR)
1989	Alexsander Karoline (USSR)
1990	Alexsander Karoline (USSR)
1991	Alexsander Karoline (USSR)
1992	Alexsander Karoline (UT)
1993	Alexsander Karoline (Russia)
1994	Alexsander Karoline (Russia)

YACHTING

America's Cup

One of sport's famous trophies; first won by the schooner *Magic* in 1870; now held approximately every four years, when challengers compete in a series of races to find which of them races against the holder; all 25 winners up to 1983 were from the United States.

Post-war winners	Winning Yacht (Skipper)
1958	*Columbia* (USA) (Briggs Cunningham)

YACHTING (cont.)

Post-war winners	Winning Yacht (Skipper)
1962	*Weatherly* (USA) (Emil Mosbacher)
1964	*Constellation* (USA) (Bob Bavier)
1967	*Intrepid* (USA) (Emil Mosbacher)
1970	*Intrepid* (USA) (Bill Ficker)
1974	*Courageous* (USA) (Ted Hood)
1977	*Courageous* (USA) (Ted Turner)
1980	*Freedom* (USA) (Dennis Conner)
1983	*Australia II* (Australia) (John Bertrand)
1987	*Stars & Stripes* (USA) (Dennis Conner)
1988	*Stars & Stripes* (USA) (Dennis Conner)[1]
1992	*America[3]* (USA) (Bill Koch)

[1] Stars and Stripes (USA) skippered by Dennis Conner won a special challenge match but on appeal the race was awarded to the New Zealand boat. However the decision was reversed by the New York Appeals court in 1989.

Admiral's Cup

A two-yearly series of races in the English Channel, around Fastnet rock and at Cowes; four national teams of three boats per team; first held in 1957.

Recent winners

1981	Great Britain
1983	West Germany
1985	West Germany
1987	New Zealand
1989	Great Britain
1991	France
1993	Germany

GENERAL KNOWLEDGE

INTERNATIONAL TIME DIFFERENCES

The time zones of the world are conventionally measured from longitude 0 at Greenwich Observatory (Greenwich Mean Time, GMT).

Each 15° of longitude east of this point is one hour ahead of GMT (eg when it is 2pm in London it is 3pm or later in time zones to the east). Hours ahead of GMT are shown by a plus sign, eg +3, +4/8.

Each 15° west of this point is one hour behind GMT (eg 2pm in London would be 1pm or earlier in time zones to the west). Hours behind GMT are shown by a minus sign, eg −3, −4/8.

Some countries adopt time zones that vary from standard time. Also, during the summer, several countries adopt Daylight Saving Time (or Summer Time), which is one hour ahead of the times shown below.

Afghanistan	+4.5	Central African	+1	Ghana	0	Lesotho	+2
Albania	+1	Republic		Gibraltar	+1	Liberia	0
Algeria	+1	Chad	+1	Greece	+2	Libya	+2
Andorra	+1	Chile	−4	Greenland	−3	Liechtenstein	+1
Angola	+1	China	+8	Grenada	−4	Lithuania	+2
Antigua and	−1	Colombia	−5	Guatemala	−6	Luxembourg	+1
Barbuda		Comoros	+3	Guinea	0	Madagascar	+3
Argentina	−3	Congo	+1	Guinea-Bissau	0	Malawi	+2
Armenia	+4	Costa Rica	−6	Guyana	−4	Malaysia	+8
Australia	+8/10	Cuba	−5	Haiti	−5	Maldives	+5
Austria	+1	Cyprus	+2	Honduras	−6	Mali	0
Bahamas	−5	Czech Republic	+1	Hong Kong	+8	Malta	+1
Bahrain	+3	Denmark	+1	Hungary	+1	Marshall Islands	+12
Bangladesh	+6	Djibouti	+3	Iceland	0	Mauritania	0
Barbados	−4	Dominica	−4	India	+5.5	Mauritius	+4
Belgium	+1	Dominican	−4	Indonesia	+7/9	Mexico	−6/8
Belize	−6	Republic		Iran	+3.5	Micronesia,	+10/11
Belorussia	+2	Ecuador	−5	Iraq	+3	Federated	
Benin	+1	Egypt	+2	Ireland	0	states of	
Bermuda	−4	El Salvador	−6	Israel	+2	Moldavia	+2
Bhutan	+6	Equatorial	+1	Italy	+1	Monaco	+1
Bolivia	−4	Guinea		Ivory Coast	0	Mongolia	+8
Botswana	+2	Eritrea	+3	Jamaica	−5	Morocco	0
Brazil	−2/5	Estonia	+2	Japan	+9	Mozambique	+2
Brunei	+8	Ethiopia	+3	Jordan	+2	Namibia	+2
Bulgaria	+2	Falkland Is	−4	Kazakhstan	+6	Nauru	+12
Burkina	0	Fiji	+12	Kenya	+3	Nepal	+5.75
Burma	+6	Finland	+2	Kirghizia	+5	Netherlands, The	+1
Burundi	+2	France	+1	Kiribati	+12	New Zealand	+12
Cambodia	+7	Gabon	+1	Kuwait	+3	Nicaragua	−5
Cameroon	+1	Gambia, The	0	Laos	+7	Niger	+1
Canada	−3/9	Georgia	+3	Latvia	+2	Nigeria	+1
Cape Verde	−1	Germany	+1	Lebanon	+2	North Korea	+9

INTERNATIONAL TIME DIFFERENCES (cont.)

Norway	+1	St Vincent and	−4	Suriname	−3	United Arab	+4
Oman	+4	the Grenadines		Swaziland	+2	Emirates	
Pakistan	+5	San Marino	+1	Sweden	+1	United Kingdom	0
Panama	−5	São Tomé and	0	Switzerland	+1	Uruguay	−3
Papua New	+10	Principe		Syria	+2	USA	−5/11
Guinea		Saudi Arabia	+3	Taiwan	+8	Uzbekistan	+5
Paraguay	−4	Senegal	0	Tajikistan	+5	Vanuatu	+11
Peru	−5	Seychelles	+4	Tanzania	+3	Venezuela	−4
Philippines	+8	Sierra Leone	0	Thailand	+7	Vietnam	+7
Poland	+1	Singapore	+8	Togo	0	Western Sahara	−1
Portugal	+1	Slovakia	+1	Tonga	+13	Western Samoa	−11
Puerto Rico	−4	Slovenia	+1	Trinidad and	−4	Yemen	+3
Qatar	+3	Solomon Is	+11	Tobago		Yugoslavia	+1
Romania	+2	Somalia	+3	Tunisia	+1	Zaire	+1/2
Russia	+2/12	South Africa	+2	Turkey	+2	Zambia	+2
Rwanda	+2	South Korea	+9	Turkmenistan	+5	Zimbabwe	+2
St Christopher-	−4	Spain	+1	Tuvalu	+12		
Nevis		Sri Lanka	+5.5	Uganda	+3		
St Lucia	−4	Sudan	+2	Ukraine	+2		

INTERNATIONAL TIME ZONES

World times at 12 noon GMT

Some countries have adopted half-hour time zones which are indicated on the map as a combination of two coded zones. For example, it is 1730 hours in India at 1200 GMT. The standard times shown are subject to variation in certain countries where Daylight Saving/Summer Time operates for part of the year.

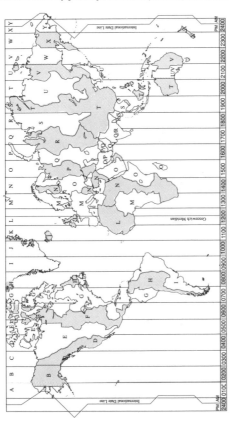

YEAR EQUIVALENTS

Gregorian equivalents are given in parentheses and are AD (=Anno Domini).

Jewish[1] (AM)

5754	(16 Sep 1993–5 Sep 1994)
5755	(6 Sep 1994–24 Sep 1995)
5756	(25 Sep 1995–13 Sep 1996)
5757	(14 Sep 1996–1 Oct 1997)
5758	(2 Oct 1997–20 Sep 1998)
5759	(21 Sep 1998–10 Sep 1999)
5760	(11 Sep 1999–29 Sep 2000)

Islamic[2] (H)

1414	(21 Jun 1993–9 Jun 1994)
1415	(10 Jun 1994–30 May 1995)
1416	(31 May 1995–18 May 1996)
1417	(19 May 1996–8 May 1997)
1418	(9 May 1997–27 Apr 1998)
1419	(28 Apr 1998–16 Apr 1999)
1420	(17 Apr 1999–5 Apr 2000)

Hindu[3] (SE)

1915	(22 Mar 1993–21 Mar 1994)
1916	(22 Mar 1994–21 Mar 1995)
1917	(22 Mar 1995–20 Mar 1996)
1918	(21 Mar 1996–21 Mar 1997)
1919	(22 Mar 1997–21 Mar 1998)
1920	(22 Mar 1998–21 Mar 1999)
1921	(22 Mar 1999–21 Mar 2000)

[1] Calculated from 3761 BC, said to be the year of the creation of the world. AM = Anno Mundi.
[2] Calculated from AD 622, the year in which the Prophet went from Mecca to Medina. H = Hegira.
[3] Calculated from AD 78, the beginning of the Saka era (SE), used alongside Gregorian dates in Government of India publications since 22 Mar 1957. Other important Hindu eras include: Vikrama era (58 BC), Kalacuri era (AD 248), Gupta era (AD 320), and Harsa era (AD 606).

MONTH EQUIVALENTS

Gregorian equivalents to other calendars are given in parentheses; the figures refer to the number of solar days in each month.

Gregorian	(Basis: Sun)	Islamic	(Basis: Moon)
	January (31)		Muharram (Sep–Oct) (30)
	February (28 or 29)		Safar (Oct–Nov) (29)
	March (31)		Rabi I (Nov–Dec) (30)
	April (30)		Rabi II (Dec–Jan) (29)
	May (31)		Jumada I (Jan–Feb) (30)
	June (30)		Jumada II (Feb–Mar) (29)
	July (31)		Rajab (Mar–Apr) (30)
	August (31)		Shaban (Apr–May) (29)
	September (30)		Ramadan (May–Jun) (30)
	October (31)		Shawwal (Jun–Jul) (29)
	November (30)		Dhu al-Qadah (Jul–Aug) (30)
	December (31)		Dhu al-Hijjah (Aug–Sep) (29 or 30)
Jewish	(Basis: Moon)	Hindu	(Basis: Moon)
	Tishri (Sep–Oct) (30)		Chaitra (Mar–Apr) (29 or 30)
	Heshvan (Oct–Nov) (29 or 30)		Vaisakha (Apr–May) (29 or 30)
	Kislev (Nov–Dec) (29 or 30)		Jyaistha (May–Jun) (29 or 30)
	Tevet (Dec–Jan) (29)		Asadha (Jun–Jul) (29 or 30)
	Shevat (Jan–Feb) (30)		Dvitiya Asadha (*certain leap years*)
	Adar (Feb–Mar) (29 or 30)		Sravana (Jul–Aug) (29 or 30)
	Adar Sheni *leap years only*		Dvitiya Sravana (*certain leap years*)
	Nisan (Mar–Apr) (29)		Bhadrapada (Aug–Sep) (29 or 30)
	Iyar (Apr–May) (29)		Asvina (Sep–Oct) (29 or 30)
	Sivan (May–Jun) (30)		Karttika (Oct–Nov) (29 or 30)
	Tammuz (Jun–Jul) (29)		Margasirsa (Nov–Dec) (29 or 30)
	Av (Jul–Aug) (30)		Pausa (Dec–Jan) (29 or 30)
	Elul (Aug–Sep) (29)		Magha (Jan–Feb) (29 or 30)
			Phalguna (Feb–Mar) (29 or 30)

CHINESE ANIMAL YEARS AND TIMES 1984–2007

Chinese	English	Years		Time of day (hours)
Shu	Rat	1984	1996	2300–0100
Niu	Ox	1985	1997	0100–0300
Hu	Tiger	1986	1998	0300–0500
Tu	Hare	1987	1999	0500–0700
Long	Dragon	1988	2000	0700–0900
She	Serpent	1989	2001	0900–1100
Ma	Horse	1990	2002	1100–1300
Yang	Sheep	1991	2003	1300–1500
Hou	Monkey	1992	2004	1500–1700
Ji	Cock	1993	2005	1700–1900
Gou	Dog	1994	2006	1900–2100
Zhu	Boar	1995	2007	2100–2300

THE SEASONS

N Hemisphere	Duration
Spring	From vernal equinox (c.21 Mar) to summer solstice (c.21 Jun)
Summer	From summer solstice (c.21 Jun) to autumnal equinox (c.23 Sept)
Autumn	From autumnal equinox (c.23 Sept) to winter solstice (c.21 Dec)
Winter	From winter solstice (c.21 Dec) to vernal equinox (c.21 Mar)

S Hemisphere	
Autumn	From autumnal equinox (c.21 Mar) to winter solstice (c.21 Jun)
Winter	From winter solstice (c.21 Jun) to spring equinox (c.23 Sept)
Spring	From spring equinox (c.23 Sept) to summer solstice (c.21 Dec)
Summer	From summer solstice (c.21 Dec) to autumnal equinox (c.21 Mar)

MONTHS (Associations of gems and flowers)

In many Western countries, the months are traditionally associated with gemstones and flowers. There is considerable variation between countries. The following combinations are widely recognized in North America and the UK.

Month	Gemstone	Flower
January	Garnet	Carnation, Snowdrop
February	Amethyst	Primrose, Violet
March	Aquamarine, Bloodstone	Jonquil, Violet
April	Diamond	Daisy, Sweet Pea
May	Emerald	Hawthorn, Lily of the Valley
June	Alexandrite, Moonstone, Pearl	Honeysuckle, Rose
July	Ruby	Larkspur, Water Lily
August	Peridot, Sardonyx	Gladiolus, Poppy
September	Sapphire	Aster, Morning Glory
October	Opal, Tourmaline	Calendula, Cosmos
November	Topaz	Chrysanthemum
December	Turquoise, Zircon	Holly, Narcissus, Poinsettia

WEDDING ANNIVERSARIES

In many Western countries, different wedding anniversaries have become associated with gifts of different materials. There is some variation between countries.

1st Cotton	6th Sugar	11th Steel	20th China	45th Sapphire
2nd Paper	7th Copper, Wool	12th Silk, Linen	25th Silver	50th Gold
3rd Leather	8th Bronze, Pottery	13th Lace	30th Pearl	55th Emerald
4th Fruit, Flowers	9th Pottery, Willow	14th Ivory	35th Coral	60th Diamond
5th Wood	10th Tin	15th Crystal	40th Ruby	70th Platinum

SIGNS OF THE ZODIAC

Spring Signs

Aries, the Ram
21 Mar-19 Apr

Gemini, the Twins
21 May-21 Jun

Taurus, the Bull
20 Apr-20 May

Summer Signs

Cancer, the Crab
22 Jun-22 July

Leo, the Lion
23 July-22 Aug

Virgo, the Virgin
23 Aug-22 Sep

Autumn Signs

Libra, the Balance
23 Sep-23 Oct

Scorpio, the Scorpion
24 Oct-21 Nov

Sagittarius, the Archer
22 Nov-21 Dec

Winter Signs

Capricorn, the Goat
22 Dec-19 Jan

Aquarius, the
Water Bearer
20 Jan-18 Feb

Pisces, the Fishes
19 Feb-20 Mar

SEVEN WONDERS OF THE ANCIENT WORLD

Originally compiled by Antipater of Sidon, a Greek poet, in the 100s BC

Name	Date built	Size	History
Pyramids of Egypt	c.2000 BC	147 m/481 ft high (the Great Pyramid at el-Gizeh)	Oldest and only surviving 'wonder'; built as royal tombs; about 80 are still standing.
Hanging Gardens of Babylon	c.600 BC	23–91 m/ 75–300 ft high	Terraced gardens adjoining Nebuchadnezzar's palace; supposedly built by the king to please his wife but also associated with the Assyrian Queen Semiramis.
Statue of Zeus at Olympia	c.400s BC	12 m/40 ft high	Carved by Phidias; marked the site of the original Olympic Games; constructed of ivory and gold; showed Zeus (Jupiter) on his throne.
Temple of Artemis (Diana) at Ephesus	c.350 BC	> 122 m/400 ft long, 18 m/ 60 ft high	Contained over 100 columns constructed of Parian marble; it took some 120 years to build; destroyed by the Goths in AD 262.
Mausoleum at Halicarnassus	c.352 BC	43 m/140 ft high	Erected by Queen Artemisia in memory of her husband King Mausolus of Caria (in Asia Minor); a few pieces remain in the British Museum.
Colossus of Rhodes	c.280 BC	36 m/117 ft high	Gigantic bronze statue of sun-god Helios (or Apollo) made by the sculptor Chares; dominated the harbour entrance at Rhodes; destroyed by an earthquake in 224 BC.
Pharos of Alexandria	c.270 BC	approx. 122 m/ 400 ft high	Marble lighthouse and watchtower on the island of Pharos in Alexandria's harbour; destroyed by an earthquake in 1375.

LABOURS OF HERCULES

Hercules undertook twelve labours for Eurystheus of Tiryns.

Order	Labour
1	To kill and flay the Nemean lion
2	To kill the monster Hydra
3	To capture the Hind of Ceryneia
4	To capture the Boar of Erymanthus
5	To clean out the stables of King Augeas of Elis
6	To remove the man-eating birds from the Stymphalian Lake
7	To capture the Cretan Bull
8	To capture the four savage mares of the Thracian king Diomedes
9	To steal the golden girdle worn by the Amazonian queen Hippolyte
10	To capture the oxen of the giant Geryon
11	To fetch the golden apples of the Hesperides
12	To capture Cerberus, the guardian of Hades

SEVEN DEADLY SINS

1	vainglory, or pride	5	gluttony
2	covetousness	6	anger
3	lust	7	sloth
4	envy